# DISCOURSES OF

## PRESIDENT GORDON B. HINCKLEY

## VOLUME 1: 1995-1999

# DISCOURSES OF

# PRESIDENT GORDON B. HINCKLEY

## VOLUME 1: 1995-1999

DESERET
BOOK
SALT LAKE CITY, UTAH

**Library of Congress Cataloging-in-Publication Data**

Hinckley, Gordon Bitner, 1910-
 [Selections. 2005]
 Discourses of president Gordon B. Hinckley.
     p.   cm.
 Includes bibliographical references and index.
 ISBN 1-59038-431-8 (hardbound : alk. paper)
 1. Church of Jesus Christ of Latter-day Saints—Sermons. 2. Mormon Church—Sermons. 3. Sermons, American. I. Title.
 BX8639.H56D572 2005
 252'.09332—dc22

                                                                    2004025335

Printed in the United States of America                              70582
Phoenix Color Corporation, Hagerstown, MD

10   9   8   7   6   5   4   3   2   1

# CONTENTS

# CONTENTS

CONTENTS

SECTION 2
MEMBER MEETINGS

# CONTENTS

# CONTENTS

## SECTION 3
### MESSAGES TO THE GENERAL PUBLIC

# CONTENTS

# PREFACE

GORDON B. HINCKLEY was ordained and set apart as President of The Church of Jesus Christ of Latter-day Saints on March 12, 1995. During the next five years, he delivered over 500 discourses in a variety of circumstances across the world. This volume is a selection of 78 of those discourses. It is divided into three sections, and the discourses are arranged in chronological order within each section. For the purposes of this collection, some of the discourses have received minor editing.

Section 1 contains all of President Hinckley's general conference addresses from 1995 to 1999. Also included are all the addresses he gave at general meetings of the Young Women and the Relief Society.

Section 2, "Member Meetings," is a representative sample of President Hinckley's messages to gatherings of Latter-day Saints in many nations. The 26 discourses in this section were given at regional conferences, missionary meetings, young adult firesides, and other meetings in North and South America, Asia, Africa, Europe, and the islands of the Pacific. This section also includes a message from a First Presidency Christmas Devotional and a Church-wide satellite broadcast on missionary work. These discourses reflect feelings President Hinckley expressed early in his presidency: "I have a desire to get out with the Latter-day Saints across the world, to look into your faces, to shake your hands wherever possible, to share with you in a more personal and intimate way my feelings concerning this sacred work, and to feel of your spirit and your love of the Lord and His mighty cause" (in Conference Report, Oct. 1995, 92; see also page 49 of this volume).

Section 3, "Messages to the General Public," contains interviews with media representatives and speeches given at civic meetings and community events. Included in this selection are his statement to the media the day after he was set apart as President of the Church; excerpts from an interview with Mike Wallace of *60 Minutes;* and his remarks at University of Utah commencement exercises, a convention of the NAACP, and the U.S. Conference of Mayors.

The discourses in this volume reveal President Hinckley's love for God's children in all parts of the world and his strong desire "to lift people, to strengthen them, to bring purpose into their lives, to provide stability in a world of ever-changing values" (see page 518).

# SECTION 1

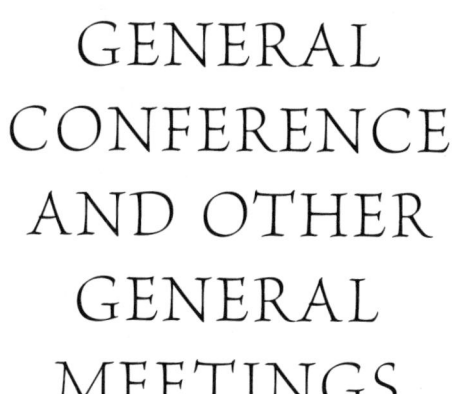

# GENERAL
# CONFERENCE
# AND OTHER
# GENERAL
# MEETINGS

# GENERAL
# YOUNG WOMEN
# MEETING

MARCH 25, 1995

$M$Y BELOVED ASSOCIATES IN this great work, you wonderful young women and your mothers, I am not here tonight as a scheduled speaker. I was not on the program originally. Nevertheless, I welcome this opportunity to say a few words of postscript to the very excellent talks to which we have listened. Much of good counsel has been given, from which each of us can benefit immensely. I hope we will never forget the things we have heard and that they will become guideposts in our lives.

I am grateful for emphasis on reading the scriptures. I hope that for you this will become something far more enjoyable than a duty—that, rather, it will become a love affair with the word of God. I promise you that as you read, your minds will be enlightened and your spirits will be lifted. At first it may seem tedious, but that will change into a wondrous experience with thoughts and words of things divine.

I think there has never been another congregation of this kind in all the world, except perhaps previous Young Women's conferences which have also originated here in the Tabernacle. There are hundreds of thousands of young women gathered this Saturday evening in halls scattered far and wide across the earth. How marvelous a thing it is to contemplate that each of you is a daughter of God, a girl with a divine birthright and a divine destiny.

When Sister Hinckley and I were much younger and less stiff and brittle, we would go to dances. She would tell you that this stopped right after we were married. I must confess that I enjoyed her company more than I enjoyed the dancing.

Back in those days there was a popular song, the opening lines of which were:

> *Somebody loves you, I want you to know,*
> *Longs to be near you wherever you go.*
> > *[Charlie Tobias and Peter De Rose,*
> > *"Somebody Loves You" (1932)]*

I have interpreted those words differently from the meaning given by the author. I wish you—each of you, wherever you are—to know that you are loved. You are loved by your Father in Heaven, of whose divine nature you have partaken. And He desires that His Holy Spirit will be near you wherever you go if you will invite it and cultivate it.

There is something of divinity within each of you. You have such tremendous potential with that quality as a part of your inherited nature. Every one of you was endowed by your Father in Heaven with a tremendous capacity to do good in the world. Train your minds and your hands that you may be equipped to serve well in the society of which you are a part. Cultivate the art of being kind, of being thoughtful, of being helpful. Refine within you the quality of mercy, which comes as a part of the divine attributes you have inherited.

Some of you may feel that you are not as attractive and beautiful and glamorous as you would like to be. Rise above any such feelings, cultivate the light you have within you, and it will shine through as a radiant expression that will be seen by others.

You need never feel inferior. You need never feel that you were born without talents or without opportunities to give them expression. Cultivate whatever talents you have, and they will grow and refine and become an expression of your true self appreciated by others.

In summary, try a little harder to measure up to the divine within each of you. As Alma said, "Awake and arouse your faculties" (Alma 32:27).

I thank you for the goodness of your lives, for the desire within your hearts to do the right thing, for the fact that you are prayerful and kind and good. We have every confidence in you. We love you. We pray for you. We leave our blessing with you in the name of Jesus Christ, amen.

# PRIESTHOOD
# SESSION

### APRIL 1, 1995

THANK YOU, BRETHREN, for the effort you have made to come to this great worldwide priesthood meeting. Wherever you may be, we thank you and commend you for your faith, for your loyalty to this the work of the Lord, for the efforts you make in your daily living to be worthy of the sacred priesthood which you bear.

This morning we all participated in a solemn assembly. That is just what the name indicates. It is a gathering of the membership where every individual stands equal with every other in exercising with soberness and in solemnity his or her right to sustain or not to sustain those who, under the procedures that arise out of the revelations, have been chosen to lead.

The procedure of sustaining is much more than a ritualistic raising of the hand. It is a commitment to uphold, to support, to assist those who have been selected.

Concerning the First Presidency, the Lord has said, "Of the Melchizedek Priesthood, three Presiding High Priests, chosen by the body, appointed and ordained to that office, and upheld by the confidence, faith, and prayer of the church" (D&C 107:22).

I emphasize those words "upheld by the confidence, faith, and prayer of the church."

Your uplifted hands in the solemn assembly this morning

became an expression of your willingness and desire to uphold us, your brethren and your servants, with your confidence, faith, and prayer. I am deeply grateful for that expression.

I thank you, each of you. I assure you, as you already know, that in the processes of the Lord there is no aspiring for office. As the Lord said to His disciples, "Ye have not chosen me, but I have chosen you, and ordained you" (John 15:16). This office is not one to be sought after. The right to select rests with the Lord. He is the master of life and death. His is the power to call. His is the power to take away. His is the power to retain. It is all in His hands.

I do not know why in His grand scheme one such as I would find a place. But having this mantle come upon me, I now rededicate whatever I have of strength or time or talent or life to the work of my Master in the service of my brethren and sisters. Again I thank you, my beloved brethren, for your actions this day. The burden of my prayer is that I will be worthy. I hope that I may be remembered in your prayers.

Now, in the ongoing of this work, administrative changes sometimes occur. The doctrine remains constant. But from time to time there are organizational and administrative changes made under provisions set forth in the revelations.

For instance, 28 years ago the First Presidency was inspired to call men to serve as regional representatives of the Twelve. At the time, that was a new calling in the Church. The Presidency stated that this was necessary because of the ever-increasing growth of the Church, which made evident a greater need to train our stake and ward leaders in the programs of the Church that they in turn might train the membership in their responsibilities before the Lord (see Conference Report, Oct. 1967, 25–26).

At that time there were 69 regional representatives. Today there are 284. The organization has become somewhat unwieldy.

More recently the Presidency were inspired to call men from the Seventy to serve in Area Presidencies. As the work grows across the world, it has become necessary to decentralize administrative authority to keep General Authorities closer to the people. We now have such Area Presidencies well established and effectively functioning.

It is now felt desirable to tighten up the organization administered by the Area Presidencies. Accordingly, we announce the release—the honorable release—of all regional representatives effective August 15 of this year. To these devoted and able brethren we express our deep appreciation for the tremendous work you have accomplished—for your loyalty, faithfulness, and devotion in advancing the cause of our Father in Heaven. I cannot say enough of good concerning these men. They have sacrificed their time and their resources. They have gone wherever they have been asked to go, whenever they have been asked to go. They have greatly assisted stake presidents and bishops with wise counsel and direction, with skillful training and instruction. We thank them one and all and pray that through the years to come the Lord will bless them with the satisfying assurance that each of them made a significant contribution to the work and that their labors have been accepted by Him.

Now we announce the call of a new local officer to be known as an Area Authority. These will be high priests chosen from among past and present experienced Church leaders. They will continue with their current employment, reside in their own homes, and serve on a Church-service basis. The term of their call will be flexible, generally for a period of approximately six years. They will be closely tied to the Area Presidencies. They will be fewer in number than have been the regional representatives. We are guided in setting up this new corps of area officers, as were our Brethren before us in the calling of regional representatives, by the provision contained in the revelation on priesthood, section 107 of the Doctrine and Covenants. After directions to the Twelve and the Seventy, the revelation states:

"Whereas other officers of the church, who belong not unto the Twelve, neither to the Seventy, are not under the responsibility to travel among all nations, but are to travel as their circumstances shall allow, notwithstanding they may hold as high and responsible offices in the church" (v. 98).

Now, I repeat that these changes will not be effective until August 15 of this year.

Now, brethren, a few words on a related matter. The Church is becoming a very large and complex organization. We now have members in more than 150 nations. There are nine million of us, and we are growing at the approximate rate of a million each three and a half years. In addition to such regular programs as sacrament meeting, home teaching, and meetings of the priesthood quorums and auxiliaries, all of which are designed to meet the needs of the living membership of the Church, we are carrying forward an enormous program involving such undertakings as the world's largest archive of genealogical and family history data; the operation of the largest private university in the nation, if not in the world, with a related seminary and institute program embracing hundreds of thousands of students; the staffing and management of the largest missionary organization of which I am aware, with the number now approaching 50,000; the carrying forward of a building program of unprecedented proportions; the operation of a very large and efficient publishing facility; and the training and motivation of the largest organization of noncompensated ecclesiastical officers to be found in any institution of which I know. I hesitate to use superlatives, but I think they fit in this case.

We are becoming a great global society. But our interest and concern must always be with the individual. Every member of this Church is an individual man or woman, boy or girl. Our great responsibility is to see that each is "remembered and nourished by the good word of God" (Moroni 6:4), that each has opportunity for growth and expression and training in the work and ways of the

Lord, that none lacks the necessities of life, that the needs of the poor are met, that each member shall have encouragement, training, and opportunity to move forward on the road of immortality and eternal life. This, I submit, is the inspired genius of this the Lord's work. The organization can grow and multiply in numbers, as it surely will. This gospel must be carried to every nation, kindred, tongue, and people. There can never be in the foreseeable future a standing still or a failure to reach out, to move forward, to build, to enlarge Zion across the world. But with all of this there must continue to be an intimate pastoral relationship of every member with a wise and caring bishop or branch president. These are the shepherds of the flock whose responsibility it is to look after the people in relatively small numbers so that none is forgotten, overlooked, or neglected.

Jesus was the true Shepherd, who reached out to those in distress, one at a time, bestowing an individual blessing upon them.

President Lee told us on more than one occasion to survey large fields and cultivate small ones. He was saying that we must know the big picture and then assiduously work on the particular niche assigned to each of us and that in doing so we concentrate on the needs of the individual.

This work is concerned with people, each a son or daughter of God. In describing its achievements we speak in terms of numbers, but all of our efforts must be dedicated to the development of the individual.

For instance, President Hunter urged us to greater temple activity. This sacred work concerns the entire human family, past and present. But it is accomplished on an individual basis, with those who have received their own ordinances standing individually as proxy for another.

Likewise, missionary service is a personal labor, with the missionary teaching and bearing witness to the investigator, who must search and pray alone in the quiet of his own soul if he or she is to gain a knowledge of the truth.

The gaining of a strong and secure testimony is the privilege and opportunity of every individual member of the Church. The Master said, "If any man will do his will, he shall know of the doctrine, whether it be of God, or whether I speak of myself" (John 7:17).

Service in behalf of others, study, and prayer lead to faith in this work and then to knowledge of its truth. This has always been a personal pursuit, as it must always be in the future.

We speak frequently of Wilford Woodruff's conversion of the United Brethren in England when some 1,800 were baptized into the Church. But let us not forget that each of them had to walk the lonely road of repentance, of faith in the Lord Jesus Christ, and of acceptance of the fact that the ancient gospel had come again to earth in this the promised dispensation of the fulness of times.

The decisions we make, individually and personally, become the fabric of our lives. That fabric will be beautiful or ugly according to the threads of which it is woven. I wish to say particularly to the young men who are here that you cannot indulge in any unbecoming behavior without injury to the beauty of the fabric of your lives. Immoral acts of any kind will introduce an ugly thread. Dishonesty of any kind will create a blemish. Foul and profane language will rob the pattern of its beauty.

"Choose the right when a choice is placed before you" is the call to each of us ("Choose the Right," *Hymns,* no. 239).

Now, in conclusion, may I say that I glory in the wonderful, courageous, victorious past of this great work. I marvel at the present, when you and I stand as watchmen upon the towers. I envision the future with hope, assurance, and certain faith.

God, our Eternal Father, lives. This is His work, designed to assist Him in "bring[ing] to pass the immortality and eternal life" of His sons and daughters of all generations of time (Moses 1:39).

Jesus is the Christ, the promised Messiah, who came to earth in the most humble of circumstances, who walked the dusty roads of Palestine teaching and healing, who died upon Golgotha's cruel cross and was resurrected the third day. This is His Church. It carries His name. We are His servants, each of us. The priesthood which we bear is His priesthood, and we exercise it in His name. It was bestowed upon Joseph Smith and Oliver Cowdery by those who held it anciently, having received it from the Lord Himself.

The gospel is the way of peace, of progress, of safety, of salvation, of exaltation. This, the last and final dispensation, was ushered in by the glorious appearance of the Father and the Son to the boy Joseph Smith. You and I, my brethren, have received this holy priesthood through the laying on of hands by those in authority. We must live worthy of it. We must safeguard it. We must honor it. We must use it in righteousness for the blessing of others. God help us to be true to the great and sacred trust which has been given to each of us, I humbly pray, as I leave my blessing with you, in the name of Jesus Christ, amen.

# Sunday Morning Session

APRIL 2, 1995

M<small>Y BELOVED BROTHERS AND</small> sisters wherever you may be, my dear friends and associates in this great work, as you can well understand, this for me is a most solemn and sacred occasion. Humbly I seek the direction of the Holy Spirit as I struggle to share with you the feelings of my heart. If in the circumstances I speak unduly much in a personal vein, I hope you will excuse me. I shall then try to put the first person singular behind me.

We have mourned in recent days the passing of our beloved friend and leader, Howard William Hunter, the 14th President of the Church and prophet to the people. His tenure in office was brief, but the impression for good that he left was tremendous. Mild of manner, quiet in his ways, he was nonetheless a man whose strong convictions of the truth of this work made him powerfully persuasive in his advocacy of the Christlike life.

He suffered much in his body before he was finally taken from us on the morning of March 3, 1995. More than 25,000 men, women, and children passed by his bier as his body lay in state in the beautiful rotunda of the Church Administration Building. With measured step they came one by one, reverently and with love for the man they had sustained only a few months before.

On Wednesday, March 8, 1995, his funeral services were held

in this historic Tabernacle and broadcast far and wide. Those services were a fitting memorial to a man of goodness and greatness who now belongs to the ages. Our hearts reach out with love and sympathy to his bereaved widow and to his sons and their families, now spanning three generations. May they be comforted, sustained, and blessed by Him who declared, "I, even I, am he that comforteth you" (Isaiah 51:12).

With President Hunter's passing, the First Presidency was dissolved. Brother Monson and I, who had served as his counselors, took our places in the Quorum of the Twelve, which became the presiding authority of the Church.

Three weeks ago today all of the living ordained Apostles gathered in a spirit of fasting and prayer in the upper room of the temple. Here we sang a sacred hymn and prayed together. We partook of the sacrament of the Lord's supper, renewing in that sacred, symbolic testament our covenants and our relationship with Him who is our divine Redeemer. The Presidency was then reorganized, following a precedent well established through generations of the past. There was no campaigning, no contest, no ambition for office. It was quiet, peaceful, simple, and sacred. It was done after the pattern which the Lord Himself had put in place.

We have received from many people expressions of congratulations and confidence. These have come from members of the Church and from those not of our faith. To one and all I express my deep appreciation. I know full well that it is not the man whom they compliment but, rather, the office.

Yesterday morning members of the Church across the world met together in a solemn assembly. You raised your hands, without compulsion and of your own free will, to confirm the action taken by the Apostles three weeks ago and to sustain those called to serve.

As you know, mine has been the special privilege to serve as a counselor to three great Presidents. I think I know something of the meaning of heavy responsibility. But with all of that, I have, during these past few days, been overwhelmed with feelings of inadequacy and total dependency upon the Lord, who is my head and whose Church this is; upon the strength of these good men who are my counselors; upon my dear Brethren of the Twelve, of the Seventy, and of the Presiding Bishopric; and upon the membership of the Church throughout the world. I search for words to express the depth of my gratitude and my appreciation and my love.

Years ago I gave a talk on the loneliness of leadership. Now for the first time I realize the full import of that loneliness. I do not know why this mantle has fallen upon my shoulders. I suppose some of you may also wonder. But we are here.

In circumstances such as these, one's searching thoughts go back over all of the years of one's life and even beyond. I am of only the third generation in the Church. My grandfather was born in Ontario, Canada, in 1828. His widowed mother eventually brought her two boys to Springfield, Illinois. From there my grandfather walked to Nauvoo, where he listened to the Prophet Joseph Smith. He was baptized. When the exodus of our people occurred in 1846, he was an 18-year-old youth of strength and capacity and faith. He was a skilled builder of wagons and a blacksmith. He was among those whom President Young requested to remain for a time in Iowa to assist those still on the westward trail. He married in 1848 and set out for this valley in the spring of 1850.

Somewhere along that wearisome trail, his young wife sickened and died. With his own hands he dug a grave, split logs to make a coffin, lovingly buried her, then tearfully took their 11-month-old child in his arms and marched on to this valley.

He was among those who repeatedly were called by President Young to undertake a variety of difficult assignments incident to the establishment of our people in these mountain valleys. He served as president of the Millard Stake of Zion when there were only a handful of stakes and when it included a vast area of central Utah, traveling thousands of miles by horse and buggy in the discharge of his ministry. He gave so generously of his substance in the establishment of schools that his once substantial estate was small at the time of his death.

My father was similarly a man of great faith who served the Church without reservation in many trusted capacities. For a number of years he presided over what was then the largest stake in the Church, with more than 15,000 members. My mother and grandmothers were likewise women of great faith whose lives were not always easy because of requirements made upon them by the Church. But they did not complain. They met their responsibilities with cheerfulness and devotion.

For these forebears I feel a great sense of gratitude and love and an almost overwhelming obligation to keep the trust which they have passed. To my beloved wife of 58 years later this month, I express appreciation. How empty our lives would be without these, our wonderful companions. How grateful I am for this precious woman who has walked at my side through sunshine and storm. We do not stand as tall as we once did. But there has been no shrinkage in our love one for another.

I likewise speak with gratitude for my children and my grandchildren and great-grandchildren, who have honored us with the goodness of their lives.

And most particularly, to each of you I express my deep appreciation. I have had opportunity to travel far and wide across this Church during the 37 years of my service as a General Authority. Everywhere I have gone, I have met wonderful people. There is so much of goodness in the lives of the Latter-day Saints. There are such tremendous expressions of faith in the service which you give. I know something of the sacrifices made by many of you. I wish I had the capacity to express my feelings of love and gratitude for you. I stand as your servant and pledge to you and to the Lord my very best effort as I ask for your continuing faith and prayers and uplifted hands.

I am fully aware that I am not a young man as I shoulder the responsibilities of this sacred office. Sister Hinckley and I are learning that the so-called golden years are laced with lead. But I think I can honestly say that I do not feel old. I cannot repudiate my birth certificate, but I can still experience a great, almost youthful exuberance in my enthusiasm for this precious work of the Almighty.

I love the people of this Church of all ages, of all races, and of many nations.

I love the children. They are very much the same the world over. Regardless of the color of their skin and of the circumstances in which they live, they carry with them a beauty that comes of innocence and of the fact that it was not long ago that they lived with their Father in Heaven. How lovely you are, wherever you are, you precious children.

I love the youth of the Church. I have said again and again that I think we have never had a better generation than this. How grateful I am for your integrity, for your ambition to train your minds and your hands to do good work, for your love for the word of the Lord, and for your desire to walk in paths of virtue and truth and goodness.

I have tremendous respect for fathers and mothers who are nurturing their children in light and truth, who have prayer in their homes, who spare the rod and govern with love, who look upon their little ones as their most valued assets to be protected, trained, and blessed.

I love the elderly who have faced into the storms of life and who, regardless of the force of the tempest, have gone forward and kept the faith. May your older years be filled with happiness and with satisfying remembrance of lives well lived.

Now, my brethren and sisters, in conclusion I wish to leave with you one thought which I hope you will never forget.

This Church does not belong to its President. Its head is the Lord Jesus Christ, whose name each of us has taken upon ourselves. We are all in this great endeavor together. We are here to assist our Father in His work and His glory, "to bring to pass the immortality and eternal life of man" (Moses 1:39). Your obligation is as serious in your sphere of responsibility as is my obligation in my sphere. No calling in this Church is small or of little consequence. All of us in the pursuit of our duty touch the lives of others. To each of us in our respective responsibilities the Lord has said:

"Wherefore, be faithful; stand in the office which I have appointed unto you; succor the weak, lift up the hands which hang down, and strengthen the feeble knees" (D&C 81:5).

"And in doing these things thou wilt do the greatest good unto thy fellow beings, and wilt promote the glory of him who is your Lord" (D&C 81:4).

Further, "And if thou art faithful unto the end thou shalt have a crown of immortality, and eternal life in the mansions which I have prepared in the house of my Father" (D&C 81:6).

All of us in this great cause are of one mind, of one belief, of one faith.

You have as great an opportunity for satisfaction in the performance of your duty as I do in mine. The progress of this work will be determined by our joint efforts. Whatever your calling, it is as fraught with the same kind of opportunity to accomplish good as is mine. What is really important is that this is the work of the Master. Our work is to go about doing good, as did He.

If in my service I have offended anyone, I offer my apology. To those who for any reason find yourselves outside the embrace of the Church you once enjoyed, I invite you to return and partake of the happiness you once knew. You will find many with outstretched arms to warmly welcome you and assist you.

I plead with our people everywhere to live with respect and appreciation for those not of our faith. There is so great a need for civility and mutual respect among those of differing beliefs and philosophies. We must not be partisans of any doctrine of ethnic superiority. We live in a world of diversity. We can and must be respectful toward those with whose teachings we may not agree. We must be willing to defend the rights of others who may become the victims of bigotry.

I call attention to these striking words of Joseph Smith spoken in 1843:

"If it has been demonstrated that I have been willing to die for a 'Mormon,' I am bold to declare before Heaven that I am just as ready to die in defending the rights of a Presbyterian, a Baptist, or a good man of any other denomination; for the same principle which would trample upon the rights of the Latter-day Saints would trample upon the rights of the Roman Catholics, or of any other denomination" (*History of the Church,* 5:498).

Now, my brethren and sisters, the time has come for us to stand a little taller, to lift our eyes and stretch our minds to a greater comprehension and understanding of the grand millennial mission of this, The Church of Jesus Christ of Latter-day Saints. This is a season to be strong. It is a time to move forward without hesitation, knowing well the meaning, the breadth, and the importance of our mission. It is a time to do what is right regardless of the consequences that might follow. It is a time to be found keeping the commandments. It is a season to reach out with kindness and love to those in distress and to those who are wandering in darkness and pain. It is a time to be considerate and good, decent and courteous toward one another in all of our relationships—in other words, to become more Christlike.

We have nothing to fear. God is at the helm. He will overrule for the good of this work. He will shower down blessings upon those who walk in obedience to His commandments. Such has been His promise. Of His ability to keep that promise none of us can doubt.

The little stone which was cut out of the mountain without hands, as seen in Daniel's vision, is rolling forth to fill the whole earth (see Daniel 2:44–45). No force under the heavens can stop it if we will walk in righteousness and be faithful and true. The Almighty Himself is at our head. Our Savior, who is our Redeemer, the Great Jehovah, the mighty Messiah, has promised: "I will go before your face. I will be on your right hand and on your left, and my Spirit shall be in your hearts, and mine angels round about you, to bear you up" (D&C 84:88).

"Therefore," said He, "fear not, little flock; do good; let earth and hell combine against you, for if ye are built upon my rock, they cannot prevail. . . .

"Look unto me in every thought; doubt not, fear not.

"Behold the wounds which pierced my side, and also the prints of the nails in my hands and feet; be faithful, keep my commandments, and ye shall inherit the kingdom of heaven" (D&C 6:34, 36–37).

Unitedly, working hand in hand, we shall move forward as servants of the living God, doing the work of His Beloved Son, our Master, whom we serve and whose name we seek to glorify.

I repeat: this, my brethren and sisters, is the work of the Almighty. He lives, our Father and our friend. It is the work of our Redeemer, who out of a love beyond comprehension gave His life for each of us. It is a divine work restored through a chosen prophet. It is a work to which we dedicate our lives as we invoke choice blessings upon you, our beloved associates, in the name of Jesus Christ, amen.

# Sunday Afternoon Session

APRIL 2, 1995

$M$Y BRETHREN AND SISTERS, just a few words in conclusion. First, I'd like to say that we have participated in a miracle. As I have listened to all who have spoken, I have noted that there has been no duplication of treatment. Every man and woman who has spoken has chosen his or her own theme to treat. There are no assignments made to any of the speakers concerning what they should say. And yet they all fit together in a pattern that is beautiful and wonderful. I have a profound feeling of gratitude to the Lord for His wonderful blessings upon us. We have listened to wise and inspired counsel. We have been taught, and we have been edified.

A week ago a conference of the young women was held in this Tabernacle. It was an inspiration to look into their faces, thousands of them. One could not do so without a feeling of peace and certitude concerning the future of this work. The theme of the conference was an appeal to the young women to read the scriptures.

I look back to my own youth. Neither young men nor young women were doing much scripture reading at that time. What a marvelous change has been wrought. A new generation is arising who are familiar with the word of the Lord. Growing up in a worldly environment that is laden with immorality and filth of every kind, our youth, for the most part, are meeting the challenge of living in the world without partaking of the evils of the world. It is with the young men as it is with the young women. Last evening this Tabernacle was filled with fathers and sons, and hundreds of thousands were gathered in other halls across the Church. It is wonderful to feel the pulse of this generation of young people. Of course, there are some who do not measure up. That has been the case since the time of the great War in Heaven, described by John the Revelator. The issue then was free agency, as it is today. Then, as now, choices had to be made.

"And there was war in heaven: Michael and his angels fought against the dragon; and the dragon fought and his angels,

"And prevailed not; neither was their place found any more in heaven.

"And the great dragon was cast out, that old serpent, called the Devil, and Satan, which deceiveth the whole world: he was cast out into the earth, and his angels were cast out with him" (Revelation 12:7–9).

That ancient struggle continues, the unrelenting battle that comes of free agency. Some, unfortunately, choose the wrong. But many, so many, choose the right, including so very many of our choice young men and young women. They deserve and need our gratitude. They need our encouragement. They need the kind of examples that we can become before them. May they be blessed as they pursue lives of virtue, of learning, of growing with faith and purpose, all the time remaining "true to the faith that [their] parents have cherished, true to the truth for which martyrs have perished" ("True to the Faith," *Hymns,* no. 254).

In the Young Women conference, emphasis was given to the words of Alma found in the 32nd chapter of the book of Alma. His teachings include these words: "Awake and arouse your faculties, even to an experiment upon my words, and exercise a particle of faith" (v. 27).

My beloved associates, far more of us need to awake and arouse our faculties to an awareness of the great everlasting truths of the gospel of Jesus Christ. Each of us can do a little better than we have been doing. We can be a little more kind. We can be a little more merciful. We can be a little more forgiving. We can put behind us our weaknesses of the past and go forth with new energy and increased resolution to improve the world about us, in our homes, in our places of employment, in our social activities.

We have work to do, you and I, so very much of it. Let us roll up our sleeves and get at it, with a new commitment, putting our trust in the Lord.

> *Come, come, ye Saints, no toil nor labor fear;*
> *But with joy wend your way.*
> *Though hard to you this journey may appear,*
> *Grace shall be as your day.*
> ["*Come, Come, Ye Saints,*" Hymns, *no. 30]*

We can do it if we will be prayerful and faithful. We can do better than we have ever done before.

The Church needs your strength. It needs your love and loyalty and devotion. It needs a little more of your time and energy.

I am not asking anyone to give more at the expense of his or her employer. We have an obligation to be men and women of absolute honesty and integrity in the service of those who employ us.

I am not asking anyone to do so at the expense of your families. The Lord will hold you responsible for your children. But I am suggesting that we spend a little less time in idleness, in the fruitless pursuit of watching some inane and empty television programs. Time so utilized can be put to better advantage, and the consequences will be wonderful. Of that I do not hesitate to assure you.

Now, my beloved brethren and sisters, as we return to our homes, may we go in safety, pondering the things we have heard these past two days. May we go with determination to try a little

23

harder to be a little better. Please know that we are not without understanding of some of your problems. We are aware that many of you carry very heavy burdens. We plead with the Lord in your behalf. We add our prayers to your prayers that you may find solutions to your problems. We leave a blessing upon you, even an apostolic blessing. We bless you that the Lord may smile with favor upon you, that there may be happiness and peace in your homes and in your lives, that an atmosphere of love and respect and appreciation may be felt among husbands and wives, children and parents. May you "look to God and live" (Alma 37:47) with happiness, with security, with peace, with faith.

At the opening of this session, the choir sang a wonderful hymn. "Faith of our fathers, holy faith, we will be true to thee till death!" ("Faith of Our Fathers," *Hymns,* no. 84). I would like to leave that thought with you: "Faith of our fathers, holy faith, we will be true to thee till death!" God bless you, my beloved associates, in this glorious work, I humbly pray in the name of Him whom we all serve, even the Lord Jesus Christ, amen.

# GENERAL
# RELIEF SOCIETY
# MEETING

I AM GREATLY HONORED IN the invitation to participate with you. My beloved companion, Marjorie, would do better in addressing the Relief Society than I. I honor her as the Relief Society member of our family, and because of her and her activities, my appreciation for this great organization is enhanced. This has been a wonderful meeting. I commend to each of you all that we have heard from these very able leaders, in whom we have total confidence.

What a mighty congregation of women you are. There are three and one-half million of you. You live in many lands, and you speak with a variety of tongues. But you understand with a single heart. Each of you is a daughter of God. Reflect on all the wondrous meaning of that one paramount fact.

He who is our Eternal Father has blessed you with miraculous powers of mind and body. He never intended that you should be less than the crowning glory of His creations.

I remind you of words spoken by the Prophet Joseph to the women of the Relief Society in April of 1842. Said he, "If you live up to your privilege, the angels cannot be restrain'd from being your associates" (in Relief Society, Minutebook 1842 Mar.–1844 Mar., p. 38, Archives of The Church of Jesus Christ of Latter-day Saints). What marvelous potential lies within you.

This evening I look into the eyes of beautiful younger women who dream of lives of accomplishment and happiness. I look into the eyes of mothers who carry in their hearts anxieties concerning their homes and their children. I look into the eyes of single parents whose burdens are so very heavy and who, in their loneliness, plead and pray for strength and companionship. I look into the eyes of grandmothers and great-grandmothers whose years are many, who have weathered the storms that have beat upon them and who have drunk deeply from the waters of life, some of them brackish, some of them sweet. I am grateful for the presence of each one of you. I am grateful for the strength that you have and for your loyalty, your faith, your love. I am thankful for the resolution which you carry in your hearts to walk in faith, to keep the commandments, to do what is right at all times and in all circumstances.

I believe this is the best season for women in all the history of the world. In opportunities for education, for the training of your hands and minds, there has never before been a time when doors were so widely opened to you as they are today.

But neither has there been a time, at least in recent history, when you have been confronted with more challenging problems. I need not remind you that the world we are in is a world of turmoil, of shifting values. Shrill voices call out for one thing or another in betrayal of time-tested standards of behavior. The moral moorings of our society have been badly shaken. So many of the youth of the world, and likewise so many of their elders, listen only to the seductive voice of self-gratification.

You single young women face tremendous challenges, and we know it is not easy for you. I cannot say enough of appreciation for your determination to live by the standards of the Church, to walk with the strength of virtue, to keep your minds above the slough of filth which seems to be moving like a flood across the world. Thank you for knowing there is a better way. Thank you for the will to say no. Thank you for the strength to deny temptation and look beyond and above to the shining light of your eternal potential.

How bitter are the fruits of casting aside standards of virtue. The statistics are appalling. More than one-fourth of all children born in the United States are born out of wedlock, and the situation grows more serious. "Of teens who give birth, 46 percent will go on welfare within four years; of unmarried teens who give birth, 73 percent will be on welfare within four years" (see Carnegie Corporation of New York, *Starting Points: Meeting the Needs of Our Youngest Children* [1994], 4, 21). I believe that it should be the blessing of every child to be born into a home where that child is welcomed, nurtured, loved, and blessed with parents, a father and a mother, who live with loyalty to one another and to their children. I am sure that none of you younger women want less than this. Stand strong against the wiles of the world. The creators of our entertainment, the purveyors of much of our literature, would have you believe otherwise. The accumulated wisdom of centuries declares with clarity and certainty that the greater happiness, the greater security, the greater peace of mind, the deeper reservoirs of love are experienced only by those who walk according to time-tested standards of virtue before marriage and total fidelity within marriage. We pray that as you walk the paths of life you will walk in ways that are straight, with the strength to conform even though those paths be narrow.

There are those who would have us believe in the validity of what they choose to call same-sex marriage. Our hearts reach out to those who struggle with feelings of affinity for the same gender. We remember you before the Lord, we sympathize with you, we regard you as our brothers and our sisters. However, we cannot condone immoral practices on your part any more than we can condone immoral practices on the part of others.

To you wives and mothers who work to maintain stable homes where there is an environment of love and respect and appreciation,

I say, the Lord bless you. Regardless of your circumstances, walk with faith. Rear your children in light and truth. Teach them to pray while they are young. Read to them from the scriptures even though they may not understand all that you read. Teach them to pay their tithes and offerings on the first money they ever receive. Let this practice become a habit in their lives. Teach your sons to honor womanhood. Teach your daughters to walk in virtue. Accept responsibility in the Church, and trust in the Lord to make you equal to any call you may receive. Your example will set a pattern for your children. Reach out in love to those in distress and need.

Encourage your children to read more and watch television less. "A study by the American Psychological Association figures that the typical child, watching 27 hours of TV a week, will view 8,000 murders and 100,000 acts of violence from age 3 to age 12" (Marc Silver, "Sex and Violence on TV," *U.S. News & World Report,* Sept. 11, 1995, 66).

Seek to establish an environment conducive to study in the home. An editorial in the *Wall Street Journal* reports on the scholastic superiority of ethnic Asians at the University of California at Berkeley. Speaking of the extraordinary accomplishments of these people, it says: "The most important factor in the rise of this new American elite is the intense and devoted family relationships that typify the Asian home. . . . They include respect for elders and high standards for children, including hard work at school and off-hours responsibilities that many times still include chores at a relative's business" ("The Asians at Berkeley," May 30, 1995, A14).

It is the home which produces the nursery stock of new generations. I hope that you mothers will realize that when all is said and done, you have no more compelling responsibility, nor any laden with greater rewards, than the nurture you give your children in an environment of security, peace, companionship, love, and motivation to grow and do well.

Now to you single mothers, whatever the cause of your present situation, our hearts reach out to you. We know that many of you live in loneliness, insecurity, worry, and fear. For most of you there is never enough money. Your constant, brooding worry is anxiety for your children and their futures. Many of you find yourselves in circumstances where you have to work and leave your children largely to their own devices. But if when they are very small there is much of affection, there is shown much of love, there is prayer together, then there will more likely be peace in the hearts and strength in the character of your children. Teach them the ways of the Lord. Declared Isaiah, "All thy children shall be taught of the Lord; and great shall be the peace of thy children" (Isaiah 54:13).

The more surely you rear your children in the ways of the gospel of Jesus Christ, with love and high expectation, the more likely that there will be peace in their lives.

Set an example for them. That will mean more than all the teaching you can give them. Do not overindulge them. Let them grow up with respect for and understanding of the meaning of labor, of working and contributing to the home and its surroundings, with some way of earning some of their own expense money. Let your sons save for missions, and encourage them to prepare themselves not only financially but spiritually and in an attitude to go out to serve the Lord without selfishness of any kind. I do not hesitate to promise that if you will do so, you will have reason to count your blessings.

I received a letter only this past Monday from which I read to you. This woman writes:

> Twenty years ago last June, I was expecting a new baby and had five other little children, nine years and under. My husband chose to leave our family and walk another path. I wish I could say I was a noble pioneer, but rather I was a naive, frightened, insecure young mother who did not know what to do and who daily made foolish mistakes. Nevertheless, I sought counsel from my leaders and obeyed, even when I

knew their advice would make my life more complicated. I decided it was not for me to question and that if some advice caused temporary pain for me, it must be something I should experience.

I remember reading President Kimball's monthly message in the *Ensign* wherein he promised that if we would read the scriptures daily that every problem we faced during the day would be answered within those holy pages. I thought, "Okay, President Kimball, you're on. I have lots of problems, and they sure do need answers." I gathered my children around, and we studied daily, we prayed, we fasted for our daddy and ourselves, we held family home evening and attended our meetings. We forgave our daddy, and I literally gave my agency back to my Heavenly Father. I told Him if I was not to have my husband for eternity as I had originally thought, I would be pleased if He would change the love I had for him as a wife into a Christlike love, because I would rather die than go another minute hating or resenting the father of my children. I did not want to teach anger, hate, or bitterness to them. I knew my husband was basically a good man, full of potential and talent. He had made a terrible mistake, and I knew he would reap his own heartaches, and he has. But my personal task at hand was to care for those soon-to-be six children and to teach them in such a way that they could not misunderstand the gospel of Jesus Christ. I felt I had borne the heartbreak of losing my husband, but I could not bear it if I lost one precious child of God who had been entrusted to my care.

I am humbly touched to report the Lord both heard and answered my prayers. The youngest of my four sons (from my first marriage) is presently serving a mission. . . . He joins his other three brothers and a sister who have seen fit to share their testimonies literally all over the world. . . . My oldest daughter married a returned missionary in the temple. . . . The three oldest boys have been elders quorum presidents and ward mission leaders; the two daughters have served in a Primary presidency and Relief Society presidency. Four of those beautiful children have found wonderful eternal companions and have been married in the temple. They are on the right track and have tasted the joy of service to a small degree.

President Hinckley, this is a miracle if ever there was a miracle. The Lord protected and nurtured those children. He answered their prayers. . . .

The Lord saw fit to provide me with a second husband, and we were sealed in the temple. We have been a family. Was the way easy? No, there were a million troubles to iron out. But with the scriptures as our "iron rod" resource, prayer as our foundation, and obedience as our determined pathway, my children are learning to trust in the Lord with all their hearts and lean not upon their own understanding (see Proverbs 3:5).

I do not share our story with you . . . to brag of myself, but I certainly can boast in the Lord. The Atonement is very real for us. Wounded hearts have been healed, confidence has been restored, peace has been tasted in a most delicious way. Indeed, as you have said, every principle God has revealed carries its own conviction of its truth. I think of my first husband; if he could only realize he has already paid the price for his mistake. . . . He missed the joy of seeing his talented children grow up in the Lord. He missed their school and Church achievements and their mission farewells and reports—all that makes life sweet. How thankful I am that I was privileged to be by their sides.

She concludes, "I know there are many single parents in the world today. How I wish I could help them see that they must never waste time reliving their own tender injuries. I have found if you cast your burden at the Savior's feet, He will carry it for you and replace anguish with love. . . . May the Lord bless you and your family always. With deepest love and appreciation," and she signs the letter.

Now to you grandmothers and great-grandmothers may I say just a word. Tremendous has been your experience. Tremendous is your understanding. You can be as an anchor in a world of shifting values. You have lived long, buffed and polished by the adversities of life through which you have passed. Quiet are your ways, deliberate your counsel. You dearly beloved women are such treasures in this topsy-turvy society. God bless you. May your waning years be filled with sunshine, with the love of those whom you love, and with love for the Lord.

I have touched lightly on some of the serious problems which confront many of you sisters.

With so much of sophistry that is passed off as truth, with so much of deception concerning standards and values, with so much of allurement and enticement to take on the slow stain of the world, we have felt to warn and forewarn. In furtherance of this, we of the First Presidency and the Council of the Twelve Apostles now issue a proclamation to the Church and to the world as a declaration and reaffirmation of standards, doctrines, and practices relative to the family which the prophets, seers, and revelators of this Church have repeatedly stated throughout its history. I now take the opportunity of reading to you this proclamation:

> We, the First Presidency and the Council of the Twelve Apostles of The Church of Jesus Christ of Latter-day Saints, solemnly proclaim that marriage between a man and a woman is ordained of God and that the family is central to the Creator's plan for the eternal destiny of His children.
>
> All human beings—male and female—are created in the image of God. Each is a beloved spirit son or daughter of heavenly parents, and, as such, each has a divine nature and destiny. Gender is an essential characteristic of individual premortal, mortal, and eternal identity and purpose.
>
> In the premortal realm, spirit sons and daughters knew and worshiped God as their Eternal Father and accepted His plan by which His children could obtain a physical body and gain earthly experience to progress toward perfection and ultimately realize his or her divine destiny as an heir of eternal life. The

divine plan of happiness enables family relationships to be perpetuated beyond the grave. Sacred ordinances and covenants available in holy temples make it possible for individuals to return to the presence of God and for families to be united eternally.

The first commandment that God gave to Adam and Eve pertained to their potential for parenthood as husband and wife. We declare that God's commandment for His children to multiply and replenish the earth remains in force. We further declare that God has commanded that the sacred powers of procreation are to be employed only between man and woman, lawfully wedded as husband and wife.

We declare the means by which mortal life is created to be divinely appointed. We affirm the sanctity of life and of its importance in God's eternal plan.

Husband and wife have a solemn responsibility to love and care for each other and for their children. "Children are an heritage of the Lord" (Psalm 127:3). Parents have a sacred duty to rear their children in love and righteousness, to provide for their physical and spiritual needs, to teach them to love and serve one another, to observe the commandments of God and to be law-abiding citizens wherever they live. Husbands and wives—mothers and fathers—will be held accountable before God for the discharge of these obligations.

The family is ordained of God. Marriage between man and woman is essential to His eternal plan. Children are entitled to birth within the bonds of matrimony, and to be reared by a father and a mother who honor marital vows with complete fidelity. Happiness in family life is most likely to be achieved when founded upon the teachings of the Lord Jesus Christ. Successful marriages and families are established and maintained on principles of faith, prayer, repentance, forgiveness, respect, love, compassion, work, and wholesome recreational activities. By divine design, fathers are to preside over their families in love and righteousness and are responsible to provide the necessities of life and protection for their families. Mothers are primarily responsible for the nurture of their children. In these sacred responsibilities, fathers and mothers are obligated to help one another as equal partners. Disability, death, or other circumstances may necessitate individual adaptation. Extended families should lend support when needed.

We warn that individuals who violate covenants of chastity, who abuse spouse or offspring, or who fail to fulfill family responsibilities will one day stand accountable before God. Further, we warn that the disintegration of the family will bring upon individuals, communities, and nations the calamities foretold by ancient and modern prophets.

We call upon responsible citizens and officers of government everywhere to promote those measures designed to maintain and strengthen the family as the fundamental unit of society.

We commend to all a careful, thoughtful, and prayerful reading of this proclamation. The strength of any nation is rooted within the walls of its homes. We urge our people everywhere to strengthen their families in conformity with these time-honored values.

May the Lord bless you, my beloved sisters. You are the guardians of the hearth. You are the bearers of the children. You are they who nurture them and establish within them the habits of their lives. No other work reaches so close to divinity as does the nurturing of the sons and daughters of God. May you be strengthened for the challenges of the day. May you be endowed with wisdom beyond your own in dealing with the problems you constantly face. May your prayers and your pleadings be answered with blessings upon your heads and upon the heads of your loved ones. We leave with you our love and our blessing, that your lives may be filled with peace and gladness. It can be so. Many of you can testify that it has been so. The Lord bless you now and through the years to come, I humbly pray in the name of our Savior, the Lord Jesus Christ, amen.

# 165th Semiannual
# General Conference

# Saturday Morning
# Session

SEPTEMBER 30, 1995

$M$Y BRETHREN AND SISTERS, it is wonderful that we have the opportunity of meeting together each six months in these great world conferences. We gather from over the earth to bear our testimonies one to another, to hear instruction, to mingle as brethren and sisters. We partake of that sociality which is so pleasant and so important a part of the culture of this great organization.

For more than a century these gatherings have originated in this historic Tabernacle. From this pulpit has gone forth the word of the Lord. Through the years the speakers have come on stage and then moved on. The personalities are different, but the spirit is the same. It is that spirit referred to when the Lord said, "He that preacheth and he that receiveth, understand one another, and both are edified and rejoice together" (D&C 50:22).

This great Tabernacle seems to grow smaller each year. We now meet with far larger groups gathered under a single roof in some regional conferences. For instance, not long ago we were in the Tacoma Washington Region. There on a Sunday morning we had the privilege of speaking to 17,328 Latter-day Saints assembled together as one congregation. The acoustics were not as good as they are in this remarkable structure.

Of course, there are far more of you participating through the wonders of the electronic media than there are here on Temple Square. Increasingly, the Tabernacle is becoming a broadcast studio from which these conference services go by radio, television, cable, satellite, and other resources to many tens of thousands of you in various parts of the world. They are now seen across the United States, Canada, and the Caribbean. They are carried to many areas of the British Isles and Europe. We hope that the time is not far distant when they can be carried live to the islands of the Pacific, to New Zealand and Australia, to the lands of Asia, to the nations of Mexico, Central America, and South America. As it is, however, more than half of the membership of the Church can, with a little effort, both see and hear me as I speak to you today.

Just below where I speak, in the basement of the Tabernacle, a large group of translators are at work so that each who wishes to hear may do so in his or her own language. I pay tribute to and express thanks for the tremendous services of these dedicated men and women who give so freely of their time and talents to this work of translation.

The little stone which was cut out of the mountain without hands is rolling forth to fill the earth (see D&C 65:2). What a wonderful thing it is to be part of this growing kingdom of our Lord. There are no political boundaries separating the hearts of the children of God, regardless of where they may live. We are all of one great family. We are sons and daughters of God. We are engaged in the service of His Beloved Son. He is our Redeemer and our Savior, and a testimony of this truth burns within our hearts. Each is entitled to such a testimony of this work. It is an individual knowledge of great fundamental truths that binds us together into what we call the Church and kingdom of God.

And so we gather each six months to renew our faith, to enlarge our understanding of things divine, to express our love and respect one for another in this great and remarkable brotherhood and sisterhood which all of us know as The Church of Jesus Christ of Latter-day Saints. With you I look forward to the services in which we shall participate today and tomorrow, praying that the Lord will bless us, each one of us, with the companionship of His Holy Spirit.

I invoke the blessings of the Lord upon all who will speak, upon all who will sing, upon all who will offer prayers, and in a very particular way, with great love and appreciation in my heart, upon all who will listen by the voice of the Spirit, in the name of Jesus Christ, amen.

# PRIESTHOOD
# SESSION

SEPTEMBER 30, 1995

Now, IF I MAY HAVE AN interest in your faith and prayers, I hope to be able to say something that is helpful. Last Saturday evening, one week ago, a great Relief Society conference was held in this Tabernacle. It was an inspiring experience to look into the faces of that vast congregation of women of strength and faith and capacity. Now it is likewise an inspiring experience to look into the faces of you brethren and feel of your strength, your faith, your loyalty, your devotion.

This has been an hour of inspiration. We have heard much of wonderful counsel that will bless our lives if we will accept it. I desire to speak of two or three matters.

The first has already been dealt with by President Monson and Brother Hillam. I wish to add my endorsement, together with a few further observations.

I speak also of missionary service. I was recently in London, England, and there we held a meeting with the missionaries serving in that area. Representatives of the British Broadcasting Corporation filmed part of the service. They are preparing a documentary of our missionary work in the British Isles.

Prior to this I had been interviewed by a representative of the BBC Radio Worldwide Service. He had seen the missionaries and noted their youthful appearance. He asked me, "How do you expect people to listen to these callow youth?"

In case some of you do not know the meaning of *callow*, it means immature, inexperienced, lacking sophistication.

I replied to the reporter with a smile, "Callow youth? It is with these missionaries today as it was with Timothy in the days of Paul. It was Paul who wrote to his young companion, saying, 'Let no man despise thy youth; but be thou an example of the believers, in word, in conversation, in charity, in spirit, in faith, in purity' (1 Timothy 4:12).

"The remarkable thing is that people do receive them and listen to them. They are wholesome. They are bright, they are alert, they are upstanding. They are clean looking, and people quickly develop confidence in them."

I might have added, "They are a miracle." They knock on doors, but not many are at home these days in a city like London. And so missionaries approach them on the street and engage them in conversation.

It is not an easy thing for a sensitive young man or woman to do this. But they come to believe in these further words of Paul to Timothy:

"For God hath not given us the spirit of fear; but of power, and of love, and of a sound mind.

"Be not thou therefore ashamed of the testimony of our Lord" (2 Timothy 1:7–8).

They recognize that fear comes not from God but from the adversary of truth. And so they develop a capacity to engage people in conversation concerning their work and their message. They and their associates will bring into the Church during this year of 1995 almost 300,000 converts. That is the equivalent of 100 new stakes of Zion and more than 500 new wards in one year.

"Callow youth?" Yes, they are lacking in sophistication. What a great blessing this is. They carry no element of deception. They speak with no element of sophistry. They speak out of their hearts with personal conviction. Each is a servant of the living God, an ambassador of the Lord Jesus Christ. Their power comes not of their learning in the things of the world. Their power comes of faith and prayer and humility. As we have been reminded, the work is not easy. It has never been easy. Long ago Jeremiah said that the Lord would gather His people one of a city and two of a family and bring them to Zion and feed them with pastors after His own heart (see Jeremiah 3:14–15). In terms of the individual missionary, the harvest is not great in most instances, but in the aggregate it becomes tremendous. The work demands courage, it demands effort, it demands dedication, it demands the humility to get on one's knees and ask the Lord for help and direction.

I throw out a challenge to every young man within this vast congregation tonight. Prepare yourself now to be worthy to serve the Lord as a full-time missionary. He has said, "If ye are prepared ye shall not fear" (D&C 38:30). Prepare to consecrate two years of your lives to this sacred service. That will, in effect, constitute a tithe on the first 20 years of your lives. Think of all that you have that is good—life itself, health, strength, food to eat and clothing to wear, parents, brothers and sisters, and friends. All are gifts from the Lord.

Of course your time is precious, and you may feel you cannot afford two years. But I promise you that the time you spend in the mission field, if those years are spent in dedicated service, will yield a greater return on investment than any other two years of your lives. You will come to know what dedication and consecration mean. You will develop powers of persuasion which will bless your entire life. Your timidity, your fears, your shyness will gradually disappear as you go forth with boldness and conviction. You will learn to work with others, to develop a spirit of teamwork. The cankering evil of selfishness will be supplanted by a sense of service to others. You will draw nearer to the Lord than you likely will in any other set of circumstances. You will come to know that without His help you are indeed weak and simple—but that with His help you can accomplish miracles.

You will establish habits of industry. You will develop a talent for the establishment of goals of effort. You will learn to work with singleness of purpose. What a tremendous foundation all of this will become for you in your later educational efforts and your life's work. Two years will not be time lost. It will be skills gained.

You will bless the lives of those you teach and their posterity after them. You will bless your own life. You will bless the lives of your family, who will sustain you and pray for you.

And above and beyond all of this will come that sweet peace in your heart that you have served your Lord faithfully and well. Your service will become an expression of gratitude to your Heavenly Father.

You will come to know your Redeemer as your greatest friend in time or eternity. You will realize that through His atoning sacrifice He has opened the way for eternal life and an exaltation above and beyond your greatest dreams.

If you serve a mission faithfully and well, you will be a better husband, you will be a better father, you will be a better student, a better worker in your chosen vocation. Love is of the essence of this missionary work. Selflessness is of its very nature. Self-discipline is its requirement. Prayer opens its reservoir of power.

And so, my dear young brethren, resolve within your hearts today to include in the program of your lives service in the harvest field of the Lord as a missionary of The Church of Jesus Christ of Latter-day Saints.

And now, brethren, I pass to another subject. Missionary work is concerned with providing saving ordinances to our Father's living children throughout the world. Temple work is primarily concerned with service in behalf of the sons and daughters of God who have passed beyond the veil of death. God is no respecter of persons. If the living in all nations are deserving of the saving ordinances of the gospel, then those of all past generations must likewise be deserving.

Our people cannot partake of all of the blessings of the gospel unless they can receive their own temple ordinances and then make these ordinances available to those of their kindred dead and others. If this is to happen, temples must be available to them. I feel very strongly about this.

Back in 1954, before I was a General Authority, President McKay called me into his office and told me of the planned construction of the Swiss Temple. He gave me an assignment to find a way by which the temple ordinances could be administered to those of various languages without multiplying the number of temple workers. Since that time I have had much to do with these sacred buildings and the ordinances administered therein.

We now have 47 working temples. Eight of these are in Utah, 16 in other areas of the United States, 2 in Canada, and 21 outside of North America. Twenty-eight of the 47 have been dedicated since I came into the First Presidency in 1981. In addition, 4 have been rededicated after very extensive remodeling. We now have under construction 6 more, located in American Fork and Vernal, Utah; St. Louis, Missouri; Hong Kong; Preston, England; and Bogotá, Colombia.

We have announced seven additional temples: for Santo Domingo in the Dominican Republic; Madrid, Spain; Guayaquil, Ecuador; Recife, Brazil; Cochabamba, Bolivia; Nashville, Tennessee; and Hartford, Connecticut. And we are working on the possibility of another—in Venezuela.

After working for years to acquire a suitable site in the Hartford area, during which time the Church has grown appreciably in areas to the north and south, we have determined that we will not at this time build a temple in the immediate area of Hartford, but rather we will build one in the area of Boston, Massachusetts, and another in White Plains, New York. In other words, there will be two to serve the needs of the people where originally it was planned one would do. We have beautiful sites in both of these new locations.

We apologize to our faithful Saints in the Hartford area. We know you will be disappointed in this announcement. You know that we and your local officers have spent countless hours searching for a suitable location that would handle the needs of the Saints of New York and New England. While we deeply regret disappointing the people in the Hartford area, we are satisfied that we have been led to the present decision and that temples will be located in such areas that those of you who reside in the Hartford area will not have too far to drive.

Additionally, we are working on six other sites. It is a tremendously ambitious program. *[Note: As of the date of publication of this book, the number of dedicated temples has increased to 119, with others in course of construction and yet others planned.]*

I have a burning desire that a temple be located within reasonable access to Latter-day Saints throughout the world. We can proceed only so fast. We try to see that each temple will be in an excellent location where there will be good neighbors over a long period of time. Real estate prices in such areas are usually high. A temple is a much more complex structure to build than an ordinary meetinghouse or stake center. It is built to a higher standard of architecture. It takes longer and costs more. The work is moving about as fast as we can go. It is my constant prayer that somehow it might be speeded up so that more of our people might have easier access to a sacred house of the Lord.

Brigham Young once said that if young people really understood the blessings of temple marriage, they would walk all the way to England if that were necessary (see *Deseret News,* Aug. 9, 1865, 355). We hope they will not have to go anywhere near that far.

These unique and wonderful buildings, and the ordinances administered therein, represent the ultimate in our worship. These ordinances become the most profound expressions of our theology. I urge our people everywhere, with all of the persuasiveness of which I am capable, to live worthy to hold a temple recommend, to secure one and regard it as a precious asset, and to make a greater effort to go to the house of the Lord and partake of the spirit and the blessings to be had therein. I am satisfied that every man or woman who goes to the temple in a spirit of sincerity and faith leaves the house of the Lord a better man or woman. There is need for constant improvement in all of our lives. There is need occasionally to leave the noise and the tumult of the world and step within the walls of a sacred house of God, there to feel His Spirit in an environment of holiness and peace.

If every man in this Church who has been ordained to the Melchizedek Priesthood were to qualify himself to hold a temple recommend and then were to go to the house of the Lord and renew his covenants in solemnity before God and witnesses, we would be a better people. There would be little or no infidelity among us. Divorce would almost entirely disappear. So much of heartache and heartbreak would be avoided. There would be a greater measure of peace and love and happiness in our homes. There would be fewer weeping wives and weeping children. There would be a greater measure of appreciation and of mutual respect among us. And I am confident the Lord would smile with greater favor upon us.

Now, brethren, I have one more matter before I conclude, and if I run overtime a little, I hope you will excuse me.

I desire to present to the priesthood of the Church my appraisal of the present condition of this great organization of which each of us is a part and in which each of us has an interest. I think you are entitled to occasionally hear such a report.

I am grateful to be able to say that the Church is in good condition. It is healthy. It is growing in numbers. As of the end of 1994 our membership stood at 9,025,000, a gain of 300,730 over the previous year. This means that we are adding a million new members each three and one-half years, and I am confident that momentum will increase. It is expanding geographically over the world. I believe that it is well managed. But we are not without problems. Too many of our people drift into inactivity. Too many fail to live the principles of the gospel. But with all of this, we have cause to rejoice as to what is occurring.

The Church has no debt. I qualify that to the extent that we have some contracts for the purchase of properties where the sellers insist on payments over a period of time. There are resources to ensure that these contracts will be covered in a timely way.

In our few business enterprises, some debt is used as a tool of management. But the ratio of debt to assets would be envied by the executives of any large organization.

The Church has been living within its means, and it will continue to do so. I am profoundly grateful for the law of tithing. To me it is a constantly recurring miracle. It is made possible by the faith of the people. It is the Lord's plan for financing the work of His kingdom.

It is so simple and straightforward. It consists of 35 words set forth in section 119 of the Doctrine and Covenants. What a contrast with the cumbersome, complex, and difficult tax codes with which we live as citizens.

There is no compulsion to pay tithing other than the commandment of the Lord, and that, of course, becomes the best of all reasons. This is the only large society of which I am aware that does not drop from its rolls those who fail to pay what might be considered their dues.

The payment of tithing carries with it the conviction of the truth of the principle.

Now, we know that these funds are sacred. We have a compelling trust to use them carefully and wisely. I have said before that I keep on the credenza in my office a genuine widow's mite, given me long ago by Brother David B. Galbraith, who at the time was the president of the Jerusalem Branch of the Church. I keep it as a reminder of the sacrifice it represents, that we are dealing with the consecration of the widow as well as the offering of the wealthy. I thank all who live honestly with the Lord in the payment of their tithes and offerings. But I know that you do not need to be thanked. Your testimony of the divinity of this law, and of the blessings that flow from its observance, is as strong as is my testimony.

Not only are we determined to live within the means of the Church, but each year we put into the reserves of the Church a portion of our annual budget. We are only doing what we have suggested every family do. Should there come a time of economic distress, we would hope to have the means to weather the storm.

We recognize the importance of consecrated voluntary service in carrying forward the programs of the Church. We have a veritable army of dedicated people who give freely of their time to assist in the work. Our Human Resources people indicate that there are 96,484 of these volunteers now serving. They represent the equivalent of 10,000 full-time employees, and their service has an annual value of $360 million. They labor in a missionary or volunteer capacity in our Church Educational System, in our family history organization, in the temples, and in various other departments and offices of the Church. We are deeply grateful and heavily indebted to them for their magnificent contribution. I am confident that the Lord is pleased with their dedicated service.

Our program of weekday religious education moves forward. Wherever the Church is organized, the seminary program is put in place. Likewise our institutes are providing a wonderful service for those of college and university age. During this 1995–1996 academic year, there are more than 583,000 students enrolled in seminaries and institutes. Many of you young men who are here this evening—I venture almost every one of you—is a beneficiary of this wonderful Church program. I'd like all of you to stand, just for a moment, who are seminary or institute enrollees. Look at that! That says it! Thank you very much.

We hope that all for whom these programs are available will take advantage of them. Knowledge of the gospel will be increased, faith will be strengthened, and you will enjoy wonderful associations and friendships with those of your own kind.

I think of the Prophet Joseph's struggle in getting out the first edition of the Book of Mormon. There were 5,000 copies in that first edition, and its printing was made possible only through the generosity of Martin Harris. You may be interested to know that last year 3,742,629 copies of the Book of Mormon were distributed. All or substantial parts of the book are printed in 85 languages. We may not be flooding the earth with the Book of Mormon, as President Benson had urged us to do, but let me say that it is no small thing to distribute three and three-quarter million copies in a single year.

It was my privilege to preside over the 150th stake of the Church, which was created in 1945, 115 years after the Church was organized. Now, an even 50 years later, there are 2,101 stakes of Zion. Seven hundred and seventy-two new wards and branches were organized during 1994, bringing the total at the close of the year to 21,774 wards and branches. It should be apparent to all why we must construct so many new buildings in which to house our people for worship and instruction. We have 375 new buildings in the course of construction at the present time. They are becoming increasingly costly to build. We hope that you will take good care of them. To you young men I make a special plea that you do all possible in this regard. We want these facilities *used* for the purposes for which they are constructed, but we do not want them *abused*. Utility costs are high. Turn off the lights when the buildings are not in use. Leave no litter about them. Keep the grounds clean and attractive. Wherever one of our buildings is found, it ought to say to those who pass, "The people who worship here are people who believe in cleanliness, order, beauty, and respectability."

I have already spoken to you about the increase in the number of temples. It is so with every aspect of the program.

I see a bright future ahead. I do not discount the fact that we will be faced with problems. This work has always been faced with problems. The work of the adversary continues against it. But we will move forward as those who have gone before us have moved forward. Every man and boy within the sound of my voice tonight has the responsibility to assist in this great work of reaching out and growing stronger.

Brethren, thank you for your faith. Thank you for your devotion. We are aware of the great trust which you place in us. We are aware of the sacred trust placed in us by the Lord. And He has likewise placed a sacred trust in each of you who holds His divine priesthood.

As I have said before, we are all in this together. Each of us has his part in the building of this kingdom. How wonderful, how very satisfying it is to know that each of us can do something to strengthen this, the work of the Almighty.

It is true. It is our Father's work. It is the Church of our Redeemer. The priesthood which we hold is a very real and a very precious thing. I leave you my testimony, my love and my blessing, and my gratitude, in the name of Jesus Christ, amen.

# Sunday Morning
# Session

OCTOBER 1, 1995

My BRETHREN AND SISTERS, thank you for your sustaining hands and hearts and for your expressions of confidence and love. My faith in this great work has been strengthened by what I have seen and heard as I have traveled among you during the past six months.

I have a desire to get out with the Latter-day Saints across the world, to look into your faces, to shake your hands wherever possible, to share with you in a more personal and intimate way my feelings concerning this sacred work, and to feel of your spirit and your love of the Lord and His mighty cause. I wish I had some way to thank you individually for the kindness you have shown us in so many ways. I know that your respect, confidence, and love are to be earned through the service that we give. I have only one desire, and that is that while the Lord gives me strength I may serve Him faithfully and well through service to His sons and daughters, you, my brethren and sisters. To that end I consecrate my strength, my time, and whatever talent I may possess.

I love this Church. I love the Prophet Joseph, to whom God, our Eternal Father, and the risen Lord spoke with that same intimacy with which I speak with you today. I feel love for all of those who accepted his testimony in those early and difficult years. Their lives in large measure constitute the early history of this work. It is a wonderful thing to have strong and deep roots. From them has grown the great worldwide movement we know as The Church of Jesus Christ of Latter-day Saints.

I thank the Lord that He planted in my heart while I was yet a boy a love for the Prophet Joseph Smith, a love for the Book of Mormon, a love for those great men and women who endured so much in establishing a foundation on which to build this cause and kingdom. I love the priesthood which is among us, this authority given to men to speak in the name of God. I am grateful for its power and authority, which reach even beyond the veil of death. I love the Saints wherever they walk in faith and faithfulness. I am thankful for the strength of your testimonies and for the goodness of your lives. I love the missionaries who are out on the front line of the world bearing testimony of the Restoration of the gospel. I pray for them that they may be protected and that they may be led to those who will receive their message.

I love the youth of this Church, so very many of them who are eager in their ways, who are searching for truth, who pray and try to do the right thing. I feel great love and respect for the women of the Relief Society, for the young women in their organization, for the Primary children, who are beautiful wherever they are regardless of the color of their skin or the circumstances in which they live.

I feel a great sense of gratitude for our bishops and those who serve with them, for our presidents of stakes and their associates, for the newly called Area Authorities, and for my brethren of the General Authorities.

I have a strong, uplifting sense of optimism concerning this work. I have lived long enough now to have seen the miracle of its growth. Mine has been the favored lot of assisting in its establishment across much of the world. Everywhere it is growing stronger. Everywhere it is touching an increasing number of lives for good.

Our statisticians tell me that if the present trend continues, then sometime in February of 1996, just a few months from now, there will be more members of the Church outside the United States than in the United States.

The crossover of that line is a wonderfully significant thing. It represents the fruit of a tremendous outreach. The God of Heaven, whose servants we are, never intended that this should be a narrow, parochial work. John the Revelator "saw another angel fly in the midst of heaven, having the everlasting gospel to preach unto them that dwell on the earth, and to every nation, and kindred, and tongue, and people" (Revelation 14:6). That angel has come. His name is Moroni. His is a voice speaking from the dust, bringing another witness of the living reality of the Lord Jesus Christ.

We have not as yet carried the gospel to every nation, kindred, tongue, and people. But we have made great strides. We have gone wherever we are permitted to go. God is at the helm, and doors will be opened by His power according to His divine will. Of that I am confident. Of that I am certain.

I cannot understand those of small vision, who regard this work as limited and provincial. They have no expanding view of it. As certainly as there is an Almighty Father in Heaven, as surely as there is His Son, our Divine Redeemer, so certainly is this work destined to reach out to people everywhere.

The story of Caleb and Joshua and the other spies of Israel has always intrigued me. Moses led the children of Israel into the wilderness. In the second year of their wandering, he chose a representative from each of the 12 tribes to search the land of Canaan and bring back a report concerning its resources and its people. Caleb represented the tribe of Judah, Joshua the tribe of Ephraim. The 12 of them went into the land of Canaan. They found it to be fruitful. They were gone 40 days. They brought back with them some of "the firstripe grapes" as evidence of the productivity of the land (Numbers 13:20).

51

They came before Moses and Aaron and all the congregation of the children of Israel, and they said concerning the land of Canaan, "Surely it floweth with milk and honey; and this is the fruit of it" (v. 27).

But 10 of the spies were victims of their own doubts and fears. They gave a negative report of the numbers and stature of the Canaanites. They concluded that "they are stronger than we" (v. 31). They compared themselves as grasshoppers to the giants they had seen in the land. They were the victims of their own timidity.

Then Joshua and Caleb stood before the people and said:

"The land, which we passed through to search it, is an exceeding good land.

"If the Lord delight in us, then he will bring us into this land, and give it us; a land which floweth with milk and honey.

"Only rebel not ye against the Lord, neither fear ye the people of the land; for they are bread for us: their defence is departed from them, and the Lord is with us: fear them not" (Numbers 14:7–9).

But the people were more willing to believe the 10 doubters than to believe Caleb and Joshua.

Then it was that the Lord declared that the children of Israel should wander in the wilderness 40 years until the generation of those who had walked with doubt and fear should pass away. The scripture records that "those men that did bring up the evil report upon the land, died by the plague before the Lord" (v. 37).

"But Joshua . . . and Caleb . . . , which were of the men that went to search the land, lived still" (v. 38). They were the only ones of that group who survived through those four decades of wandering and who had the privilege of entering the promised land concerning which they had reported in a positive manner.

We see some around us who are indifferent concerning the future of this work, who are apathetic, who speak of limitations, who express fears, who spend their time digging out and writing about what they regard to be weaknesses which really are of no consequence. With doubt concerning its past, they have no vision concerning its future.

Well was it said of old, "Where there is no vision, the people perish" (Proverbs 29:18). There is no place in this work for those who believe only in the gospel of doom and gloom. The gospel is good news. It is a message of triumph. It is a cause to be embraced with enthusiasm.

The Lord never said that there would not be troubles. Our people have known afflictions of every sort as those who have opposed this work have come upon them. But faith has shown through all their sorrows. This work has consistently moved forward and has never taken a backward step since its inception. I think of the boy Joseph, persecuted and ridiculed by those his senior. But the pain of the wounds of that persecution was tempered by the declaration of Moroni, who told him that God had a work for him to do and that his name "should be had for good and evil among all nations, kindreds, and tongues, or that it should be both good and evil spoken of among all people" (Joseph Smith—History 1:33).

He and his brother Hyrum were murdered June 27, 1844. Their enemies thought that this would end the cause for which they had given their lives. Little did they realize that the blood of the martyrs would give nurture to the young roots of the Church.

I stood the other day on the old docks of Liverpool, England. There was practically no activity the Friday morning when we were there. But once this was a veritable beehive. During the 1800s, tens of thousands of our people walked over the same stone paving on which we walked. They came from across the British Isles and from the lands of Europe, converts to the Church. They came with testimony on their lips and faith in their hearts. Was it difficult to leave their homes and step into the unknown of a new world? Of course it was. But they did it with optimism and enthusiasm. They boarded sailing vessels. They knew the crossing at best was hazardous. They soon found out that for the most part it was miserable. They lived in cramped quarters week after week. They endured storms, disease, sickness. Many died on the way and were buried at sea. It was an arduous and fearsome journey. They had doubts, yes. But their faith rose above those doubts. Their optimism rose above their fears. They had their dream of Zion, and they were on their way to fulfill it.

With a great, overpowering spirit of optimism, based on a solid bedrock of faith, they built this Tabernacle in which we meet this day. Through 40 years they constructed the temple just to the east of us. Through all their travail was a shining, bright, and wonderful vision concerning the growth of this work.

I can scarcely comprehend the magnitude of Brigham Young's faith in leading thousands of people into the wilderness. He had never seen this country, except as he had seen it in vision. It was an act of boldness almost beyond comprehension. For him their coming here was all part of the grand pattern of the growth and destiny of this work. To those who followed him it was the pursuit of a great dream.

So it was in the latter part of the last century. It seemed the whole world stood against us. But the faithful knew there was sunlight behind those dark clouds and that if they held on the storm would pass.

Today we walk in the sunlight of goodwill. There is a tendency on the part of some to become indifferent. There are those who drift off, seeking the enticements of the world, forsaking the cause of the Lord. I see others who think it is all right to lower their standards, perhaps in small ways. In this very process they lose the cutting edge of enthusiasm for this work. For instance, they think the violation of the Sabbath is a thing of unimportance. They neglect their meetings. They become critical. They engage in backbiting. Before long they have drifted from the Church.

The Prophet Joseph once declared, "Where doubt is, there faith has no power" (*Lectures on Faith* [1985], 46).

I invite any who may have so drifted to come back to the strong and solid moorings of the Church. This is the work of the Almighty. Whether we as individuals go forward will depend on us. But the Church will never fail to move forward. I remember an old song rendered in stirring tones by a male chorus: "Start me with ten who are stouthearted men, and I'll soon give you ten thousand more" (Oscar Hammerstein, "Stouthearted Men").

When the Lord took Moses unto Himself, He then said to Joshua, "Be strong and of a good courage; be not afraid, neither be thou dismayed: for the Lord thy God is with thee whithersoever thou goest" (Joshua 1:9). This is His work. Never forget it. Embrace it with enthusiasm and affection.

Let us not be afraid. Jesus is our leader, our strength, and our king.

This is an age of pessimism. Ours is a mission of faith. To my brethren and sisters everywhere, I call upon you to reaffirm your faith, to move this work forward across the world. You can make it stronger by the manner in which you live. Let the gospel be your sword and your shield. Each of us is a part of the greatest cause on earth. Its doctrine came of revelation. Its priesthood came of divine bestowal. Another witness has been added to its testimony of the Lord Jesus Christ. It is literally the little stone of Daniel's dream which was "cut out of the mountain without hands [to] roll forth, until it has filled the whole earth" (D&C 65:2).

"Brethren, shall we not go on in so great a cause? Go forward and not backward. Courage, brethren; and on, on to the victory!" (D&C 128:22). So wrote the Prophet Joseph in a psalm of faith.

How glorious is the past of this great cause. It is filled with heroism, courage, boldness, and faith. How wondrous is the present as we move forward to bless the lives of people wherever they will hearken to the message of the servants of the Lord. How magnificent will be the future as the Almighty rolls on His glorious work, touching for good all who will accept and live His gospel and even reaching to the eternal blessing of His sons and daughters of all generations through the selfless work of those whose hearts are filled with love for the Redeemer of the world.

Back in the days of the Great Depression, an old sign dangled by one staple from a piece of rusting barbed wire. The owner of the farm had written:

*Burned out by drought,*
*Drowned out by flud waters,*
*Et out by jackrabbits,*
*Sold out by sheriff,*
*Still here!*

So it is with us. There have been makers of threats, naysayers, and criers of doom. They have tried in every conceivable way to injure and destroy this Church. But we are still here, stronger and more determined to move it forward. To me it is exciting. It is wonderful. I feel like Ammon of old, who said: "Now have we not reason to rejoice? Yea, I say unto you, there never were men that had so great reason to rejoice as we, since the world began; yea, and my joy is carried away, even unto boasting in my God; for he has all power, all wisdom, and all understanding" (Alma 26:35).

I invite every one of you, wherever you may be as members of this Church, to stand on your feet and with a song in your heart move forward, living the gospel, loving the Lord, and building the kingdom. Together we shall stay the course and keep the faith, the Almighty being our strength. In the name of Jesus Christ, amen.

# Sunday Afternoon
# Session

OCTOBER 1, 1995

THIS HAS BEEN A MOST remarkable thing, this conference. We have listened to 28 different speakers. No one was assigned a topic on which to speak. Each was free to choose his or her message. There is always the risk of repetition in that. But isn't it remarkable that all of it seems to have been woven together into a beautiful fabric of expression of faith and testimony. I am grateful for what we have heard. I will be a better man if I will put into my life the things of which I have been reminded in this conference, and I would like to suggest that each of you will be a better man or woman if you will put into your lives something of what you have heard in this great conference.

Brethren and sisters, I know that you are a praying people. That is a wonderful thing in this day and time when the practice of prayer has slipped from many lives. To call upon the Lord for wisdom beyond our own, for strength to do what we ought to do, for comfort and consolation, and for the expression of gratitude is a significant and wonderful thing. We know that you pray for us, and we appreciate your prayers. They sustain us; they remind us of the great trust which you have placed in us. I want you to know that we pray for you always. We pray for you that you may be happy and that in living the gospel there may be love and peace in your homes and growing goodness in your lives. That is what this is all about, for God sent His Only Beloved Son "that whosoever believeth in him should not perish, but have everlasting life" (John 3:16). The great purpose of the work in which we are engaged is to help each of us along the way of immortality and eternal life.

Please know of our great love for you. I thank the Lord every morning of my life for the Restoration of the gospel and its meaning in the lives of faithful Latter-day Saints.

You parents, love your children. Cherish them. They are so precious. They are so very, very important. They are the future. You need more than your own wisdom in rearing them. You need the help of the Lord. Pray for that help, and follow the inspiration which you receive.

Now, as we say good-bye to you at the conclusion of this conference, please know of our love for each of you. Even those who transgress, we want you to know that we love you. We cannot condone the sin, but we love the sinner.

God bless you. I leave my blessing upon you, that as you walk in faith there may be peace in your hearts and goodness and gladness in your lives and that the Spirit of the Lord may dwell with you in your homes to bring nurture to you and those you love most dearly, in the name of Jesus Christ, amen.

# General
# Young Women
# Meeting

WHAT A MAGNIFICENT SIGHT this is. This great Tabernacle is filled with bright and beautiful young women. Many thousands more are assembled in Church halls far and wide. Thank you for the effort you have made to gather together this evening. It has been a wonderful meeting. The talks have been uplifting and inspiring, as has been the music of this beautiful choir and the opening prayer. If you will remember what you have heard and if you will follow the counsel given you, your lives will know much of happiness.

I pray for the Spirit of the Lord to guide me as I speak to you. I regard this as a great opportunity to tell you how I feel. You are young women 12 to 18 years of age, of whom your Father in Heaven and all of us who know you expect great things. You are part of this marvelous generation, preparing to take your places in the challenging world that lies ahead.

You constantly are faced with difficult choices. Your problems are not new, but they are intensified. You are subjected to temptations that are attractive and appealing. You represent the future of this Church, and the adversary of truth would like to injure you, would like to destroy your faith, would like to lead you down paths that are beguiling and interesting but deadly.

We have a hymn that I love to hear the youth of the Church sing:

> *Shall the youth of Zion falter*
> *In defending truth and right?*
> *While the enemy assaileth,*
> *Shall we shrink or shun the fight?*
> *No!*
> *True to the faith that our parents have cherished,*
> *True to the truth for which martyrs have perished,*
> *To God's command,*
> *Soul, heart, and hand,*
> *Faithful and true we will ever stand.*
> *["True to the Faith," Hymns, no. 254]*

I wish to talk to you about being true to the faith, about being true to yourselves and your associates, about being true to your parents and your heritage, about being true to the Church and to our Heavenly Father and His Son, the Lord Jesus Christ.

Let me first speak about being true to ourselves. Our thirteenth article of faith says that we believe in being honest and true.

We believe in being true. How very important it is to be true to ourselves. Each of us has a thing we call conscience. We know the difference between right and wrong. We do not have to be instructed concerning what is good and what is evil. I think we know that. We know when we have done the wrong thing, and we suffer pangs of conscience. We know when we have done the right thing, and we experience a sense of happiness. To be true to ourselves means being an example of righteous living in all situations and circumstances.

Being true to ourselves means being honest. It means being honest in school. We cannot afford to cheat or do anything of that kind. Suppose that you needed a lifesaving operation. You would not want that operation performed by a surgeon who had cheated in medical school, would you? Of course not. We go to school to learn and to equip ourselves for the work which we will do in the future. It is imperative that we take advantage of the opportunity to learn. The Lord has said concerning us of this Church that He expects us to study and learn. I know of no other church that has scripture instructing its people to pursue secular knowledge as well as spiritual knowledge.

I urge each of you young women to get all of the schooling you can get. You will need it for the world into which you will move. Life is becoming so exceedingly competitive. Experts say that the average man or woman, during his or her working career, can expect to have five different jobs. The world is changing, and it is so very important that we equip ourselves to move with that change. But there is a bright side to all of this. No other generation in all of history has offered women so many opportunities. Your first objective should be a happy marriage, sealed in the temple of the Lord, and followed by the rearing of a good family. Education can better equip you for the realization of those ideals.

Be honest in your lives. As a Latter-day Saint you cannot do shoplifting or anything of the kind. It was said a long time ago that honesty is the best policy. The finger of the Lord wrote on tablets of stone: "Thou shalt not steal. . . . Thou shalt not covet" (Exodus 20:15, 17).

We must be true to ourselves in matters of personal virtue. You and I as members of this Church cannot become involved in immorality. The Lord has said by way of commandment, "Let virtue garnish thy thoughts unceasingly" (D&C 121:45). He is saying to us that we cannot even think about immoral matters. Why? Because evil thoughts lead to evil deeds. Then He has said that if we will let virtue garnish our thoughts, we shall stand with confidence in the presence of God. Think of that. He goes on to say the Holy Ghost shall be our constant companion. Our dominion shall be an everlasting dominion. (See D&C 121:45–46.) What

61

marvelous and remarkable promises these are, and they are given to those who walk in virtue.

We cannot afford to be tainted by moral sin. We live in a world where temptation is constantly being thrown at us, particularly at you young people. It is on television. It is in magazines. It is in books. It is on videos which are readily available. Stay away from these things. They will only hurt you. When it comes to the moral law, you know what is expected of you. If you find yourself slipping under the pressure of circumstances, discipline yourself. Stop before it is too late. You will be forever grateful that you did.

Be true to yourselves and the best you have within you. That best is very good. Shakespeare said, "To thine ownself be true, and it must follow, as the night the day, thou canst not then be false to any man" (*Hamlet,* act 1, scene 3).

Many young women at your age suffer from lack of self-esteem. Contrary to what you may think, an immoral act of any kind will only lower your self-esteem. Be true to yourself and your respect for yourself will increase. Know that yours is a divine birthright. Cultivate a good opinion of yourself. Others may make cutting remarks concerning you. This is only a sign of their ignorance and not of your qualities. Walk with that dignity which is becoming a young woman who is a daughter of God.

Do not become involved in illegal drugs. Do not touch them. Never experiment with them. I plead with you, with every one of you, to shun them as you would poison. You are young women. A great future is ahead of you. Your lives are radiant with promise. Most of you will someday wish to be married and have children. The use of illegal drugs could place a terrible handicap not only upon you, but also upon your children. I do not hesitate to say that if you tamper with these things, you will regret it. If you discipline yourselves to avoid them, you will have reason to rejoice.

Be true to yourselves, my dear friends. Be loyal to one another, your friends and associates. Look for the good in those about you, and emphasize that good. Never go around gossiping about your associates or speaking unkind words concerning them. Such words will only backfire to hurt you. Jehovah has commanded, "Thou shalt not bear false witness" (Exodus 20:16).

Reach out to help one another. All of us need help from time to time. We need encouragement. We need friends who will stand by us through thick and thin. I ask each of you to be that kind of a friend.

Some of you may have read in the March issue of the *New Era* the story of a handicapped girl named Jenni. She was lonely and not very attractive. One day she said to her classmates, "I need a friend. I need someone who will eat lunch with me. Who will be my friend?"

One girl stood and said, "I will be your friend," and then another did likewise. They ate lunch with her. They encouraged her. They helped her. They brought new life into the dark world of this handicapped girl. And in the process they brought new gladness into their own lives. (See Victor W. Harris, "The Miracle of Jenni," *New Era*, Mar. 1996, 12–14.)

Be true to your parents and your heritage. Regrettably, there are a few parents who act in a way that does serious injustice to their children. But these are relatively few. No one has a greater interest in your welfare, in your happiness, in your future than do your mothers and fathers. They are of a prior generation, that is true. But they were once the age that you are now. Your problems are not substantially different from what theirs were. If they occasionally place restrictions on you, it is because they see danger down the road. Listen to them. What they ask you to do may not be to your liking, but you will be much happier if you do it. Your mother is your best friend. Never forget that. She gave you life itself. She cared for you, nurtured you, nursed you when you were sick, and looked after your every need. Listen to her now. Talk with her candidly and confidentially. You will find that she will keep your confidence and that her wisdom will prove to be wonderful.

Many of you are descended from pioneers in this Church. They struggled so hard; they paid such a terrible price for their faith. Be true to them and true always to the Church they loved so much. I wish that each of you would remember that tonight you heard me say that this Church is true. Other churches also do much good, but this is the "true and living Church" of the Lord Jesus Christ, whose name it bears (see D&C 1:30). Be true to it. Cling to it. If you will do so, it will become as an anchor in the midst of a stormy sea. It will be a light to your lives and a foundation upon which to build them. I give you my solemn testimony that this Church will never be led astray. It is in the hands of God, and should any of its leaders ever attempt to lead it astray, His is the power to remove them. He has said that He has restored His work for the last time, "never again to be destroyed nor given to other people" (D&C 138:44; see also Daniel 2:44–45).

I hope all of you who are eligible are attending seminary. This organization provides wonderful opportunities to learn the doctrines that will make you happy. It provides wonderful opportunities for socializing with those of your own kind.

Look to the Church and its leaders for counsel and direction. We have only one desire, and that is that you be happy, that your lives be challenging and satisfying, that you be saved from pitfalls of evil which could destroy you, that you will be the kind of people who will carry high the torch of eternal truth and hand it on to the generation which will succeed you.

The truths of this gospel are everlasting and eternal. Philosophies change. Customs change. Culture changes. But with all of these changes, there are gospel fundamentals that have never changed and never will change.

How lucky can you be to be a member of The Church of Jesus Christ of Latter-day Saints! Here you find choice and wonderful friends. Here you find able and faithful teachers. Here you find opportunities for service. For instance, where else is there any service to compare with being baptized for the dead? You, each one of you, may have that opportunity of going to the Lord's holy house, there to be baptized in behalf of someone who is helpless to go forward in the world beyond without the service you can give. That individual might have been a woman of great power and influence when she was upon the earth. But without the ordinance of baptism she is stopped in her eternal progress. Yours is the opportunity to free her. What an unselfish and wonderful thing this is. You, through a little effort, can become the one to unlock the gate which will permit that individual to move forward on the way of immortality and eternal life. There is not another organization in all the world that offers this opportunity. It affords the means by which to give the most unselfish kind of service. You will receive no thanks in this life for that which you do in being baptized for the dead. But you will receive a satisfaction in your heart of having done something totally unselfish and much appreciated. Be true to the Church.

Be true to our Eternal Father and His Beloved Son, the Lord Jesus Christ.

Never forget who you are. As you have sung tonight, you are in very deed a child of God. He is your Eternal Father. He loves you. You can go to Him in prayer. He has invited you to do so. Every one of you knows this, and what a wonderful thing this is. He is the greatest of all. He is the Creator and Governor of the universe. And yet He will listen to your prayer!

He wants His sons and daughters to be happy. Sin never was happiness. Transgression never was happiness. Disobedience never was happiness. The way of happiness is found in the plan of our Father in Heaven and in obedience to the commandments of His Beloved Son, the Lord Jesus Christ.

Now let me mention a related matter as I mention the name of the Father and the Son. I refer to the habit—yes, it has become a habit—of many young people in junior high and high school to profane the name of Deity in their everyday conversation. Jehovah wrote on the tablets of stone: "Thou shalt not take the name of the Lord thy God in vain, for [he] will not hold him guiltless [who] taketh his name in vain" (Exodus 20:7).

Let me tell you of an experience I had when I was a little boy in the first or second grade. I came home from school one day, threw my books on the table, and took the name of the Lord in vain in expressing my relief that school was out for the day.

My mother heard me. She was shocked. She took me by the hand and led me to the bathroom. There she got a clean washcloth and a clean bar of soap. She told me to open my mouth and then proceeded to wash the inside of my mouth with that terrible soap. I blubbered and protested. She stayed at it for a while and then said, "Don't let me ever hear such words from your lips again."

The taste was terrible. The reprimand was worse. I have never forgotten it, and I hope that I have never used the Lord's name in vain since that time.

When President Spencer W. Kimball underwent surgery years ago, he was wheeled from the operating room to the intensive care room. The attendant who pushed the gurney which carried him stumbled and let out an oath using the name of the Lord. President Kimball, who was barely conscious, said weakly, "Please! Please! That is my Lord whose names you revile."

There was a deathly silence, then the young man whispered with a subdued voice, "I am sorry." (See *The Teachings of Spencer W. Kimball,* ed. Edward L. Kimball [1982], 198.)

And while I am speaking of language, may I plead with you young women never to indulge in dirty, sleazy talk of any kind. There is so much of it, and it is so common. There is no need to use such language. It only advertises to others that your vocabulary is so deficient that you cannot express yourself without picking words out of the gutter. Do not do it. Please do not do it. Do not use such filthy language, and do not profane the name of the Lord.

Be true to our Eternal Father and His Beloved Son. When all else fails, our Lord is there to help us. He has said, "Come unto me, all ye that labour and are heavy laden, and I will give you rest" (Matthew 11:28). Each of you has burdens. Let the Lord help you in carrying those burdens. Again He has said, "Cast your burden on me, for my yoke is easy, and my burden is light" (see Matthew 11:29–30). He stands ready to help each of us with every burden. He loves us so much that He shed drops of blood in Gethsemane, then permitted evil and wicked men to take Him, to compel Him to carry the cross up to Golgotha to suffer beyond any power of description terrible pain when He was nailed to the cross, to be lifted up on the cross, and to die for each of us.

He was the one perfect man, without blemish, to walk the earth. He was the Savior and Redeemer of mankind. Because of His sacrifice, because of His Atonement, all of us will at some time arise in the Resurrection, and beyond that there will be marvelous opportunities to go forward on the road of immortality and eternal life.

He invites us to come unto Him. He has said to each of us, "Ask, and it shall be given you; seek, and ye shall find; knock, and it shall be opened unto you" (Matthew 7:7).

Pray to the Father in His name. None of us can really make it alone. We need help, the kind of help that can come in answer to prayer.

I know that you young women pray. I compliment you on this. I know that you are trying to live the gospel. I know that you are trying to live lives of honesty and virtue, of service and kindness and love toward others. I know that you pray for us, and I assure you that we pray for you.

You are so very important. This work is so much the stronger because of you. Whenever you step over the line in an immoral act or in doing any other evil thing, the Church is that much weaker because of what you have done. When you stand true and faithful, it is that much stronger. Each one of you counts.

Now, in conclusion I wish to add one other thought. If any of you has stepped over the line, please do not think all is lost. The Lord reaches out to help you, and there are many willing hands in the Church also who will help you. Put all evil behind you. Pray about the situation, talk with your parents if you can, and talk with your bishop. You will find that he will listen and do so confidentially. He will help you. We all stand ready to help you.

Repentance is one of the first principles of the gospel. Forgiveness is a mark of divinity. There is hope for you. Your lives are ahead, and they can be filled with happiness, even though the past may have been marred by sin. This is a work of saving and assisting people with their problems. This is the purpose of the gospel of Jesus Christ.

The prophet Isaiah declared:

"Wash you, make you clean; put away the evil of your doings from before mine eyes; cease to do evil. . . .

"Come now, and let us reason together, saith the Lord: though your sins be as scarlet, they shall be as white as snow; though they be red like crimson, they shall be as wool" (Isaiah 1:16, 18).

This is the time, this is the very hour, to repent of any evil in the past, to ask for forgiveness, to stand a little taller, and then to go forward with confidence and faith.

And finally, in all of living have much of fun and laughter. Life is to be enjoyed and not just endured.

I leave my blessing upon you. Please know that we love you. Please know that we have confidence in you. Live the gospel, be true to the faith, cling to the Church, honor your parents, love the Lord, and walk as a child of God. That you may do so and taste much of happiness is my prayer in your behalf, with love in my heart, in the name of Jesus Christ, amen.

# PRIESTHOOD
# SESSION

APRIL 6, 1996

W<small>E HAVE HAD A WONDERFUL</small> meeting. The Spirit of the Lord has been with us. I hope that each of us has gained much from what we have heard.

We are a blessed people. Where else in all the world can men and boys, each ordained to the holy priesthood, meet together as we do tonight? We are a vast congregation of hundreds of thousands—yes, of millions—bound together in a great brotherhood. It is a tremendous and remarkable thing. I hope each of us treasures that which we have.

A week ago tonight this Tabernacle was filled with beautiful and bright young women. It was the annual Young Women conference of the Church, and I was asked to speak. A number of those in attendance, and particularly the girls, said, "We wish you would tell the boys the same thing. They need to know what you've told us." Well, I'm not going to tell you quite the same thing. If you wish to read it, it will be in the May issue of the *Ensign* magazine.

I wish to begin this evening by reading a dream which President Joseph F. Smith had as a young man. As some of you know, President Joseph F. Smith was the sixth President of the Church. He served from 1901 to 1918, a period of 17 years.

He was the son of Hyrum Smith, who was the brother of the

69

Prophet Joseph Smith. He was born at Far West, Missouri, on November 13, 1838. When the Saints were driven out of Missouri, he was brought to Illinois as an infant. His father was killed in Carthage Jail at the time the Prophet Joseph was murdered. As a boy not yet six years of age, he heard a knock on the window of his mother's home in Nauvoo. It was a horseman to tell his mother that her husband had been killed at Carthage that afternoon. What a sobering and terrible experience that was for a little boy.

At the age of 9 this fatherless lad drove an ox team with his mother across the plains to this valley. At the age of 15 he was called on a mission to Hawaii. He made his way to San Francisco and there worked in a shingle mill to earn enough money to get to the islands.

Hawaii was not a tourist center then. It was peopled largely by the native Hawaiians. They were, for the most part, poor but generous with what they had. He learned to speak their language and to love them. He never lost his love for the Hawaiian people, nor did they for him. I give you this as background for the dream which he had when he was serving there as a very young man. I quote his words:

> I was very much oppressed, once, [when I was] on a mission. I was almost naked and entirely friendless, except the friendship of a poor, benighted . . . people. I felt as if I was so debased in my condition of poverty, lack of intelligence and knowledge, just a boy, that I hardly dared look a . . . man in the face.
>
> While in that condition I dreamed [one night] that I was on a journey, and I was impressed that I ought to hurry— hurry with all my might, for fear I might be too late. I rushed on my way as fast as I possibly could, and I was only conscious of having just a little bundle, a handkerchief with a small bundle wrapped in it. I did not realize just what it was, when I was hurrying as fast as I could; but finally I came to a wonderful mansion. . . . I thought I knew that was my destination. As

I passed towards it, as fast as I could, I saw a notice, "Bath." I turned aside quickly and went into the bath and washed myself clean. I opened up this little bundle that I had, and there was a pair of white, clean garments, a thing I had not seen for a long time, because the people I was with did not think very much of making things exceedingly clean. But my garments were clean, and I put them on. Then I rushed to what appeared to be a great opening, or door. I knocked and the door opened, and the man who stood there was the Prophet Joseph Smith. He looked at me a little reprovingly, and the first words he said: "Joseph, you are late." Yet I took confidence and [replied]:

"Yes, but I am clean—I am clean!"

He clasped my hand and drew me in, then closed the great door. I felt his hand just as tangible as I ever felt the hand of man. I knew him, and when I entered I saw my father, and Brigham [Young] and Heber [C. Kimball], and Willard [Richards], and other good men that I had known, standing in a row. I looked as if it were across this valley, and it seemed to be filled with a vast multitude of people, but on the stage were all the people that I had known. My mother was there, and she sat with a child in her lap; and I could name over as many as I remember of their names, who sat there, who seemed to be among the chosen, among the exalted. . . .

[When I had this dream,] I was alone on a mat, away up in the mountains of Hawaii—no one was with me. But in this vision I pressed my hand up against the Prophet, and I saw a smile cross his countenance. . . .

When I awoke that morning I was a man, although only a boy. There was not anything in the world that I feared [after that]. I could meet any man or woman or child and look them in the face, feeling in my soul that I was a man every whit. That vision, that manifestation and witness that I enjoyed at that time has made me what I am, if I am anything that is good, or clean, or upright before the Lord, if there is anything good in me. That has helped me out in every trial and through every difficulty. [ *Gospel Doctrine,* 5th ed. (1939), 542–43]

The core of that meaningful dream is found in the reproof given by Joseph Smith to young Joseph F. Said the Prophet, "Joseph, you are late."

Replied Joseph F., "Yes, but I am clean—I am clean!"

The result of that dream was that a boy was changed into a man. His declaration "I am clean" gave him self-assurance and courage in facing anyone or any situation. He received the strength that comes from a clear conscience fortified by the approbation of the Prophet Joseph.

There is something in this for every man and boy assembled in this vast congregation tonight.

Are you beset with doubts and fears? Has discouragement pulled you down? Do you need added wisdom and strength to go forward with your life?

I call to mind the words of Tennyson's Sir Galahad: "My strength is as the strength of ten, / Because my heart is pure" (Alfred, Lord Tennyson, "Sir Galahad").

Everything looks better when there is cleanliness. In Joseph F. Smith's dream, he could look into the eyes of the Prophet and say, "I am clean." Can you, my brethren, each of you tonight? We have a saying that used to be heard more commonly: "Cleanliness is next to godliness."

When I was a boy living here in Salt Lake City, most homes were heated with coal stoves. Black smoke belched forth from almost every chimney. As winter came to a close, black soot and grime were everywhere, both inside and outside of the house.

There was a ritual through which we passed each year, not a very pleasant one, as we viewed it. It involved every member of the family. It was known as spring-cleaning. When the weather warmed after the long winter, a week or so was designated as cleanup time. It was usually when there was a holiday and included two Saturdays.

My mother ran the show. All of the curtains were taken down and laundered. Then they were carefully ironed. The windows were washed inside and out, and oh, what a job that was in that big two-story house.

Wallpaper was on all of the walls, and Father would bring home numerous cans of wallpaper cleaner. It was like bread dough, but it was a pretty pink in color when the container was opened. It had an interesting smell, a pleasant, refreshing kind of smell. We all pitched in. We would knead some of the cleaning dough in our hands, climb a ladder, and begin on the high ceiling and then work down the walls. The dough was soon black from the dirt it lifted from the paper. It was a terrible task, very tiring, but the results were like magic. We would stand back and compare the dirty surface with the clean surface. It was amazing to us how much better the clean walls looked.

All of the carpets were taken up and dragged out to the back-yard, where they were hung over the clothesline, one by one. Each of us boys would have what we called a carpet beater, a device made of light steel rods with a wooden handle. As we beat the carpet, the dust would fly, and we would have to keep going until there was no dust left. We detested that work. But when all of it was done and everything was back in place, the result was wonderful. The house was clean, our spirits renewed. The whole world looked better.

This is what some of us need to do with our lives. Isaiah said:

"Wash you, make you clean; put away the evil of your doings from before mine eyes; cease to do evil;

"Learn to do well. . . .

"Come now, and let us reason together, saith the Lord: though your sins be as scarlet, they shall be as white as snow; though they be red like crimson, they shall be as wool" (Isaiah 1:16–18).

"Be ye clean that bear the vessels of the Lord" (D&C 133:5). Thus has He spoken to us in modern revelation. Be clean in body.

Be clean in mind. Be clean in language. Be clean in dress and manner.

I speak particularly to the boys, but I hope the men will also listen and hear. We all constantly need reminding. Our bodies are sacred. They were created in the image of God. They are marvelous, the crowning creation of Deity. No camera has ever matched the wonder of the human eye. No pump was ever built that could run so long and carry such a heavy duty as the human heart. The ear and the brain constitute a miracle. The capacity to pick up sound waves and convert them into language is almost beyond imagination. Look at your finger, and contemplate the wonder of it. Clever men have tried to match it but have never fully succeeded. These, with others of our parts and organs, represent the divine, omnipotent genius of God, who is our Eternal Father.

I cannot understand why anyone would knowingly wish to injure his body. And yet it happens around us every day as men and boys drink alcoholic beverages and use illegal drugs. What a scourge these are. For a little temporary lift, they take into their systems that which robs them of self-control, becomes habit-forming, is terribly expensive, enslaves, and yields no good.

I think of a young man who was recently convicted of automobile homicide because he killed an innocent victim while driving drunk. He was a young man of great potential. There is no telling what he might have become, but today he sits in prison, not only in the misery of his surroundings but also in the torture of his conscience. Our Father in Heaven, who loves us, has reminded us of the evils of these things and has warned us against them.

Stay away from alcohol, my brethren. Never get involved in a so-called beer bust. Do not get entrapped with illegal drugs. They could destroy you. They could make of you a slave, and the cravings that would follow would impoverish you in getting money to buy more drugs to satisfy those cravings.

You hold the priesthood of God. You are someone special. You have had bestowed upon you a power sacred and divine. It is totally wrong for you to partake of alcohol or drugs that are forbidden by the law.

Be clean in mind, and then you will have greater control over your bodies. It was said of old, "As [a man] thinketh in his heart, so is he" (Proverbs 23:7). Unclean thoughts lead to unclean acts.

I remember going to President McKay years ago to plead the cause of a missionary who had become involved in serious sin. I said to President McKay, "He did it on an impulse." The President said to me, "His mind was dwelling on these things before he transgressed. The thought was father to the deed. There would not have been that impulse if he had previously controlled his thoughts."

The finger of the Lord wrote on the tablets of stone, "Thou shalt not commit adultery" (Exodus 20:14). I believe that fornication is included within that term.

Of course you are tempted. It seems as if the whole world has become obsessed with sex. In a very beguiling and alluring way, it is thrown at you constantly. You are exposed to it on television, in magazines and books, in videos, even in music. Turn your back on it. Shun it. I know that is easy to say and difficult to do. But each time that you do so, it will be so much the easier the next time. What a wonderful thing it will be if someday you can stand before the Lord and say, "I am clean."

The Lord has given a commandment in our time that applies to each of us. He has said, "Let virtue garnish thy thoughts unceasingly." And with this He has given a promise: "Then shall thy confidence wax strong in the presence of God" (D&C 121:45). I believe He is saying that if we are clean in mind and body, the time will come when we can stand confidently before the Lord just as Joseph F. Smith stood before the Prophet Joseph and said, "I am clean." There will be a feeling of confidence, and there will also be smiles of approval.

As a holder of the priesthood, you cannot, you must not be led into the vicious trap of immoral behavior. Of course you are to socialize with young women, to date, to have fun of a wholesome kind in a hundred ways. But there is a line which you must not cross. It is the line that separates personal cleanliness from sin. I need not get clinical in telling you where that line is. You know. You have been told again and again. You have a conscience within you. Stay on the Lord's side of the line.

Be clean in language. There is so much of filthy, sleazy talk these days. I spoke to the young women about it. I speak to you also. It tells others that your vocabulary is so extremely limited that you cannot express yourself without reaching down into the gutter for words. Dirty talk is unbecoming any man who holds the priesthood, be he young or old.

Nor can you as a priesthood holder take the name of the Lord in vain. Said Jehovah to the children of Israel, "Thou shalt not take the name of the Lord thy God in vain; for the Lord will not hold him guiltless that taketh his name in vain" (Exodus 20:7).

That commandment, engraved by the finger of the Lord, is as binding upon us as it was upon those to whom it was originally given. The Lord has said in modern revelation, "Remember that that which cometh from above is sacred, and must be spoken with care, and by constraint of the Spirit" (D&C 63:64).

A filthy mind expresses itself in filthy and profane language. A clean mind expresses itself in language that is positive and uplifting and in deeds that bring happiness into the heart.

Be clean in dress and manner. I do not expect you to look like missionaries all of the time. But let me say that the clean and conservative dress and grooming of our missionaries has become as a badge of honor recognized wherever they go. The age in which we are living now has become an age of sloppy dress and sloppy manners. But I am not so concerned about what you wear as I am that it be clean. Remember Joseph F. Smith's dream. As he was hurrying toward the mansion, he had a little bundle wrapped in a handkerchief. When he bathed himself and opened it, he found that it contained clean clothing. Whenever you administer or pass the sacrament, look your very best. Be sure of your personal cleanliness.

I urge you to be clean in manner, to be courteous, to be respectful, to be honest, to be young men and older men of integrity.

It is amazing what courtesy will accomplish. It is tragic what a lack of courtesy can bring. We see it every day as we move in the traffic of the cities in which we live. A moment spent in letting someone else get into the line does good for the one who is helped, and it also does good for the one who helps. Something happens inside of us when we are courteous and deferential toward others. It is all part of a refining process which, if persisted in, will change our very natures.

On the other hand, anger over a little traffic problem, with swearing and filthy gestures, demeans those who make them and offends those at whom they are aimed. To practice the kind of self-discipline which can control one's temper in the little things that happen almost every day is an expression of emotional cleanliness.

Honesty—what a precious jewel this is. Again this is a manifestation of cleanliness in thought and action. Insurance adjusters can tell you of false claims made by so many who dishonestly try to get compensation to which they are not entitled. Cheating is so common a phenomenon in school.

"Thou shalt not steal. . . . Thou shalt not covet" (Exodus 20:15, 17). These mandates are likewise among the commandments written by the finger of the Lord on the tablets of stone. I am always pained when I read in a newspaper of some who are members of this Church who have been involved in a scam operation designed to take from others through dishonest means that which they covet for themselves.

Said the Lord, "Let all things be done in cleanliness before me"

(D&C 42:41). I believe that includes a proscription against any kind of dishonesty.

Brethren, have I belabored the point? I hope not. If so, it is only because I feel so strongly concerning the obligations placed upon us by the Lord. He expects His people to be clean from the sins of the world.

If any here have been guilty of any of these, let us repent forthwith. Confess to the Lord, and if the sin is egregious, confess to your bishop. He will help you. There can be repentance, and there can be forgiveness. The Lord has stated, "Behold, your sins are forgiven you; you are clean before me; therefore, lift up your heads and rejoice" (D&C 110:5).

In that revelation which is known as the "Olive Leaf," the Lord stated:

"And I give unto you, who are the first laborers in this last kingdom, a commandment that you assemble yourselves together, and organize yourselves, and prepare yourselves, and sanctify yourselves; yea, purify your hearts, and cleanse your hands and your feet before me, that I may make you clean;

"That I may testify unto your Father, and your God, and my God, that you are clean from the blood of this wicked generation; that I may fulfil this promise, this great and last promise, which I have made unto you" (D&C 88:74–75).

In conclusion I return to where I started, with the dream of a poor boy who was sleeping alone on a mountain and saw a mansion toward which he hurried. Before entering, he stopped to cleanse himself and dress himself in clean garments. He was reproved for being late. He replied, "Yes, but I am clean!" The Prophet Joseph smiled, and Joseph F. Smith, that young missionary, eventually succeeded to the office of prophet and President himself. What a testimony. God bless us to walk with clean hands and pure hearts and be worthy of His smile of approbation, I humbly ask in the name of Jesus Christ, amen.

# Sunday Morning
# Session

APRIL 7, 1996

Now, MY BROTHERS AND SISTERS, if I may say a few words. First I'd like to say that it's wonderful to see all of you gathered in the Tabernacle this Easter morning. You're a wonderful sight. It is a remarkable thing to contemplate the many more who are assembled in more than 3,000 halls in various parts of the world.

I regret that many who wish to meet with us in the Tabernacle this morning are unable to get in. There are very many out on the grounds. This unique and remarkable hall, built by our pioneer forebears and dedicated to the worship of the Lord, comfortably seats about 6,000. Some of you seated on those hard benches for two hours may question the word *comfortably.*

My heart reaches out to those who wish to get in and could not be accommodated. About a year ago I suggested to the Brethren that perhaps the time has come when we should study the feasibility of constructing another dedicated house of worship on a much larger scale that would accommodate three or four times the number who can be seated in this building.

We recognize, of course, that we can never build a hall large enough to accommodate all the membership of this growing Church. We've been richly blessed with other means of communication, and the availability of satellite transmission makes it possible to carry the proceedings of the conference to hundreds of thousands throughout the world.

But there are still those in large numbers who wish to be seated where they can see in person those who are speaking and participating in other ways. The structure we envision will not be a sports arena. It will be a great hall with fixed seating and excellent acoustics. It will be a dedicated house of worship, and that will be its primary purpose. It will be fashioned in such a way that only a portion or the entire hall may be used, according to need. It will accommodate not only religious services but will serve other Church purposes, such as the presentation of sacred pageants and things of that kind. It will also accommodate some community cultural events that will be in harmony with its purpose.

The architectural and engineering studies have not gone far enough for us to make a detailed announcement, but the results thus far are encouraging, and we're hopeful that they will materialize.

Now for a moment I wish to speak of a personal matter. It was a year ago at this conference when in a solemn assembly you raised your hands to sustain me in this great and sacred calling. My heart swells with gratitude for your expressions of confidence. I am humbled, I am overwhelmed by your words of kindness, loyalty, and love. I think I understand, in a measure at least, the magnitude of this responsibility. I have no desire other than to do that which the Lord would have done. I am His servant, called to serve His people. This is His Church. We are only custodians of that which belongs to Him.

I am deeply grateful for the two good and able men who stand at my side as counselors and who have been so loyal and helpful. I am grateful for my Brethren of the Quorum of the Twelve Apostles. Nowhere else will you find a more dedicated and able body of men who love the Lord and seek to do His will. I am likewise grateful for the Quorums of the Seventy and the Presiding

Bishopric. I am grateful for the Area Authorities, for stake presidents and bishops and those who preside over quorums, for faithful mission presidents and temple presidents. I am thankful for the auxiliary organizations and for the strength and capacity and dedication of those who preside over the Relief Society, the Young Women, the Sunday School, and the Primary organizations.

I am thankful for every member of this Church who walks in faith and faithfulness. We are all in this together as Latter-day Saints bound by a common love for our Master, who is the Son of God, the Redeemer of the world. We are a covenant people who have taken upon ourselves His holy name.

The Church is the stronger or the weaker as each member is strong or weak in his or her faith and performance.

During this past year I have traveled extensively. I am determined that while I have strength I will get out among the people at home and abroad to express my appreciation, to give encouragement, to build faith, to teach, to add my testimony to theirs and at the same time to draw strength from them. I thank all of those who are assisting in this.

I intend to keep moving with energy for as long as I can. I wish to mingle with the people I love. Recently I have met with many of our youth, thousands of them. These have been wonderfully reassuring experiences. It is an inspiration to look into the eyes of young men and women who love the Lord, who want to do the right thing, who want to build lives that are productive and fruitful of great good. They are working hard to develop skills that will bless them and the society of which they will become a part. They are serving missions for the Church in unprecedented numbers. They are clean, bright, able, and happy. Surely the Lord must love those of this choice generation of youth who learn and serve in His Church. I love them, and I want them to know that. Life is not easy for them. I think that never before has evil been presented in so attractive and beguiling a manner by those who with sinister designs seek to grow wealthy on the tragedies of lives that become blighted and marred as they partake of these evil goods.

I salute fathers and mothers who are loyal to one another and who nurture their children in faith and love. There has been a wonderful response to the proclamation on the family, which we issued last October (see *Ensign,* Nov. 1995, 102). We hope you will read it and reread it.

This work is growing across the world in a remarkable and wonderful way. The Lord is opening the doors of the nations. He is touching the hearts of the people. The equivalent of 100 new stakes of Zion are coming into the Church each year. This brings with it significant challenges. As has been widely noted, we have passed the line where we now have more members of the Church outside the United States than we have in the United States.

Thank you, my brothers and sisters, for the goodness of your lives. I thank you for your efforts in trying to measure up to the very high standards of this, the Lord's Church. Thank you for your faith. Thank you for your sustaining hands and hearts. Thank you for your prayers.

As everyone here knows, there is only one reason for any of us serving, and that is to assist our Father in Heaven in His declared work and glory to bring to pass the immortality and eternal life of His sons and daughters (see Moses 1:39).

There is one grand key in this vast divine program, and that is the redemption of mankind by the Lord Jesus Christ. It is that of which I now wish to speak briefly.

This is Easter morning. This is the Lord's day, when we celebrate the greatest victory of all time, the victory over death.

Those who hated Jesus thought they had put an end to Him forever when the cruel spikes pierced His quivering flesh and the cross was raised on Calvary. But this was the Son of God, with whose power they did not reckon. Through His death came the Resurrection and the assurance of eternal life. None of us can fully understand the pain He bore as He prayed in Gethsemane and subsequently hung in ignominy between two thieves while those who looked at Him taunted Him and said, "He saved others; himself he cannot save" (Matthew 27:42; Mark 15:31).

With sorrow unspeakable, those who loved Him placed His wounded, lifeless body in the new tomb of Joseph of Arimathea. Gone was hope from the lives of His Apostles, whom He had loved and taught. He to whom they had looked as Lord and Master had been crucified and His body laid in a sealed tomb. He had taught them of His eventual death and Resurrection, but they had not understood. Now they were forlorn and dejected. They must have wept and wondered as the great stone was rolled to seal the burial place.

The Jewish Sabbath passed. Then came a new day, a day that ever after was to be the Lord's day. In their sorrow, Mary Magdalene and the other women came to the tomb. The stone was no longer in place. Curiously they looked inside. To their astonishment the tomb was empty.

Distraught and fearful, Mary ran to Simon Peter and to the other disciple whom Jesus loved. She cried, "They have taken away the Lord out of the sepulchre, and we know not where they have laid him" (John 20:2).

They came running, and their fears were confirmed. Disconsolate, they looked and then "went away again unto their own home" (John 20:10).

> But Mary stood without at the sepulchre weeping: and as she wept, she stooped down, and looked into the sepulchre,
>
> And seeth two angels in white sitting, the one at the head, and the other at the feet, where the body of Jesus had lain.
>
> And they say unto her, Woman, why weepest thou? She saith unto them, Because they have taken away my Lord, and I know not where they have laid him.

And when she had thus said, she turned herself back, and saw Jesus standing, and knew not that it was Jesus.

Jesus saith unto her, Woman, why weepest thou? whom seekest thou? She, supposing him to be the gardener, saith unto him, Sir, if thou have borne him hence, tell me where thou hast laid him, and I will take him away.

Jesus saith unto her, Mary. She turned herself, and saith unto him, Rabboni; which is to say, Master.

Jesus saith unto her, Touch me not; for I am not yet ascended to my Father: but go to my brethren, and say unto them, I ascend unto my Father, and your Father; and to my God, and your God. [John 20:11–17]

She who had loved Him so much, she who had been healed by Him was the first to whom He appeared. There followed others, even, as Paul declares, up to 500 brethren at one time (see 1 Corinthians 15:6).

Now the Apostles understood what He had tried to teach them. Thomas, on feeling of His wounds, declared, "My Lord and my God" (John 20:28).

Can anyone doubt the veracity of that account? No event of history has been more certainly confirmed. There is the testimony of all who saw and felt and spoke with the risen Lord. He appeared on two continents, in two hemispheres, and taught the people before His final ascension. Two sacred volumes, two testaments speak of this most glorious of all events in all of human history. But these are only accounts, the faithless critic says, to which we reply that beyond these is the witness and the testimony, borne by the power of the Holy Ghost, of the truth and validity of this most remarkable event. Through the centuries, untold numbers have paid with the sacrifice of their comforts, their fortunes, their very lives for the convictions they carried in their hearts of the reality of the risen, living Lord.

And then comes the ringing testimony of the Prophet of this dispensation that in a wondrous theophany he saw and was spoken to by the Almighty Father and the risen Son. That vision, glorious beyond description, became the wellspring of this, The Church of Jesus Christ of Latter-day Saints, with all the keys, authority, and power found therein, and the sustaining comfort to be found in the testimony of its people.

There is nothing more universal than death and nothing brighter with hope and faith than the assurance of immortality. The abject sorrow that comes with death, the bereavement that follows the passing of a loved one are mitigated only by the certainty of the Resurrection of the Son of God that first Easter morning.

What meaning would life have without the reality of immortality? Otherwise life would become only a dismal journey of getting and spending, only to end in utter and hopeless oblivion.

"O death, where is thy sting? O grave, where is thy victory?" (1 Corinthians 15:55).

The pain of death is swallowed up in the peace of eternal life. Of all the events in the chronicles of humanity, none is of such consequence as this.

Contemplating the wonder of the Atonement wrought in behalf of all mankind, the Prophet Joseph Smith declared in words descriptive and beautiful:

"Let the mountains shout for joy, and all ye valleys cry aloud; and all ye seas and dry lands tell the wonders of your Eternal King! And ye rivers, and brooks, and rills, flow down with gladness. Let the woods and all the trees of the field praise the Lord; and ye solid rocks weep for joy! And let the sun, moon, and the morning stars sing together, and let all the sons of God shout for joy! And let the eternal creations declare his name forever and ever! And again I say, how glorious is the voice we hear from heaven, proclaiming in our ears, glory, and salvation, and honor, and immortality, and eternal life; kingdoms, principalities, and powers!" (D&C 128:23).

Whenever the cold hand of death strikes, there shines through the gloom and the darkness of that hour the triumphant figure of the Lord Jesus Christ, He, the Son of God, who by His matchless and eternal power overcame death. He is the Redeemer of the world. He gave His life for each of us. He took it up again and became the firstfruits of them that slept. He, as King of Kings, stands triumphant above all other kings. He, as the Omnipotent One, stands above all rulers. He is our comfort, our only true comfort, when the dark shroud of earthly night closes about us as the spirit departs the human form.

Towering above all mankind stands Jesus the Christ, the King of glory, the unblemished Messiah, the Lord Emmanuel. In the hour of deepest sorrow we draw hope and peace and certitude from the words of the angel that Easter morning: "He is not here: for he is risen, as he said" (Matthew 28:6). We draw strength from the words of Paul, "As in Adam all die, even so in Christ . . . all [are] made alive" (1 Corinthians 15:22).

> *I stand all amazed at the love Jesus offers me,*
> *Confused at the grace that so fully he proffers me.*
> *I tremble to know that for me he was crucified,*
> *That for me, a sinner, he suffered, he bled and died.*
> *Oh, it is wonderful that he should care for me*
> *Enough to die for me!*
> *Oh, it is wonderful, wonderful to me!*
> *["I Stand All Amazed," Hymns, no. 193]*

He is our King, our Lord, our Master, the living Christ, who stands on the right hand of His Father. He lives! He lives, resplendent and wonderful, the living Son of the living God. Of this we bear solemn testimony this day of rejoicing, this Easter morning, when we commemorate the miracle of the empty tomb, in the name of Him who rose from the dead, even the Lord Jesus Christ, amen.

# SUNDAY AFTERNOON SESSION

## APRIL 7, 1996

THIS HAS BEEN A WONDERFUL conference. The Spirit of the Lord has been with us. We have heard much of wisdom and inspiration. Our testimonies of this divine work have been strengthened. Many of us, I hope, have resolved within our hearts to live more fully the principles of the gospel.

Surely we have been blessed in the talks that have been given. The prayers have been inspiring, and the music has been wonderful. We are so greatly blessed with dedicated musicians in the Church. They add so substantially to the spirit of the conference. Every choir and chorus has performed exceptionally well.

I wish to say a particular word about this Tabernacle Choir, which has sung to us today. I came across a letter written by Wilford Woodruff and his counselors, George Q. Cannon and Joseph F. Smith, under date of February 11, 1895, 101 years ago. It was addressed to the choir at that time. It reads:

"We desire to see this choir not only maintain the high reputation it has earned at home and abroad, but become the highest exponent of the 'Divine Art' in all the land; and the worthy head, example and leader of all other choirs and musical bodies in the Church, inspiring musicians and poets with purest sentiment and song and harmony, until its light shall shine forth to the world undimmed, and nations shall be charmed [by] its music."

The letter goes on: "This choir is and should be a great auxiliary to the cause of Zion. By means of its perfection in the glorious realm of song, it may unstop the ears of thousands now deaf to the truth, soften their stony hearts, and inspire precious souls with a love for that which is divine. Thus removing prejudice, dispelling ignorance and shedding forth the precious light of heaven to tens of thousands who have been, and are still, misled concerning us" (in James R. Clark, comp., *Messages of the First Presidency of The Church of Jesus Christ of Latter-day Saints,* 6 vols. [1965–75], 3:267–68).

Such has been the responsibility resting upon this choir for more than a century. Personnel changes have occurred through the years, but the quality of performance has only improved. This choir is one of the great treasures of the Church. I think it is one of the great treasures of America. I regard it as the outstanding choir in all the world. May it continue its great mission of providing lofty and inspiring music at home and abroad. I thank, in behalf of the entire Church, the officers, directors, organists, and members of this dedicated body of talented and gifted musicians who give so generously of their time.

Now I think I might venture to mention another matter. Months ago I was invited to be interviewed by Mike Wallace, a tough senior reporter for the CBS *60 Minutes* program, which is broadcast across America to more than 20 million listeners each week.

I recognized that if I were to appear, critics and detractors of the Church would also be invited to participate. I knew we could not expect that the program would be entirely positive for us.

On the other hand, I felt that it offered the opportunity to present some affirmative aspects of our culture and message to many millions of people. I concluded that it was better to lean into the stiff wind of opportunity than to simply hunker down and do nothing. It has been an interesting experience. The program's crews have photographed hours of eyeball-to-eyeball interview (if you'll pardon that expression), dialogue, and formal talks in various settings. They have interviewed other members of the Church, as well as our critics. From all of this I assume they have distilled a presentation of about a quarter of an hour.

We have no idea what the outcome will be—that is, I don't. We will discover this this evening when it is aired in this valley. If it turns out to be favorable, I will be grateful. Otherwise, I pledge I'll never get my foot in that kind of trap again. In the Salt Lake City area it will be released at 6:00 p.m. and in many other areas across the nation at 7:00 p.m. local time.

In the prayer of dedication at the Kirtland Temple, which prayer was received by revelation according to the Prophet, he petitioned the Lord in these words:

"Remember all thy church, O Lord, . . . that the kingdom, which thou hast set up without hands, may become a great mountain and fill the whole earth;

"That thy church may come forth out of the wilderness of darkness, and shine forth fair as the moon, clear as the sun, and terrible as an army with banners" (D&C 109:72–73).

We are witnessing the answer to that remarkable pleading. Increasingly, the Church is being recognized at home and abroad for what it truly is. There are still those, not a few, who criticize and rebel, who apostatize and lift their voices against this work. We have always had them. They speak their piece as they walk across the stage of life, and then they are soon forgotten. I suppose we always will have them as long as we are trying to do the work of the Lord. The honest in heart will detect that which is true and that which is false. We go forward, marching as an army with banners emblazoned with the everlasting truth. We are a cause that is militant for truth and goodness. We are a body of Christian soldiers "marching as to war, with the cross of Jesus going on before" ("Onward, Christian Soldiers," *Hymns,* no. 246).

Everywhere we go, we see great vitality in this work. There is enthusiasm wherever it is organized. It is the work of the Redeemer. It is the gospel of good news. It is something to be happy and excited about.

Brothers and sisters, let us now return to our homes with increased resolution in our hearts to live the gospel more fully, to serve with greater diligence, and to stand for truth with enthusiasm and without fear. As a servant of the Lord, I leave my blessing upon you. May you be happy as you walk with faith, I humbly pray, in the name of Him whom we all love and serve, even the Lord Jesus Christ, amen.

# SATURDAY MORNING
# SESSION

OCTOBER 5, 1996

WE HAVE GATHERED HERE in the historic Tabernacle on Temple Square in Salt Lake City. Others are joining us in thousands of other halls and in their homes across America and across the world. We are deeply grateful for the means of communication afforded us by which we can speak to you and in most cases you can hear and see us. We feel of your warmth, your brotherhood, your faith, your sustaining prayers. Thank you, one and all.

Following a previous conference, we received a letter from England. May I read it? The writer says:

> This last weekend, just a short while after our 40th wedding anniversary, we had the great pleasure to gather our children and grandchildren together to watch the general conference broadcast in our own home. . . .
>
> We had the wonderful blessing of being able to stand and raise our arms to the square as a family and sustain a living prophet, his counselors, together with the Quorum of the Twelve, and in our own home too!
>
> We give you our report: the voting was unanimous and in the affirmative, with not a single abstaining or dissenting voice.
>
> Our family of three sons have served honorable missions, to their great credit. Upon returning home they married fine and

honorable young ladies in the temple, and together they are raising 10 beautiful children. All the adults serve in leadership positions, and my wife and I are also delighted to be serving on a Church-service mission. . . . How sweet have been the Lord's blessings to all of our family.

All our family thank you for the inspiring instruction and uplifting talks that were given, and without hesitation we tell you that the tears flowed freely as we truly sat at the feet of the Lord's servants. As we basked in the joy of having your presence in our home, we felt empty when the broadcast finished; it was like saying good-bye to loved ones. We all knelt down in prayer and felt the warm assurance of the Spirit all around us.

It is an awesome responsibility to say a few words as we begin the conference. You have gathered to be encouraged, to be inspired, to be lifted and directed as members of the Church. We are all assembled together as believers in this, the cause of Christ. Each of us is His servant in building His kingdom in anticipation of the time when He will come as King of Kings and Lord of Lords.

You have gathered to be helped with your temporal concerns, your failures, and your victories. You have come to hear the word of the Lord taught by those who, not of their own choosing, have been called as teachers in this great work.

You have prayed that you might hear things that will help you with your problems and add strength to your faith. I assure you that we have prayed also. We have prayed for inspiration and direction. There is a constant prayer in our hearts that we will not fail the great trust the Lord has placed in us and the trust which you have placed in us. We have prayed that we might be prompted to say those words which will build faith and testimony and which will become answered prayers for those who will hear.

We are reassured by the word of the Lord that "he that preacheth [by the Spirit] and he that receiveth [by the Spirit], understand one another, and both are edified and rejoice together" (D&C 50:22).

One hundred and fifty years ago our people were leaving Nauvoo and threading their way across the prairies of Iowa. None of us, I am confident, can appreciate the measure of sacrifice which they made in leaving their comfortable homes to brave the tempests of the wilderness on a journey that would not end until they reached this valley of the Great Salt Lake. Their suffering was immeasurable. They died by the hundreds for this cause of which each one of us is a part.

I was in Palmyra this past summer, and in Nauvoo, and in Council Bluffs, Iowa, which they had called Kanesville out of respect and love for a loyal friend. I stood where the Grand Encampment assembled when they reached the Missouri River. I have been over the trail from the Missouri to this valley a number of times. For me it is always a sacred experience. I am so deeply grateful for our inheritance. We shall remember it in a special way next year when we commemorate the arrival of our pioneer forebears in this valley.

Ours is the blessing to live in a better season. The terrible persecutions of the past are behind us. Today we are looked upon with respect by people across the world. We must always be worthy of that respect. We must earn it, or we will not have it. We will be reminded of that principle during this conference.

I invite you to listen, listen if you will by the power of the Spirit, to the speakers who will address you today and tomorrow as well as this evening. If you will do so, I do not hesitate to promise that you will be uplifted, your resolution to do what is right will be stronger, you will find solutions to your problems and your needs, and you will be led to thank the Lord for what you have heard.

We have become as a great family spread across this vast world. We speak different tongues. We live under a variety of circumstances. But in the heart of each of us beats a common testimony:

You and I know that God lives and is at the helm of this, His holy work. We know that Jesus is our Redeemer, who stands at the head of this Church which carries His name. We know that Joseph Smith was a prophet and is a prophet who stands at the head of this, the dispensation of the fulness of times. We know that the priesthood was restored upon his head and that it has come down to us in this day in an unbroken line. We know that the Book of Mormon is a true testament of the reality and divinity of the Lord Jesus Christ. Our testimony of these and other matters will be strengthened, our faith will be deepened as we participate together in this great and sacred convocation.

For this I pray in the name of Jesus Christ, amen.

# PRIESTHOOD
# SESSION

OCTOBER 5, 1996

$M$Y DEAR BRETHREN, we have received good counsel this evening.

Since we met last April, I have been much out among our people. I have determined that for so long as I have the strength to do so, I will get out and meet with the Saints I love, both the youth and the adults. I have in recent months participated in many meetings with more than 300,000 Latter-day Saints in 17 different nations. We have traveled from sea to sea across the United States and extensively in Asia and in Europe. I do not enjoy travel. I weary of it. Jet lag, for me, is a very real thing. But I do enjoy looking into the faces and shaking the hands of faithful Latter-day Saints, and I thank those who have made this possible.

As I have gone about the world, I have had opportunity for interviews with representatives of the media. This is always a worrisome undertaking because one never knows what will be asked. These reporters are men and women of great capacity who know how to ask questions that come at you like a javelin. It is not exactly an enjoyable experience, but it represents an opportunity to tell the world something of our story. As Paul said to Festus and Agrippa, "This thing was not done in a corner" (Acts 26:26).

We have something that this world needs to hear about, and these interviews afford an opportunity to give voice to that.

One of the most extensive interviews was with Mr. Mike Wallace of the CBS *60 Minutes* program. I express appreciation to Senator Orrin Hatch, Willard Marriott Jr., and Steve Young (who ought to be here this evening—and probably *is,* somewhere), who participated in this program.

Millions saw the outcome this last Easter Sunday, as Elder Haight said this morning. The editors of the program distilled about 15 minutes out of many hours of filming.

I developed a deep respect for Mr. Wallace. He is a very able professional. He was courteous, respectful, incisive in his questions—one who might be described as a tough, streetwise reporter with long experience but a gentleman in the best sense of the word.

I first met him at a luncheon at the Harvard Club in New York about a year ago. He then came to Salt Lake City on two different occasions and interviewed me at great length in my office. I have thought this evening to read parts of those interviews as they were recorded—his questions and my extemporaneous answers just as they were given and without editing except to delete areas in the interest of time and add in brackets an occasional needed word. I do so in the spirit of reaffirming the position of this Church on a number of different and significant matters of general concern.

*[Note: A more extensive transcript of President Hinckley's interview with Mike Wallace is included in Section 3 of this book (pages 483–513). For this reason, President Hinckley's report of the interview is not included here.]*

I wish to say that none of us ever need hesitate to speak up for this Church, for its doctrine, for its people, for its divine organization and divinely given responsibility. It is true. It is the work of God. The only things that can ever embarrass this work are acts of disobedience to its doctrine and standards by those of its membership. That places upon each of us a tremendous responsibility. This work will be judged by what the world sees of our behavior. God give us the will to walk with faith, the discipline to do what is right at all times and in all circumstances, the resolution to make of our lives a declaration of this cause before all who see us, I humbly pray in the name of Jesus Christ, amen.

# SUNDAY MORNING SESSION

OCTOBER 6, 1996

HALF, POSSIBLY MORE THAN HALF, of the adult members of the Church are women. It is to them that I wish particularly to speak this morning. I do so with the hope that the men will also hear.

First let me say to you sisters that you do not hold a second place in our Father's plan for the eternal happiness and well-being of His children. You are an absolutely essential part of that plan.

Without you the plan could not function. Without you the entire program would be frustrated. As I have said before from this pulpit, when the process of creation occurred, Jehovah, the Creator, under instruction from His Father, first divided the light from the darkness and then separated the land from the waters. There followed the creation of plant life, followed by the creation of animal life. Then came the creation of man, and culminating that act of divinity came the crowning act, the creation of woman.

Each of you is a daughter of God, endowed with a divine birthright. You need no defense of that position.

As I go about from place to place, I am interviewed by representatives of the media. Invariably they ask about the place of women in the Church. They do so in an almost accusatory tone, as if we denigrate and demean women. I invariably reply that I know of no other organization in all the world which affords women so many opportunities for development, for sociality, for the accomplishment of great good, for holding positions of leadership and responsibility.

I wish all of these reporters could have been in the Tabernacle a week ago Saturday when the general Relief Society meeting was held. It was an inspiration to look into the faces of that vast gathering of the daughters of God, women of faith and ability, women who know what life is about and have something of a sense of the divinity of their creation. I wish they could have heard that great chorus of young women from Brigham Young University, who touched our hearts with the beauty of their singing. I wish they could have heard the stirring messages of the Relief Society general presidency, each of whom spoke on a phase of the subject "faith, hope, and charity."

What able people these women are. They express themselves with power and conviction and great persuasiveness. President Faust concluded that service with a wonderful talk.

If those reporters who are prone to raise this question could have sat in that vast congregation, they would have known, even without further inquiry, that there is strength and great capacity in the women of this Church. There is leadership and direction, a certain spirit of independence, and yet great satisfaction in being a part of this, the Lord's kingdom, and of working hand in hand with the priesthood to move it forward.

Many of you are here today who were in that meeting. Today you are seated with your husbands, men whom you love and honor and respect and who in turn love and honor and respect you. You know how fortunate you are to be married to a good man who is your companion in life and who will be your companion throughout eternity. Together, as you have served in many capacities and reared your families and provided for them, you have faced a variety of storms and come through them all with your heads held high. Most of you are mothers, and very many of you are grandmothers and even great-grandmothers. You have walked the sometimes painful, sometimes joyous path of parenthood. You have walked hand in hand with God in the great process of bringing children into the world that they might experience this estate along the road of immortality and eternal life. It has not been easy rearing a family. Most of you have had to sacrifice and skimp and labor night and day. As I think of you and your circumstances, I think of the words of Anne Campbell, who wrote as she looked upon her children:

> *You are the trip I did not take;*
> *You are the pearls I cannot buy;*
> *You are my blue Italian lake;*
> *You are my piece of foreign sky.*
> *["To My Child," in Charles L. Wallis,*
> *ed.,* The Treasure Chest *(1965), 54]*

You sisters are the real builders of the nation wherever you live, for you have created homes of strength and peace and security. These become the very sinew of any nation.

Unfortunately a few of you may be married to men who are abusive. Some of them put on a fine face before the world during the day and come home in the evening, set aside their self-discipline, and on the slightest provocation fly into outbursts of anger.

No man who engages in such evil and unbecoming behavior is worthy of the priesthood of God. No man who so conducts himself is worthy of the privileges of the house of the Lord. I regret that there are some men undeserving of the love of their wives and children. There are children who fear their fathers and wives who fear their husbands. If there be any such men within the hearing of my voice, as a servant of the Lord I rebuke you and call you to repentance. Discipline yourselves. Master your temper. Most of the things that make you angry are of very small consequence. And what a terrible price you are paying for your anger. Ask the Lord to forgive you. Ask your wife to forgive you. Apologize to your children.

There are many women among us who are single. Generally this is not of their own choice. Some have never had the opportunity to marry one with whom they would wish to spend eternity.

To you single women who wish to be married, I repeat what I recently said in a meeting for singles in this Tabernacle:

> Do not give up hope. And do not give up trying. But do give up being obsessed with it. The chances are that if you forget about it and become anxiously engaged in other activities, the prospects will brighten immeasurably. . . .
>
> I believe that for most of us the best medicine for loneliness is work, service in behalf of others. I do not minimize your problems, but I do not hesitate to say that there are many others whose problems are more serious than are yours. Reach out to serve them, to help them, to encourage them. There are so many boys and girls who fail in school for want of a little personal attention and encouragement. There are so many elderly people who live in misery and loneliness and fear for whom a simple conversation would bring a measure of hope and happiness. [Salt Lake Valley single adult fireside, Sept. 22, 1996]

Included among the women of the Church are those who have lost their husbands through abandonment, divorce, and death. Great is our obligation to you. As the scriptures declare, "Pure religion and undefiled before God and the Father is this, To visit the fatherless and widows in their affliction, and to keep himself unspotted from the world" (James 1:27).

I received a letter from one who counts herself fortunate, and indeed fortunate she is. She writes:

101

Although I have been raising our four boys as a single parent, . . . I am not alone. I have a wonderful "ward family" that has rallied around us. . . .

My Relief Society president has been there for me through my greatest hardships, encouraging my spiritual growth, personal prayer, and temple attendance.

Our bishop has been generous in providing needed food and clothing and has helped send two of the boys to camp. He has had interviews with all of us and given each of us blessings and needed encouragement. He has helped me to budget and do what I can to help my family.

Our home teachers have come regularly and even gave the boys blessings as they started the new school year.

Our stake president and his counselors have checked in on us on a regular basis by taking time to visit with us at church, on the phone, or in our home.

This Church is true, and my boys and I are living proof that God loves us and that a "ward family" can make all the difference.

Our priesthood leaders have been instrumental in keeping the boys active in Church and in the Scouting program. [One] is an Eagle Scout and is receiving his fourth palm this week. [Another] is an Eagle with three palms. And [a third] has just turned in his Eagle papers this week. The youngest is a Webelos and loves Cub Scouts.

We are always met with loving hearts and warm handshakes. The Christlike attitude of the stake and our ward has helped us through trials we never imagined possible.

Life has been hard, . . . but we put on the whole armor of God as we kneel in family prayer . . . , asking for help and guidance and sharing thanks for the blessings we have received. I pray daily for the constant companionship of the

Holy Ghost to guide me as I raise these boys to be missionaries and encourage them to be true to the gospel and the
priesthood they hold.

I am proud to say I am a member of The Church of Jesus
Christ of Latter-day Saints. I know this Church is true. I sustain my Church leaders. We are doing well, and I thank everyone for their love and prayers and acceptance.

What a great letter that is! How much it says about the way this
Church functions and should function throughout the world. I
hope that every woman who finds herself in the kind of circumstances in which this woman lives is similarly blessed with an understanding and helpful bishop, with a Relief Society president who
knows how to assist her, with home teachers who know where their
duty lies and how to fulfill it, and with a host of ward members who
are helpful without being intrusive.

I have never met the woman whose letter I have read.
Notwithstanding the cheerful attitude she conveys, I am sure there
has been much of struggle and loneliness and, at times, fear. I
notice that she works to provide for her needs and the needs of her
boys, who are in their teens. I assume her income is inadequate,
because she indicates that the bishop has helped them with food
and clothing.

Some years ago President Benson delivered a message to the
women of the Church. He encouraged them to leave their employment and give their individual time to their children. I sustain the
position which he took.

Nevertheless, I recognize, as he recognized, that there are some
women (it has become very many, in fact) who have to work to provide for the needs of their families. To you I say, do the very best
you can. I hope that if you are employed full-time you are doing it
to ensure that basic needs are met and not simply to indulge a taste
for an elaborate home, fancy cars, and other luxuries. The greatest
job that any mother will ever do will be in nurturing, teaching,

lifting, encouraging, and rearing her children in righteousness and truth. None other can adequately take her place.

It is well-nigh impossible to be a full-time homemaker and a full-time employee. I know how some of you struggle with decisions concerning this matter.

I repeat, do the very best you can. You know your circumstances, and I know that you are deeply concerned for the welfare of your children. Each of you has a bishop who will counsel with you and assist you. If you feel you need to speak with an understanding woman, do not hesitate to get in touch with your Relief Society president.

To the mothers of this Church, every mother who is here today, I want to say that as the years pass, you will become increasingly grateful for that which you did in molding the lives of your children in the direction of righteousness and goodness, integrity and faith. That is most likely to happen if you can spend adequate time with them.

For you who are single parents, I say that many hands stand ready to help you. The Lord is not unmindful of you. Neither is His Church.

May He bless you, my beloved sisters who find yourselves in the situation of single parenthood. May you have health, strength, vitality to carry the heavy burden that is yours. May you have loving friends and associates to bear you up in your times of trial. You know the power of prayer as perhaps few others do. Many of you spend much time on your knees speaking with your Father in Heaven, with tears running down your cheeks. Please know that we also pray for you.

With all that you have to do, you are also asked to serve in the Church. Your bishop will not ask you to do anything that is beyond your capacity. And as you so serve, a new dimension will be added to your life. You will find new and stimulating associations. You will find friendship and sociality. You will grow in knowledge and understanding and wisdom and in your capacity to do. You will become a better mother because of the service you give in the work of the Lord.

Now, in conclusion I wish to say a word to you older women, many of whom are widows. You are a great treasure. You have passed through the storms of life. You have weathered the challenges now facing your younger sisters. You are mature in wisdom, in understanding, in compassion, in love and service.

There is a certain beauty that shines through your countenances. It is the beauty that comes of peace. There may still be struggle, but there is mature wisdom to meet it. There are health problems, but there is a certain composure concerning them. The bad memories of the past have largely been forgotten, while the good memories return and bring sweet and satisfying enrichment to life.

You have learned to love the scriptures, and you read them. Your prayers, for the most part, are prayers of thanksgiving. Your greetings are words of kindness. Your friendship is a sturdy staff on which others may lean.

What a resource are the women of The Church of Jesus Christ of Latter-day Saints. You love this Church; you accept its doctrine; you honor your place in its organization; you bring luster and strength and beauty to its congregations. How thankful we are to you. How much you are loved, respected, and honored.

I salute my own beloved companion. It will soon be 60 years ago that we walked from the Salt Lake Temple as husband and wife, with love for one another. That love has strengthened through all of these years. We have faced many problems during our years of marriage. Somehow, with the blessing of the Lord, we have survived them all.

It is becoming physically harder to stand tall and straight as we did in our younger years. No matter—we still have one another, and we still stand together, even though we lean a little. And when the time for separation comes, there will be much of sorrow, but there will also be the comfort that will come from the assurance that she is mine and I am hers for the eternity that lies ahead.

And so, my beloved sisters, please know how much we appreciate you. You bring a measure of wholeness to us. You have great strength. With dignity and tremendous ability, you carry forward the remarkable programs of the Relief Society, the Young Women, and the Primary. You teach Sunday School. We walk at your side as your companions and your brethren with respect and love, with honor and great admiration. It was the Lord who designated that men in His Church should hold the priesthood. It was He who has given you your capabilities to round out this great and marvelous organization, which is the Church and kingdom of God. I bear testimony before the entire world of your worth, of your grace and goodness, of your remarkable abilities and tremendous contributions, and I invoke the blessings of heaven upon you, in the name of the Lord Jesus Christ, amen.

# SUNDAY AFTERNOON SESSION

### OCTOBER 6, 1996

JUST A FEW WORDS AS WE bring to a close this great general conference of the Church. It's been a wonderful occasion. The weather has favored us here in Salt Lake City. This is a beautiful season of the year, with the fall flowers in bloom. The harvest is largely in, and by and large it has been good. We are grateful for the mercies of the Lord upon us.

We have been able to meet together in peace and comfort and security here in the sacred precincts of Temple Square, where our forebears built so well that we might be so comfortable.

We have had unprecedented coverage of the conference, reaching across the continents and the oceans to people far and wide.

Though we are far removed from some of you, we feel of your brotherhood and express our great appreciation for you.

Most importantly, we have enjoyed a remarkable and wonderful outpouring of the Spirit of the Lord. The Brethren and the sisters have spoken to us, and we have been blessed by their messages.

I hope that we will long remember what we have heard. I hope that we will take the time to read the talks which will be reprinted in the *Ensign*. I hope that each of us may have been touched in a personal way by something that was said and that as a result of that, there will be a turnabout in any unseemly attitude or action.

As Brother Ballard has reminded us, this is an anniversary year, and next year will be another anniversary year when we commemorate the arrival of the Mormon pioneers in this valley in 1847. There will be much of remembering. It will all be to the good. All of us need to be reminded of the past. It is from history that we gain knowledge which can save us from repeating mistakes and on which we can build for the future.

These are days for remembering and celebrating the past. These are anniversary days.

I think of what occurred in this Tabernacle 140 years ago this Sunday. I spoke of it from this pulpit some years back, but I wish to mention it again as we bring to a close this conference.

I take you back to the general conference of October 1856. On Saturday of that conference, Franklin D. Richards and a handful of associates arrived in the valley. They had traveled from Winter Quarters with strong teams and light wagons and had been able to make good time. Brother Richards immediately sought out President Young. He reported that there were hundreds of men, women, and children scattered over the long trail from Scottsbluff to this valley. Most of them were pulling handcarts. They were accompanied by two wagon trains which had been assigned to assist them. They had reached the area of the last crossing of the North Platte River. Ahead of them lay a trail that was uphill all the way to the Continental Divide, with many, many miles beyond that. They were in desperate trouble. Winter had come early. Snow-laden winds were howling across the highlands of what is now western Nebraska and Wyoming. Our people were hungry; their carts and their wagons were breaking down, their oxen dying. The people themselves were dying. All of them would perish unless they were rescued.

I think President Young did not sleep that night. I think visions of those destitute, freezing, dying people paraded through his mind.

The next morning he came to the old Tabernacle which stood on this square. He said to the people:

I will now give this people the subject and the text for the Elders who may speak. . . . It is this. . . . Many of our brethren and sisters are on the plains with handcarts, and probably many are now seven hundred miles from this place, and they must be brought here, we must send assistance to them. The text will be, "to get them here." . . .

That is my religion; that is the dictation of the Holy Ghost that I possess. It is to save the people. . . .

I shall call upon the Bishops this day. I shall not wait until tomorrow, nor until the next day, for 60 good mule teams and 12 or 15 wagons. I do not want to send oxen. I want good horses and mules. They are in this Territory, and we must have them. Also 12 tons of flour and 40 good teamsters, besides those that drive the teams. . . .

I will tell you all that your faith, religion, and profession of religion, will never save one soul of you in the Celestial Kingdom of our God, unless you carry out just such principles as I am now teaching you. *Go and bring in those people now on the plains.* [In LeRoy R. Hafen and Ann W. Hafen, *Handcarts to Zion: The Story of a Unique Western Migration, 1856–1860* (1960), 120–21]

That afternoon, food, bedding, and clothing in great quantities were assembled by the women.

The next morning, horses were shod, and wagons were repaired and loaded.

The following morning, Tuesday, 16 mule teams pulled out and headed eastward. By the end of October there were 250 teams on the road to give relief.

Wonderful sermons have been preached from this pulpit, my brethren and sisters. But none has been more eloquent than that spoken by President Young in those circumstances.

Stories of the beleaguered Saints and of their suffering and death will be repeated again and again next year. Stories of their rescue need to be repeated again and again. They speak of the very essence of the gospel of Jesus Christ.

I am grateful that those days of pioneering are behind us. I am thankful that we do not have brethren and sisters stranded in the snow, freezing and dying, while trying to get to this, their Zion in the mountains. But there are people, not a few, whose circumstances are desperate and who cry out for help and relief.

There are so many who are hungry and destitute across this world who need help. I am grateful to be able to say that we are assisting many who are not of our faith but whose needs are serious and whom we have the resources to help. But we need not go so far afield. We have some of our own who cry out in pain and suffering and loneliness and fear. Ours is a great and solemn duty to reach out and help them, to lift them, to feed them if they are hungry, to nurture their spirits if they thirst for truth and righteousness.

There are so many young people who wander aimlessly and walk the tragic trail of drugs, gangs, immorality, and the whole brood of ills that accompany these things. There are widows who long for friendly voices and that spirit of anxious concern which speaks of love. There are those who were once warm in the faith but whose faith has grown cold. Many of them wish to come back but do not know quite how to do it. They need friendly hands reaching out to them. With a little effort, many of them can be brought back to feast again at the table of the Lord.

My brethren and sisters, I would hope, I would pray that each of us, having participated in this great conference, would resolve to seek those who need help, who are in desperate and difficult circumstances, and lift them in the spirit of love into the embrace of the Church, where strong hands and loving hearts will warm them, comfort them, sustain them, and put them on the way of happy and productive lives.

I leave with you, my beloved friends, my co-workers in this wonderful cause, my testimony of the truth of this work, the work of the Almighty, the work of the Redeemer of mankind. I leave with you my love and my blessing, in the name of Jesus Christ, amen.

# 167TH ANNUAL GENERAL CONFERENCE

# SATURDAY MORNING SESSION

APRIL 5, 1997

$M$Y BELOVED BRETHREN AND SISTERS, if I may make a few preliminary remarks. We welcome you wherever you may be throughout the world. With much of love we greet you. This is both a general conference and a world conference. One hundred sixty-seven years have passed since the Church was organized. From that day until this it has steadily and consistently grown until, at the end of 1996, the membership reached nearly 9,700,000. We have become a great concourse of people. We should reach the 10 million mark by the end of this year.

In these opening remarks, I intend to briefly mention three or four matters that I hope will be of interest to each of you.

For those far afield, I may say that we are speaking from the historic Tabernacle on Temple Square in Salt Lake City. We hope to break ground on July 24 for a new place of assembly which we have not yet named, where, at least for many years to come, all who desire to attend the general conference may do so. It will be constructed on the block directly north of Temple Square. It will seat up to four times as many as the Tabernacle.

It will be used for general conference and for other purposes that are in harmony with the reasons for which it is being built. The stage will be such that it can accommodate a large pageant. We may not fill it initially, but we are building for the long term.

This remarkable Tabernacle has served us well and will continue to do so. The Tabernacle Choir broadcasts will continue from here, and many meetings will be held here. This building has remarkable properties, different from other structures. It is unique and wonderful. However, there are today regional conferences involving only six or seven stakes where we have many more people than the Tabernacle will accommodate.

Now, as we speak of construction projects, we remind you that we are moving forward with the building of new temples. On June 1–5 the St. Louis Missouri Temple will be dedicated. This fall the temple in Vernal, Utah, will be dedicated.

Work is on schedule in Preston, England; Bogotá, Colombia; Guayaquil, Ecuador; Cochabamba, Bolivia; Santo Domingo, Dominican Republic; Recife, Brazil; and Madrid, Spain. The approval process is moving forward in Boston, Massachusetts. While delayed, planning for a temple in Nashville, Tennessee, continues. Preliminary work is under way in Billings, Montana, and White Plains, New York, as well as Monterrey, Mexico. The search for a suitable property continues in Venezuela. We are pleased to announce today that ground has been acquired in Albuquerque, New Mexico, for the construction of a temple and also in Campinas, Brazil, where the need is great. Other sites are under consideration. I hope to see temples so located that members of the Church can travel to one of these sacred houses within a reasonable distance of their homes.

Though I live with it, this matter of temple construction is a thing of awesome wonder to me. We are trying to build in such a way and in such places across the world that these houses of the Lord may stand and serve through the Millennium.

The next item: the general Relief Society presidency will be released at this conference. These women have done a great and significant work. They have served for more than eight years, giving unselfishly of their time and their rich talents. They have given remarkable leadership to the women of the Church and also have participated on other boards and committees of which they have been members. We are deeply grateful to them. Formal action on this matter will be taken when President Monson presents the General Authorities and general officers of the Church immediately after my remarks.

I come now to the Brethren of the Seventy. As you know, we have two Quorums of Seventy who serve as General Authorities, with jurisdiction across the Church. The First is comprised of those who serve to age 70. We will sustain four Brethren in this quorum this morning. Additionally, we are calling a group of wise and mature men with long experience in the Church and with freedom to go wherever circumstances dictate as members of the Second Quorum of the Seventy. These Brethren will serve for periods of from three to five years. In every sense they will be General Authorities.

We also have a faithful cadre of Brethren serving as Area Authorities. These have been called wherever the Church is organized. They are faithful and devoted men. They are men who love the Church and who have served in many capacities. As we have traveled at home and abroad, we have worked with many of them and have been deeply impressed with their remarkable capacity.

The Lord made provision at a general level for a First Presidency, a Quorum of the Twelve Apostles, Quorums of the Seventy, and the Presiding Bishopric. At a local level the revelations speak of stake presidents and bishops. We have had in between the general and local authorities, for a period of time, the regional representatives—now, more recently, these Area Authorities. We have determined to present to the conference the names of these Area Authorities to be ordained Seventies. They will then have a quorum relationship presided over by the Presidents of the Seventy. They will be known as Area Authority Seventies, to serve for a period of years in a voluntary capacity in the area in which they reside. They are called by the First Presidency and will work under the general direction of the Quorum of the Twelve, the Presidents of the Seventy, and the Area Presidencies in that part of the world in which they live.

They will continue with their present employment, reside in their own homes, and serve on a Church-service basis. Those residing in Europe, Africa, Asia, Australia, and the Pacific will become members of the Third Quorum of Seventy. Those in Mexico, Central America, and South America will become members of the Fourth Quorum. Those residing in the United States and Canada will become members of the Fifth Quorum.

They may be assigned to *(a)* preside at stake conferences and train stake presidencies, *(b)* create or reorganize stakes and set apart stake presidencies, *(c)* serve as counselors in Area Presidencies, *(d)* chair regional conference planning committees, *(e)* serve on area councils presided over by the Area Presidency, *(f)* tour missions and train mission presidents, and *(g)* complete other duties as assigned.

Consistent with their ordination as Seventies, they become officers of the Church with a specific and definite tie to a quorum. While there will be only limited opportunities for them to come together in quorum meetings, the Presidents of the Seventy will communicate with them, will instruct them, receive reports, and do other things of that kind. They will now have a sense of belonging that they have not experienced up to this time. As Seventies they are called to preach the gospel and to be especial witnesses of the Lord Jesus Christ as set forth in the revelations. Though all Seventies have equal scriptural authority, members of the First and Second Quorums are designated General Authorities, while members of the Third, Fourth, and Fifth are designated Area Authorities.

Although the ordination to the office of Seventy is without term, a Seventy is called to serve in a quorum for a designated period of years. At the conclusion of this service, he will return to activity in his respective ward and stake and will meet with his high priests group.

We welcome most warmly these Brethren into quorum membership and activity. They have our confidence, our love, and our esteem.

With these respective quorums in place, we have established a pattern under which the Church may grow to any size with an organization of Area Presidencies and Area Authority Seventies, chosen and working across the world according to need.

Now, the Lord is watching over His kingdom. He is inspiring its leadership to care for its ever-growing membership. Immediately following my remarks, President Monson will present the General Authorities, the Area Authorities, and the general officers of the Church for your sustaining vote. I need not remind you that this is a very sacred and important matter.

We are living in a wonderful season of the work of the Lord. The work is growing ever stronger. It is expanding across the world. Each of us has an important part to play in this great undertaking. People in more than 160 nations, speaking a score of languages and more, worship our Father in Heaven and our Redeemer, His Beloved Son. This is their great work. It is their cause and their kingdom.

May I, in closing, repeat the words of Jacob: "But behold, I, Jacob, would speak unto you that are pure in heart. Look unto God with firmness of mind, and pray unto him with exceeding faith, and he will console you in your afflictions, and he will plead your cause, and send down justice upon those who seek your destruction" (Jacob 3:1).

May we be faithful and true, doing our duty to move forward the eternal work of the Lord, blessing our Father's children wherever we can touch their lives, is my humble prayer, in the name of Jesus Christ, amen.

# PRIESTHOOD
# SESSION

I ENDORSE THAT WHICH HAS BEEN said this evening. I hope that you have listened well and taken note.

President Monson has spoken on retaining the convert. I endorse what he has said and wish to speak somewhat further on this same subject. I feel very strongly about it.

Each year a substantial number of people become members of the Church, largely through missionary efforts. Last year there were 321,385 converts, comprised of men, women, and children. This is a large enough number—and then some—in one single year to constitute 100 new stakes of Zion. One hundred new stakes per year. Think of it! This places upon each of us an urgent and pressing need to fellowship those who join our ranks.

It is not an easy thing to become a member of this Church. In most cases it involves setting aside old habits, leaving old friends and associations, and stepping into a new society which is different and somewhat demanding.

With the ever-increasing number of converts, we must make an increasingly substantial effort to assist them as they find their way. Every one of them needs three things: a friend, a responsibility, and nurturing with "the good word of God" (Moroni 6:4). It is our duty and opportunity to provide these things.

To illustrate, I think I would like to share with you one of my failures. I suppose some people think I have never experienced failure. I have. Let me tell you of one such instance.

Sixty-three years ago, while serving as a missionary in the British Isles, my companion and I taught, and it was my pleasure to baptize, a young man. He was well educated. He was refined. He was studious. I was so proud of this gifted young man who had come into the Church. I felt he had all of the qualifications someday to become a leader among our people.

He was in the course of making the big adjustment from convert to member. For a short period before I was released, mine was the opportunity to be his friend. Then I was released to return home. He was given a small responsibility in the branch in London. He knew nothing of what was expected of him. He made a mistake. The head of the organization where he served was a man I can best describe as being short on love and strong on criticism. In a rather unmerciful way, he went after my friend who had made the simple mistake.

The young man left our rented hall that night smarting and hurt by his superior officer. He said to himself, "If that is the kind of people they are, then I am not going back."

He drifted into inactivity. The years passed. The war came on, and he served in the British forces. His first wife died. After the war he married a woman whose father was a Protestant minister. That did not help his belief.

When I was in England, I tried desperately to find him. His file contained no record of a current address. I came home and finally, after a long search, was able to track him down.

I wrote to him. He responded, but with no mention of the gospel.

When next I was in London, I again searched for him. The day I was to leave, I found him. I called him, and we met in the underground station. He threw his arms around me as I did around him.

117

I had very little time before I had to catch my plane, but we talked briefly and with what I think was a true regard for one another. He gave me another embrace before I left. I determined that I would never lose track of him again. Through the years I wrote to him, letters that I hoped would give encouragement and incentive to return to the Church. He wrote in reply without mentioning the Church.

The years passed. I grew older as did he. He retired from his work and moved to Switzerland. On one occasion when I was in Switzerland, I went out of my way to find the village where he lived. We spent the better part of a day together—he, his wife, my wife, and myself. We had a wonderful time, but it was evident that the fire of faith had long since died. I tried every way I knew, but I could not find a way to rekindle it. I continued my correspondence. I sent him books, magazines, recordings of the Tabernacle Choir, and other things, for which he expressed appreciation.

He died a few months ago. His wife wrote me to inform me of this. She said, "You were the best friend he ever had."

Tears coursed my cheeks when I read that letter. I knew I had failed. Perhaps if I had been there to pick him up when he was first knocked down, he might have made a different thing of his life. I think I could have helped him then. I think I could have dressed the wound from which he suffered. I have only one comfort: I tried. I have only one sorrow: I failed.

The challenge now is greater than it has ever been because the number of converts is greater than we have ever before known. A program for retaining and strengthening the convert will soon go out to all the Church. I plead with you, brethren; I ask of you, each of you, to become a part of this great effort. Every convert is precious. Every convert is a son or daughter of God. Every convert is a great and serious responsibility.

Moroni, long ago, spoke of these people with whom we deal in this day and time. Said he:

"Neither did they receive any unto baptism save they came forth with a broken heart and a contrite spirit, and witnessed unto the church that they truly repented of all their sins.

"And none were received unto baptism save they took upon them the name of Christ, having a determination to serve him to the end" (Moroni 6:2–3).

I believe, my brethren, that these converts have a testimony of the gospel. I believe they have faith in the Lord Jesus Christ and know of His divine reality. I believe they have truly repented of their sins and have a determination to serve the Lord.

Moroni continues concerning them after they are baptized: "And after they had been received unto baptism, and were wrought upon and cleansed by the power of the Holy Ghost, they were numbered among the people of the church of Christ; and their names were taken, that they might be remembered and nourished by the good word of God, to keep them in the right way, to keep them continually watchful unto prayer, relying alone upon the merits of Christ, who was the author and the finisher of their faith" (Moroni 6:4).

In these days as in those days, converts are "numbered among the people of the church . . . [to] be remembered and nourished by the good word of God, to keep them in the right way, to keep them continually watchful unto prayer." Brethren, let us help them as they take their first steps as members.

This is a work for everyone. It is a work for home teachers and visiting teachers. It is a work for the bishopric, for the priesthood quorums, for the Relief Society, the young men and young women, even the Primary.

I was in a fast and testimony meeting only last Sunday. A 15- or 16-year-old boy stood before the congregation and said that he had decided to be baptized.

Then one by one, boys of the teachers quorum stepped to the microphone to express their love for him, to tell him that he was doing the right thing, and to assure him that they would stand with him and help him. It was a wonderful experience to hear those young men speak words of appreciation and encouragement to their friend. I am satisfied that all of those boys, including the one who was baptized last week, will go on missions.

In a recent press interview I was asked, "What brings you the greatest satisfaction as you see the work of the Church today?"

My response: "The most satisfying experience I have is to see what this gospel does for people. It gives them a new outlook on life. It gives them a perspective that they have never felt before. It raises their sights to things noble and divine. Something happens to them that is miraculous to behold. They look to Christ and come alive."

Now, brethren, I ask each of you to please help in this undertaking. Your friendly ways are needed. Your sense of responsibility is needed. The Savior of all mankind left the ninety and nine to find the one lost. That one who was lost need not have become lost. But if he is out there somewhere in the shadows, and if it means leaving the ninety and nine, we must do so to find him. (See Luke 15:3–7.)

Now, I think that is all I will say this evening about this, except to say that in my view nothing is of greater importance.

I now wish to move to another subject.

I wish to speak to the young men. I have as my text Paul's letters to his young friend and associate Timothy. I have quoted from these letters extensively to missionaries, and now I speak to you as missionaries yet to be.

I picture Paul as the old, battered teacher of truth. He writes to his young friend, in whom he has confidence and for whom he has a great love.

He says, among other things, "We both labour and suffer reproach, because we trust in the living God, who is the Saviour of all men, specially of those that believe" (1 Timothy 4:10).

Paul was persecuted and driven; he was hated and despised. Eventually his life was taken because he fearlessly bore witness of the Redeemer of all men.

We must be prepared to do likewise.

As Nephi proclaimed, "We talk of Christ, we rejoice in Christ, we preach of Christ, we prophesy of Christ, and we write according to our prophecies, that our children may know to what source they may look for a remission of their sins" (2 Nephi 25:26).

Writes Paul further to Timothy, "Let no man despise thy youth; but be thou an example of the believers, in word, in conversation, in charity, in spirit, in faith, in purity" (1 Timothy 4:12).

Those whom we teach will overlook our youth if in our conversations in charity, in spirit, in faith, and in the purity of our lives, we reflect the Spirit of Christ. We cannot indulge in swearing. We cannot be guilty of profanity; we cannot indulge in impure thoughts, words, and acts and have the Spirit of the Lord with us.

Paul goes on to say, "Neglect not the gift that is in thee, which was given thee by prophecy, with the laying on of the hands of the presbytery" (1 Timothy 4:14).

Who are the presbytery? They are the elders of the Church. Each of you deacons, teachers, and priests has been ordained by one having the proper authority, in most cases by your fathers or bishops. You have been given a great and precious gift. You can speak truth. You must speak truth. You can bear testimony of the great and good things of the gospel. This is your gift. Neglect it not!

Paul continues, "Take heed unto thyself, and unto the doctrine; continue in them: for in doing this thou shalt both save thyself, and them that hear thee" (1 Timothy 4:16).

As you work with your associates to help them with their faith, you will save them and also yourselves.

Again, Paul's counsel to Timothy: "Keep thyself pure" (1 Timothy 5:22).

Those are simple words. But they are ever so important. Paul is saying, in effect, stay away from those things which will tear you down and destroy you spiritually. Stay away from television shows which lead to unclean thoughts and unclean language. Stay away from videos which will lead to evil thoughts. They won't help you. They will only hurt you. Stay away from books and magazines which are sleazy and filthy in what they say and portray. Keep thyself pure.

Continuing with the words of Paul: "For the love of money is the root of all evil" (1 Timothy 6:10). It is the love of money and the love of those things which money can buy which destroys us. We all need money to supply our needs. But it is the love of it which hurts us, which warps our values, which leads us away from spiritual things and fosters selfishness and greed.

And now I come to Paul's great statement:

"For God hath not given us the spirit of fear; but of power, and of love, and of a sound mind.

"Be not thou therefore ashamed of the testimony of our Lord" (2 Timothy 1:7–8).

It is not God who has given us the spirit of fear; this comes from the adversary. So many of us are fearful of what our peers will say, that we will be looked upon with disdain and criticized if we stand for what is right. But I remind you that "wickedness never was happiness" (Alma 41:10). Evil never was happiness. Sin never was happiness. Happiness lies in the power and the love and the sweet simplicity of the gospel of Jesus Christ.

We need not be prudish. We need not slink off in a corner, as it were. We need not be ashamed. We have the greatest thing in the world, the gospel of the risen Lord. Paul gives us a mandate: "Be not thou therefore ashamed of the testimony of our Lord" (2 Timothy 1:8).

As deacons, teachers, and priests ordained to the holy priesthood, we can stand tall and, without equivocation or fear, declare our testimony of Jesus Christ.

Further from Paul: "Study to shew thyself approved unto God, a workman that needeth not to be ashamed" (2 Timothy 2:15).

If we were called upon to stand before God and give an accounting of ourselves, could we do it without embarrassment? This is Paul's great plea to his young friend. It is his plea to each of you. He goes on to say, "Shun profane and vain babblings: for they will increase unto more ungodliness" (2 Timothy 2:16).

He is warning against just fooling around, wasting our time, talking about useless things. Idleness leads to evil.

He continues, "Flee also youthful lusts: but follow righteousness, faith, charity, peace, with them that call on the Lord out of a pure heart" (2 Timothy 2:22).

It was Sir Galahad who said, "My strength is as the strength of ten, / Because my heart is pure" (Alfred, Lord Tennyson, "Sir Galahad").

We cannot say it frequently enough. Turn away from youthful lusts. Stay away from drugs. They can absolutely destroy you. Avoid them as you would a terrible disease, for that is what they become. Avoid foul and filthy talk. It can lead to destruction. Be absolutely honest. Dishonesty can corrupt and destroy. Observe the Word of Wisdom. You cannot smoke; you must not smoke. You must not chew tobacco. You cannot drink liquor. You hold the priesthood of God. You must rise above these things which beckon with a seductive call. Be prayerful. Call on the Lord in faith, and He will hear your prayers. He loves you. He wishes to bless you. He will do so if you live worthy of His blessing.

You face great challenges that lie ahead. You are moving into a world of fierce competition. You must get all of the education you can. The Lord has instructed us concerning the importance of education. It will qualify you for greater opportunities. It will equip you to do something worthwhile in the great world of opportunity that lies ahead. If you can go to college and that is your wish, then do it.

If you have no desire to attend college, then go to a vocational or business school to sharpen your skills and increase your capacity.

Prepare now to go on a mission. It will not be a burden. It will not be a waste of time. It will be a great opportunity and a great challenge. It will do something for you that nothing else will do for you. It will sharpen your skills. It will train you in leadership. It will bring testimony and conviction into your heart. You will bless the lives of others as you bless your own. It will bring you nearer to God and to His Divine Son as you bear witness and testimony of Him. Your knowledge of the gospel will strengthen and deepen. Your love for your fellowman will increase. Your fears will fade as you stand boldly in testimony of the truth.

We love you, boys, our dear young associates in this great work. We pray for you that you may be faithful and true. We count on you to prepare yourselves to take our places in the great work of moving forward the work of God. Get on your knees and pray every day, night and morning. Look to your fathers and mothers, and follow their counsel. Look to your bishop and his counselors. They will lead you in the direction you should go. "Look to God and live" (Alma 37:47).

You have come into the world in a great season in this, the work of the Lord. No other generation has had quite the same opportunities that you have and will have. Begin now to establish those goals which will bring you happiness—education in your chosen skill or branch of learning, whatever it may be; a mission in which to surrender yourself entirely to the Lord to do His work; future marriage in the house of the Lord to a wonderful and delightful companion of whom you will be worthy because of the way you have lived.

May the Lord bless you, my dear young friends. May His watch care be over you to preserve and protect and guide you. He has a great work for you. Do not fail Him. I leave my love and my blessing with you in the name of Jesus Christ, amen.

# SUNDAY MORNING SESSION

I WISH TO SAY SOMETHING IN recapitulation of what we have already heard and seen on this, the birthday of the Church. As we have been reminded a number of times, this is a great anniversary year, and I wish to go on record concerning the magnitude of what our forebears accomplished and what this means to us. It is a story with which most of you are familiar, but it is worth another telling.

It is a story so large in scope, so fraught with human suffering and the workings of faith, that it will never grow old or stale.

Whether you are among the posterity of the pioneers or whether you were baptized only yesterday, each is the beneficiary of their great undertaking.

What a wonderful thing it is to have behind us a great and noble body of progenitors! What a marvelous thing to be the recipients of a magnificent heritage that speaks of the guiding hand of the Lord, of the listening ear of His prophets, of the total dedication of a vast congregation of Saints who loved this cause more than life itself! Small wonder that so many hundreds of thousands of us—yea, even millions—will pause this coming July to remember them, to celebrate their wondrous accomplishments, and to rejoice in the miraculous thing that has grown from the foundation they laid.

Permit me to quote to you from Wallace Stegner, not a member of the Church but a contemporary at the University of Utah who later became professor of creative writing at Stanford and a Pulitzer Prize winner. He was a close observer and a careful student. He wrote this concerning these forebears of ours:

> They built a commonwealth, or as they would have put it, a Kingdom. But the story of their migration is more than the story of the founding of Utah. In their hegira they opened up southern Iowa from Locust Creek to the Missouri, made the first roads, built the first bridges, established the first communities. They transformed the Missouri at Council Bluffs from a trading post and an Indian agency into an outpost of civilization, founded settlements on both sides of the river and made Winter Quarters . . . and later Kanesville . . . into outfitting points that rivaled Independence, Westport, and St. Joseph. . . . Their guide books and trail markers, their bridges and ferries, though made for the Saints scheduled to come later, served also for the Gentiles.

He continues:

> The Mormons were one of the principal forces in the settlement of the West. Their main body opened southern Iowa, the Missouri frontier, Nebraska, Wyoming, Utah. Samuel Brannan's group of eastern Saints who sailed around the Horn in the ship *Brooklyn,* and the Mormon Battalion that marched 2,000 miles overland from Fort Leavenworth to San Diego, were secondary prongs of the Mormon movement; between them, they contributed to the opening of the Southwest and of California. Battalion members were at Coloma when gold gleamed up from the bedrock of Sutter's millrace. . . . Brigham Young's colonizing Mormons, taking to wheels again after the briefest stay, radiated outward from the Salt Lake, Utah, and Weber Valleys and planted settlements that reached from Northern Arizona to the Lemhi River in Idaho, and from Fort Bridger in Wyoming to Genoa in Carson Valley . . . , and in the Southwest down

126

through St. George and Las Vegas to San Bernardino. [*The Gathering of Zion: The Story of the Mormon Trail* (1964), 6–7]

That is a capsule account of their remarkable achievements.

In a period of seven years, our people, who had fled the extermination order of Governor Boggs of Missouri, came to Illinois and built the largest city then in the state. It was on the shores of the Mississippi, where the river makes a great sweeping bend. Here they constructed brick homes, a school, chartered a university, erected an assembly hall, and built their temple, reportedly the most magnificent structure then in the entire state of Illinois. But hatred against them continued to enflame. It culminated in the death of their leader, Joseph Smith, and his brother Hyrum, who were shot and killed at Carthage on June 27, 1844.

Brigham Young knew they could not stay there. They determined to move west, to a faraway place where, as Joseph Smith had said, "the devil cannot dig us out" (*Teachings of the Prophet Joseph Smith*, sel. Joseph Fielding Smith [1972], 332). On February 4, 1846, wagons rolled down Parley's Street to the river. Here they were ferried across and began to roll over the soil of Iowa. The weather subsequently turned bitter cold. The river froze; they crossed on the ice. Once they said good-bye to Nauvoo, they consigned themselves to the elements of nature and to the mercy of God.

When the ground thawed, it was mud—deep and treacherous mud. Wagons sank to their axles, and teams had to be doubled and tripled to move them. They cut a road where none had been before.

Finally reaching the Grand Encampment on the Missouri, they built hundreds of shelters, some very crude and others more comfortable. It was anything to get out of the treacherous weather.

All during that winter of 1846 in those frontier establishments, forges roared and anvils rang with the making of wagons. My own grandfather, barely out of his teens, became an expert blacksmith and wagon builder. No vocation was more useful in those days than that of the ability to shape iron. He would later build his own wagon and with his young wife and baby and his half-brother set off for the West. Somewhere on that long journey, his wife sickened and died, and his half-brother died on the same day. He buried them both, tearfully said good-bye, tenderly picked up his child, and marched on to the valley of the Great Salt Lake.

In the spring of 1847, the wagons of the first company pulled out of Winter Quarters and headed west. Generally they followed a route along the north side of the Platte River. Those going to California and Oregon followed a route on the south side. The road of the Mormons later became the right-of-way of the Union Pacific Railroad and the transcontinental highway.

As we all know, on July 24, 1847, after 111 days, they emerged from the mountain canyon into the Salt Lake Valley. Brigham Young declared, "This is the right place" (in B. H. Roberts, *A Comprehensive History of the Church*, 3:224).

I stand in reverent awe of that statement. They might have gone on to California or Oregon, where the soil had been tested, where there was ample water, where there was a more equable climate. Jim Bridger had warned them against trying to grow crops in the Salt Lake Valley. Sam Brannan had pleaded with Brigham to go on to California. Now they looked across the barren valley, with its saline waters shimmering in the July sun to the west. No plow had ever broken the sun-baked soil. Here stood Brigham Young, 46 years of age, telling his people this was the right place. They had never planted a crop or known a harvest. They knew nothing of the seasons. Thousands of their numbers were coming behind them, and there would yet be tens of thousands. They accepted Brigham Young's prophetic statement.

Homes soon began to spring from the desert soil. Trees were planted, and the miracle is that they grew. Construction of a new temple was begun, a task that was to last unremittingly for 40 years.

From that 1847 beginning to the coming of the railroad in 1869, they came by the tens of thousands to their Zion in the mountains. Nauvoo was evacuated. Its temple was burned by an arsonist, and its walls later fell in a storm.

Missionary work had begun in England in 1837. It spread from there to Scandinavia and gradually to Germany and other countries. All who were converted wanted to go to Zion.

That gathering was not a haphazard operation. Church agents were responsible for every detail. Ships were commissioned to bring the immigrants to New Orleans, New York, and Boston. The ultimate goal was always the same: the valley of the Great Salt Lake, from which place many of them would spread in all directions to found new cities and settlements, more than 350 of them in the Rocky Mountain area.

Hundreds died on that long trail. They died of cholera and black canker, of sheer exhaustion and hunger and the bitter cold.

Most noble, as we've heard, among those who paid a terrible price were the Willie and Martin handcart companies of 1856.

There were not wagons enough to carry all who were converted in England and western Europe. If they were to come to Zion, they would have to walk, pulling a small cart behind them. Hundreds did so and traveled faster than did the ox teams. But these two companies in 1856 literally walked with death. They started late, and no one knew they were coming. Their carts were not ready. A few who could afford wagons were assigned to travel with them to give assistance. They started west, singing as they went. Little did they know what lay ahead of them.

They walked beside the Platte, ever westward. Near Fort Laramie their troubles began. Snow commenced falling. Their rations were reduced. They knew they were in desperate circumstances as they slowly crept over the high plains of Wyoming. Some 200 perished in that terrible, tragic march.

Legion are the stories of those who were there and who

suffered almost unto death and who carried all of their lives the scars of that dreadful experience. It was a tragedy without parallel in the western migration of our people.

When all is said and done, no one can imagine, no one can appreciate or understand how desperate were their circumstances. I wish to pay tribute to the people of the Riverton Wyoming Stake, who have done so much to identify and complete the temple work for and memorialize those who walked that march of death and terrible suffering. I could recount story after story, but there is no time for that. I mention very briefly only one.

At Rock Creek Hollow, on property the Church now owns, is the common grave of 13 who perished in one night. Among them was a nine-year-old girl from Denmark who was traveling alone with another family. Her name was Bodil Mortensen.

In October of 1856 wind-driven heavy snow was already two feet deep as those of the James G. Willie Company tried to find some shelter from the terrible storm. Bodil went out and gathered brush with which to make a fire. Returning, she reached her cart with the brush in her arm. There she died, frozen to death. Starvation and bitter cold drained from her emaciated body the life she had fought for.

We thank the Lord today that all of this is now behind us, as much as a century and a half behind us.

We stand today as the recipients of their great effort. I hope we are thankful. I hope we carry in our hearts a deep sense of gratitude for all that they have done for us.

It is now 1997, and the future is ahead. As great things were expected of them, so are they of us. We note what they did with what they had. We have so much more, with an overwhelming challenge to go on and build the kingdom of God. There is so much to do. We have a divine mandate to carry the gospel to every nation, kindred, tongue, and people. We have a charge to teach and baptize in the name of the Lord Jesus Christ. Said the resurrected

Savior, "Go ye into all the world, and preach the gospel to every creature" (Mark 16:15).

We are engaged in a great and consuming crusade for truth and goodness. Fortunately we live in a season of goodwill. There has come down to us an inheritance of respect and honor to our people. We must grasp the torch and run the race.

Our people are found in positions of responsibility across the world. Their good reputation enhances the work of the Lord. Wherever we may be, whatever the circumstances in which we live, "if there [be] anything virtuous, lovely, or of good report or praiseworthy, [let us] seek after these things" (Articles of Faith 1:13).

The little stone envisioned by Daniel is rolling forth in majesty and power. There are some who still scorn. Let us live above it. There are still those who regard us as a peculiar people. Let us accept that as a compliment and go forth showing by the virtue of our lives the strength and goodness of the wonderful thing in which we believe.

At a time when families all across the world are falling apart, let us solidify our own, let us strengthen them, let us nurture them in righteousness and truth.

With so great an inheritance, we can do no less than our very best. Those who have gone before expect this of us. We have a mandate from the Lord. We have a vision of our cause and purpose.

Let us seek out the righteous of the earth who will listen to our message of salvation. Let us bring light and truth and understanding to a generation that is prone in its disillusionment to look for other things.

God has blessed us with wonderful facilities in which to teach the living truth. We now have meetinghouses scattered across the continents. Let us use them to nurture our people with "the good word of God" (Jacob 6:7).

We now have temples far and wide and are building more, that the great work of salvation for the dead may go forward with an ever-increasing momentum.

Our forebears laid a solid and marvelous foundation. Now ours is the great opportunity to build a superstructure, all fitly framed together with Christ as the chief cornerstone.

My beloved brethren and sisters, how blessed we are! What a wonderful inheritance we have! It involved sacrifice, suffering, death, vision, faith, and knowledge and a testimony of God the Eternal Father and His Son, the risen Lord Jesus Christ.

The covered wagons of long ago have been replaced by airplanes that thread the skies. The horse and buggy have been replaced by air-conditioned automobiles that speed over ribbons of highway. We have great institutions of learning. We have vast treasures of family history. We have houses of worship by the thousands. Governments of the earth look upon us with respect and favor. The media treat us well. This, I submit, is our great season of opportunity.

We honor best those who have gone before when we serve well in the cause of truth. May the Almighty smile with favor upon us as we seek to do His will and go forward as "a chosen generation, a royal priesthood, an holy nation, a peculiar people" (1 Peter 2:9).

For this I humbly pray, as I both look back to the past and forward to the future in this anniversary year and leave my testimony and blessing with you in the name of Him who is our Master, even the Lord Jesus Christ, amen.

# Sunday Afternoon Session

## April 6, 1997

T HIS HAS BEEN A WONDERFUL conference. The Spirit of the Lord has been here. The music has been inspirational. The talks and prayers have touched us with a desire to do better. We have appreciated all who have spoken and wish that all of the General and Area Authorities and general officers might have been heard from. That would have taken about a week.

We have been reminded that ours is a great inheritance. The past is behind us. It is the future with which we must be concerned. We face great opportunities and great challenges. Our critics at home and abroad are watching us. In an effort to find fault, they listen to every word we say, hoping to entrap us. We may stumble now and again. But the work will not be materially hindered. We will stand up where we fell and go forward.

We have nothing to fear and everything to gain. God is at the helm. We will seek His direction. We will listen to the still, small voice of revelation. And we will go forward as He directs.

His Church will not be misled. Never fear that. If there were any disposition on the part of its leaders to do so, He could remove them. All of us are beholden to Him for life and voice and strength.

Let us be good citizens of the nations in which we live. Let us be good neighbors in our communities. Let us acknowledge the diversity of our society, recognizing the good in all people. We need not make any surrender of our theology. But we can set aside any element of suspicion, of provincialism, of parochialism.

"We believe in God, the Eternal Father, and in His Son, Jesus Christ, and in the Holy Ghost" (Articles of Faith 1:1). This is our primary declaration of faith. We speak unabashedly of the living reality of the Lord Jesus Christ. We declare without equivocation the fact of His great act of Atonement for all mankind. That act brought assurance of universal resurrection and opened the way to exaltation in our Father's kingdom.

This is the burden of our declaration to the world. It is the substance of our theology. It is the wellspring of our faith. Let no one ever say that we are not Christians.

To those who have been released during this conference, we express our deep gratitude for your past performance. You have done so very, very well. Thank you for your great contributions. To those of you newly sustained, we wish for you great satisfaction and happiness in the work which you will do. All of us at some time will be released by one process or another. It matters not where we serve in this great cause, but how we serve.

Brigham Young and a handful of others are remembered from our pioneer history. But what of the unsung, the unheralded, the unrecognized who lived the gospel, loved the Lord, and did their daily work without fanfare or applause? Will their eternal reward be any less? I think not.

So it is with us. We each make our own contribution, and that contribution adds up to the building of the cause. Your contribution is as acceptable as ours. Jesus said, "If any man desire to be first, the same shall be last of all, and servant of all" (Mark 9:35).

Brethren and sisters, we're all part of one great family. Each has a duty; each has a mission to perform. And when we pass on, it will be reward enough if we can say to our beloved Master, "I have fought a good fight, I have finished my course, I have kept the faith" (2 Timothy 4:7).

May each of you go safely to your homes. May you live together in love and appreciation and respect one for another. May you know the smile of heaven upon your lives.

Our love reaches out to you. We love you very much. We leave our blessing with you. We do so as servants of the living God and in the name of our divine Redeemer. God be with you till we meet again, as we conclude this great and wonderful conference, is my humble prayer in the name of Jesus Christ, amen.

# 167TH SEMIANNUAL GENERAL CONFERENCE

# SATURDAY MORNING SESSION

OCTOBER 4, 1997

$M$Y BELOVED BRETHREN AND SISTERS, it is a great pleasure to welcome you again to a general conference of the Church. You have come from far and wide. You have come with the expectation of being inspired and blessed and of drawing nearer to the Lord. The Tabernacle is filled to capacity. I am pleased to report that we broke ground last July 24th for the large new assembly building which is going up on the block to the north of us. It will seat some 21,000, about three and a half times the capacity of this Tabernacle. We have been promised that it will be ready to use for the April conference of the year 2000. We will have a great new building for a great new century.

We meet today under very favorable circumstances. For the most part the world is at peace, and what a priceless boon this is. We walk, generally, in an environment of goodwill. It is true that many do not care for us, and some few may even hate us, using every opportunity to lash out against us. But these are few, and they are largely ineffectual. Never before has the Church had a better reputation than it has now. This is because of you, my brethren and sisters. The opinions of people concerning us for the most part arise out of personal and individual experiences. It is your friendliness, your concern for others, and the good examples of your lives that result in the opinions held by others concerning the Latter-day Saints.

The media have been kind and generous to us. This past year of pioneer celebrations has resulted in very extensive, favorable press coverage. There have been a few things we wish might have been different. I personally have been much quoted, and in a few instances misquoted and misunderstood. I think that's to be expected. None of you need worry because you read something that was incompletely reported. You need not worry that I do not understand some matters of doctrine. I think I understand them thoroughly, and it is unfortunate that the reporting may not make this clear. I hope you will never look to the public press as the authority on the doctrines of the Church.

Notwithstanding these occasional blips, we have been treated very well, and we are grateful to the writers and the editors who have dealt with us honestly and generously.

Two weeks ago this morning I had the opportunity to speak to the Religion Newswriters Association. They were gracious and receptive. There was nothing of contention or argument. I have great respect for these people and great appreciation.

Now the sun is setting on our celebration, and there is much serious work to be done. I intend to speak more of this tomorrow morning.

We are releasing at this conference a number of the Seventy and also the presidency of the Young Women of the Church. This is in conformity with a policy of five years of service.

These faithful and able brothers and sisters have served so very well. Without complaint of any kind they have gone wherever they were sent. They have freely given of their talents and devotion in carrying forward the work of the Lord at home and abroad. This cause is much the stronger because of their efforts.

To their spouses and families, particularly in the case of the Young Women presidency, we express thanks for enduring the inconveniences of sharing their wives and mothers with the entire Church.

We extend our love and blessing to each one who is being released and wish for them continuing satisfaction concerning the service they have given and much of happiness wherever their paths lead them.

At this time I wish only to invite the Spirit of the Lord to be with us as we go forward with another great conference. May all who speak be inspired in their remarks. May the prayers lift our thoughts to high and sacred levels. May the music bring beauty and spiritual nourishment to each of us.

I wish that all of the General Authorities could speak to us. Unfortunately, that is not possible. But we shall all be as one as our hearts reach out to you, our beloved brothers and sisters, in testimony of this great work. God is our Father, who watches over His kingdom. Jesus is the Christ, whose name this Church bears. He stands at its head. The gospel has been restored and is moving with power across the earth. Our faith is made secure by the things which we know to be true.

May the blessings of the Lord attend us I humbly pray in the name of Jesus Christ, amen.

# Priesthood
# Session

NOW BRETHREN, IT BECOMES my privilege to speak to you, and I will repeat some things that have been said during this conference with the hope of giving emphasis to them. This has been a wonderful meeting, and if the counsel we have received is heeded, we shall all be the better for it.

I believe that no member of the Church has received the ultimate which this Church has to give until he or she has received his or her temple blessings in the house of the Lord. Accordingly, we are doing all that we know how to do to expedite the construction of these sacred buildings and make the blessings received therein more generally available.

With the dedication of the St. Louis Temple last June, we have 50 working temples. We will soon dedicate the Vernal Utah Temple. The next dedication is scheduled for June of 1998 in Preston, England.

I am pleased to report that the temples in Colombia; Ecuador; the Dominican Republic; Bolivia; Spain; Recife and Campinas, Brazil; Mexico; Boston; New York; and Albuquerque are all moving forward either in planning or in various stages of construction. Our previously announced plan to construct a temple in Venezuela is also going forward, and we are hopeful of acquiring a site in the very near future. We continue to work on permits of various kinds, against some opposition, for temples in Billings, Montana, and Nashville, Tennessee.

I am now pleased to announce our intent to build temples in Houston, Texas, and in Porto Alegre, Brazil. All of this speaks of our great interest in vigorously moving forward this important work. Altogether I think we have about 17 temples in some course of construction, and that is a prodigious undertaking.

But there are many areas of the Church that are remote, where the membership is small and not likely to grow very much in the near future. Are those who live in these places to be denied forever the blessings of the temple ordinances? While visiting such an area a few months ago, we prayerfully pondered this question. The answer, we believe, came bright and clear.

We will construct small temples in some of these areas, buildings with all of the facilities to administer all of the ordinances. They would be built to temple standards, which are much higher than meetinghouse standards. They would accommodate baptisms for the dead, the endowment service, sealings, and all other ordinances to be had in the Lord's house for both the living and the dead.

They would be presided over, wherever possible, by local men called as temple presidents, just as stake presidents are called. They would have an indefinite period of appointment. They would live in the area, in their own homes. One counselor would serve as temple recorder, the other as temple engineer. All ordinance workers would be local people who would serve in other capacities in their wards and stakes.

Patrons would be expected to have their own temple clothing, thereby making unnecessary the construction of very costly laundries. A simple laundry would take care of baptismal clothing. There would be no eating facilities.

These structures would be open according to need, maybe only one or two days a week—that would be left to the judgment of the temple president. Where possible, we would place such a building on the same grounds as the stake center, using the same parking lot for both facilities, thereby effecting a great savings.

One of these small temples can be constructed for about the same cost it takes just to maintain a large temple for a single year. It can be constructed in a relatively short time, several months. I repeat that none of the essentials would be missing. Every ordinance performed in the house of the Lord would be available. These small buildings would have at least half the capacity of some of our much larger temples. They could be expanded when needed.

Now, as you hear me say these things, I think stake presidents in many areas will say this is exactly what we need. Well, let us know of your needs, and we will give them prayerful and careful consideration, but please don't expect things to happen all at once. We need a little experience for this undertaking.

The operation of such temples will require some measure of sacrifice on the part of our faithful local Saints. They not only will serve as ordinance workers; it will be expected that they will clean the buildings and take care of them. But the burden will not be heavy; in view of the blessings, it will be light indeed. There will be no paid employees; all of the work of operation will represent faith and devotion and dedication.

We are planning such structures immediately in Anchorage, Alaska; in the LDS colonies in northern Mexico; and in Monticello, Utah. In areas of greater Church membership we will build more of the traditional temples, but we are developing plans that will reduce the costs without any reduction in terms of the work to be performed therein. We are determined, brethren, to take the temples to the people and afford them every opportunity for the very precious blessings that come of temple worship.

Now, so much for that matter. What I say next you have heard me say before, and you have heard others speak of it. I hope we keep talking about it and then doing something about it. I do so because I am so concerned with it.

With the increase of missionary work throughout the world, there must be a comparable increase in the effort to make every convert feel at home in his or her ward or branch. Enough people will come into the Church this year to constitute more than 100 new average-size stakes. Unfortunately, with this acceleration in conversions, we are neglecting some of these new members. I am hopeful that a great effort will go forward throughout the Church, throughout the world, to retain every convert who comes into the Church.

This is serious business. There is no point in doing missionary work unless we hold on to the fruits of that effort. The two must be inseparable.

I should like to read you a letter. It is of a kind that we occasionally receive. A man writes:

> I feel compelled to write to you after reading your comments from the April general conference. I was especially moved by your comments on "Converts and Young Men." I was reading the article on the Internet and was touched by your words. Your perception of converts and their special needs was especially moving to me since I was a convert to the Church. I wanted to write to you and tell you that I agree with all of your statements and that had more members been aware of the needs of a convert I would probably have stayed in the Church.
>
> I was converted to The Church of Jesus Christ of Latter-day Saints in 1994. This was after a long period of time in which I was searching for the true church. I had explored just about every denomination and church but never found what I was looking for. From my first contact with the missionaries, I knew that they were presenting something to me that would change my life. I listened to what they had to say, and I heard what I was looking for all those years. I don't know if there

are words to describe how I felt after hearing their message. I was finally at peace. It all made sense. I earnestly studied the Church and felt as if I had found a "home." I decided to be baptized on October 8, 1994. It was one of the greatest days of my life.

However, after my baptism, things with the Church changed. I suddenly was thrown into an environment where I was supposed to know what was going on. I now was not the focus of attention but just another member. I was treated as if I was in the Church for years.

I had been told that there would be six discussions following my joining the Church. They never took place. At this same time, I was feeling intense pressure from my fiancée to not be in the Church. She was extremely anti-Mormon [in her] beliefs and didn't want me to be a part of it. We fought often about the Church. I thought that I could make her see my side of the story. I thought that if I just had more time to participate in the Church, she wouldn't think of it as a bad thing or as a cult. I thought that she would see from my example that this was the true Church and she would come to accept it.

I used the missionaries for a lot of support. They helped . . . to think of ways to convince my fiancée that I had made the right decision. That worked until the missionaries were transferred. They moved away, and I was basically left alone. At least, that is how I thought. I looked to the members for support, but there was none. The bishop helped, but he could only do so much. I gradually lost my "warm, fuzzy feeling" about the Church. I felt like a stranger. I began to doubt the Church and its message. Eventually, I started to listen more to my fiancée. Then I made a decision that maybe I had rushed into the Church too quickly. I wrote my bishop and asked that my name be removed from the Church records. I allowed this to be done. That was a low point in my life.

Now it's two years since I left the Church. I have gone back to [my old church] and haven't been involved with The

Church of Jesus Christ of Latter-day Saints since then. I am constantly praying and asking God to guide me. I know in my heart that He will guide me to His true Church. However, I don't know if that is The Church of Jesus Christ of Latter-day Saints or if it even exists at all. I regret that I left the Church and had my name removed from the records, but at the time I felt that there was no other option. The experience left a bad impression with me, and it would be difficult to overcome.

As the Church prepares to implement a program for the retention of new converts, I wanted you to know . . . that I think a lot of new converts may have similar experiences to mine. I know that there are people who are joining the Church against the advice of friends and family. This is a big step for them, and they should be supported at this critical time. I know from my past that had the support been there, I would not be writing this letter to you.

Thank you for your time, [and he signs the letter].

What a tragedy. What a terrible tragedy. I believe the writer still has a testimony of this work. That testimony has been with him since the time he was baptized, but he has felt neglected and of no consequence to anyone.

Someone has failed, failed miserably. I say to bishops throughout the world that with all you have to do—and we recognize that it is much—you cannot disregard the converts. Most of them do not need very much. As I have said before, they need a friend. They need something to do, a responsibility. They need nurturing with the good word of God. They come into the Church with enthusiasm for what they have found. We must immediately build on that enthusiasm. You have people in your wards who can be friends to every convert. They can listen to them, guide them, answer their questions, and be there to help in all circumstances and in all conditions. Brethren, this loss must stop. It is unnecessary. I am satisfied the Lord is not pleased with us. I invite you, every one of you, to make this a matter of priority in your administrative work. I invite every member to reach out in friendship and love for those who come into the Church as converts.

You will hear much about this in the months to come. I mention it now only to give my wholehearted endorsement.

Permit me now to speak of another matter. I wish to speak to every boy who is listening tonight. And I express appreciation for what the other Brethren have said to them.

First, let me say that we honor and respect you young men. You represent a marvelous generation in this Church. I have said again and again that I believe this is the best generation we have ever had. You and the young women are tremendous. You study the scriptures. You pray. You attend seminary at sacrifice to yourselves. You try to do the right thing. You have testimonies of this work, and most of you live accordingly. I compliment you most generously! I express to you our great love for you. I wish only to say one or two things, adding to the things I have previously said, which I hope will be encouraging as you go forward with your lives.

I could wish for you nothing better than to see in your lives total loyalty to the Church, total faith in its divine mission, total love for the work of the Lord with a desire to move it forward, and total dedication in performing your duties as members of the Aaronic Priesthood.

You live in a world of terrible temptations. Pornography, with its sleazy filth, sweeps over the earth like a horrible, engulfing tide. It is poison. Do not watch it or read it. It will destroy you if you do. It will take from you your self-respect. It will rob you of a sense of the beauties of life. It will tear you down and pull you into a slough of evil thoughts and possibly of evil actions. Stay away from it. Shun it as you would a foul disease, for it is just as deadly. Be virtuous in thought and in deed. God has planted in you, for a purpose, a divine urge which may be easily subverted to evil and destructive ends. When you are young, do not get involved in steady dating. When you reach an age where you think of marriage, then is the time to become so involved. But you boys who are in high school don't need this, and neither do the girls.

We receive letters, we constantly deal with people who, under the pressures of life, marry while very young. There is an old saying, "Marry in haste, repent at leisure." How true that is.

Have a wonderful time with the young women. Do things together, but do not get too serious too soon. You have missions ahead of you, and you cannot afford to compromise this great opportunity and responsibility.

The Lord has said, "Let virtue garnish thy thoughts unceasingly" (D&C 121:45).

Stay away from alcohol. Graduation from high school is no reason for a beer bust. Better stay away and be thought a prude than go through life regretting it ever afterwards. Stay away from drugs. You cannot afford to touch them. They will utterly destroy you. The euphoria will quickly pass, and the deadly, strangling clutches of this evil thing will embrace you in their power. You will become a slave, a debauched slave. You will lose control of your life and your actions. Do not experiment with them. Stay free of them!

Walk in the sunlight, strength, and virtue of self-control and of absolute integrity.

Get all the schooling you can. Education is the key that unlocks the door of opportunity. God has placed upon this people a mandate to acquire knowledge "even by study and also by faith" (D&C 88:118; see also D&C 109:7, 14).

You are a peculiar people. Of course you are. You have bypassed the things of the world. You are on your way to something higher and better. You have education to be obtained. You have marriage before you as a great and sacred opportunity in the house of the Lord.

You have missions to perform. Each of you should plan for missionary service. You may have some doubts. You may have some fears. Face your doubts and your fears with faith. Prepare yourselves to go. You have not only the opportunity; you have the responsibility. The Lord has blessed and favored you in a remarkable and wonderful way. Is it too much to ask that you give two years totally immersed in His service?

My young brethren, you are something special. You must rise above the ordinary. You must put on the whole armor of God and walk with virtue. You know what is right. You know what is wrong. You know when and how to make the choice. You know that there is a power in heaven on which you can call in your time of extremity and need. Pray with fervency and with faith. Pray to the God of heaven, whom you love and who loves you. Pray in the name of the Lord Jesus Christ, who gave His very life for you. Stand up and walk as becomes the sons of God.

We love you. We pray for you. We count on you so very, very much. May you be watched over and safeguarded and blessed of the Lord.

Now I wish to say something to bishops and stake presidents concerning missionary service. It is a sensitive matter. There seems to be growing in the Church an idea that all young women as well as all young men should go on missions. We need some young women. They perform a remarkable work. They can get in homes where the elders cannot.

I confess that I have two granddaughters on missions. They are bright and beautiful young women. They are working hard and accomplishing much good. Speaking with their bishops and their parents, they made their own decisions to go. They did not tell me until they turned in their papers. I had nothing to do with their decision to go.

Now, having made that confession, I wish to say that the First Presidency and the Council of the Twelve are united in saying to our young sisters that they are not under obligation to go on missions. I hope I can say what I have to say in a way that will not be offensive to anyone. Young women should not feel that they have a

147

duty comparable to that of young men. Some of them will very much wish to go. If so, they should counsel with their bishop as well as their parents. If the idea persists, the bishop will know what to do.

I say what has been said before, that missionary work is essentially a priesthood responsibility. As such, our young men must carry the major burden. This is their responsibility and their obligation.

We do not ask the young women to consider a mission as an essential part of their life's program. Over a period of many years, we have held the age level higher for them in an effort to keep the number going relatively small. Again to the sisters I say that you will be as highly respected, you will be considered as being as much in the line of duty, your efforts will be as acceptable to the Lord and to the Church whether you go on a mission or do not go on a mission.

We constantly receive letters from young women asking why the age for sister missionaries is not the same as it is for elders. We simply give them the reasons. We know that they are disappointed. We know that many have set their hearts on missions. We know that many of them wish this experience before they marry and go forward with their adult lives. I certainly do not wish to say or imply that their services are not wanted. I simply say that a mission is not necessary as a part of their lives.

Now, that may appear to be something of a strange thing to say in priesthood meeting. I say it here because I do not know where else to say it. The bishops and stake presidents of the Church have now heard it. And they must be the ones who make the judgment in this matter.

That is enough on that subject.

Now, in closing, I simply want to express my love for each of you. You men and boys provide the leadership for this great organization, which is moving across the world in a marvelous and miraculous manner. I have not the slightest concern about the future. This Church has become a great builder of leaders. One sees them everywhere. Converts of only a few years are serving as bishops and stake presidents and in other capacities. What a wonderful thing you are doing, my brethren.

Husbands, live the gospel. Be kind to your wives. You cannot serve acceptably in the Church if there is conflict at home. Fathers, be kind to your children. Be companionable with them. As hard as you may labor in gathering the necessities of the world, no asset you will ever have will compare with the love and loyalty of the woman with whom you joined hands over the altar in the temple and the affection and respect of your children.

May each of you be blessed in your vocational pursuits, whatever they may be, so long as they are honorable. May you look upon the Church as your great and good friend, your refuge when the world appears to be closing around you, your hope when things are dark, your pillar of fire by night and your cloud by day as you thread the pathways of your lives. May the Lord be mindful of you and merciful and kind to you. May you find great joy in that which you do in His service is my humble prayer, with an expression of love and affection for each of you, in the name of Jesus Christ, amen.

# Sunday Morning Session

OCTOBER 5, 1997

THE CELEBRATIONS OF 1997 are largely over. The last wagon has rolled to a stop. The last handcart has come to rest. We have had a wonderful year, when we have commemorated the great migration of our forebears to these western valleys.

We have bowed in remembrance of their sacrifices, the many who died along the way and who were lovingly placed in graves whose location we know not.

We have shared, to a very small degree, the terrible suffering of those caught in the Wyoming snows of 1856.

We have seen the fulfillment of Isaiah's promise, "The wilderness and the solitary place shall be glad for them; and the desert shall rejoice, and blossom as the rose" (Isaiah 35:1).

We cannot detract from their accomplishments. We cannot add to their glory. We can only look back with reverence, appreciation, respect, and resolution to build on what they have done.

The time has now come to turn about and face the future. This is a season of a thousand opportunities. It is ours to grasp and move forward. What a wonderful time it is for each of us to do his or her small part in moving the work of the Lord on to its magnificent destiny.

"And this gospel of the kingdom shall be preached in all the world for a witness unto all nations; and then shall the end come" (Matthew 24:14).

Something, my brothers and sisters, is happening in this Church, something wonderful. As we walk in the small world of our individual wards and branches, we are scarcely aware of it. And yet it is real, and it is tremendous. We are growing. We are expanding. Enough people will come into the Church this year to constitute more than 600 new wards or branches.

A month from now we will reach the 10 million mark in membership. It took over a century, 117 years, from the organization of the Church in 1830 to 1947, to reach one million. More of our members now live outside the U.S. than in the U.S. We have been out among our people. It has been glorious to meet with them, to speak with them, to share testimonies with them. They are enthusiastic.

We were recently with the Navajo Nation at Window Rock in Arizona. It was the first time that a President of the Church had met with and spoken to them in their capital. It was difficult to hold back the tears as we mingled with these sons and daughters of Father Lehi. In my imagination I have seen him weeping for his progeny who for so long have walked in poverty and pain.

But the shackles of darkness are falling. Some of them now are men and women of achievement. They have partaken of the fruits of education. They have come to know and love the gospel. They have become pure and delightsome.

But there is so much more to do among them. Alcohol and drugs literally destroy many of them. We must do more to help. As I look to the future, I envision the Spirit of the Lord being poured out upon these people. Education will unlock the door of opportunity, and the gospel will bring new light and understanding into their lives.

We have been with thousands of these wonderful people in South America. We recently flew from Asunción, Paraguay, to

Guayaquil, Ecuador, over the high and forbidding peaks and narrow valleys of that vast area. Everywhere there were Indian villages and small cities. Our missionaries are working with these good people, bringing the light of the everlasting gospel into their lives. Many years ago Sister Hinckley and I took the little train that runs from Cuzco, Peru, to Puno on Lake Titicaca. In Puno we met with a little handful of native members, the first General Authority ever to do so. Today we have two stakes of Zion in Puno, their stake presidents and bishops drawn from their number.

We have now been in all the nations of South America and Central America, and we have seen miracles, with great gatherings of 30,000, 40,000, and 50,000 in football stadiums. These are all Latter-day Saints. In each case as we left there was a great waving of handkerchiefs, with tears in their eyes and tears in ours.

In the nation of Brazil alone there will be approximately 50,000 people join the Church this year. That is the equivalent of 16 or 17 new stakes in just 12 months. The São Paulo Temple cannot accommodate all who wish to come. We are building three new temples in that nation and will yet have to build others.

These are strong and wonderful Latter-day Saints in whose hearts beat the same testimonies of Jesus and this work as beat in yours.

We must construct meetinghouses by the score to accommodate the needs of these ever increasing numbers.

I stand in amazement, knowing the history of this Church, when I realize there is not a city in the United States or Canada of any consequence which does not have a Latter-day Saint congregation. It is the same in Mexico. It is the same in Central and South America. Likewise in New Zealand and Australia, in the islands of the sea, and in Japan, Korea, Taiwan, the Philippines.

In Europe our congregations are everywhere. What a remarkable thing it is to contemplate that each Sabbath there are more than 24,000 wards and branches across the world in which the same lessons are taught and the same testimonies are borne.

Now, what of the future? What of the years that lie ahead? It looks promising indeed. People are beginning to see us for what we are and for the values we espouse. The media generally treat us well. We enjoy a good reputation, for which we are grateful.

If we will go forward, never losing sight of our goal, speaking ill of no one, living the great principles we know to be true, this cause will roll on in majesty and power to fill the earth. Doors now closed to the preaching of the gospel will be opened. The Almighty, if necessary, may have to shake the nations to humble them and cause them to listen to the servants of the living God. Whatever is needed will come to pass.

The key to the great challenges facing us and to the success of the work will be the faith of all who call themselves Latter-day Saints. Our standards are certain and unequivocal. We need not quibble about them. We need not rationalize them. They are set forth in the Decalogue, written by the finger of the Lord on Mount Sinai. They are found in the Sermon on the Mount, spoken by the Lord Himself. They are found elsewhere in His teachings, and they are found plainly set forth in the words of modern revelation. From the beginning these have served as our code of conduct. They must continue to so serve.

The future will be essentially the same as the past, only much brighter and greatly enlarged. We must continue to reach out across the world, teaching the gospel at home and abroad. A divine mandate rests heavily upon us. We cannot run from it. We cannot avoid it.

Declared the risen Lord to those He loved:

"Go ye into all the world, and preach the gospel to every creature.

"He that believeth and is baptized shall be saved; but he that believeth not shall be damned" (Mark 16:15–16).

The figure of Moroni, atop many of our temples, is a constant reminder of the vision of John the Revelator:

"And I saw another angel fly in the midst of heaven, having the everlasting gospel to preach unto them that dwell on the earth, and to every nation, and kindred, and tongue, and people,

"Saying with a loud voice, Fear God, and give glory to him; for the hour of his judgment is come: and worship him that made heaven, and earth, and the sea, and the fountains of waters" (Revelation 14:6–7).

There must be no diminution in our effort to carry the gospel to the people of the earth. In the future even more of our young men must prepare themselves to go out in service to the Lord. Our Christian acts must precede them and accompany them wherever necessary. I am grateful for the humanitarian aid we have been able to extend to the poor and the unfortunate. This very day hungry children are eating food in North Korea because of the aid which you have sent. In a world where there is so much of hunger and suffering, where death walks hand in hand with little children, we must continue and enlarge our efforts, not permitting politics or other factors to hold back the hand of mercy.

As we look to the future we must extend the great work carried forward in the temples, both for the living and the dead. If this people cannot be saved without their dead, as the Prophet Joseph declared, then we must make it possible for many more to accomplish this work. We now have 50 operating temples. We need twice that number, and as I explained last evening, we have in place a program to reach that goal to accommodate the needs of the people. Those on the other side, who are not dead but who are alive as to the spirit, will rejoice and be made glad as they awaken and go forward on their way to "immortality and eternal life" (Moses 1:39).

But there are many other things we must do as we move forward the work to a new and promising century. Simply put, we must be better Latter-day Saints. We must be more neighborly. We cannot live a cloistered existence in this world. We are a part of the whole of humanity.

A lawyer cometh unto Jesus, asking, "Master, which is the great commandment in the law?

"Jesus said unto him, Thou shalt love the Lord thy God with all thy heart, and with all thy soul, and with all thy mind.

"This is the first and great commandment.

"And the second is like unto it, Thou shalt love thy neighbour as thyself.

"On these two commandments hang all the law and the prophets" (Matthew 22:36–40).

Let us love the Lord, yes, with all our strength and power. And let us also love our neighbors. Let us banish from our lives any elements of self-righteousness. Many regard us with suspicion, as having only one interest, and that is to convert them. Conversion is more likely to come as a consequence of love. Let us be friendly. Let us be helpful. Let us live the Golden Rule. Let us be neighbors of whom it might be said, "He or she was the best neighbor I ever had."

And as we move forward into a wonderful future, there are what some may regard as the lesser commandments but which are also of such tremendous importance.

I mention the Sabbath day. The Sabbath of the Lord is becoming the play day of the people. It is a day of golf and football on television, of buying and selling in our stores and markets. Are we moving to mainstream America, as some observers believe? In this I fear we are. What a telling thing it is to see the parking lots of the markets filled on Sunday in communities that are predominately LDS.

Our strength for the future, our resolution to grow the Church across the world, will be weakened if we violate the will of the Lord in this important matter. He has so very clearly spoken anciently and again in modern revelation. We cannot disregard with impunity that which He has said.

We must observe the Word of Wisdom. As we read our newspapers, as we watch the television news, these remarkable words first spoken in 1833 come to life before our very eyes: "In consequence of evils and designs which do and will exist in the hearts of conspiring men in the last days, I have warned you, and forewarn you" (D&C 89:4). People are becoming increasingly health conscious. We have a running start on the world, a code so simple and easily understood. Not long ago I met Dr. James E. Enstrom of the University of California at Los Angeles. He is not a member of the Church. He speaks with complete objectivity. His studies indicate that actuarially speaking, Latter-day Saints live about 10 years longer than their peers.

Who can set a price on 10 years of life? What a remarkable and wonderful blessing is this Word of Wisdom.

Reporters whom I have met simply cannot believe that we pay 10 percent of our income as tithing. I explain that this is a spiritual phenomenon. We pay because we are obedient to the commandment of the Lord. We pay because we have faith in His munificent promises. Let us teach our children while they are yet young of the great opportunity and responsibility of paying tithing. If we do so, there will be another generation, and yet another, who will walk in the ways of the Lord and merit His promised blessing.

Perhaps our greatest concern is with families. The family is falling apart all over the world. The old ties that bound together father and mother and children are breaking everywhere. We must face this in our own midst. There are too many broken homes among our own. The love that led to marriage somehow evaporates, and hatred fills its place. Hearts are broken; children weep. Can we not do better? Of course we can. It is selfishness that brings about most of these tragedies. If there is forbearance, if there is forgiveness, if there is an anxious looking after the happiness of one's companion, then love will flourish and blossom.

As I look to the future, I see little to feel enthusiastic about concerning the family in America and across the world. Drugs and alcohol are taking a terrible toll, which is not likely to decrease. Harsh language one to another, indifference to the needs of one another—all seem to be increasing. There is so much of child abuse. There is so much of spouse abuse. There is growing abuse of the elderly. All of this will happen and get worse unless there is an underlying acknowledgment, yes, a strong and fervent conviction, concerning the fact that the family is an instrument of the Almighty. It is His creation. It is also the basic unit of society.

I lift a warning voice to our people. We have moved too far toward the mainstream of society in this matter. Now, of course there are good families. There are good families everywhere. But there are too many who are in trouble. This is a malady with a cure. The prescription is simple and wonderfully effective. It is love. It is plain, simple, everyday love and respect. It is a tender plant that needs nurturing. But it is worth all of the effort we can put into it.

Now, in closing, I see a wonderful future in a very uncertain world. If we will cling to our values, if we will build on our inheritance, if we will walk in obedience before the Lord, if we will simply live the gospel, we will be blessed in a magnificent and wonderful way. We will be looked upon as a peculiar people who have found the key to a peculiar happiness.

"And many people shall go and say, Come ye, and let us go up to the mountain of the Lord, to the house of the God of Jacob; and he will teach us of his ways, and we will walk in his paths: for out of Zion shall go forth the law, and the word of the Lord from Jerusalem" (Isaiah 2:3).

Great has been our past, wonderful is our present, glorious can be our future.

*Arise, O glorious Zion,*
*Thou joy of latter days,*
*Whom countless Saints rely on*
*To gain a resting place.*
*Arise and shine in splendor*
*Amid the world's deep night,*
*For God, thy sure defender,*
*Is now thy life and light.*
          *["Arise, O Glorious Zion,"*
          Hymns, *no. 40]*

We have glimpsed the future, we know the way, we have the truth. God help us to move forward to become a great and mighty people spread over the earth, counted in the millions, but all of one faith and of one testimony and of one conviction, I humbly pray in the name of our great Redeemer and Savior, even Jesus Christ, amen.

# Sunday Afternoon
# Session

I THINK I WILL LEAVE THE TEXT that I prepared and just talk with you a little bit and express my deep appreciation to you.

We need these conferences. We need them to remind us of our responsibilities and obligations. We must never forget that spirituality must be the dominant feature of the Church.

A recent magazine article praised us as a well-run financial institution of great wealth. It grossly exaggerated the figures.

The money the Church receives from faithful members is consecrated. It is the Lord's purse. Our Church facilities are money consuming and not money producing. We are not a financial institution. We are the Church of Jesus Christ. The funds for which we are responsible involve a sacred trust to be handled with absolute honesty and integrity and with great prudence as the dedicated consecrations of the people.

We feel a tremendous responsibility to you who make these contributions. We feel an even greater responsibility to the Lord, whose money this is.

Now, brothers and sisters, we pray that all of you may return safely to your homes. Please be careful. Drive with great care. Ponder the things you have heard. May your experience be similar to that of the people of King Benjamin, who all cried with one voice, saying, "We believe all the words which thou hast spoken unto us; and also, we know of their surety and truth, because of the Spirit of the Lord Omnipotent, which has wrought a mighty change in us, . . . that we have no more disposition to do evil, but to do good continually" (Mosiah 5:2).

Let us counsel with the Lord in all our undertakings. Let us be better neighbors. Let us be better employers and employees. Let us be men and women of integrity and honesty in business, in education, in government, in the professions, whatever is our place in life.

I have a confession to make, my brothers and sisters. It is simply this: I love you. I love the people of this Church. I love all who are faithful. I love all who follow the ways of the Lord. It is a humbling thing to preside over the Church. I can never forget the words of Jesus: he that would be first among you, let him be the "servant of all" (Mark 9:35; D&C 50:26).

Thank you for your prayers, your trust, your confidence. I am deeply grateful for all who have generously assisted in helping us to do our duty.

In closing, I would like to read a word or two from Mormon—great words:

"But behold, that which is of God inviteth and enticeth to do good continually; wherefore, every thing which inviteth and enticeth to do good, and to love God, and to serve him, is inspired of God. . . .

"For behold, the Spirit of Christ is given to every man, that he may know good from evil; wherefore, I show unto you the way to judge; for every thing which inviteth to do good, and to persuade to believe in Christ, is sent forth by the power and gift of Christ; wherefore ye may know with a perfect knowledge it is of God" (Moroni 7:13, 16).

And then these great words, which become the *summum bonum* of it all: "Whatsoever thing ye shall ask the Father in my name, which is good, in faith believing that ye shall receive, behold, it shall be done unto you" (Moroni 7:26). I believe those words.

We are proud to be one with you in moving forward this mighty work. We are all in this together. Every man and woman has a part to play. God give us the strength and the will to play it well.

"God be with you till we meet again" (*Hymns,* no. 152), my beloved associates. I have sung those simple words in a thousand places across the world since I began my ministry 39 years ago. I sing them again today with love and affection. God bless you, my dear friends, I ask in the name of Jesus Christ, amen.

# 168th Annual General Conference

# Saturday Morning Session

April 4, 1998

My beloved brethren and sisters, we welcome you most warmly to this general conference, which has become a great world conference of the Church.

These proceedings will be heard and seen across this nation and Canada and in much of the remainder of the world. I think there is nothing to compare with it. I commend and thank all who have to do with the complicated logistics of this great undertaking.

We are met to worship the Lord, to declare His divinity and His living reality. We are met to reaffirm our love for Him and our knowledge of His love for us. No one, regardless of what he or she may say, can diminish that love.

There are some who try. For instance, there are some of other faiths who do not regard us as Christians. That is not important. How we regard ourselves is what is important. We acknowledge without hesitation that there are differences between us. Were this not so, there would have been no need for a restoration of the gospel. President Packer and Elder Ballard recently spoke of this in other settings.

I hope we do not argue over this matter. There is no reason to debate it. We simply, quietly, and without apology testify that God has revealed Himself and His Beloved Son in opening this full and final dispensation of His work.

We must not become disagreeable as we talk of doctrinal differences. There is no place for acrimony. But we can never surrender or compromise that knowledge which has come to us through revelation and the direct bestowal of keys and authority under the hands of those who held them anciently. Let us never forget that this is a restoration of that which was instituted by the Savior of the world. It is not a reformation of perceived false practice and doctrine that may have developed through the centuries.

We can respect other religions and must do so. We must recognize the great good they accomplish. We must teach our children to be tolerant and friendly toward those not of our faith. We can and do work with those of other religions in the defense of those values which have made our civilization great and our society distinctive.

For instance, there recently came to my office a Protestant minister who is a most effective leader in the unending battle against pornography. We are grateful for him. We join with him and his associates. We give financial support to his organization.

We can and do work with those of other religions in various undertakings in the everlasting fight against social evils which threaten the treasured values which are so important to all of us. These people are not of our faith, but they are our friends, neighbors, and co-workers in a variety of causes. We are pleased to lend our strength to their efforts.

But in all of this there is no doctrinal compromise. There need not be and must not be on our part. But there is a degree of fellowship as we labor together.

As we carry forward our distinctive mission, we work under a mandate given us by the risen Lord, who has spoken in this last and final dispensation. This is His unique and wonderful cause. We bear testimony and witness of Him. But we need not do so with arrogance or self-righteousness.

As Peter expressed it, we are "a chosen generation, a royal priesthood, an holy nation, a peculiar people." Why? That we might "shew forth the praises of him who hath called [us] out of darkness into his marvellous light" (1 Peter 2:9).

A holier-than-thou attitude is not becoming to us. I am in receipt of a letter from a man in our community who is not a member of the Church. In it he says that his little daughter has been ostracized by her schoolmates who are Latter-day Saints. He sets forth another instance of a child who, it is alleged, had a religious medal ripped from his neck by an LDS child. I hope this is not true. If it is, I apologize to those who have been offended.

Let us rise above all such conduct and teach our children to do likewise. Let us be true disciples of the Christ, observing the Golden Rule, doing unto others as we would have them do unto us. Let us strengthen our own faith and that of our children while being gracious to those who are not of our faith. Love and respect will overcome every element of animosity. Our kindness may be the most persuasive argument for that which we believe.

Now, one other matter. A week ago I was in Palmyra, New York. I there dedicated two buildings. One was a restoration of the small log home in which the Joseph Smith Sr. family first lived in that area. It was in this humble home that the 14-year-old Joseph determined to go into the nearby grove to ask of God and experienced an incomparable vision of the Father and the Son.

It was in this home that Moroni, the angel, appeared to the boy Joseph, calling him by name and telling him that God had a work for him to do and that his "name should be had for good and evil among all nations, kindreds, and tongues, or that it should be both good and evil spoken of among all people" (Joseph Smith—History 1:33).

How could a farm boy, largely without formal education, have dared to say such a thing? And yet it has all come to pass and will continue to increase as this restored gospel is taught across the world.

While in Palmyra, I also dedicated the E. B. Grandin Building, where the first edition of the Book of Mormon was printed in 1829 and 1830. It was a bold undertaking to print what Mr. Grandin first regarded as a fraud, and to print an edition of 5,000, which was very large for the time. I am pleased to remind you that since that time we have printed more than 88 million copies of this remarkable volume.

I am grateful that we have this old building, purchased by a generous member of the Church and donated to the Church. Its very presence confirms the validity of the book, this remarkable testament of the Son of God.

Who, having read it, can honestly refute its divine origin? Critics may try to explain it away. The harder they try, the more plausible becomes the true account of its coming forth as a voice speaking from the dust.

How grateful I am for the testimony with which God has blessed me of the divine calling of Joseph Smith, of the reality of the First Vision, of the restoration of the priesthood, of the truth of this, The Church of Jesus Christ of Latter-day Saints.

And so, my beloved brothers and sisters, let us rejoice together now as we celebrate with appreciation the wondrous doctrines and practices which have come as a gift from the Lord in this most glorious time of His work. This is the Easter season, when we remember His glorious Resurrection, of which we bear witness. Let us ever be grateful for these most precious gifts and privileges and act well our part as those who love the Lord. I invite you to listen to the words which will go forth from this pulpit, to be delivered by those who have been called as your servants. May we be blessed I humbly pray in the name of Jesus Christ, amen.

# PRIESTHOOD SESSION

A WEEK AGO PRESIDENT FAUST and the Young Women general presidency spoke to the young women of the Church in this Tabernacle.

As I looked at that gathering of beautiful young women, the question moved through my mind, "Are we rearing a generation of young men worthy of them?"

Those girls are so fresh and vibrant. They are beautiful. They are bright. They are able. They are faithful. They are virtuous. They are true. They are simply wonderful and delightful young women.

And so tonight, in this great priesthood meeting, I wish to speak to you young men, their counterpart. The title of my talk: "Living Worthy of the Girl You Will Someday Marry."

The girl you marry will take a terrible chance on you. She will give her all to the young man she marries. He will largely determine the remainder of her life. She will even surrender her name to his name.

As Adam declared in the Garden of Eden:

"This is now bone of my bones, and flesh of my flesh. . . .

"Therefore shall a man leave his father and his mother, and shall cleave unto his wife: and they shall be one flesh" (Genesis 2:23–24).

As members of The Church of Jesus Christ of Latter-day Saints, as young men holding the priesthood of God, you have a tremendous obligation toward the girl you marry. Perhaps you are not thinking much of that now. But the time isn't far away when you will think of it, and now is the time to prepare for that most important day of your lives when you take unto yourself a wife and companion equal with you before the Lord.

That obligation begins with absolute loyalty. As the old Church of England ceremony says, you will marry her "for richer or for poorer, in sickness and in health, for better or for worse." She will be yours and yours alone, regardless of the circumstances of your lives. You will be hers and hers alone. There can be eyes for none other. There must be absolute loyalty, undeviating loyalty one to another. Hopefully you will marry her forever, in the house of the Lord, under the authority of the everlasting priesthood. Through all the days of your lives, you must be as true one to another as the polar star.

The girl you marry can expect you to come to the marriage altar absolutely clean. She can expect you to be a young man of virtue in thought and word and deed.

I plead with you boys tonight to keep yourselves free from the stains of the world. You must not indulge in sleazy talk at school. You must not tell sultry jokes. You must not fool around with the Internet to find pornographic material. You must not dial a long-distance telephone number to listen to filth. You must not rent videos with pornography of any kind. This salacious stuff simply is not for you. Stay away from pornography as you would avoid a serious disease. It is as destructive. It can become habitual, and those who indulge in it get so they cannot leave it alone. It is addictive.

It is a five-billion-dollar business for those who produce it. They make it as titillating and attractive as they know how. It seduces and destroys its victims. It is everywhere. It is all about us. I plead with you young men not to get involved in its use. You simply cannot afford to.

The girl you marry is worthy of a husband whose life has not been tainted by this ugly and corrosive material.

Look upon the Word of Wisdom as more than a commonplace thing. I regard it as the most remarkable document on health of which I know. It came to the Prophet Joseph Smith in 1833, when relatively little was known of dietary matters. Now the greater the scientific research, the more certain becomes the proof of Word of Wisdom principles. The evidence against tobacco is now overwhelming, yet we see a tremendous increase in its use by young men and women. The evidence against liquor is just as great.

To me it is an ironic thing that service stations offer beer sales. An individual can get as drunk on beer and be as dangerous on the road as he can on any other alcoholic substance. It is simply a matter of how much he drinks. How absolutely inconsistent it is for a service station, where you get gas so you can drive, to also sell beer that can cause you to drive "under the influence" and become a terrible menace on the highway.

Stay away from it. It will do you no good. It could do you irreparable harm. Suppose you drink and drive and cause the death of someone. You will never get over it as long as you live. It will haunt you night and day. The one simple thing to do is simply to not touch it.

Likewise, stay away from illegal drugs. They can absolutely destroy you. They will take away your powers of reason. They will enslave you in a vicious and terrible way. They will destroy your mind and your body. They will build within you such cravings that you will do anything to satisfy them.

Would any girl in her right mind ever wish to marry a young man who has a drug habit, who is the slave of alcohol, who is addicted to pornography?

Avoid profanity. It is all around you in school. Young people seem to pride themselves on using filthy and obscene language as well as indulging in profanity, taking the name of our Lord in vain.

It becomes a vicious habit which, if indulged in while you are young, will find expression throughout your life. Who would wish to be married to a man whose speech is laden with filth and profanity?

There is another serious thing to which many young men become addicted. This is anger. With the least provocation they explode into tantrums of uncontrolled rage. It is pitiful to see someone so weak. But even worse, they are prone to lose all sense of reason and do things which bring later regret.

We hear much these days of the phenomenon called road rage. Drivers become provoked over some small irritation. They fly into a rage, even resulting in murder. A life of regret follows.

As the writer of Proverbs has said, "He that is slow to anger is better than the mighty; and he that ruleth his spirit than he that taketh a city" (Proverbs 16:32).

If you have a temper, now is the time to learn to control it. The more you do so while you are young, the more easily it will happen. Let no member of this Church ever lose control of himself in such an unnecessary and vicious manner. Let him bring to his marriage words of peace and composure.

I constantly deal with those cases of members of the Church who have been married in the temple and who later divorce and then apply for a cancellation of their temple sealing. When first married, they are full of great expectations, with a wonderful spirit of happiness. But the flower of love fades in an atmosphere of criticism and carping, of mean words and uncontrolled anger. Love flies out the window as contention enters. I repeat, my brethren, if any of you young men have trouble controlling your temper, I plead with you to begin the work of making that correction now. Otherwise you will bring only tears and sorrow into the homes which you will someday establish. Jacob, in the Book of Mormon, condemns his people for their wickedness in marriage. Says he: "Behold, ye have done greater iniquities than the Lamanites, our brethren. Ye have broken the hearts of your tender wives, and lost the confidence of your children, because of your bad examples before them; and the sobbings of their hearts ascend up to God against you. And because of the strictness of the word of God, which cometh down against you, many hearts died, pierced with deep wounds" (Jacob 2:35).

Work for an education. Get all the training that you can. The world will largely pay you what it thinks you are worth. Paul did not mince words when he wrote to Timothy, "But if any provide not for his own, and specially for those of his own house, he hath denied the faith, and is worse than an infidel" (1 Timothy 5:8).

It is your primary obligation to provide for your family.

Your wife will be fortunate indeed if she does not have to go out and compete in the marketplace. She will be twice blessed if she is able to remain at home while you become the breadwinner of the family.

Education is the key to economic opportunity. The Lord has laid a mandate upon us as a people to acquire learning "by study, and also by faith" (D&C 109:14). It is likely that you will be a better provider if your mind and hands are trained to do something worthwhile in the society of which you will become a part.

Be modest in your wants. You do not need a big home with a big mortgage as you begin your lives together. You can and should avoid overwhelming debt. There is nothing that will cause greater tensions in marriage than grinding debt, which will make of you a slave to your creditors. You may have to borrow money to begin ownership of a home. But do not let it be so costly that it will preoccupy your thoughts day and night.

When I was married, my wise father said to me, "Get a modest home, and pay off the mortgage so that if economic storms should come, your wife and children will have a roof over their heads."

The girl who marries you will not wish to be married to a tightwad. Neither will she wish to be married to a spendthrift. She is entitled to know all about family finances. She will be your partner. Unless there is full and complete understanding between you and your wife on these matters, there likely will come misunderstandings and suspicions that will cause trouble that can lead to greater problems.

She will wish to be married to someone who loves her, who trusts her, who walks beside her, who is her very best friend and companion. She will wish to be married to someone who encourages her in her Church activity and in community activities which will help her to develop her talents and make a greater contribution to society. She will want to be married to someone who has a sense of service to others, who is disposed to contribute to the Church and to other good causes. She will wish to be married to someone who loves the Lord and seeks to do His will. It is well, therefore, that each of you young men plan to go on a mission, to give unselfishly to your Father in Heaven a tithe of your life, to go forth with a spirit of total unselfishness to preach the gospel of peace to the world wherever you may be sent. If you are a good missionary, you will return home with the desire to continue to serve the Lord, to keep His commandments, and to do His will. Such behavior will add immeasurably to the happiness of your marriage.

As I have said, you will wish to be married in one place and one place only. That is the house of the Lord. You cannot give to your companion a greater gift than that of marriage in God's holy house, under the protective wing of the sealing covenant of eternal marriage. There is no adequate substitute for it. There should be no other way for you.

Choose carefully and wisely. The girl you marry will be yours forever. You will love her and she will love you through thick and thin, through sunshine and storm. She will become the mother of your children. What greater thing in all this world can there be than to become the father of a precious child, a son or daughter of God, our Father in Heaven, for whom we are given the rights and responsibilities of mortal stewardship.

How precious a thing is a baby. How wonderful a thing is a child. What a marvelous thing is a family. Live worthy of becoming a father of whom your wife and children will be proud.

The Lord has ordained that we should marry, that we shall live together in love and peace and harmony, that we shall have children and rear them in His holy ways.

And so, my dear young men, you may not think seriously about it now. But the time will come when you will fall in love. It will occupy all of your thoughts and be the stuff of which your dreams are made. Make yourself worthy of the loveliest girl in all the world. Keep yourself worthy through all the days of your life. Be good and true and kind one to another. There is so much of bitterness in the world. There is so much of pain and sorrow that come of angry words. There is so much of tears that follow disloyalty. But there can be so much of happiness if there is an effort to please and an overwhelming desire to make comfortable and happy one's companion.

When all is said and done, this is what the gospel is about. The family is a creation of God. It is the basic creation. The way to strengthen the nation is to strengthen the homes of the people.

I am satisfied that if we would look for the virtues in one another and not the vices, there would be much more of happiness in the homes of our people. There would be far less of divorce, much less of infidelity, much less of anger and rancor and quarreling. There would be more of forgiveness, more of love, more of peace, more of happiness. This is as the Lord would have it.

Young men, now is the time to prepare for the future. And in that future for most of you is a beautiful young woman whose greatest desire is to bond with you in a relationship that is eternal and everlasting.

You will know no greater happiness than that found in your

home. You will have no more serious obligation than that which you face in your home. The truest mark of your success in life will be the quality of your marriage.

God bless you, my dear young men. I could wish for you nothing more wonderful than the love, the absolute total love of a companion of whom you are proud and worthy in every respect. This choice will be the most important of all the choices you make in your life. I pray that heaven may smile upon you in the choice you make, that you may be guided, that you may live without regret, in the name of Jesus Christ, amen.

# Sunday Morning
# Session

APRIL 5, 1998

Now, MY DEAR FRIENDS, I pray for the direction of the Holy Spirit. It is three years now since you sustained me as President of the Church. May I say a few words of a personal nature? From the bottom of my heart I thank you for your love and support, for your prayers and faith. I am no longer a young man filled with energy and vitality. I am an old man trying to catch up with Brother Haight! I'm given to meditation and prayer. I would enjoy sitting in a rocker, swallowing prescriptions, listening to soft music, and contemplating the things of the universe. But such activity offers no challenge and makes no contribution.

I wish to be up and doing. I wish to face each day with resolution and purpose. I wish to use every waking hour to give encouragement, to bless those whose burdens are heavy, to build faith and strength of testimony. Through the great kindness of a generous friend, I have been permitted to travel over the earth during these three years, visiting among our people in scores of nations. They have gathered by the thousands and tens of thousands. In one place there were more than 200 buses which brought them to the stadium.

I have been among the affluent but more so among the poor—the poor of the earth and the poor of the Church. Some of their eyes are of a slightly different tilt than mine and their skin of a different color, but all of this disappears and becomes meaningless when I am among them. They all become our Father's sons and daughters, children with a divine birthright. We speak various languages, but we all understand the common tongue of brotherhood.

It is wearisome to travel far to reach them. But it is difficult to leave them after being with them. Everyplace we go is only for a brief visit, a meeting scheduled to fit with other meetings. I wish we could stay longer. At the conclusion of the meeting we spontaneously sing "God Be with You Till We Meet Again" (*Hymns*, no. 152). Handkerchiefs come out to dry tears and then are waved in affectionate farewell. Most recently we held 11 large meetings in different cities in Mexico in just seven days.

It is the presence of wonderful people which stimulates the adrenaline. It is the look of love in their eyes which gives me energy.

I could spend all day in my office, doing so year after year, dealing with mountains of problems, many of them of small consequence. I do spend a good deal of time there. But I feel a greater mission, a higher responsibility to be out among the people. These thousands, hundreds of thousands, even millions now, all have one thing in common. They have an individual and personal testimony that this is the work of the Almighty, our Heavenly Father; that Jesus, the Lord, who died on the cross of Calvary and was resurrected, lives, a distinct and real and individual personality; that this is Their work, restored in this last, wonderful dispensation of time; that the ancient priesthood has been restored with all of its keys and powers; that the Book of Mormon has spoken from the dust in testimony of the Redeemer of the world.

This thing which we call testimony is the great strength of the Church. It is the wellspring of faith and activity. It is difficult to explain. It is difficult to quantify. It is an elusive and mysterious thing, and yet it is as real and powerful as any force on the earth. The Lord described it when He spoke to Nicodemus and said, "The wind bloweth where it listeth, and thou hearest the sound thereof, but canst not tell whence it cometh, and whither it goeth: so is every one that is born of the Spirit" (John 3:8). This thing which we call testimony is difficult to define, but its fruits are plainly evident. It is the Holy Spirit testifying through us.

Personal testimony is the factor which turns people around in their living as they come into this Church. This is the element which motivates the membership to forsake all in the service of the Lord. This is the quiet, encouraging voice which sustains without pause those who walk in faith down to the last days of their lives.

It is a mysterious and wonderful thing, a gift from God to man. It overrides wealth or poverty when one is called to serve. This testimony which is carried in the hearts of our people motivates to an impelling duty. It is found in young and old. It is found in the seminary student, in the missionary, in the bishop and the stake president, in the mission president, in the Relief Society sister, in every General Authority. It is heard from those who hold no office other than membership. It is of the very essence of this work. It is what is moving the work of the Lord forward across the world. It impels to action. It demands that we do what we are asked to do. It brings with it the assurance that life is purposeful, that some things are of far greater importance than others, that we are on an eternal journey, that we are answerable unto God.

Emily Dickinson captured an element of it when she wrote:

> *I never saw a Moor—*
> *I never saw the Sea—*
> *Yet know I how the Heather looks*
> *And what a Billow be.*
>
> *I never spoke with God*
> *Nor visited in Heaven—*
> *Yet certain am I of the spot*
> *As if the [chart] were given.*
> [The Complete Poems of Emily
> Dickinson, *Thomas H. Johnson,*
> *ed. (1960), 480]*

It is this element, weak and somewhat feeble at first, which moves every investigator in the direction of conversion. It pushes every convert toward security in the faith. This is the thing which caused our forebears to leave England and the lands of Europe, to cross the seas with harrowing experiences, to walk what seemed endlessly beside plodding oxen or frail handcarts in the direction of these mountains of the West. They struggled, they worked, they died by the thousands on that fateful journey. That spirit of testimony has come down to us, who are the inheritors of their precious faith.

Wherever the Church is organized its power is felt. We stand on our feet and say that we know. We say it until it almost appears to be monotonous. We say it because we do not know what else to say. The simple fact is that we *do* know that God lives, that Jesus *is* the Christ, and that this is Their cause and Their kingdom. The words are simple; the expression comes from the heart. It is at work wherever the Church is organized, wherever there are missionaries teaching the gospel, wherever there are members sharing their faith.

It is something that cannot be refuted. Opponents may quote scripture and argue doctrine endlessly. They can be clever and persuasive. But when one says, "I know," there can be no further argument. There may not be acceptance, but who can refute or deny the quiet voice of the inner soul speaking with personal conviction?

Let me tell you a story that I heard recently in Mexico. In Torreón I was driven about in the fine automobile that belonged to the man of whom I speak. His name is David Castañeda.

Thirty years ago he, his wife, Tomasa, and their children lived on a dry little run-down ranch near Torreón. They owned 30 chickens, 2 pigs, and 1 thin horse. The chickens provided a few eggs to sustain them and the means whereby to earn an occasional peso. They walked in poverty. Then the missionaries called on them. Sister Castañeda said, "The elders took the blinders from our eyes

177

and brought light into our lives. We knew nothing of Jesus Christ. We knew nothing of God until they came."

She had two years of schooling, her husband none. The elders taught them, and they were eventually baptized. They moved into the little town of Bermejillo. They were fortuitously led into the junk business, buying wrecked automobiles. This led to association with insurance companies and others. They gradually built a prosperous business in which the father and his five sons worked. With simple faith they paid their tithing. They put their trust in the Lord. They lived the gospel. They served wherever called to do so. Four of their sons and three of their daughters filled missions. The youngest son is presently serving in Oaxaca. They have now built a very substantial business and have been prospered therein. They have been taunted by their critics. Their answer is a testimony of the power of the Lord in their lives.

Some 200 of their family and friends have joined the Church due to their influence. Over 30 sons and daughters of family and friends have served missions. They donated the land on which a chapel now stands.

The children, now grown to maturity, and the parents take turns going to Mexico City each month, there to work in the temple. They stand as a living testimony of the great power of this work of the Lord to lift and change people. They are typical of thousands upon thousands throughout the world who experience the miracle of Mormonism as a testimony of the divinity of the work comes into their lives.

This witness, this testimony, can be the most precious of all the gifts of God. It is a heavenly bestowal when there is the right effort. It is the opportunity, it is the responsibility of every man and woman in this Church to obtain within himself or herself a conviction of the truth of this great latter-day work and of those who stand at its head, even the living God and the Lord Jesus Christ.

Jesus pointed the way for the acquisition of such a testimony when He said:

"My doctrine is not mine, but his that sent me.

"If any man will do his will, he shall know of the doctrine, whether it be of God, or whether I speak of myself" (John 7:16–17).

We grow in faith and knowledge as we serve, as we study, as we pray.

When Jesus fed the 5,000, they recognized and wondered at the miracle He had performed. Some came back again. To these He taught the doctrine of His divinity, of Himself as the Bread of Life. He accused them of not being interested in the doctrine but rather only in the satisfaction of the hunger of their bodies. Some, on hearing Him and His doctrine, said, "This is an hard saying; who can hear it?" (John 6:60). Who can believe what this man is teaching?

"From that time many of his disciples went back, and walked no more with him.

"Then said Jesus unto the twelve [I think with some feeling of discouragement], Will ye also go away?

"Then Simon Peter answered him, Lord, to whom shall we go? thou hast the words of eternal life.

"And we believe and are sure that thou art that Christ, the Son of the living God" (John 6:66–69).

This is the great question, and the answer thereto, which we must all face. If not to Thee, then "Lord, to whom shall we go? thou hast the words of eternal life. And we believe and are sure that thou art that Christ, the Son of the living God."

It is this conviction, this quiet, inward certainty of the reality of the living God, of the divinity of His Beloved Son, of the Restoration of their work in this time, and of the glorious manifestations which have followed which become for each of us the foundation of our faith. This becomes our testimony.

As I mentioned earlier in this conference, I've recently been in Palmyra, New York. Of the events which occurred in that area, one is led to say, "They either happened or they did not. There can be no gray area, no middle ground."

And then the voice of faith whispers, "It all happened. It happened just as he said it happened."

Nearby is the Hill Cumorah. From there came the ancient record from which was translated the Book of Mormon. One must accept or reject its divine origin. Weighing of the evidence must lead every man and woman who has read with faith to say, "It is true."

And so it is with other elements of this miraculous thing which we call the Restoration of the ancient gospel, the ancient priesthood, and the ancient Church.

This testimony is now, as it has always been, a declaration, a straightforward assertion of truth as we know it. Simple and powerful is the statement of Joseph Smith and Sidney Rigdon concerning the Lord, who stands at the head of this work:

"And now, after the many testimonies which have been given of him, this is the testimony, last of all, which we give of him: That he lives!

"For we saw him, even on the right hand of God; and we heard the voice bearing record that he is the Only Begotten of the Father—

"That by him, and through him, and of him, the worlds are and were created, and the inhabitants thereof are begotten sons and daughters unto God" (D&C 76:22–24).

It is in this spirit that I add my own witness. Our Eternal Father lives. He stands as the great God of the universe, ruling in majesty and power. And yet He is my Father, to whom I may go in prayer with the assurance that He will hear, listen, and answer.

Jesus is the Christ, His immortal Son, who under His Father's direction was the Creator of the earth. He was the great Jehovah of the Old Testament, who condescended to come into the world as the Messiah, who gave His life on Calvary's cross in His wondrous Atonement because He loved us. The work in which we are engaged is Their work, and we are Their servants, who are answerable to Them, of which I testify in the sacred name of Jesus Christ, amen.

# SUNDAY AFTERNOON SESSION

APRIL 5, 1998

I HAVE LOOKED DOWN FROM MY seat and seen on the front row in the Tabernacle a group of Otavalo Indians from the highlands of Ecuador, and I want to express my appreciation to these wonderful people, these faithful Latter-day Saints who have come so very, very far to participate with us in this conference. Thank you very much, brothers and sisters.

In case you do not know where Otavalo is, you go to Quito, then you drive up across the equator and come to villages in the highlands of the great mountains of Ecuador, and there are these peaceful and wonderful people.

As we conclude this great gathering, which has reached across the nation and bridged the seas, I express in humility and with thanksgiving my deep appreciation for all who have participated, including those who have listened. The music has been wonderful. The prayers have been inspirational. The talks have been prepared and delivered under the promptings of the Holy Spirit. We have rejoiced together with grateful hearts. Now it becomes our duty and responsibility, as we return to our homes, to translate into our daily lives the truths which we have heard spoken.

Now, in conclusion I wish to make an announcement. As I have previously indicated, in recent months we have traveled far out among the membership of the Church. I have been with many who have very little of this world's goods. But they have in their hearts a great burning faith concerning this latter-day work. They love the Church. They love the gospel. They love the Lord and want to do His will. They are paying their tithing, modest as it is. They make tremendous sacrifices to visit the temples. They travel for days at a time in cheap buses and on old boats. They save their money and do without to make it all possible.

They need nearby temples—small, beautiful, serviceable temples.

Accordingly, I take this opportunity to announce to the entire Church a program to construct some 30 smaller temples immediately. They will be in Europe, in Asia, in Australia and Fiji, in Mexico and Central and South America and Africa, as well as in the United States and Canada. They will have all the necessary facilities to provide the ordinances of the Lord's house.

This will be a tremendous undertaking. Nothing even approaching it has ever been tried before. These will be in addition to the 17 buildings now going forward in England; Spain; Ecuador; Bolivia; the Dominican Republic; Brazil; Colombia; Billings, Montana; Houston, Texas; Boston, Massachusetts; White Plains, New York; and Albuquerque, New Mexico, and the smaller temples in Anchorage, Alaska; Monticello, Utah; and Colonia Juárez, Mexico. This will make a total of 47 new temples in addition to the 51 now in operation. I think we had better add 2 more to make it an even 100 by the end of this century, being 2,000 years "since the coming of our Lord and Savior Jesus Christ in the flesh" (D&C 20:1). In this program we are moving on a scale the like of which we have never seen before.

I will not give you the specific cities at this time. Stake presidents will be advised as property is secured. I am confident the membership of the Church will do a lot of speculating as to whether one of these will be in their city.

If temple ordinances are an essential part of the restored gospel, and I testify that they are, then we must provide the means by which they can be accomplished. All of our vast family history endeavor is directed to temple work. There is no other purpose for it. The temple ordinances become the crowning blessings the Church has to offer.

I can only add that when these 30 or 32 are built, there will be more yet to come.

May God bless the faithful Latter-day Saints. May you be prospered as you live the commandments. May all be honest, and even generous, in the payment of tithes and offerings, and may the windows of heaven be opened and blessings be showered down upon us as a people as we walk with boldness and in faith before the Lord to accomplish His eternal work.

I was deeply touched by Brother Ronald Poelman's talk on tithing. He and I lived in the same ward when we were boys. We had the same bishop. We paid a little tithing as boys, and the Lord, I can testify, has blessed us through the years that have passed. I can see in my mind's eye his dear mother kneeling with her family and pleading with the Lord and thanking Him for the great privilege that was theirs to impart of their meager substance in obedience to His commandment.

May there be peace and harmony and love in our homes and in our families. May the testimony of the living, hallowed truth of this great work be reflected in our lives. May we all rejoice together in praising Him from whom all blessings flow, our glorious leader and our great Redeemer.

This is my humble prayer, my beloved brethren and sisters, as we come to the close of this great and significant and historic conference. God help us to be Latter-day Saints in the finest expression of that word is my humble prayer, in the name of Jesus Christ, amen.

# GENERAL RELIEF SOCIETY MEETING

SEPTEMBER 26, 1998

My DEAR SISTERS, I WISH TO tell you at the outset how much we appreciate the women of this Church. You are an essential part of it, a most important part of it. It could not function properly without you.

You provide inspiration. You provide balance. You constitute a vast reservoir of faith and good works. You are an anchor of devotion and loyalty and accomplishment. No one can gainsay the great part you play in the onward rolling of this work across the earth. You teach in the organizations and do it so very well. Your preparation is an example to all of us. Each of you is a part of this vast enterprise, the Relief Society, a great family of sisters, more than four million strong. In your worldwide membership lies the power to accomplish incalculable good.

You are the keepers of the homes. You give encouragement to your husbands. You teach and nurture your children in faith. For some of you life is difficult and even bitter. But you complain so very little and do so very much. How deeply indebted we are to you!

Speaking of the Relief Society, President Joseph F. Smith said on one occasion:

"This organization is divinely made, divinely authorized,

divinely instituted, divinely ordained of God to minister for the salvation of the souls of women and of men. Therefore there is not any organization that can compare with it, . . . that can ever occupy the same stand and platform that this can. . . .

"Make [Relief Society] first, make it foremost, make it the highest, the best and the deepest of any organization in existence in the world. You are called by the voice of the Prophet of God to do it, to be uppermost, to be the greatest and the best, the purest and the most devoted to the right" (Minutes of the General Board of Relief Society, Mar. 17, 1914, Archives of The Church of Jesus Christ of Latter-day Saints, 54–56).

A great challenge!

At the marriage of each of our daughters and granddaughters, my wife has presented a special gift. It is not a vacuum cleaner or dishes or anything utilitarian. It is a seven-generation family history chart of her maternal line, beautifully framed. It is made up of photographs of her maternal great-great-grandmother, of her great-grandmother, of her grandmother, her mother, herself, her daughter, and her newly married granddaughter.

Every woman in that picture for seven generations has been a Relief Society worker. This beautiful family history chart becomes an ever-present reminder to the younger ones of this generation of the great responsibility they carry, of the great obligation they have to move forward this work in the tradition of their mothers and grandmothers in service in the Relief Society organization.

You and your forebears have walked in the light of the Lord. From the beginning it has been your most important responsibility to see that no one goes hungry, to see that no one goes without adequate clothing, that no one goes without shelter. It has been and is your responsibility to visit your sisters wherever they may be found, to give encouragement as they may need it, to assure them of love and concern and interest. It is and has been your opportunity to tear away the curtain of darkness that enshrouds those who are illiterate and to bring into their lives the light of understanding as you teach them to read and to write.

It is and has been your opportunity to mingle together as sisters who love and honor and respect one another, to bring the blessings of pleasant sociality into the lives of tens of thousands who, without you, would be left in very bleak and lonely circumstances.

I pulled a book from my shelf the other evening. I read again the life of Mary Fielding Smith, wife of Hyrum Smith, sister-in-law of Joseph Smith, mother and grandmother of two Presidents of the Church. A convert to the Church, originally from England and then from Canada, she came to Kirtland in her late 30s. There she met and married Hyrum Smith, who was left with six children after the death of his first wife.

Mary loved him and brought an added dimension into his life. In that process she set a course which brought her happiness only to be followed by immeasurable sorrow, for there was laid upon her a terrifying and fearful responsibility which took her from Nauvoo across Iowa to Winter Quarters and, in 1848, on the long trail that led to the Salt Lake Valley. At the age of 51 she was worn out, weary from the struggle. She passed away September 21, 1852.

Her life is the epitome of the Relief Society woman of those days. In fact, some of her experiences predated the organization of the society in 1842.

Mary's boy Joseph was born at a time when her husband was snatched away by the mob militia then terrorizing Far West. Hyrum and the Prophet Joseph were taken to Liberty, Missouri, where they were imprisoned. Under the compulsion of Governor Lilburn W. Boggs's extermination order, she left Missouri with the stepchildren for whom she had taken responsibility, as well as her own son. Her sister Mercy placed Mary, who was seriously ill, on a bed in a wagon box with her infant boy cradled at her side.

In February 1839, when winter was still upon the land, they

traveled east across the state and then across the Mississippi to Quincy, Illinois, bumping along in a springless wagon where every jolt brought pain.

When her husband and the Prophet escaped from Liberty Jail and came to Quincy, life again improved. The Saints moved to what became Nauvoo and established their beautiful city on the Mississippi. But their peace was short-lived. Her little boy was less than six years old when a knock came at night on her window and a man said, "Sister Smith, your husband has been killed!"

Joseph F. never forgot his mother's weeping through the night.

Her world was shattered. She was on her own now with a large family to care for. In the summer of 1846, they bade their comfortable home good-bye and rode a flatboat across the Mississippi. Taking matters into her own hands, she was able to trade, borrow, and barter for ox teams and wagons.

While living in Winter Quarters, she and her brother went down the Missouri River to purchase provisions and clothing. They had two wagons, each having two yoke of oxen. Camping for the night, they discovered in the morning that their two best oxen were gone. Young Joseph and his uncle spent the entire morning looking for the lost animals. They found nothing. Disheartened, he returned to tell his mother. Their situation was desperate, terribly so. As he approached, he saw her on her knees praying fervently, speaking with the Lord about their problem. When she arose to her feet, there was a smile on her face. She told her son and her brother to get their breakfast and she would look around. Following a little stream of water, and disregarding the words of a man who was in the area, she went directly along the bank of the river.

Pausing, she called to her son and brother. She pointed to their oxen, which had been tied to a clump of willows growing in the bottom of a deep gulch. The thief, who had tried to misdirect her, lost his prize, and they were saved.

Mary's faith imprinted itself in her son's boyish heart. He never forgot it. He never doubted her closeness to the Lord.

All of you are familiar with her experience when one of her oxen, exhausted and worn, lay down to die while they were en route to these valleys in the West. In a mixture of utter desperation and simple faith, she secured consecrated oil and asked her brother and an associate to administer to the ox. They did so. It rose to its feet with a renewal of strength and carried them for the remainder of their long journey.

Such was the faith, sweet and simple and beautiful, which graced this woman's life. She walked in the light of the Lord. She lived by that light. It guided her in all of her actions. It became the lodestar of her life. She exemplified the tremendous faith of the women of this Church—the women of the Relief Society, who today on a thousand fronts carry on the dedicated work of this remarkable organization.

Now there is an added challenge for you sisters of this day. Never before, at least not in our generation, have the forces of evil been so blatant, so brazen, so aggressive as they are today. Things we dared not speak about in earlier times are now constantly projected into our living rooms. All sensitivity is cast aside as reporters and pundits speak with a disgusting plainness of things that can only stir curiosity and lead to evil.

Some to whom we have looked as leaders have betrayed us. We are disappointed and disillusioned. And their activity is only the tip of the iceberg. In successive layers beneath that tip is a great mass of sleaze and filth, of dissolute and dishonest behavior.

There is a reason for it. I feel it is simple to define. I believe our problems, almost every one, arise out of the homes of the people. If there is to be reformation, if there is to be a change, if there is to be a return to old and sacred values, it must begin in the home. It is here that truth is learned, that integrity is cultivated, that self-discipline is instilled, and that love is nurtured.

The home is under siege. So many families are being destroyed. Where are the fathers who should be presiding in love in those homes? Fortunate indeed is the woman who is married to a good man, who is loved by him, and who in turn loves him—a man who loves his children, provides for them, teaches them, guides them, rears and protects them as they walk the stormy course from babyhood to adulthood.

It is in the home that we learn the values by which we guide our lives. That home may be ever so simple. It may be in a poor neighborhood, but with a good father and a good mother, it can become a place of wondrous upbringing. My wife likes to tell of Sam Levenson. In his book *Everything But Money* he speaks of growing up in a crowded New York tenement where the environment was anything but good. Here in this slum, his mother reared her eight precocious children. He said, "The moral standard of the home had to be higher than that of the street." His mother would say to them when they acted the way they acted on the street, "You are not on the street; you are in our home. This is not a cellar nor a poolroom. Here we act like human beings" ([1966], 145).

If anyone can change the dismal situation into which we are sliding, it is you. Rise up, O women of Zion. Rise to the great challenge which faces you.

Stand above the sleaze and the filth and the temptation which is all about you.

You women who are single, and some of you who are married, who are out in the workplace, may I give you a word of caution. You work alongside men. More and more, there are invitations to go to lunch, ostensibly to talk about business. You travel together. You stay in the same hotel. You work together.

Perhaps you cannot avoid some of this, but you can avoid getting into compromising situations. Do your job, but keep your distance. Don't become a factor in the breakup of another woman's home. You are members of The Church of Jesus Christ of Latter-day

Saints. You know what is expected of you. Stay away from that which is tempting. Avoid evil—its very appearance.

You who are wives and mothers are the anchors of the family. You bear the children. What an enormous and sacred responsibility that is. I am told that between 1972 and 1990 there were 27 million abortions in the United States alone. What is happening to our appreciation of the sanctity of human life? Abortion is an evil, stark and real and repugnant, which is sweeping over the earth. I plead with the women of this Church to shun it, to stand above it, to stay away from those compromising situations which make it appear desirable. There may be some few circumstances under which it can occur, but they are extremely limited and for the most part improbable. You are the mothers of the sons and daughters of God, whose lives are sacred. Safeguarding them is a divinely given responsibility which cannot be lightly brushed aside.

Nurture and cultivate your marriage. Guard it, and work to keep it solid and beautiful. Divorce is becoming so common, even rampant, that studies show in a few years half of those now married will be divorced. It is happening, I regret to say, even among some who are sealed in the house of the Lord. Marriage is a contract, it is a compact, it is a union between a man and a woman under the plan of the Almighty. It can be fragile. It requires nurture and very much effort. I regret to acknowledge that some husbands are abusive, some are unkind, some are thoughtless, some are evil. They indulge in pornography and bring about situations which destroy them, destroy their families, and destroy the most sacred of all relationships.

I pity the man who at one time looked into the eyes of a beautiful young woman and held her hand across the altar in the house of the Lord as they made sacred and everlasting promises one to another, but who, lacking in self-discipline, fails to cultivate his better nature, sinks to coarseness and evil, and destroys the relationship which the Lord has provided for him.

Sisters, guard your children. They live in a world of evil. The forces are all about them. I am proud of so many of your sons and daughters who are living good lives. But I am deeply concerned about many others who are gradually taking on the ways of the world. Nothing is more precious to you as mothers, absolutely nothing. Your children are the most valuable thing you will have in time or all eternity. You will be fortunate indeed if, as you grow old and look at those you brought into the world, you find in them uprightness of life, virtue in living, and integrity in their behavior.

I think the nurture and upbringing of children is more than a part-time responsibility. I recognize that some women must work, but I fear that there are far too many who do so only to get the means for a little more luxury and a few fancier toys.

If you must work, you have an increased load to bear. You cannot afford to neglect your children. They need your supervision in studying, in working inside and outside the home, in the nurturing that only you can adequately give—the love, the blessing, the encouragement, and the closeness of a mother.

Families are being torn asunder everywhere. Family relationships are strained as women try to keep up with the rigors of two full-time jobs.

I have many opportunities to speak with leaders who decry what is going on—gangs on the streets of our cities, children killing children, spending their time in practices that can lead only to prison or to death. We face a great, overwhelming tide of children born to mothers without husbands. The futures of such children are almost inevitably blighted from the day they are born. Every home needs a good father and a good mother.

We cannot build prisons fast enough in this country to accommodate the need.

I do not hesitate to say that you who are mothers can do more than any other group to change this situation. All of these problems find their root in the homes of the people. It is broken homes that lead to a breakup in society.

And so tonight, my beloved sisters, my message to you, my challenge to you, my prayer is that you will rededicate yourselves to the strengthening of your homes.

Three years ago, in this same meeting, I read for the first time in public the proclamation on the family given by the First Presidency and the Council of the Twelve Apostles. I hope every one of you has a copy and that you occasionally read it carefully and prayerfully. It sets forth our great concepts of marriage and family, of a man and a woman in a sacred bond under the eternal plan of the Almighty.

Now, in closing, I wish to reemphasize my deep gratitude, my profound appreciation for the women of this Church and the tremendous sons and daughters you are teaching, training, helping to take their places in the world. But the task will never be finished. It will never be complete. May the light of the Lord shine upon you. May the Lord bless you in your great and sacred work.

I leave my blessing, my testimony, and my love with you in the name of the Lord Jesus Christ, amen.

# SATURDAY MORNING SESSION

OCTOBER 3, 1998

$M$Y BROTHERS AND SISTERS, we welcome you most warmly. We welcome you to this great conference. There are some 6,000 of us here in the Tabernacle and millions more in other halls across the world. We are all one great family. We have one Lord, one faith, one baptism. In fulfillment of the words of Peter, we are "a chosen generation, a royal priesthood, an holy nation, a peculiar people; that [we] should shew forth the praises of him who hath called [us] out of darkness into his marvellous light" (1 Peter 2:9).

For the most part, we are a happy people. We are mindful of and continue to pray for those who are experiencing hardship due to natural or man-caused calamity. But even those among our number who are bowed down with sorrow and pain go forward in faith with the certain assurance that God lives and is watching over His children.

The Tabernacle this morning is filled. Once it was considered very large and commodious. Now, with the growth of the Church, it will not accommodate our people. I was in the Astrodome in Houston, Texas, only two weeks ago for a regional conference. We had somewhere in the neighborhood of 20,000 people in attendance—three times as many as we can get into this building.

I am deeply grateful that we are moving forward with

construction of a wonderful new facility adjoining Temple Square on the block to the north of us. It is an immense structure. I am grateful that we have followed the promptings to build it. I believe that the Lord would have us do so and that He has revealed His will in this undertaking.

Workmen are working on the placement of the huge king beam, which marks the beginning of the roof structure. Things are moving forward according to schedule. Six hundred people are at work on the project now, and this number will grow.

The building will seat some 21,000, plus 1,000 in the theater which will be a part of it. Through the generations that lie ahead, it will ring with the voices of the prophets. It will be primarily a house of worship. But it will also be a place of art. There will be concerts and other public offerings that will be uplifting and wholesome and spiritual. Barring some unforeseen circumstances, the building will be ready for the general conference of April in the year 2000. It will be a gift to the Master, whose birth we will commemorate at that season.

As we contemplate these things, we think of our brothers and sisters in distant lands. We have met hundreds of thousands of you, have looked into your faces, have felt of your spirits. You are so very precious to this work. The Lord has gathered you "one of a city, and two of a family," as prophesied by Jeremiah. He is teaching you with pastors after His own heart. (See Jeremiah 3:14–15.) We pray for you, we visit you, we respect and admire you, we love you. We are all part of a great family—10 million strong—worshipping with one heart and one voice at the feet of our Master, the Son of God.

Wherever you are, no matter how distant, you have the opportunity of participating in this conference. You will receive it by satellite in very many places. You will receive it by videotape in some places that cannot be reached by satellite. And for a few in faraway places, you will have it as the written word in our Church magazines.

No matter where we are, no matter our circumstances, we all can be faithful Latter-day Saints. We can pray and worship the Lord in the privacy of our own closet. We can sing anthems of praise to the Almighty even when we are alone. We can study the scriptures. We can live the gospel. We can pay our tithes and offerings though the amount be ever so small. We can walk in faith. We can strive to live lives patterned after the life of our Master.

Now, brothers and sisters, I invite all of you to listen to those whom you have sustained as General Authorities and general officers of the Church, as with prayer and faith and in humility, testimony is borne to you. May we all be inspired together. May our hearts be lifted in praise to our Redeemer, I humbly pray in His holy name, even the name of Jesus Christ, amen.

# Priesthood Session

$M$Y BRETHREN, IT IS A tremendous opportunity and an awesome responsibility to speak to you.

I wish to speak initially to the younger men who are here tonight. Thank you for your presence, wherever you may be gathered. Thank you for attending seminary as well as your Sunday meetings. I honor you for your desire to learn of the gospel, to deepen your scholarship in studying the word of the Lord. I thank you for the desire you carry in your hearts to serve missions. I thank you for your dreams of marrying in the temple and rearing honorable families of your own.

You are not "dead-end" kids. You are not wasting your lives in drifting aimlessly. You have purpose. You have design. You have plans that can only lead to growth and strength.

When your energies are harnessed, when your dreams are focused, marvelous things happen. I recently received a proclamation from a group of LDS young men from the northern area of California. They are from 19 stakes, and as they gathered in the mountains they visited the scene of a pioneer tragedy. As the boys pondered the things they saw and the reminders of their inheritance, they were invited to sign a Mormon Trail Scout

Encampment Proclamation. I should like to read this pledge to you:

> Be it known to all that we are Boy Scouts . . . and bearers of the Aaronic Priesthood of God. We pledge our allegiance to the values and principles that guided the men of the Mormon Battalion and the Latter-day Saint pioneer men and women who helped establish this state of California. As their grateful sons, we rejoice in our heritage of service.
>
> On this 18th day of July 1998, we pledge to become converted to the gospel of Jesus Christ. We will study the scriptures. We will pray for strength to obey. We will work. We will strive with all our hearts to follow the example of Jesus.
>
> We will magnify the priesthood we have been given by serving other people. We will keep ourselves worthy to administer the sacrament of the Lord's supper. Wherever there is a need for help, like our forefathers, we will step forward.
>
> We will prove ourselves worthy of the greater, Melchizedek Priesthood. We commit ourselves to the Lord's army and will go forth as full-time missionaries to invite all to come unto Christ.
>
> We are young men of the covenant. We will prepare ourselves to receive the covenant of eternal marriage. We pray for righteous wives and children whom we will honor and protect with our own lives.
>
> Be it known that whatever the risks, whatever the temptations, whatever the state of the world around us, as our forefathers were faithful, so we will be. Like those who have gone before, we will turn away from self-aggrandizement and set aside personal gain in order to build a peaceful society, governed by God.
>
> At all times and in all places, we will be true to our pledge.

I compliment every boy who signed this pledge. I pray that not one will ever default on the promises he has made to himself, to the Church, and to the Lord.

What a different world this would be if every young man could and would sign such a statement of promise. There would be no lives wasted with drugs. There would be no gangs with children killing children and young men headed either for prison or death. Education would become a prize worth working for. Service in the Church would become an opportunity to be cherished. There would be greater peace and love in the homes of the people. There would be no viewing of pornography, no reading of sleazy literature. You would honor and respect the girls with whom you associate, and they would never have any fear about being alone with you in any set of circumstances. It would be as if the stripling warriors of Helaman had recruited the youth of the world to their way of living.

On the agenda of your lives, of course, would be a mission. You would gladly go wherever you might be sent to do the work of the Lord, giving it your full time and attention, your strength and energy and love.

Permit me to read to you parts of a letter from a young man now serving a mission. It is written to his family, and I hope I do not violate propriety in reading it to this great gathering. I will not disclose the name of the writer or the mission in which he serves. He says:

> This past year has been great! I transferred out of the mission office and came to this small branch. My life has changed dramatically since that last transfer. I have in the past few months learned what is really important. I have learned what matters. I have learned to forget myself. I have learned to work effectively. I have learned to love others. I have learned that God loves me and that I love Him. In short, I have learned to live what I believe. . . .
>
> I have learned about people and things. I have watched tears of joy come to those who never knew they were children of God. I have seen the prayers of the penitent be answered. I

199

have seen people absorb the gospel of Jesus Christ and want to change into new persons, all because of a feeling. . . .

I often dream about the plan of salvation. I think about the marvelous work and a wonder that has taken place. I think about the power and force of angels that stand among us. I wonder at times how many of these are around me helping to bear testimony in a language I never thought could be fully understood.

I ponder upon the peaceable things of immortal glory visioned by Enoch. . . . I am thankful to God to be who I am. My greatest blessing in life is to be alive—alive in the service of our God. In this, I find great peace and joy.

Now, my dear young friends, I hope all of you are pointed in the direction of missionary service. I cannot promise you fun. I cannot promise you ease and comfort. I cannot promise you freedom from discouragement, from fear, from downright misery at times. But I can promise you that you will grow as you have never grown in a similar period during your entire lives. I can promise you a happiness that will be unique and wonderful and lasting. I can promise you that you will reevaluate your lives, that you will establish new priorities, that you will live closer to the Lord, that prayer will become a real and wonderful experience, that you will walk with faith in the outcome of the good things you do.

God bless you young men, the boys, of this, His great Church. May each of you walk with a higher resolve, a determination to be Latter-day Saints in every meaning of the word. May achievement, accomplishment, and service become your reward in the fascinating and wonderful life which lies ahead of you.

Now, brethren, I should like to talk to the older men, hoping that there will be some lesson for the younger men as well.

I wish to speak to you about temporal matters.

As a backdrop for what I wish to say, I read to you a few verses from the 41st chapter of Genesis.

Pharaoh, the ruler of Egypt, dreamed dreams which greatly troubled him. The wise men of his court could not give an interpretation. Joseph was then brought before him.

Pharaoh said unto Joseph, In my dream, behold, I stood upon the bank of the river:

And, behold, there came up out of the river seven kine, fat-fleshed and well favoured; and they fed in a meadow:

And, behold, seven other kine came up after them, poor and very ill favoured and leanfleshed. . . .

And the lean and the ill favoured kine did eat up the first seven fat kine. . . .

And I saw in my dream . . . seven ears came up in one stalk, full and good:

And, behold, seven ears, withered, thin, and blasted with the east wind, sprung up after them:

And the thin ears devoured the seven good ears. . . .

And Joseph said unto Pharaoh, . . . God hath shewed Pharaoh what he is about to do.

The seven good kine are seven years; and the seven good ears are seven years: the dream is one. . . .

. . . What God is about to do he sheweth unto Pharaoh.

Behold, there come seven years of great plenty throughout all the land of Egypt:

And there shall arise after them seven years of famine. . . .

. . . And God will shortly bring it to pass. [Genesis 41:17–20, 22–26, 28–30, 32]

Now, brethren, I want to make it very clear that I am not prophesying, that I am not predicting years of famine in the future. But I am suggesting that the time has come to get our houses in order.

So many of our people are living on the very edge of their incomes. In fact, some are living on borrowings.

We have witnessed in recent weeks wide and fearsome swings in the markets of the world. The economy is a fragile thing. A stumble in the economy in Jakarta or Moscow can immediately affect the entire world. It can eventually reach down to each of us as individuals. There is a portent of stormy weather ahead to which we had better give heed.

I hope with all my heart that we shall never slip into a depression. I am a child of the Great Depression of the thirties. I finished the university in 1932, when unemployment in this area exceeded 33 percent.

My father was then president of the largest stake in the Church in this valley. It was before our present welfare program was established. He walked the floor worrying about his people. He and his associates established a great wood-chopping project designed to keep the home furnaces and stoves going and the people warm in the winter. They had no money with which to buy coal. Men who had been affluent were among those who chopped wood.

I repeat, I hope we will never again see such a depression. But I am troubled by the huge consumer installment debt which hangs over the people of the nation, including our own people. In March 1997 that debt totaled $1.2 trillion, which represented a 7 percent increase over the previous year.

In December of 1997, 55 to 60 million households in the United States carried credit card balances. These balances averaged more than $7,000 and cost $1,000 per year in interest and fees. Consumer debt as a percentage of disposable income rose from 16.3 percent in 1993 to 19.3 percent in 1996.

Everyone knows that every dollar borrowed carries with it the penalty of paying interest. When money cannot be repaid, then bankruptcy follows. There were 1,350,118 bankruptcies in the United States last year. This represented a 50 percent increase from 1992. In the second quarter of this year, nearly 362,000 persons filed for bankruptcy, a record number for a three-month period.

We are beguiled by seductive advertising. Television carries the enticing invitation to borrow up to 125 percent of the value of one's home. But no mention is made of interest.

President J. Reuben Clark Jr., in the April 1938 general conference, said from this pulpit, "Once in debt, interest is your companion every minute of the day and night; you cannot shun it or slip away from it; you cannot dismiss it; it yields neither to entreaties, demands, or orders; and whenever you get in its way or cross its course or fail to meet its demands, it crushes you" (in Conference Report, Apr. 1938, 103).

I recognize that it may be necessary to borrow to get a home, of course. But let us buy a home that we can afford and thus ease the payments which will constantly hang over our heads without mercy or respite for as long as 30 years.

No one knows when emergencies will strike. I am somewhat familiar with the case of a man who was highly successful in his profession. He lived in comfort. He built a large home. Then one day he was suddenly involved in a serious accident. Instantly, without warning, he almost lost his life. He was left a cripple. Destroyed was his earning power. He faced huge medical bills. He had other payments to make. He was helpless before his creditors. One moment he was rich; the next he was broke.

Since the beginnings of the Church, the Lord has spoken on this matter of debt. To Martin Harris, through revelation, He said: "Pay the debt thou hast contracted with the printer. Release thyself from bondage" (D&C 19:35).

President Heber J. Grant spoke repeatedly on this matter from this pulpit. He said:

"If there is any one thing that will bring peace and contentment into the human heart, and into the family, it is to live within our means. And if there is any one thing that is grinding and discouraging and disheartening, it is to have debts and obligations that one cannot meet" (*Gospel Standards,* comp. G. Homer Durham [1941], 111).

We are carrying a message of self-reliance throughout the Church. Self-reliance cannot obtain when there is serious debt hanging over a household. One has neither independence nor freedom from bondage when he is obligated to others.

In managing the affairs of the Church, we have tried to set an example. We have, as a matter of policy, stringently followed the practice of setting aside each year a percentage of the income of the Church against a possible day of need.

I am grateful to be able to say that the Church, in all its operations, in all its undertakings, in all of its departments, is able to function without borrowed money. If we cannot get along, we will curtail our programs. We will shrink expenditures to fit the income. We will not borrow.

One of the happiest days in the life of President Joseph F. Smith was the day the Church paid off its long-standing indebtedness.

What a wonderful feeling it is to be free of debt, to have a little money against a day of emergency put away where it can be retrieved when necessary.

President Faust would not tell you this himself. Perhaps I can tell it, and he can take it out on me afterward. He had a mortgage on his home drawing 4 percent interest. Many people would have told him he was foolish to pay off that mortgage when it carried so low a rate of interest. But the first opportunity he had to acquire some means, he and his wife determined they would pay off their mortgage. He has been free of debt since that day. That's why he wears a smile on his face, and that's why he whistles while he works.

I urge you, brethren, to look to the condition of your finances. I urge you to be modest in your expenditures; discipline yourselves in your purchases to avoid debt to the extent possible. Pay off debt as quickly as you can, and free yourselves from bondage.

This is a part of the temporal gospel in which we believe. May the Lord bless you, my beloved brethren, to set your houses in order. If you have paid your debts, if you have a reserve, even though it be small, then should storms howl about your head, you will have shelter for your wives and children and peace in your hearts. That's all I have to say about it, but I wish to say it with all the emphasis of which I am capable.

I leave with you my testimony of the divinity of this work and my love for each of you, in the name of the Redeemer, the Lord Jesus Christ, amen.

# Sunday Morning Session

## October 4, 1998

$M$Y BELOVED BROTHERS AND SISTERS, it is a tremendous honor to speak on this occasion.

We are interviewed frequently by the media these days. As many of you know, I recently appeared on the *Larry King Live* television program. I consented to do so because I felt that while there were possible hazards in it, there also was a great opportunity to speak to the world on issues before us.

In the course of the show Mr. King asked me point-blank, "What is your role? You're the leader of a major religion. What's your role?"

I replied: "My role is to declare doctrine. My role is to stand as an example before the people. My role is to be a voice in defense of the truth. My role is to stand as a conservator of those values which are important in our civilization and our society. My role is to lead."

This reply was extemporaneous. I never expected that question. But in the spirit of that response I have thought this morning that I would like to raise a half-dozen or so questions we are invariably asked by those of the media and other churches. For this occasion I must be necessarily brief. Every one of these issues is worthy of a full discourse.

I have chosen these questions at random, not putting them in any special order except for the first. I do not wish to argue with anyone. I respect the religion of every man and woman and honor them in their desire to live it. I simply wish to set forth, as simply as I know how, my response to what people are asking about us.

*Question 1: What is the Mormon doctrine of Deity, of God?*

Since the time of the First Vision, people have raised this question, and they continue to raise it and will do so for so long as they believe in the God of their tradition, while we bear testimony of the God of modern revelation.

The Prophet Joseph declared, "It is the first principle of the Gospel to know for a certainty the Character of God, and to know that we may converse with him as one man converses with another" (*Teachings of the Prophet Joseph Smith*, sel. Joseph Fielding Smith [1976], 345).

"We believe in God, the Eternal Father, and in His Son, Jesus Christ, and in the Holy Ghost" (Articles of Faith 1:1). This first article of faith epitomizes our doctrine. We do not accept the Athanasian Creed. We do not accept the Nicene Creed or any other creed based on tradition and the conclusions of men.

We do accept, as the basis of our doctrine, the statement of the Prophet Joseph Smith that when he prayed for wisdom in the woods, "the light rested upon me [and] I saw two Personages, whose brightness and glory defy all description, standing above me in the air. One of them spake unto me, calling me by name and said, pointing to the other—*This is My Beloved Son. Hear Him!*" (Joseph Smith—History 1:17).

Two beings of substance were before him. He saw Them. They were in form like men, only much more glorious in Their appearance. He spoke to Them. They spoke to him. They were not amorphous spirits. Each was a distinct personality. They were beings of flesh and bone whose nature was reaffirmed in later revelations which came to the Prophet.

Our entire case as members of The Church of Jesus Christ of Latter-day Saints rests on the validity of this glorious First Vision. It was the parting of the curtain to open this, the dispensation of the fulness of times. Nothing on which we base our doctrine, nothing we teach, nothing we live by is of greater importance than this initial declaration. I submit that if Joseph Smith talked with God the Father and His Beloved Son, then all else of which he spoke is true. This is the hinge on which turns the gate that leads to the path of salvation and eternal life.

Are we Christians? Of course we are Christians. We believe in Christ. We worship Christ. We take upon ourselves in solemn covenant His holy name. The Church to which we belong carries His name. He is our Lord, our Savior, our Redeemer through whom came the great Atonement with salvation and eternal life.

*Question 2: What is your Church's attitude toward homosexuality?*

In the first place, we believe that marriage between a man and a woman is ordained of God. We believe that marriage may be eternal through exercise of the power of the everlasting priesthood in the house of the Lord.

People inquire about our position on those who consider themselves so-called gays and lesbians. My response is that we love them as sons and daughters of God. They may have certain inclinations which are powerful and which may be difficult to control. Most people have inclinations of one kind or another at various times. If they do not act upon these inclinations, then they can go forward as do all other members of the Church. If they violate the law of chastity and the moral standards of the Church, then they are subject to the discipline of the Church, just as others are.

We want to help these people, to strengthen them, to assist them with their problems and to help them with their difficulties. But we cannot stand idle if they indulge in immoral activity, if they try to uphold and defend and live in a so-called same-sex marriage situation. To permit such would be to make light of the very serious and sacred foundation of God-sanctioned marriage and its very purpose, the rearing of families.

*Question 3: What is your position on abortion?*

According to the Centers for Disease Control and Prevention, there were more than 1,200,000 abortions performed in 1995 in the United States alone. What has happened to our regard for human life? How can women, and men, deny the great and precious gift of life, which is divine in its origin and nature?

How wonderful a thing is a child. How beautiful is a newborn babe. There is no greater miracle than the creation of human life.

Abortion is an ugly thing, a debasing thing, a thing which inevitably brings remorse and sorrow and regret.

While we denounce it, we make allowance in such circumstances as when pregnancy is the result of incest or rape, when the life or health of the mother is judged by competent medical authority to be in serious jeopardy, or when the fetus is known by competent medical authority to have serious defects that will not allow the baby to survive beyond birth.

But such instances are rare, and there is only a negligible probability of their occurring. In these circumstances, those who face the question are asked to consult with their local ecclesiastical leaders and to pray in great earnestness, receiving a confirmation through prayer before proceeding.

There is a far better way.

If there is no prospect of marriage to the man involved, leaving the mother alone, there remains the very welcome option of placing the child for adoption by parents who will love it and care for it. There are many such couples in good homes who long for a child and cannot have one.

*Question 4: What is the Church's position on polygamy?*

We are faced these days with many newspaper articles on this subject. This has arisen out of a case of alleged child abuse on the part of some of those practicing plural marriage.

I wish to state categorically that this Church has nothing whatever to do with those practicing polygamy. They are not members of this Church. Most of them have never been members. They are in violation of the civil law. They know they are in violation of the law. They are subject to its penalties. The Church, of course, has no jurisdiction whatever in this matter.

If any of our members are found to be practicing plural marriage, they are excommunicated, the most serious penalty the Church can impose. Not only are those so involved in direct violation of the civil law, they are in violation of the law of this Church. An article of our faith is binding upon us. It states, "We believe in being subject to kings, presidents, rulers, and magistrates, in obeying, honoring, and sustaining the law" (Articles of Faith 1:12). One cannot obey the law and disobey the law at the same time.

There is no such thing as a "Mormon fundamentalist." It is a contradiction to use the two words together.

More than a century ago God clearly revealed unto His prophet Wilford Woodruff that the practice of plural marriage should be discontinued, which means that it is now against the law of God. Even in countries where civil or religious law allows polygamy, the Church teaches that marriage must be monogamous and does not accept into its membership those practicing plural marriage.

*Question 5: To what do you attribute the growth of the Church?*

We are growing. We are growing in a wonderful way. Between natural growth and converts baptized, we are adding about 400,000 per year. On a base of 10 million, that is about 4 percent, which is exceptionally good for a church.

People are looking for a solid anchor in a world of shifting values. They want something they can hold to as the world about them increasingly appears to be in disarray.

They are welcomed as new converts and are made to feel at home. They feel the warmth of the fellowship of the Saints.

They are put to work. They are given responsibility. They are made to feel a part of the great onward movement of this, the work of God.

And, of course, we have missionaries to assist them in their search for truth.

They soon discover that much is expected of them as Latter-day Saints. They do not resent it. They measure up, and they like it. They expect their religion to be demanding, to require reformation in their lives. They meet the requirements. They bear testimony of the great good that has come to them. They are enthusiastic and faithful.

*Question 6: What about spouse and child abuse?*

We condemn most strongly abusive behavior in any form. We denounce the physical, sexual, verbal, or emotional abuse of one's spouse or children. Our proclamation on the family declares: "Husband and wife have a solemn responsibility to love and care for each other and for their children. . . . Parents have a sacred duty to rear their children in love and righteousness, to provide for their physical and spiritual needs. . . . Husbands and wives—mothers and fathers—will be held accountable before God for the discharge of these obligations" (*Ensign,* Nov. 1995, 102).

We are doing all we know how to do to stamp out this terrible evil. When there is recognition of equality between the husband and the wife, when there is acknowledgment that each child born into the world is a child of God, then there will follow a greater sense of responsibility to nurture, to help, to love with an enduring love those for whom we are responsible.

No man who abuses his wife or children is worthy to hold the priesthood of God. No man who abuses his wife or children is worthy to be a member in good standing in this Church. The abuse of one's spouse and children is a most serious offense before God, and any who indulge in it may expect to be disciplined by the Church.

*Question 7: How does the Church finance its operations?*

Brother Faust has spoken on that very ably this morning. Those in the outside world wonder how we are able to do so much. They speak and write of the Church as having great wealth and tremendous assets.

We do have assets. We have houses of worship that dot the earth. We are building a large number of new ones every year. We carry on a great program of higher education, of seminaries and institutes. We have an unequaled family history facility. We foster a tremendous missionary organization that entails the maintenance of mission homes and other facilities in addition to the cost of maintaining the missionaries, which is borne by the missionaries themselves and their families. We carry on other programs, all of which require money.

But all of these and more are money consuming and not money creating. It costs a great deal to operate this Church. Its worldwide operations are financed through the consecrated tithes of faithful members. What a wonderful and glorious principle is the law of tithing. It is so simple to understand and follow. It is the Lord's law of finance.

I thank the Lord from the bottom of my heart for the faith of those who pay their honest tithes. Are they the poorer for it? We testify that somehow under the divine providence of the Lord, He makes it up to us and does so generously. It is not a tax. It is a voluntary offering given in confidentiality. It is a principle that carries with it a remarkable promise. God has stated that He will "open you the windows of heaven, and pour you out a blessing, that there shall not be room enough to receive it" (Malachi 3:10). That is *His* promise. He has the capacity to fulfill that promise. And it is my testimony that He does so.

Well, that is all I have time for now. There could be many other items. These are only a sample of questions that those of a curious world ask of us.

We have to know this, you and I who subscribe to the doctrines of this Church, that this is God's work, directed by the Lord Jesus Christ, that it operates according to Their plan and Their pattern, and that it carries with it Their blessings.

Why are we such a happy people? It is because of our faith, the quiet assurance that abides in our hearts that our Father in Heaven, overseeing all, will look after His sons and daughters who walk before Him with love and appreciation and obedience. We will ever be a happy people if we will so conduct our lives. Sin never was happiness. Transgression never was happiness. Falsehood in word or behavior never was happiness. Happiness lies in obedience to the teachings and commandments of God, our Eternal Father, and His Beloved Son, the Lord Jesus Christ.

As I have said before from this pulpit, my brothers and sisters, we love you. We love you for your faith and goodness. We love you for your willingness to do whatever you are asked to do. We love you for your obedience to the will of the Lord.

Knowing this work to be true, we go forward, each of us. May we make a renewed effort to put on the whole armor of God and look to Him is my humble prayer in the name of our Redeemer, the Lord Jesus Christ, amen.

# Sunday Afternoon Session

### OCTOBER 4, 1998

J_UST A WORD IN CONCLUSION._ We've been here a long time for those in the Tabernacle seated on the hard benches. I look forward to our holding conference in the new building, where the chairs will be upholstered.

We have had a wonderful conference. The Lord has blessed us, and we are deeply grateful. As we return to our homes, may we reflect upon the things which we have heard. Where there is need for reformation in our lives, may we make those adjustments which will lead to such. Where we have been stirred in our hearts, may we respond to the Spirit which has touched us. Where we have been lax in our duty, may we have the self-discipline to stand tall and do what is expected of us.

I am pleased to report, my brethren and sisters, concerning the program of constructing smaller temples which has been mentioned in this conference many times. We dedicated the first of these in Monticello, Utah, a few months ago. We built a temple there so that we might learn from it. We have learned a few things, and we have been deeply gratified by the response of the Saints in that area and by their great enthusiasm for the beautiful structure which has come into their midst.

We will dedicate a number of new temples beginning the first of the year. Some of these will be larger, some smaller. During the last conference I expressed the hope that we would build 30 new temples during the next two years. I am sure that many thought this was just wishful dreaming on my part. It seemed totally unrealistic.

I am grateful to be able to say that our building people—our architects, our engineers, our designers and furnishings experts—advise me that in all likelihood we will have 100 or more temples operating in the year 2000, nearly twice the number we have today. I assure you that nobody is sleeping on the job—no one who has anything to do with this immense project. I speak of these temples as smaller temples. Actually they do not look small; they look large. They are beautiful. They are built of the best materials and in the best fashion of which we know. Each will be a house of the Lord, dedicated to His holy purposes.

We shall not stop at these. We shall go on building. We know there are so very many locations where they are needed in order that you, the faithful Saints of this Church, may go to receive your own blessings and to extend those blessings to those who have passed beyond the veil of death. We pray that our people will be worthy to use them. Where repentance is needed, now is the time to turn about and prepare ourselves for their use.

My brothers and sisters, these are momentous times in which we are living as Saints of the Most High. With the generous blessing of the Lord, with His revealed will before us, with the faithful Saints throughout the world, we find it possible to do that which was thought to be impossible only a very short time ago.

I have now been an officer in this Church for a very long time. I am an old man who cannot deny the calendar. I'm getting worried about that anatomy lesson Brother Nelson just gave us. I have lived long enough and served in enough different capacities to have removed from my mind, if such were necessary, any doubt of the divinity of this, the work of God. We respect those of other churches. We desire their friendship and hope to render meaningful service with them. We know they all do good, but we unabashedly state—and this frequently brings criticism upon us—that this is the true and living Church of our Father in Heaven and His Son, the Lord Jesus Christ.

Now before I sit down, I want to pay a moment's tribute to this great choir to which we've listened today. They are magnificent. They are doing a great work. They are better than they've ever been, and they must go on improving. Their best today will not be good enough tomorrow. Keep it up, dear friends.

Let us go on rearing our children in righteousness and truth. Let us be good neighbors and good friends, loving and reaching out to those not of our faith as well as those who are of our faith. May the smiles of heaven rest upon you, my beloved associates, as I leave with you my witness and my testimony and my love for each of you wherever you may be across this broad world, is my humble prayer and word of benediction in the name of Jesus Christ, amen.

# 169TH ANNUAL GENERAL CONFERENCE

# SATURDAY MORNING SESSION

APRIL 3, 1999

Welcome to conference! We again welcome you, my brothers and sisters, to this great world conference. Six months between conferences once seemed like a long time. Now it seems to pass ever so rapidly. We gather together again as a great family, more than 10 million strong, to listen and learn from those who are called to lead, to renew our faith and build our resolution to live better, and to mingle together in pleasant sociality.

We are a happy and blessed people, working to build the cause and kingdom of God on earth. Regardless of race or nationality, whether we be poor or rich, old or young, we meet to share our common testimony of the Lord, in whose name we worship.

I am pleased to report that the Church is in good condition. The work continues to move forward; I will point out just two or three areas.

We now have approximately 60,000 missionaries. Come July there will be 333 missions. We are trying to fulfill the mandate of the Lord when He said, "Go ye therefore, and teach all nations, baptizing them in the name of the Father, and of the Son, and of the Holy Ghost" (Matthew 28:19).

Additionally, there are 137,629 volunteers and missionaries in nonproselyting activities. These are, for the most part, mature individuals who contribute their time and talents without compensation of any kind but with a great love for the work of the kingdom. Their united contribution is the equivalent of 15,174 full-time employees, with a payroll value of $531 million. What a remarkable thing this is!

Our family history work goes forward with increasing momentum. There is a tremendous interest in one's roots everywhere. As the years pass, all of this will lead to the fulfillment of the great purpose for which this work is done. The hearts of the children are being turned to their fathers, that the purposes of the Lord may be fulfilled.

We are constructing temples on a scale never before dreamed of to carry forward this work to its destined conclusion. Since last October we have dedicated temples in Anchorage, Alaska; Colonia Juárez, Mexico; and Madrid, Spain. It is anticipated that we will dedicate 14 more during the remainder of this year.

This is a tremendous undertaking, with many problems, but no matter the difficulty, things work out, and I am confident we will reach our goal.

We are constructing chapels in large numbers to accommodate the needs of our people. There is an old proverb that says it is an ill wind that blows no good. The economic problems that have afflicted Asia and other parts of the world have brought lower real estate prices, thus permitting us to acquire building sites at lower costs.

In many areas of the Church, sacrament meeting attendance is up and the level of activity is increasing.

I mention these items simply to indicate the robust growth of the work throughout the world.

We are prone to speak of large numbers such as the total membership of the Church. But we must never forget that we are all individuals with our own needs and problems, our own hopes and dreams, our own faith and convictions. Some are strong, some weak, but we all try. We have problems to deal with—they are serious and difficult. We need one another to build and strengthen each other. We must never lose sight of the fact that we are to "succor the weak, lift up the hands which hang down, and strengthen the feeble knees" (D&C 81:5).

We must never forget that we live in a world of great diversity. The people of the earth are all our Father's children and are of many and varied religious persuasions. We must cultivate tolerance and appreciation and respect one another. We have differences of doctrine. This need not bring about animosity or any kind of holier-than-thou attitude.

At this moment our hearts reach out to the brutalized people of Kosovo. It is difficult for us to understand how those who claim to be Christians can act so barbaric to those of another faith. I am grateful that we are rushing humanitarian aid to the victims of these atrocities.

I am pleased to report that the Church is better known and better understood. Generally the media have been kind to us. They have dealt honestly with us. There are exceptions, of course, and this we regret. The old images of the past continue to be dragged forth by those who deal in sensationalism and exploitation. But television images fade almost immediately with the tremendous amount of information given. Yesterday's newspaper is soon forgotten. Meanwhile the Church goes forward on its appointed mission in the direction of its appointed destiny.

We will work together with patience, never losing sight of the great mission given us by Him who is our leader and whose Church this is.

Now I invite you to listen to the Brethren and sisters. All who speak feel the responsibility in so doing. Much of prayer and effort have gone into that which will be said. May our faith be increased in the great, salient underpinnings of our doctrine and our practice as members of this great Church of Jesus Christ of Latter-day Saints, I humbly pray in the name of Jesus Christ, amen.

# PRIESTHOOD
# SESSION

APRIL 3, 1999

$M$Y DEAR BRETHREN, IT IS A tremendous honor and responsibility to speak to you. I pray the Lord will bless me.

What a tremendous brotherhood this is, composed of hundreds of thousands of men and boys who have been ordained to the priesthood of God. What a mighty concourse this would be if we were all to come together in one great gathering. It would astonish the world. There is nothing like it of which I am aware.

You are the backbone of the Church, my brethren. From your ranks come the bishops and branch presidents, the district and stake presidents, the Area Authority Seventies, and all of the General Authorities.

You young men are the substance of a great missionary program whose influence is felt throughout the world. Altogether, you are men and boys who have taken on the whole armor of God to move forward His work in the earth.

Whenever we gather in one of these meetings, I am sorry that we cannot accommodate all who wish to come. From the moment the doors of the Tabernacle were opened tonight, there was a flood of young men and their fathers. Hopefully the new hall will be finished a year from now, and we will be able to accommodate all who wish to come.

And to you brethren who are taking advantage of the broadcast and satellite transmission of these proceedings, we feel at one with you.

I think, my brethren, that our Father in Heaven smiles down upon us. I think it must be of great comfort to Him to look upon the hundreds of thousands of men and boys who love Him, who carry in their hearts a testimony of Him and His Beloved Son, who give leadership and direction to His Church, who stand as heads of families where there is righteousness and where truth is taught and exemplified.

We have become a great body of men, young and old. There is scarcely anything we cannot accomplish if we work unitedly together with one mind and one purpose and one heart.

I hope that each of us is aware of the tremendous thing that has come to us with ordination to the priesthood. This is the authority of God in the earth. It comes from Him as a divine bestowal. It carries with it the power and the authority to govern in the affairs of the Church. It carries with it the power and the authority to bless in the name of the Lord, to lay hands upon the sick and call down the powers of heaven. It is sacred and holy. It partakes of the divine. Its authority is expressed in mortality and reaches beyond the veil of death.

I hope we are worthy of the priesthood we bear. I plead with you, every one of you, to conduct your lives in such a way as to be worthy of it.

As we have been reminded, this is a season of great evil in the world. No one needs to be reminded of that. We are constantly exposed to the muck and filth of pornography, to salacious and evil behavior totally unbecoming anyone who holds the priesthood of God.

It is a challenge to work in the world and live above its filth.

Dishonesty is rampant. It is manifest in cheating that goes on in schools, in the operation of clever schemes, in businesses that rob and defraud. Temptations are everywhere about us; unfortunately, some succumb to these.

Brethren, be strong. Rise above the evils of the world. We need not be prudish. We need not adopt a holier-than-thou attitude. We need only let our personal integrity, our sense of right and wrong, and simple honesty govern our actions.

Let us live the gospel in our homes. Let there be an honest manifestation of love between husbands and wives, between children and their parents. Control the voice of anger. Be absolutely loyal one to another.

Simply "do what is right [and] let the consequence follow" (*Hymns*, no. 237). So live that each morning you may kneel in prayer, seeking the direction and guidance of the Holy Spirit, as well as its protective power, as you go about your work of the day. So live that each night, before retiring, you may come before the Lord in prayer without shame or embarrassment or the need to plead for forgiveness. I do not hesitate to say that God will bless you if you will do so. Someday you will grow old and look back upon your life. You will be able to say, "I lived with integrity. I cheated no one, not even myself. I reveled in the companionship of my wife, who is the mother of our children. I am proud of those children. I am grateful to God for His manifest blessings."

If such can be your lot, I promise that when the shades of old age gather about you, there will be tears of gratitude in your eyes and the throbbing of a thankful heart beating in your breast.

Now, some years ago, more than 10 years ago, I spoke from this pulpit concerning the bishops of the Church. I wish to return briefly to that subject again tonight.

I carry in my heart a deep appreciation for our bishops. I am profoundly grateful for the revelation of the Almighty, under which this office was created and functions.

As all of you are aware, last fall a terrible storm hit Central America. For six days and nights, Hurricane Mitch locked in over that area and particularly over Honduras. The winds blew ferociously, and the rains fell without letup. Rivers swelled and took with them houses that had been built along their banks. More than 200 bridges were washed out in Honduras, destroying means of travel. The soil from the highlands washed towards the sea in a deluge of filthy mud. Houses were filled to the tops of the windows. Yards and streets were filled. People fled in terror, leaving all behind them.

One of our bishops secured a big truck and went about gathering his people, taking them to higher ground. When the truck could no longer get through, he somehow secured a boat. He was looking after his flock.

I went down there to see what had happened and to give comfort, where possible. I beheld a miracle. I witnessed in operation the simple and marvelously effective organization of this Church.

Every member of this Church has a bishop or a branch president. I have only commendation for other relief efforts which came in from across the world. But I have unending admiration for the wonderful manner in which the Church operated. The bishops appealed to their stake presidents, who appealed to the Area Presidency, who appealed to headquarters here in Salt Lake City. Within hours great quantities of basic foodstuffs, medicine, and clothing were on their way from our storehouses.

A warehouse was rented in San Pedro Sula in the area of the greatest damage. It was the bishops who marshaled their people to work shifts in the warehouse putting into plastic bags enough food to take care of a family for a week, clothing to put on their backs, medicine to safeguard them against disease. Every bishop knew his own people. He, with his Relief Society president, knew their needs. These were not faceless strangers working as employees of government. They were friends, each a member of a ward family small enough that they knew one another's needs. There was no argument, no greedy grasping for food and clothing. Everything was orderly. It was systematic. It was friendly. It was motivated by love and concern, and it was done quickly to meet an immediate need. It was the gospel at work in a quiet and magnificent manner.

The waters finally subsided, but mud was left in a thick and ugly coating on everything. Nothing became more valuable than shovels and wheelbarrows. And together, again under the direction of the bishops, the mud was cleaned from the houses.

We visited a meetinghouse on a Saturday. There were many people there, with a bishop, a loving father to his flock, giving direction. The pews, which had been floating in the water, were taken out and carefully cleaned. Mud was scraped from the walls and the floors. Then the mops came out and the polishing cloths, and before nightfall that Saturday evening, the building had been made ready for worship services on the Sabbath.

I stand in humble gratitude and respect and admiration for the bishops of this Church. In the most dire of circumstances, I watched them in La Lima, Honduras. I spoke with them, shook their hands, loved them. How thankful I am for these men who, without regard for their own comfort, give of their time, of their wisdom, of their inspiration in presiding over our wards throughout the world. They receive no compensation other than the love of their people. There is no rest for them on the Sabbath nor very much at other times. They are the ones closest to the people, best acquainted with their needs and circumstances.

The requirements of their office are today as they were in the days of Paul, who wrote to Timothy:

"A bishop then must be blameless, the husband of one wife, vigilant, sober, of good behaviour, given to hospitality, apt to teach;

"Not given to wine, no striker [that is, not a bully or a violent person], . . . not a brawler, not covetous" (1 Timothy 3:2–3).

In his letter to Titus, Paul adds that "a bishop must be blameless, as the steward of God; . . .

"Holding fast the faithful word as he hath been taught, that he may be able by sound doctrine both to exhort and to convince the gainsayers" (Titus 1:7, 9).

All during the years of my childhood and youth, even until the time I was ordained an elder and came home from a mission, I had only one bishop. He was a remarkable man. He served for 25 years. We knew him, and he knew us. We always addressed him as "Bishop Duncan," and he always called us by our first names. We had great respect for him—an almost awesome respect. But we had no fear of him. We knew that he was our friend. His was a very large ward, and how very well he served his people.

I spoke at his funeral. Next to my own father, he probably had the greatest influence on my young life. How grateful I am for him.

Since then, I have had a number of bishops. Without exception, every one of them has been a dedicated and inspired leader.

Now let me say a few words directly to the bishops who are with us this night. And much of what I say to you might be echoed to the stake presidents and others in similar callings. I hope you know that I carry in my heart a great feeling of love for you. I know that your people love you. Tremendous is your trust. In calling you we have placed in you our total confidence. We expect you to stand as the presiding high priest of the ward, a counselor to the people, a defender and helper of those in trouble, a comfort to those in sorrow, a supplier to those in need. We expect you to stand as a guardian and protector of the doctrine that is taught in your ward, of the quality of the teaching, of the filling of the many offices which are necessary.

Your personal behavior must be impeccable. You must be a man of integrity, above reproach of any kind. Your example will set the tone for the direction your people follow. You must be fearless in denouncing evil, willing to take a stand for the right, uncompromising in your defense of truth. While all of this requires firmness, it must be done with kindness and love.

You are the father of the ward and the guardian of your people.

You must reach out to them in their times of sorrow and sickness and distress. You stand as president of the Aaronic Priesthood and with your counselors must give leadership to the deacons and the teachers and the priests to see that they grow in "the nurture and admonition of the Lord" (Ephesians 6:4).

You are a husband to your wife, her beloved companion, her protector and provider. You are a father to your children and must nurture them with love and teach them with appreciation.

You may expect that the adversary will work on you. You, of all men, must exercise self-discipline, standing far apart from sin and evil of any kind in your own life. You must shun pornography, shut off the television set when it carries salacious entertainment, be pure in thought and deed.

You cannot use your office to further your business interests among your people, lest some accuse you of benefiting from your service as bishop.

You stand as a common judge in Israel. This is almost a terrifying responsibility. In some instances, you must determine even the eligibility of your people to be members of the Church. You must determine their worthiness to receive baptism, their worthiness to be ordained to the Aaronic Priesthood, their eligibility to serve missions, and above all, their qualifications to enter the house of the Lord and partake of the blessings there to be had. You are to see that none goes hungry or without clothing or shelter. You must know the circumstances of all over whom you preside.

You must be a comforter and a guide to your people. Your door must be ever open to any cries of distress. Your back must be strong in sharing their burdens. You must reach out in love, even to the wrongdoer.

My brethren, I invoke the blessings of the Almighty upon you in the great responsibility which you carry. May God bless you with health and strength. May He touch your mind with wisdom and understanding, with appreciation and love. May the interests of your people be the dominant concern of your life, without sacrificing the demands of your employment or the proper attention given your family.

I thank the Lord for each of you. I love you for what you do. I pray for you, every one of you, wherever you may be. I plead with you to shield yourselves from the darts of the adversary. I counsel you to put on the whole armor of God.

May the blessings of heaven come down upon your wives and your children. Someday you will be released. That will be a day of sadness. The memories of your people will remain throughout your life. They will sanctify your days and bring peace and rest and gladness. God bless you, my beloved brethren, I humbly pray, in the name of Jesus Christ, amen.

# SUNDAY MORNING
# SESSION

APRIL 4, 1999

$M$Y BROTHERS AND SISTERS, I feel so deeply grateful as I stand before you. Of all men, I feel so richly blessed. I am blessed by your love. Wherever I go, you are so very kind to me. I am blessed by your faith. Your tremendous service, your devotion, your loyalty— all become a part of my own faith. How really wonderful you are. It is plainly evident that the gospel, when lived, makes people better than they otherwise would be.

How unselfish you are with your time and your means. All across this broad world you serve to build our Father's kingdom and to move His work forward.

I telephoned a man last week. He is retired. He has served as a mission president, and he and his wife are now serving as missionaries. I asked him if they would be willing to go to preside over a new temple. He broke down with emotion. He was overcome. He could not talk. He and his wife will leave their children and grandchildren for another long period to serve the Lord in another capacity. Will they miss their grandchildren? Of course they will. But they will go, and they will serve faithfully.

How deeply grateful I am for the devotion and the loyalty of the members of the Church throughout the earth who respond to every call, no matter the inconvenience, no matter what comfort they must forgo.

But of all the things for which I feel grateful, I am most thankful this Easter morning for the gift of my Lord and my Redeemer. This is Easter, when, with all of Christendom, we commemorate the Resurrection of Jesus Christ.

This was not an ordinary thing. It was the greatest event in human history. I do not hesitate to say that.

"If a man die, shall he live again?" asked Job (Job 14:14). There is no question of greater importance than this.

Those of us who live in comfort and security seldom give any thought to death. Our minds are on other things. Yet there is nothing more certain, nothing more universal, nothing more final than the closure of mortal life. No one can escape it, not one.

I have stood at the tomb of Napoleon in Paris, at the tomb of Lenin in Moscow, and before the burial places of many others of the great leaders of the earth. In their time they commanded armies; they ruled with almost omnipotent power; their very words brought terror into the hearts of people. I have reverently walked through some of the great cemeteries of the world. I have reflected quietly and thoughtfully as I have stood in the military cemetery in Manila in the Philippines where are buried some 17,000 Americans who gave their lives in the Second World War and where are remembered another 35,000 who died in the terrible battles of the Pacific and whose remains were never found. I have walked with reverence through the British cemetery on the outskirts of Rangoon, Burma, and noted the names of hundreds of young men who came from the villages, towns, and great cities of the British Isles and gave their lives in hot and distant places. I have strolled through old cemeteries in Asia and Europe and yet other places and reflected on the lives of those who were once buoyant and happy, who were creative and distinguished, who gave much to the world in which they lived. They have all passed into the oblivion of the grave. All who have lived upon the earth before us are now gone. They have left all behind as they have stepped over the threshold of silent death. None has escaped. All have walked their way to "the undiscover'd country from whose bourn no traveler returns" (*Hamlet*, act 3, scene 1). Shakespeare so described it.

But Jesus the Christ changed all that. Only a God could do what He did. He broke the bonds of death. He too had to die, but on the third day following His burial, He rose from the grave, "the firstfruits of them that slept" (1 Corinthians 15:20), and in so doing brought the blessing of the Resurrection to every one of us.

Contemplating this wondrous thing, Paul declared: "O death, where is thy sting? O grave, where is thy victory?" (1 Corinthians 15:55).

Two weeks ago I was in Jerusalem, that great and ancient city where Jesus walked 2,000 years ago. Standing on a high point, I looked down upon the Old City. I thought of Bethlehem, a few miles to the south, where He was born in a lowly manger. He who was the Son of God, the Only Begotten Son, left His Father's celestial courts to take on mortality. At His birth angels sang and Wise Men came to bestow gifts. He grew as did other boys in Nazareth of Galilee. There He "increased in wisdom and stature, and in favour with God and man" (Luke 2:52).

With Mary and Joseph He visited Jerusalem when He was 12. On their journey home, they missed Him. They came back to Jerusalem and found Him in the temple conversing with the learned doctors. When Mary upbraided Him for not being with them, He answered, "Wist ye not that I must be about my Father's business?" (Luke 2:49). His words were a premonition of His future ministry.

That ministry began with His baptism in the river Jordan at the hands of His cousin John. When He arose from the water, the Holy Ghost descended upon Him in the form of a dove, and His Father's voice was heard, saying, "This is my beloved Son, in whom I am well pleased" (Matthew 3:17). That declaration became the affirmation of His divinity.

He fasted for 40 days and was tempted of the devil, who sought to take Him from His divinely appointed mission. To the adversary's invitation He responded, "Thou shalt not tempt the Lord thy God" (Matthew 4:7), again declaring His divine sonship.

He walked the dusty roads of Palestine. He had no home that He could call His own, no place to rest His head. His message was the gospel of peace; His teachings were those of generosity and love: "If any man will sue thee at the law, and take away thy coat, let him have thy [cloak] also" (Matthew 5:40).

He taught with parables. He performed miracles the like of which were never performed before or since. He healed those whose sickness was of long standing. He caused the blind to see, the deaf to hear, the lame to walk. He raised the dead, and they lived again to speak His praises. Surely no man had ever done such before.

A few followed Him, but most hated Him. He spoke of the scribes and Pharisees as hypocrites, as whited sepulchres. They plotted against Him. He drove the money changers from the house of the Lord. They doubtless joined those who planned to destroy Him. But He was not deterred. He "went about doing good" (Acts 10:38).

Was not all of this enough to make His memory immortal? Was it not enough to place His name among and even above those of the great men who have walked the earth and who have been remembered for what they said or did? Certainly He would have been ranked among the great prophets of all time.

But all of this was not enough for the Son of the Almighty. It was but prelude to greater things to come. They came in a strange and terrible way.

He was betrayed, arrested, condemned to death, to die in awful agony by crucifixion. His living body was nailed to a cross of wood.

In unspeakable pain His life slowly ebbed away. While yet He breathed, He cried out, "Father, forgive them; for they know not what they do" (Luke 23:34).

The earth shook as His spirit passed. The centurion who had seen it all declared in solemnity, "Truly this was the Son of God" (Matthew 27:54).

Those who loved Him took His body from the cross. They dressed it and placed it in a new tomb offered by Joseph of Arimathea. The tomb was sealed with a great stone at its opening, and a guard was set.

His friends must have wept. The Apostles He loved and whom He had called as witnesses of His divinity wept. The women who loved Him wept. None had understood what He had said about rising the third day. How could they understand? This had never happened before. It was totally unprecedented. It was unbelievable, even for them.

There must have been a terrible sense of dejection and hopelessness and misery as they thought of their Lord, taken from them in death.

But that was not the end. On the morning of the third day, Mary Magdalene and the other Mary returned to the tomb. To their utter amazement, the stone was rolled away and the tomb was open. They peered inside. Two beings in white sat at either end of the burial site. An angel appeared to them and said:

"Why seek ye the living among the dead?

"He is not here, but is risen: remember how he spake unto you when he was yet in Galilee,

"Saying, The Son of man must be delivered into the hands of sinful men, and be crucified, and the third day rise again" (Luke 24:5–7).

These simple words—"He is not here, but is risen"—have become the most profound in all literature. They are the declaration of the empty tomb. They are the fulfillment of all He had spoken concerning rising again. They are the triumphant response to the query facing every man, woman, and child who was ever born to earth.

The risen Lord spoke to Mary, and she replied. He was not an apparition. This was not imagination. He was real, as real as He had been in mortal life. He did not permit her to touch Him. He had not yet ascended to His Father in Heaven. That would happen shortly. What a reunion it must have been, to be embraced by the Father, who loved Him and who also must have wept for Him during His hours of agony.

He would appear to two men on the road to Emmaus. He would converse with them and eat with them. He would meet with His Apostles behind closed doors and teach them. Thomas was not present on the first occasion. On the second occasion the Lord invited him to feel of His hands and His side. In utter wonder he exclaimed, "My Lord and my God" (John 20:28). He spoke with 500 at one time.

Who can dispute the documentation of these facts? There is no record of any repudiation of the testimony of those who had these experiences. There is abundant evidence that they bore witness of these events throughout their lives, even giving their own lives in affirmation of the reality of the things they had experienced. Their word is clear, and their testimony is secure.

Men and women by the millions through the centuries have accepted that testimony. Countless numbers have lived and died in affirmation of its truth, which has come to them by the power of the Holy Ghost and which they could not in truth deny. Surely no event of human history has been tested more widely as to its validity.

And there is another witness. This biblical companion, the Book of Mormon, testifies that He appeared not only to those of the Old World but also to those of the New. For had He not at one time declared, "Other sheep I have, which are not of this fold: them also I must bring, and they shall hear my voice; and there shall be one fold, and one shepherd"? (John 10:16).

To those of this hemisphere He appeared following His Resurrection. At His descent through the clouds of heaven, the voice of God the Eternal Father was heard again in solemn declaration: "Behold my Beloved Son, in whom I am well pleased, in whom I have glorified my name—hear ye him" (3 Nephi 11:7).

Here again He called Twelve Apostles who would become witnesses of His name and divinity. He taught the people and blessed and healed them as He had done in Palestine, and peace reigned in the land for 200 years as the people sought to live by that which He had taught them.

And if all of this is not enough, there is the testimony, sure and certain and unequivocal, of the great prophet of this dispensation, Joseph Smith. As a boy he went into the woods to pray, seeking light and understanding. And there appeared before him two Personages, whose brightness and glory defy all description, standing above him in the air. One of them spoke to him, calling him "by name and said, pointing to the other—*This is My Beloved Son. Hear Him!*" (Joseph Smith—History 1:17).

This same Joseph declared on a subsequent occasion:

"We beheld the glory of the Son, on the right hand of the Father, and received of his fulness. . . .

"And now, after the many testimonies which have been given of him, this is the testimony, last of all, which we give of him: That he lives!" (D&C 76:20, 22).

And so on this wonderful Easter morning, as the servants of the Almighty, as prophets and apostles in His great cause, we lift our voices in witness and testimony of our immortal Savior. He came to earth as the Son of the Everlasting Father. He did as Isaiah prophesied He must do. He bore "our griefs, and carried our sorrows. . . .

". . . He was wounded for our transgressions, he was bruised for our iniquities: the chastisement of our peace was upon him; and with his stripes we are healed" (Isaiah 53:4–5).

In everlasting immortality He arose the third day from the rock-hewn grave. He spoke with many. His Father repeatedly affirmed His divine sonship.

Thanks be to the Almighty. His glorified Son broke the bonds of death, the greatest of all victories. As Paul declared, "For as in Adam all die, even so in Christ shall all be made alive" (1 Corinthians 15:22).

He is our triumphant Lord. He is our Redeemer, who atoned for our sins. Through His redeeming sacrifice all men shall rise from the grave. He has opened the way whereby we may gain not only immortality but also eternal life.

As an Apostle of the Lord Jesus Christ, I bear witness and testimony of these things this Easter day. I speak in solemnity and reverence and gratitude, in the name of the Lord Jesus Christ, amen.

# Sunday Afternoon
# Session

APRIL 4, 1999

My BRETHREN AND SISTERS, these have been two glorious days. The inspiration and power of the Holy Ghost have rested upon us. We rejoice together. As we conclude this conference, we have every reason to thank the Lord for His blessings.

The music has been wonderful. We have been lifted and edified by the choirs and choruses which have sung for us. The prayers have drawn us nearer to the Lord, and those who have spoken to us have done so by the power of the Holy Ghost.

Now the curtains are gradually closing on this notable and exceptional century. In one respect it has been a shameful period in the history of the world. It has been the worst of all centuries, with more of war, more of man's inhumanity to man, more of conflict and trouble than any other century in the history of the world. It has been the bloodiest of all seasons. It has been a time when the adversary of truth has brought his evil influence of destruction and misery and pain to millions upon millions, as witness what is going on in Yugoslavia. The Father of us all must weep as He looks down upon His quarrelsome children.

But in a larger sense this has been the best of all centuries. In the long history of the earth there has been nothing like it. The life expectancy of man has been extended by more than 25 years. Think of it. It is a miracle. The fruits of science have been manifest everywhere. By and large, we live longer, we live better. This is an age of greater understanding and knowledge. We live in a world of great diversity. As we learn more of one another, our appreciation grows. This has been an age of enlightenment. The miracles of modern medicine, of travel, of communication are almost beyond belief. All of this has opened new opportunities for us which we must grasp and use for the advancement of the Lord's work.

And above all of these marvelous gifts is the Restoration of the gospel of Jesus Christ with all of the wonderful authority and blessings that have come therewith. This is verily the dispensation of the fulness of times, bringing with it that which will never again be taken from the earth.

I believe that Peter was speaking of us when he said, "But ye are a chosen generation, a royal priesthood, an holy nation, a peculiar people; that ye should shew forth the praises of him who hath called you out of darkness into his marvellous light" (1 Peter 2:9).

Now, brethren and sisters, let us return to our homes with resolution in our hearts to do a little better than we have done in the past. We can all be a little kinder, a little more generous, a little more thoughtful of one another. We can be a little more tolerant and friendly to those not of our faith, going out of our way to show our respect for them. We cannot afford to be arrogant or self-righteous. It is our obligation to reach out in helpfulness, not only to our own but to all others as well. Their interest in and respect for this Church will increase as we do so.

I am deeply grateful that as a Church we are extending humanitarian aid when there is sore distress. We have done a great deal and have blessed the lives of many people who are not of our faith but who also are children of our Father. We will continue to do so for as long as we have the means. To all who have contributed to this effort we express our thanks.

Let us continually work to strengthen our families. Let husbands and wives cultivate a spirit of absolute loyalty one to another. Let us not take one another for granted, but let us constantly work to nurture a spirit of love and respect for each other. We must guard against faultfinding, anger, and disrespect one for another.

Parents, safeguard your families. Bring up your children in light and truth as the Lord has commanded. Shower them with love, but do not spoil them. Share your testimony with them. Read the scriptures together. Guide and protect them. You have no greater blessing and no greater responsibility than those whom the Lord has placed in your care. Pray together. There is no substitute for family prayer when all kneel together before the Lord.

Let us be a people of honesty and integrity, doing the right thing at all times and in all circumstances.

Great are our blessings. Tremendous is our responsibility. Let us get on our knees and plead with the Lord for direction. Then let us stand on our feet, square up our shoulders, and march forward without fear to enlarge among people everywhere the righteousness of the Lord.

In closing now, I feel impressed to announce that among all of the temples we are constructing, we plan to rebuild the Nauvoo Temple. A member of the Church and his family have provided a very substantial contribution to make this possible. We are grateful to him. It will be a while before it happens, but the architects have begun their work. This temple will not be busy much of the time; it will be somewhat isolated. But during the summer months, we anticipate it will be very busy. And the new building will stand as a memorial to those who built the first such structure there on the banks of the Mississippi.

I repeat what I have said before. I love you. I leave my blessing and my testimony of this great and wonderful latter-day work. God be with you till we meet six months from now, I pray in the name of Jesus Christ, amen.

# 169TH SEMIANNUAL GENERAL CONFERENCE

# SATURDAY MORNING SESSION

OCTOBER 2, 1999

MY BELOVED BRETHREN AND SISTERS, we welcome you to this great world conference of the Church. We are grateful for your presence and for the efforts you have made to be here. We are grateful for the association of our brothers and sisters assembled in thousands of halls across the world.

The Church grows ever larger. It touches more and more lives for good. It is spreading over the earth in a wonderful way.

I take the opportunity this morning to advise you briefly of the progress we are making toward the goal of 100 working temples in the year 2000.

Since the first of this year we have dedicated temples in Anchorage, Alaska; Colonia Juárez, Mexico; Madrid, Spain; Bogotá, Colombia; Guayaquil, Ecuador; Spokane, Washington; Columbus, Ohio; and Bismarck, North Dakota—eight in all. Between now and the end of the year, we will dedicate temples in Columbia, South Carolina; Detroit, Michigan; Halifax, Nova Scotia; Regina, Saskatchewan; Billings, Montana; Edmonton, Alberta; and Raleigh, North Carolina—seven more. At the conclusion of 1999, we anticipate that there will be 68 operating temples.

It has been a wonderful experience to participate in these

dedicatory services. Most satisfying of all has been the enthusiasm of the people. The spirit of temple work rests upon them. They are so grateful to have a house of the Lord nearer their homes. Some of them have traveled so very far in the past. Many of them still do. As we have gathered in these sacred services, while consecrating these hallowed buildings, we have seen many with tears in their eyes.

Boys and girls in large numbers have attended these services. They have been reminded that these temples are not only for their parents but also for them. When 12 years of age, they may enter the house of the Lord and stand as proxies in baptisms for those beyond the veil of death. What a great and unselfish service this is. What a wonderful thing for our youth to be involved in this totally selfless act in behalf of others who are powerless to help themselves.

Going hand in hand with this increased temple activity is an increase in our family history work. The computer, in its various ramifications, is accelerating the work, and people are taking advantage of the new techniques being offered to them. How can one escape the conclusion that the Lord is in all of this? As computer facilities improve, the number of temples grows to accommodate the accelerated family history work.

Hundreds and hundreds of thousands of nonmembers have attended the open houses associated with these new temples. They have done so with reverence and respect. In many cases the temples are, without question, the finest buildings in the cities in which they are located. People marvel at their beauty. But among many things, they are most impressed with pictures of the Savior they see in these holy houses. They will no longer regard us as a non-Christian people. They must know that the central figure in all of our worship is the Lord Jesus Christ.

This building of so many temples has been and is a tremendous undertaking. You cannot believe what is involved in it unless you are closely associated with the process. Every one of these buildings, large or small, is constructed in the best manner of which we know, using the very best of materials. Their cost is much more than that of a chapel. This is because they are built to higher standards. I express appreciation to the very many dedicated men and women who are working on this tremendous project.

Every ordinance which is given in the Salt Lake Temple, the largest in the Church, is also given in every other temple, including these smaller structures. The fact is that they are not so small. They are commodious, and they are beautiful. They represent the ultimate in our worship and the ultimate in blessings offered.

We plan to break ground later this month for the Nauvoo Temple. Many people are excited, and many are contributing to this historic undertaking.

We shall go on with the work of dedication next year. It will be a very busy season. We anticipate the dedication of perhaps as many as 42 more. When we finish the year 2000, if present plans materialize, we will have not only the 100 which we have striven for, but more beyond that.

We shall not stop then. We may not build at the same pace, but we shall go on for as long as the Lord wills that it be done.

Brethren and sisters, it is a glorious season in this work. God, our Eternal Father, is blessing His cause, His kingdom, and His people. The resources of the Church, including the facilities for temple work, are increasing.

In view of the fact that we do not build a temple until there are sufficient people in the area, until there are sufficient tithe payers, and until there is sufficient faith, the very construction of these sacred buildings becomes an indicator of the increase of faith and obedience to the principles of the gospel.

May we enjoy the blessings of the Lord as we go forward in this great work, which affects not only the living but the great multitude of the dead of all generations. For this I humbly pray in the name of Jesus Christ, amen.

# PRIESTHOOD SESSION

OCTOBER 2, 1999

MY BELOVED BRETHREN, I commend you, wherever you may be. As usual, the Tabernacle is filled to capacity this evening. Next spring we shall be able to accommodate all of you who wish to sit together in these great Saturday evening priesthood gatherings, and what a blessing that will be.

As we conclude this meeting, I wish to speak for a few minutes on the subject of "why we do some of the things we do."

Now, I recognize that this is a rather strange-sounding title, but this is the only meeting where we can discuss Church procedures and Church business. I pray for the guidance of the Holy Spirit.

The Church is an ecclesiastical organization. It is an eleemosynary society. It is concerned primarily with worship of the Lord Jesus Christ. Our great mission is to testify of His living reality. We should not be involved with anything not in harmony with this major objective. We should be involved with whatever is in harmony with this objective.

We do many things which on the surface do not appear to be associated with this overriding pattern. I'm going to speak of two or three of these. Among these is the operation of Brigham Young University. People ask why we sponsor such a large and costly institution that is basically concerned with secular education. The question is appropriate. This sponsorship has a doctrinal root.

The Lord has decreed in revelation:

> Teach ye diligently and my grace shall attend you, that you may be instructed more perfectly in theory, in principle, in doctrine, in the law of the gospel, in all things that pertain unto the kingdom of God, that are expedient for you to understand;
>
> Of things both in heaven and in the earth, and under the earth; things which have been, things which are, things which must shortly come to pass; things which are at home, things which are abroad; the wars and the perplexities of the nations, and the judgments which are on the land; and a knowledge also of countries and of kingdoms—
>
> That ye may be prepared in all things when I shall send you again to magnify the calling whereunto I have called you, and the mission with which I have commissioned you. [D&C 88:78–80]

It is apparent that we are obligated not only to learn of ecclesiastical matters but also of secular matters. There is a tradition in the Church that deals with these things. There was the School of the Prophets in Kirtland. The Seventies Hall in Nauvoo was used for educational purposes. A university was projected in Nauvoo.

When the Saints arrived in these western valleys, academies were established for the training of the young. The University of Utah was chartered in 1850 by our pioneer forebears. Brigham Young University came along later, outlasting most of the Church academies. It has grown until its present enrollment numbers more than 27,000. That is a large number of students, but it is a very small fraction of the young people of the Church worthy of a university education. We can accommodate only a relatively few. If we cannot give to all, why should we give to any? The answer is that if we cannot give to all, let us give to as many as we can. The number who can be accommodated on campus is finite, but the influence of the university is infinite. Tremendous efforts are being made to enlarge and extend that influence.

How fortunate are those who have the opportunity to attend. I almost become angry when I hear of complaining among the students or the faculty. I am grateful to be able to say that with very few exceptions those who come to learn and those who teach are appreciative and mindful of the great blessing that is theirs.

Moreover, the university has brought much favorable notice to the Church. Its sponsoring organization, the Church, is widely recognized. It has become known for standards and ideals which have been written about and talked about and which have let the world know of those things in which we believe. Its academic programs and its athletic programs have both brought honor to the university and the Church. And as generations of students move through its halls and on to graduation and then out across the world, they will bring honor to their alma mater and its sponsor, The Church of Jesus Christ of Latter-day Saints.

We shall continue to support BYU and its Hawaii campus. We shall continue to support Ricks College. We are not likely to build other university campuses. We wish that we might build enough to accommodate all who desire to attend. But this is out of the question. They are so terribly expensive. But we shall keep these as flagships testifying to the great and earnest commitment of this Church to education, both ecclesiastical and secular, and while doing so prove to the world that excellent secular learning can be gained in an environment of religious faith.

Backing up these institutions will be our other schools, our institutes of religion, scattered far and wide, and the great seminary system of the Church.

It is hoped that through these our youth, wherever they may be, may experience some of the good to be had at BYU.

Now, the next question: "Why is the Church in business?"

We have a few business interests. Not many. Most of these were begun in very early days when the Church was the only organization that could provide the capital that was needed to start certain business interests designed to serve the people in this remote area. We have divested ourselves long since of some of these where it was felt there was no longer a need. Included in these divestitures, for instance, was the old Consolidated Wagon and Machine Company, which did well in the days of wagons and horse-drawn farm machinery. The company outlived its usefulness.

The Church sold the banks which it once held. As good banking services developed in the community, there was no longer any need for Church-owned banks.

Some of these business interests directly serve the needs of the Church. For instance, our business is communication. We must speak with people across the world. We must speak at home to let our stand be known and abroad to acquaint others with our work. And so we own a newspaper, the *Deseret News,* the oldest business institution in Utah.

We likewise own television and radio stations. These provide a voice in the communities which they serve. I may add that we are sometimes embarrassed by network television presentations. Our people do the best they can to minimize the impact of these.

We have a real estate arm designed primarily to ensure the viability and the attractiveness of properties surrounding Temple Square. The core of many cities has deteriorated terribly. This cannot be said of Salt Lake City, although you may disagree as you try to get to the Tabernacle these days. We have tried to see that this part of the community is kept attractive and viable. With the beautiful grounds of Temple Square and the adjoining block to the east, we maintain gardens the equal of any in the world. This area will become even more attractive when the facility now being constructed on Main Street is completed and the large Conference Center to the north is finished.

Are these businesses operated for profit? Of course they are. They operate in a competitive world. They pay taxes. They are important citizens of this community. And they produce a profit, and from that profit comes the money which is used by The Church of Jesus Christ of Latter-day Saints Foundation to help with charitable and worthwhile causes in this community and abroad and, more particularly, to assist in the great humanitarian efforts of the Church.

These businesses contribute one-tenth of their profit to the Foundation. The Foundation cannot give to itself or to other Church entities, but it can use its resources to assist other causes, which it does so generously. Millions of dollars have been so distributed. Thousands upon thousands have been fed. They have been supplied with medicine. They have been supplied with clothing and shelter in times of great emergency and terrible distress. How grateful I feel for the beneficence of this great Foundation, which derives its resources from the business interests of the Church.

I have time to discuss one other question: "Why does the Church become involved in issues that come before the legislature and the electorate?"

I hasten to add that we deal only with those legislative matters which are of a strictly moral nature or which directly affect the welfare of the Church. We have opposed gambling and liquor and will continue to do so. We regard it as not only our right but our duty to oppose those forces which we feel undermine the moral fiber of society. Much of our effort, a very great deal of it, is in association with others whose interests are similar. We have worked with Jewish groups, Catholics, Muslims, Protestants, and those of no particular religious affiliation, in coalitions formed to advocate positions on vital moral issues. Such is currently the case in California, where Latter-day Saints are working as part of a coalition to safeguard traditional marriage from forces in our society which are attempting to redefine that sacred institution. God-sanctioned marriage between a man and a woman has been the basis of civilization for thousands of years. There is no justification to redefine what marriage is. Such is not our right, and those who try will find themselves answerable to God.

Some portray legalization of so-called same-sex marriage as a civil right. This is not a matter of civil rights; it is a matter of morality. Others question our constitutional right as a church to raise our voice on an issue that is of critical importance to the future of the family. We believe that defending this sacred institution by working to preserve traditional marriage lies clearly within our religious and constitutional prerogatives. Indeed, we are compelled by our doctrine to speak out.

Nevertheless, and I emphasize this, I wish to say that our opposition to attempts to legalize same-sex marriage should never be interpreted as justification for hatred, intolerance, or abuse of those who profess homosexual tendencies, either individually or as a group. As I said from this pulpit one year ago, our hearts reach out to those who refer to themselves as gays and lesbians. We love and honor them as sons and daughters of God. They are welcome in the Church. It is expected, however, that they follow the same God-given rules of conduct that apply to everyone else, whether single or married.

I commend those of our membership who have voluntarily joined with other like-minded people to defend the sanctity of traditional marriage. As part of a coalition that embraces those of other faiths, you are giving substantially of your means. The money being raised in California has been donated to the coalition by individual members of the Church. You are contributing your time and talents in a cause that in some quarters may not be politically correct but which nevertheless lies at the heart of the Lord's eternal plan for His children, just as those of many other churches are doing. This is a united effort.

I think that is all I need to say on that and the other matters on which I have commented. I have tried to explain why we do some of the things that we do. I hope I have been helpful.

Now, in conclusion I wish to say that I love the priesthood of this Church. It is a vital, living thing. It is the very heart and strength of this work. It is the power and authority by which God, our Eternal Father, accomplishes His work on the earth. It is the authority by which men speak in His name. It is the authority by which they govern His Church.

I love the boys who hold the Aaronic Priesthood. Every young man who does so, walking in obedience to the commandments of the Lord, may expect to have the guidance of the Holy Spirit in his life. That Spirit will bless him in his studies and other pursuits and will lead him in efforts that will bless him and bless the lives of others all about him.

Boys, I endorse and repeat what has been said here this night; live worthy of the priesthood you hold. Never do anything that will make you unworthy. Observe the Word of Wisdom. It is not difficult, and it will bring you promised blessings. Avoid drugs. They will utterly destroy you. They will take from you control and discipline over your minds and bodies. They will enslave you and place a vicious and deadly grip upon you that will be almost impossible to break.

Stay away from pornography. It too will destroy you. It will cloud your minds with evil and destroy your capacity to appreciate the good and the beautiful.

Avoid alcohol as you would a loathsome disease. Beer will do to you what hard liquor will do. Each contains alcohol in varying amounts.

Shun immorality. It will blight your life if you indulge in it. It will destroy your self-respect. It will rob you of pleasant opportunities and make you unworthy of the companionship of lovely young women.

As you look forward and plan your lives, include a mission. You have an obligation to do so. It may be a difficult experience, but it will enrich and give balance to your life, and it will bless the lives of others in a way beyond your power to comprehend.

So much depends upon you, my very dear young friends.

May God bless you as you go forward with your lives, walking in obedience to His commandments.

This, I remind every man and boy in this vast audience tonight, is the Church and kingdom of the Almighty God. As our history has amply demonstrated, it is not a cause of ease nor a work without effort, even sacrifice. We shall go on pursuing the path which the Lord has marked out before us. We shall try to be strong and faint not as we pursue those programs and practices which have been established and maintained through generations of time.

Brethren, what a tremendous organization we are all a part of. We shall go forward and never flag or be deterred in our efforts to build this kingdom and establish righteousness in the earth. May God grant us wisdom, strength, and resolution, I humbly pray in the name of our Redeemer, the Lord Jesus Christ, amen.

# Sunday Morning
# Session

OCTOBER 3, 1999

WHAT AN EXCITING AND WONDERFUL thing it is to step across the threshold of the centuries. This will be our experience before long. Even more exciting is our opportunity to bridge the millennium that is drawing to a close and greet a new thousand years. I am overwhelmed with a grand and solemn sense of history as I contemplate this period.

It is only two millennia since the Savior walked the earth. It is a wonderful acknowledgment of His place in history that the calendar now in use throughout most of the world places His birth as the meridian of time. All that went before is reckoned back from that date. All that has happened since is measured forward from that date.

Every time anyone uses a date, he knowingly or unknowingly acknowledges the coming to earth of the Son of God. His birth, as it has been popularly determined, marks the center point of the ages, the meridian of time recognized throughout the earth. As we use these dates we pay no attention to it. But if we pause to think, we must recognize that He is the one sublime figure in all the history of the world on which our measurement of time is based.

In the centuries before He came to earth there was prophecy of His coming. Isaiah declared, "For unto us a child is born, unto us a son is given: and the government shall be upon his shoulder: and his name shall be called Wonderful, Counsellor, The mighty God, The everlasting Father, The Prince of Peace" (Isaiah 9:6).

King Benjamin, more than a century before the Savior's birth, said this to his people:

> For behold, the time cometh, and is not far distant, that with power, the Lord Omnipotent who reigneth, who was, and is from all eternity to all eternity, shall come down from heaven among the children of men, and shall dwell in a tabernacle of clay, and shall go forth amongst men, working mighty miracles, such as healing the sick, raising the dead, causing the lame to walk, the blind to receive their sight, and the deaf to hear, and curing all manner of diseases. . . .
>
> And he shall be called Jesus Christ, the Son of God, the Father of heaven and earth, the Creator of all things from the beginning; and his mother shall be called Mary. [Mosiah 3:5, 8]

It is small wonder that angels sang at His birth and Wise Men traveled far to pay Him homage.

He was the one perfect man to walk the earth. He fulfilled the law of Moses and brought a new canon of love to the world.

His mother was mortal, and from her came an inheritance of the flesh. His Father was immortal, the great God of the universe, through whom came His divine nature.

The magnificent expression of His love came in His death, when He gave His life as a sacrifice for all men. That Atonement, wrought in unspeakable pain, became the greatest event of history, an act of grace for which men gave nothing but which brought the assurance of the Resurrection to all who have or would walk the earth.

No other act in all of human history compares with it. Nothing that has ever happened can match it. Totally unselfish and with unbounded love for all mankind, it became an unparalleled act of mercy for the whole human race.

Then with the Resurrection that first Easter morn came the triumphal declaration of immortality. Well was Paul able to declare, "For as in Adam all die, even so in Christ shall all be made alive" (1 Corinthians 15:22). He not only granted the blessing of the Resurrection to all, but opened the way to eternal life to those who observe His teachings and commandments.

He was and is the great central figure of human history, the zenith of the times and seasons of all men.

Before His death, He had ordained His Apostles. They carried on for a period. His Church was set in place.

The centuries rolled on. A cloud of darkness settled over the earth. Isaiah described it: "For, behold, the darkness shall cover the earth, and gross darkness the people" (Isaiah 60:2).

It was a season of plunder and suffering, marked by long and bloody conflict. Charlemagne was crowned emperor of the Romans in the year 800.

It was an age of hopelessness, a time of masters and serfs.

The first thousand years passed, and the second millennium dawned. Its earlier centuries were a continuation of the former. It was a time fraught with fear and suffering. The great and deadly plague of the 14th century began in Asia. It spread to Europe and on up to England. Everywhere it went there was sudden death. Boccaccio said of its victims, "At noon [they] dined with their relatives and friends, and at night [they] supped with their ancestors in the next world!" (*The Decameron of Giovanni Boccaccio,* trans. Richard Aldington [1930], 6). It struck terror into the hearts of people. In five years it took the lives of 25 million, one-third the population of Europe.

Periodically it reappeared with its dark and ghoulish hand striking indiscriminately. But this was also a season of growing enlightenment. As the years continued their relentless march, the sunlight of a new day began to break over the earth. It was the Renaissance, a magnificent flowering of art, architecture, and literature.

Reformers worked to change the church, notably such men as Luther, Melanchthon, Hus, Zwingli, and Tyndale. These were men of great courage, some of whom suffered cruel deaths because of their beliefs. Protestantism was born, with its cry for reformation. When that reformation was not realized, the reformers organized churches of their own. They did so without priesthood authority. Their one desire was to find a niche in which they might worship God as they felt He should be worshipped.

While this great ferment was stirring across the Christian world, political forces were also at work. Then came the American Revolutionary War, resulting in the birth of a nation whose constitution declared that government should not reach its grasping hand into matters of religion. A new day had dawned, a glorious day. Here there was no longer a state church. No one faith was favored above another.

After centuries of darkness and pain and struggle, the time was ripe for the Restoration of the gospel. Ancient prophets had spoken of this long-awaited day.

All of the history of the past had pointed to this season. The centuries, with all of their suffering and all their hope, had come and gone. The Almighty Judge of the nations, the living God, determined that the times of which the prophets had spoken had arrived. Daniel had foreseen a stone which was cut out of the mountain without hands and which became a great mountain and filled the whole earth (see Daniel 2:34–35).

"And in the days of these kings shall the God of heaven set up a kingdom, which shall never be destroyed: and the kingdom shall not be left to other people, but it shall break in pieces and consume all these kingdoms, and it shall stand for ever" (Daniel 2:44).

Isaiah and Micah had spoken long before when with prophetic vision they saw our time:

"And it shall come to pass in the last days, that the mountain of the Lord's house shall be established in the top of the mountains, and shall be exalted above the hills; and all nations shall flow unto it.

"And many people shall go and say, Come ye, and let us go up to the mountain of the Lord, to the house of the God of Jacob; and he will teach us of his ways, and we will walk in his paths: for out of Zion shall go forth the law, and the word of the Lord from Jerusalem" (Isaiah 2:2–3; see also Micah 4:2).

Paul had written of the whole procession of time, the parade of the centuries, saying, "Let no man deceive you by any means: for that day shall not come, except there come a falling away first" (2 Thessalonians 2:3).

He had further said of this day, "That in the dispensation of the fulness of times he might gather together in one all things in Christ, both which are in heaven, and which are on earth; even in him" (Ephesians 1:10).

Peter foresaw the whole grand panorama of the centuries when he declared with prophetic vision:

"Repent ye therefore, and be converted, that your sins may be blotted out, when the times of refreshing shall come from the presence of the Lord;

"And he shall send Jesus Christ, which before was preached unto you:

"Whom the heaven must receive until the times of restitution of all things, which God hath spoken by the mouth of all his holy prophets since the world began" (Acts 3:19–21).

All of these and others pointed to this glorious season, this most wonderful season in all the annals of human history, when there should come a day of restitution of true doctrine and true practice.

That glorious day dawned in the year 1820, when a boy, earnest and with faith, walked into a grove of trees and lifted his voice in prayer, seeking that wisdom which he felt he so much needed.

There came in response a glorious manifestation. God the

Eternal Father and the risen Lord Jesus Christ appeared and spoke with him. The curtains which had been closed for much of two millennia were parted to usher in the dispensation of the fulness of times.

There followed the restoration of the holy priesthood, first the Aaronic and then the Melchizedek, under the hands of those who had held it anciently. Another testament, speaking as a voice from the dust, came forth as a second witness to the reality and the divinity of the Son of God, the great Redeemer of the world.

Keys of divine authority were restored, including those keys which were necessary to bind together families for time and eternity in a covenant which death could not destroy.

The stone was small in the beginning. It was hardly noticeable. But it has grown steadily and is rolling forth to fill the earth.

My brethren and sisters, do you realize what we have? Do you recognize our place in the great drama of human history? This is the focal point of all that has gone before. This is the season of restitution. These are the days of restoration. This is the time when men from over the earth come to the mountain of the Lord's house to seek and learn of His ways and to walk in His paths. This is the summation of all of the centuries of time since the birth of Christ to this present and wonderful day:

> *The morning breaks, the shadows flee;*
> *Lo, Zion's standard is unfurled!*
> *The dawning of a brighter day . . .*
> *Majestic rises on the world.*
> *["The Morning Breaks,"*
> Hymns, *no. 1]*

The centuries have passed. The latter-day work of the Almighty, that of which the ancients spoke, that of which the prophets and apostles prophesied, is come. It is here. For some reason unknown to us, but in the wisdom of God, we have been privileged to come to earth in this glorious age. There has been a great flowering of science. There has been a veritable explosion of learning. This is the greatest of all ages of human endeavor and human accomplishment. And more importantly, it is the season when God has spoken, when His Beloved Son has appeared, when the divine priesthood has been restored, when we hold in our hand another testament of the Son of God. What a glorious and wonderful day this is.

God be thanked for His generous bestowal upon us. We thank Him for this wondrous gospel, whose power and authority reach even beyond the veil of death.

Given what we have and what we know, we ought to be a better people than we are. We ought to be more Christlike, more forgiving, more helpful and considerate to all around us.

We stand on the summit of the ages, awed by a great and solemn sense of history. This is the last and final dispensation toward which all in the past has pointed. I bear testimony and witness of the reality and truth of these things. I pray that every one of us may sense the awesome wonder of it all as we look forward shortly to the passing of a century and the death of a millennium.

Let the old year go. Let the new year come. Let another century pass. Let a new one take its place. Say good-bye to a millennium. Greet the beginning of another thousand years.

And so we shall go forward on a continuing path of growth and progress and enlargement, touching for good the lives of people everywhere for as long as the earth shall last.

At some stage in all of this onward rolling, Jesus Christ will appear to reign in splendor upon the earth. No one knows when that will be. Not even the angels in heaven will know of the time of His return. But it will be a welcome day.

> *Come, O thou King of Kings!*
> *We've waited long for thee,*
> *With healing in thy wings,*
> *To set thy people free.*

*Come, thou desire of nations, come;*
*Let Israel now be gathered home.*
   *["Come, O Thou King of Kings,"*
   Hymns, *no. 59]*

May God bless us with a sense of our place in history and, having been given that sense, with our need to stand tall and walk with resolution in a manner becoming the Saints of the Most High, is my humble prayer in the name of Jesus Christ, amen.

# SUNDAY AFTERNOON SESSION

OCTOBER 3, 1999

MY BRETHREN AND SISTERS, as we conclude this great conference, we experience considerable emotion. If present plans hold, this is the last time we will meet in this Tabernacle for general conference. With few exceptions, a half-dozen perhaps, for 132 years our conferences have been held here.

This Tabernacle was conceived in 1863 and was first used for the October 1867 conference. There was no gallery in the building at that time. This was added for the April conference of 1870.

What a remarkable and wonderful structure this has been. But it has grown too small for our needs. At the time of its building it was a tremendous undertaking, built to accommodate all who wished to attend conference. It replaced the old Tabernacle, which was built to the south of us and which seated about 2,500.

We salute President Brigham Young on his boldness in undertaking the construction of this unique and remarkable building at a time when this was still frontier territory. The concept of the design was original. Its builders knew of nothing else quite like it.

These large sandstone pillars were first constructed to form an oval, 250 feet east to west. On these pillars was placed a great bridgework of timbers. For most of the roof structure they spanned 150 feet. There were no interior supporting pillars. The doomsayers predicted that when the interior scaffolding was removed, the whole roof would come down. The roof structure was nine feet thick. It was formed by a great latticework of timbers pinned together with wooden pegs. Green rawhide was then wrapped around these timbers so that when it dried it tightened the grip on the pegs.

Sheeting was then applied on the roof, and this was covered with shingles. The interior was lathed and then plastered, the hair of cattle being mixed with the plaster to give it strength.

The scaffolding was removed, and the roof remained solid. It has so remained for a century and a third, although the shingles were replaced with aluminum some years ago.

The Tabernacle has served the needs of this Church and community through all of these years. General conferences of the Church have been held here. The voices of prophets have spoken out from this podium. The law and the testimony have been quoted and declared. Numerous other Church meetings have been held here. In this magnificent old structure the funeral services of beloved leaders have been conducted. Presidents of the nation and other distinguished men have spoken from where I now stand.

This has been home to the Tabernacle Choir since the structure was completed. More recently it has been home also to the Mormon Youth Chorus and Symphony. It was the first home of the Utah Symphony. Handel's *Messiah* has been presented here over a period of many years. Countless concerts of various kinds, a variety of musical ensembles, and many distinguished soloists have all entertained the public in this great and singular hall.

What a remarkable and useful building it has been. What great purposes it has served. I know of no other structure like it in all the world.

It is true that with electronic means we can broadcast to wherever we wish to be heard. But looking at a television screen is not the same as being in the hall with the speakers and singers.

The new hall, which we are erecting on the adjoining block and which we have named the Conference Center, will seat 21,000—with its adjoining theater, 22,000—nearly three and one-half times the capacity of this Tabernacle. I do not know if we will fill it, but I do know that we have spoken to much larger gatherings of Latter-day Saints. For instance, in Santiago, Chile, we spoke to 57,500 in a great football stadium; in Buenos Aires, Argentina, to 50,000; in Manila in the Philippines, in a great coliseum, we spoke to 35,000 gathered under one roof.

This Tabernacle will continue to be used for a great variety of purposes. It is expected that the choir will go on originating its weekly broadcast here. This building will continue to accommodate various Church gatherings, public gatherings, and serve a variety of purposes.

The new hall will take some getting accustomed to. But it will be more pleasant. It will be air-conditioned. The seating will be more comfortable than these hard wooden pews. My fear is that too many will fall asleep. It is not of the same design as this Tabernacle, but it is also of a unique and wonderful kind. It represents the very latest in architectural and engineering skills. Parking will be improved.

We anticipate that next April we will meet in a new hall as we usher in a new century and a new millennium. The building may not be complete at that time. The organ probably will not be finished. There will be other construction details needing attention. It will likely be dedicated a year from this conference.

It is a very large and a truly magnificent structure, designed and built to the highest seismic codes. It is constructed with reinforced concrete with a granite veneer. That granite is the same stone that was used in the building of the Salt Lake Temple, including the blemishes which you will recognize in both buildings.

And so, in terms of general conference, we bid good-bye to an old and wonderful friend. We hope it will be around and that it will be useful for a very long time to come. It is a bold step we are taking. But this boldness is in harmony with the tremendous outreach of the Church across the world.

We have no desire to outdo Brigham Young or his architects—William H. Folsom, Henry Grow, and Truman O. Angell. We wish only to build on the tremendous foundation which President Young laid in pioneering this marvelous work here in the valleys of the West.

As today we close the doors of this Tabernacle and look forward to opening the doors of the new Conference Center next April, we do so with love, with appreciation, with respect, with reverence—really with affection—for this building and for those who have gone before us, who built so well, and whose handiwork has served so long.

A building develops a personality of its own. The Spirit of the Lord has been in this structure. It is sacred unto us. We hope, we anticipate, we pray that the new structure will likewise radiate the same spirit.

Now I leave with words that have been spoken so often from this great assembly hall—my testimony, my blessing, and my love—with you, my dear associates in this great cause. This work is true. You know that, as do I. It is God's work. You know that also. It is the restored gospel of Jesus Christ. It is the way to happiness, the plan for peace and righteousness.

God, our Eternal Father, lives. His Son, our Redeemer, the resurrected Savior of the world, lives. They appeared to the boy Joseph Smith to part the curtains in opening a great work of restoration, ushering in the dispensation of the fulness of times. The Book of Mormon is true. It speaks as a voice from the dust in testimony of the divinity of the Lord. The priesthood, with its keys, its authority, and all of its blessings, is upon the earth.

And we are partakers of these precious gifts. And so, as we might say to an old friend, good-bye. May the blessings of God rest

261

upon this sacred and wonderful hall. And may we, as those who have come here frequently to partake of the Spirit felt here, live worthy of the title Latter-day Saints is my humble prayer in the name of the Lord Jesus Christ, amen.

# SECTION 2

# MEMBER MEETINGS

# REGIONAL CONFERENCE— PRIESTHOOD LEADERSHIP SESSION

### APRIL 22, 1995

THIS IS A TREMENDOUS PICTURE in Boston, this hall filled with men who hold the priesthood, on a Saturday afternoon. To think that on a Saturday afternoon you would be here, all dressed up, eager, attentive, wonderful. Thank you for being here, brethren, thank you very much.

I feel profoundly grateful for the faithful Latter-day Saints everywhere, men who love the Lord and who love their wives and treat them properly; men who love their children and treat them properly; men who pray, who get on their knees and pray. That's a tremendous thing in this day and time. It's an unusual thing. It's a wonderful thing. Thank you very much for the good men that you are.

I'm glad to have heard Brother Maxwell. He always says something of significance. I appreciate him and enjoy listening to him. Thank you very much.

It's always a pleasure to travel with Brother Maxwell. He is such a delightful man, a wonderful man. And he says things in such an interesting, challenging, and unique way. I feel deeply honored for the privilege of being here with him today.

Well, I don't know what to say to you except to tell you to keep the faith. You men are leaders. Every man here today is a leader.

That's because you are responsible for the well-being of someone other than yourself. Every man here—be he a stake president, a bishop, a counselor, an elders quorum president, whatever—has responsibility for the faith and the well-being of others. And I'd like to talk with you a little about leadership because it's so very, very important in this Church. It's one of the great miracles of our time, in my judgment, that we are going all over this world—we are now in 150 nations—and wherever we go we find the butcher, the baker, the candlestick maker and make of him a bishop, a stake president, an elders quorum president, whatever. The development of leadership in this Church is so basic and so fundamental. As with the priest so with the people, to paraphrase an old statement. As with us so will the Church go and grow and strengthen in the lives of the people. To me it is a miracle—no seminaries in which we train priests, nothing of that kind. We just take people as we find them and add to their strength and add to their capacity and add to their ability to govern in the affairs of the kingdom of God.

What can I do to improve myself as a leader? One of the great blessings of my life, brethren, has been to work with good men. I count that as a most precious thing. Men from whom I hope I have learned a few things. My mission president for most of my mission was a member of the Council of the Twelve, Joseph F. Merrill. I was called to become his assistant when he presided over the European Mission in London. He didn't smile much. He was dean of the School of Mines and Engineering at the University of Utah. He had that wonderful capacity that most deans have of being a bit gruff and grim and frightening. But he was a great man. He reminded me of some of these trees we have seen today—rough, shaggy bark but hardwood that's true and strong and good and solid. He was my mission president, a great man. Each morning we studied Brother Talmage together: Articles of Faith and Jesus the Christ. Over a period of many months I sat at his feet, three of us did, his wife and two elders, and heard him. And I learned something of the way the Council of the Twelve operates from him, and I have always appreciated what I learned from him.

And then I came home, and I've had the opportunity since of working closely with President Grant and President George Albert Smith, President David O. McKay, President Joseph Fielding Smith, President Harold B. Lee, President Spencer W. Kimball, President Ezra Taft Benson, President Howard W. Hunter, and a lot of other great men such as John A. Widtsoe, Albert E. Bowen, Stephen L. Richards, Henry D. Moyle—men of that caliber who served in the Council of the Twelve and in the Presidency of the Church, such as J. Reuben Clark. Great men. Nothing very pretentious about them, really. Nothing very pretentious about any of them. They walked their way quietly and tried to do what was right in standing as examples before the people of this Church and declaring without fear of man the great basic, fundamental doctrines of the restored gospel of Jesus Christ. Wonderful men.

Out of that experience, I'd like to just talk with you a little about what I can do, and you can do, to become a more effective leader in this Church. I want to emphasize, as I have said publicly before, in this last conference, that you have as serious a responsibility in your sphere of action in terms of your calling as I do in my sphere of action and in terms of my calling. I believe that. This Church isn't Gordon B. Hinckley's Church; it's the Lord's Church, and you and I are His servants, helping our Father in Heaven to accomplish His purposes. His great purpose is "to bring to pass the immortality and eternal life of man" (Moses 1:39). And you do not have just a little job. You have a big job. You elders quorum presidents—I like to stand back in tremendous admiration of presidencies in the elders quorums. How many are there of you here? All of you who are in elders quorum presidencies, stand up. You have a tremendous job. For every man who is active in the Church you have at least one or two not active, right? You're sparse. You wouldn't be sparse if they were all active, would you? Same thing with all of you. Thank you very much, brethren.

Are you accomplishing anything? Do you feel you are making some headway? I hope so. Maybe not very rapidly—"one of a city, and two of a family," almost as Jeremiah predicted (Jeremiah 3:14). But to get these men who once saw the light of the gospel back into activity, what a challenge. Well, as leaders, we begin with ourselves. That's where we begin.

Number one: I can make myself worthy of the call. I'm going to make a suggestion to you. We all do a lot of studying, but most of us don't do much meditation. We don't take time to think. I'd like to suggest that next fast day, which isn't very far away, everybody in this hall set aside an hour or two. Sit by yourself. Go in the bedroom, and lock the door. Go out in the yard under a tree. Go in your study, if you have one, and shut the door, and think about yourself and your worthiness. Read from this great book of which Brother Maxwell has spoken [the Book of Mormon]. Read a little of that. Read King Benjamin and then Mosiah. Read what they say, and think about it, meditate on it. There's a great word that's used: ponder. Ponder. What do we mean by ponder? Well, I think it simply means quietly thinking things through. Ponder what you have read. Ponder your life. Are you worthy? Are you living the commandments? Are you doing a little cheating? That isn't right; you can't do that. You hold the priesthood. Are you doing a little looking at pornography? You can't do that. You hold the priesthood. Are you wasting your time in fruitless things? You can't do that. You're preparing for eternity. Are you dishonest with your employer in any way? You can't do that. You hold the priesthood. You're a leader. You're an example to others. Square up your life. Think about it, brethren. Think about it.

Take an hour or two to ponder how you're doing. Before you break your fast, go off by yourself, do a little scripture reading, and think about yourself and your responsibilities as a leader in this

Church for the well-being, the faith, the temporal welfare of those for whom you are responsible.

President McKay, I remember, said to us once, in speaking to the Council of the Twelve when I was in that circle, "Brethren, we need to meditate more." Those were his words. We need to take time to meditate. It's so hard. We have been cruising the highways in this part of the world. We started down at White Plains on Friday, and we were up to Hartford yesterday and drove here today, and I've had one impression—the whole world's going mad. Traffic! Everywhere you go! People! I hope they all know where they are going, because they are paying a lot for gasoline. But we don't meditate. We don't take time to think. We passed a sign somewhere on one of these roads—we were following President Hutchins, and that isn't easy—but we passed a sign on one of these roads that said Walden's Pond, with an arrow. And I thought, "Poor old Henry Thoreau would go crazy if he saw what was happening on the highways around his pond." The speed at which we live. Slow down, at least for an hour or two, and think of Bill Jones or whatever your name is. How am I? How am I? What am I doing to qualify for the responsibility that has been given me? Think of it, brethren, and if you're by yourself and it's quiet, get on your knees, and talk with the Lord about it, and ask Him to help you, because you need it. We all need it. I need it. Brother Maxwell needs it. We all need it. We can't do this work alone. We can't do it without the help of the Lord. And we have to be worthy of His help if we are going to accomplish it.

President McKay used to tell a story of General Gordon on a campaign in Africa. Every morning there was a white handkerchief dropped at his tent door, in the front, on the ground. And the whole army under his direction knew that when that flag was on the ground in front of his tent, General Gordon was in communing with the Lord, and nobody, regardless of the emergency, dared disturb him during that time. Try it. Something will happen if you try it. I'm not asking you to spend all day. You better get up and help your wife with her responsibilities. But try an hour or two. Think of yourself in terms of your wife and your children. Just reflect on it and ponder. I don't want to overstate it, but I believe that it would be wonderfully fruitful. Think of your relationships with people in your business and your office, people with whom you associate. Do you like to cuff them around, or do you treat them with respect?

Joseph Anderson was a General Authority, a Seventy. He lived to be 102, the oldest General Authority ever, I guess, as a General Authority. Joseph Anderson was first secretary to President Grant, beginning way back about 1922, and he was a great secretary. He served with President Grant until President Grant died. I heard Joseph say this in a meeting which we had in the temple with all of the General Authorities, when he bore his testimony. He said he went up to see President Grant when he was very ill, in his old age, and President Grant looked at Joseph, his secretary for all these years, and said, "Joseph, have I ever been unkind to you? Have I ever abused you in any way?" And Joseph said, "No, President Grant, you have never been unkind to me in all these years." And tears rolled down President Grant's cheeks, and he said, "Joseph, I'm glad I have never been unkind to you." He had nothing to repent of in that matter. President Grant died the next day. Kindness, civility, decency, honesty, integrity in our relationships—these are the qualities we need.

Number two: I can learn the requirements of my office. It's a complex Church. Somehow we have built a great, complex organization to accomplish our purposes. We have done the best we know how, and I think it's been done under the inspiration of the Lord, and the accomplishments have been tremendous, but it isn't always easy to understand. How can I qualify myself? Well, if you have a handbook—and you should have a handbook—read it thoughtfully. Underline it. I write in every book I read and put markings. I have some beautiful leather-bound books. I don't dare read them for fear I'll destroy them. I get paperbacks of the same title, some of the old ones, and mark them up. But I have to mark things up. It reminds me of when I was on a mission in England many years ago. We held street meetings in Hyde Park, Regent's Park, and Clapham Common in London. I remember one Cockney heckler saying, "Eeeee, he says he believes the Bible. He's got half of it crossed out!"

Study the handbook, and study the scriptures. Read the great sections on priesthood in the Doctrine and Covenants—section 20, section 42, section 84, section 107. You're a priesthood officer. Those comprise the constitution of your priesthood responsibility. Read them, and study them, and gain from them, and then read something of the life of the Lord. Do it rather regularly.

When I arrived in the mission field 62 years ago, my companion met me at the train station in Preston, Lancashire, and we went to our digs at 15 Wadham Road in that city, and the next morning he said, "Now, we are going to study the Bible. We are going to study the Gospel of John. You and I together are going to study the Gospel of John." And we began with that great verse, "In the beginning was the Word, and the Word was with God, and the Word was God. . . . And the Word was made flesh, and dwelt among us, (and we beheld his glory, the glory as of the only begotten of the Father)" (John 1:1, 14). It did something for me. Try to read the Gospel of John once each year. It's good for you.

Read the Book of Mormon. Read that fifth testimony, as we call it—3 Nephi, beginning with chapter 11, when the Lord appeared among the Nephites. Read it. Read the last words of Moroni, that great, challenging testimony at the end of this marvelous book.

I love Moroni. My heart reaches out to Moroni, that great, lonely figure who wandered for years and years, with all of his people gone. He saw them go down by the thousands, walking in their evil ways and forsaking the Lord and going to destruction. He and his father were left alone, and then his father died, and Moroni walked alone. These great final words of his always touch me: "Despair cometh because of iniquity" (Moroni 10:22). Moroni was a man of hope, of optimism, forward-looking. Despair cometh of iniquity. "And now I speak unto all the ends of the earth—that if the day cometh that the power and gifts of God shall be done away among you, it shall be because of unbelief" (Moroni 10:24). That's as applicable to us today as it was in his day. "I exhort you to remember these things; for the time speedily cometh that ye shall know that I lie not, for ye shall see me at the bar of God; and the Lord God will say unto you: Did I not declare my words unto you, which were written by this man, like as one crying from the dead, yea, even as one speaking out of the dust? . . . And God shall show unto you, that that which I have written is true" (Moroni 10:27, 29). Marvelous. Read those things, and ponder them in your hearts.

Number three: I can gather around me help. You don't need to do it all yourself. You can't, if you do it right. There isn't enough of you. You need help. Remember those words of Jethro, whose son-in-law was Moses. Jethro was talking to Moses. He had been watching him for a while, and the people were bringing all their complaints to Moses. Jethro finally said to his son-in-law, and I guess sons-in-law don't pay much attention to what their fathers-in-law say, nevertheless, he said it: "Moses, [and I'm paraphrasing] you can't do it. You can't keep this up. You don't have the strength to keep this up. You need help. You don't need to listen to everyone's complaint on an individual basis, all these murmuring Israelites. You can't do it. Divide up the work. Get some help—leaders of 10s and 50s and 100s. Let them handle the little problems, and you save your energy for the big problems." (See Exodus 18:13–26.) Now, that's good counsel for us today, brethren. You men who are presidents, give your counselors work to do. Share the load. Wear them out. If you do so, you can release them with honor and get some new ones—or turn them over and wear them out on the other side. Delegate to your counselors. You will discover something. You'll discover that they can do some things better than you can. And in that process you will help them, and you will help yourself.

I remember when I was made a stake president. I called two wonderful men as counselors—wonderful men. We had to build a new stake center, and in those days we had to put up half the money. You people are being spoiled today; the Church puts up all the money from the tithing funds of the Church to build and maintain these buildings. We had to put up 50 percent, and we also operated a stake farm, a big stake farm. I said to my counselors, "Brother Alldredge, the new building is your responsibility. I'll come up and use a hammer and pound some nails to help, but it's your job to get that stake center built." And I said to President Erickson, "The stake farm is your responsibility, and if I get a call in the middle of the night that our cattle are in the neighbor's corn, I'm simply going to tell the caller to call you, even at three o'clock in the morning." Well, they did it, and they did a far better job than I could have done.

Use your counselors. Spread the load. You'll do wonders for them. They will grow in strength, and you will have more time to do that which you alone should do. Delegate responsibility. It isn't easy. Some of us like to do everything hands on, micromanage all the time, everything. It isn't easy to delegate responsibility, do you know that? But it's good. It's worth working at. Every president in this Church has counselors for a reason—for a great reason, in the wisdom of the Lord. Now, the Seventies are a little different. It takes seven of them, but everywhere else, it's a president and two counselors, and that's how it works from the top down. In the First Presidency meeting which we hold every Tuesday, Wednesday, Thursday, and Friday at eight o'clock in the morning, President Monson, President Faust, and I meet together with a secretary who makes a record of everything. We pray together, and I ask President

Faust what he has to present, and he does so, and President Monson, and then I present those matters which I have to present. As far as I'm concerned, when they are given a responsibility I have total confidence that they will take care of it and take care of it well, and I forget it. I believe in that. I know; I've been a counselor a lot of years in my life, and to have been given the confidence of your leader is a wonderful thing and a great motivator to get the job done and done right. Brethren, delegate responsibility. You can't do it alone.

Next, fourth, I can call on the Lord for help. I've had an interesting experience on this trip. I've been working over a problem for a long time. I tell you this by way of testimony. And I think that being gone for three or four days, I begin to see the answer to that problem. I have prayed about it, I have worried about it, I have wondered about it, I have laid awake nights about it. I woke up at four o'clock this morning and couldn't get to sleep, thinking about it.

Call on the Lord for help. I remember President Harold B. Lee, on one occasion, right after he became President. A stake president from Florida came and asked to meet with the First Presidency, and he said, "I have about 10 families in my stake who are in very serious trouble because of the dishonesty of a developer of a subdivision in which they bought homes. They are going to lose their homes. They are all going to lose their homes. We've got to have some help." And President Lee said to the president, "I am afraid we can't help you, President. We can't do for one individual in the Church what we can't do for all." And the stake president left dejected and returned to his home. The next day President Lee came into the presidency meeting and said these interesting words. He had been thinking through the night. He said, "Yesterday, Harold B. Lee spoke. Today, the Lord is speaking. We are going to help those people. We are going to send our chief legal counsel down there to see what can be done to untangle this mess and help

274

those people save their homes." That was an interesting statement: "Yesterday, Harold B. Lee was speaking. Today, the Lord is speaking." Pray and listen. Most of us pray the way we order groceries by telephone: pick up the phone, place the order, and hang up.

I want to make you a promise that if you do those four simple things, things will look up for you. I don't hesitate to promise that. You will see greater results in your life. The Lord bless you. Please know of our great love for you, our great appreciation, our great respect for you. Practice those four simple little things of meditation, instructing yourself in your duties, sharing the load, and sharing your problems with your Father in Heaven, who stands ready to help you. Don't forget, it was the Lord who said—and again I'm paraphrasing, "Come unto me, and take upon yourselves my yoke. Let me do that for you. I'll take this burden from your shoulders if you will, in fact, listen to my counsel" (see Matthew 11:28–29).

"And the Lord thy God shall lead thee by the hand, and give thee answer to thy prayers" (D&C 112:10). That's the promise of the revelation. May you be blessed in your great and sacred responsibilities as leaders in The Church of Jesus Christ of Latter-day Saints, I humbly pray in His holy name, even the name of Jesus Christ, amen.

# Heber City and Springville, Utah

# Regional Conference

MAY 14, 1995

Sister Anderson's reference to a ladder reminds me of a story my father told when I was a boy. He said that a boy came down to breakfast one morning and said to his father, "I was dreaming about you last night."

"You were?"

"Yes."

"What were you dreaming?"

He said, "I was dreaming that I was climbing a ladder heavenward, and on each rung of the ladder I had to write one of my sins as I went up."

And his father said, "Yes, where do I come into your dream?"

And the boy said, "As I was going up, I met you coming down for more chalk."

It's nice to be with you, brothers and sisters. Wonderful to be with you, this great, vast congregation of Latter-day Saints, all shined up on Mother's Day. My, you look good. You're so bright and clean. Look at these boys, all polished, hair combed, shirts and ties, smiles—wonderful. These lovely girls, all polished and beautiful. And these parents—they look a little tired, but glad you're here. Thank you for making the effort to be here in this great regional conference of eight stakes of Zion, the people of eight stakes of

Zion assembled here this morning in this vast congregation. You're frightening almost, to look into the faces of so very, very many of you. Thank you for coming. Thank you for being the kind of people that you are. Thank you for your faith.

It's just wonderful to look into the faces of people of this kind and be able to say, "Here are good people. Here are people who pray. Here are people who actually get on their knees night and morning to express thanks to the Lord and ask for His blessings. Here are people who give a tenth of their income without any questions, without any quibbling, without any selfishness, to move forward the work of the Lord. Here are people who believe in the principles of chastity and virtue and try to live lives in harmony with the law of the Lord concerning these matters. Here are fathers who regard their children as sons and daughters of God and their wives as their companions, walking equally at their sides. And here are women who know that their children are the most treasured possessions of their lives and that nothing in all this world is more important than these children and the establishment of good homes."

You are members of The Church of Jesus Christ of Latter-day Saints. Thank you for trying to live the gospel. I know you're not perfect. None of us is. There was only one perfect man who ever walked the earth, and that was the Son of God. But we are trying to walk in His footsteps and be the kind of people that He would have us be. Thank you, my brothers and sisters, for your efforts in this regard.

Now, it is Mother's Day, isn't it? It surely is. I'd like to read you this that I clipped from a rather unlikely source, the Wall Street Journal, some years ago: "The most creative job in the entire world: It involves tastes, fashions, decorating, recreation, education, transportation, psychology, romance, cuisine, designing, literature, handicrafts, art, horticulture, economics, government, community relations, pediatrics, geriatrics, entertainment, maintenance, purchasing, direct mail, law, accounting, religion, energy, and management. Anyone who can handle all those has to be somebody special. She is. She's a home-maker."

How very, very true that is. In this age when more and more women are turning to daily work, how tremendous it is once in a while to just stop and recognize that the greatest job that any woman will ever do will be in nurturing and teaching and lifting and encouraging and rearing her children in righteousness and truth. There is no other thing that will compare with that, regardless of what she does. And I hope that the women of the Church will not slight their greatest responsibility in favor of a lesser responsibility. To the mothers of this Church, every mother who is here this day, I want to say that as the years pass, you will become increasingly grateful for that which you did in molding the lives of your children in the direction of righteousness and goodness and integrity and faith. My beloved sisters, I believe that with all of my heart.

My mother died 65 years ago. That's a long time. As the years pass, although I have forgotten a lot of detail, her face looms before me, as it were, as a guide and a strength in my life. I wouldn't be here without her; that goes without saying, of course it does. She disciplined us—never, I think, took a strap to us, or a switch, that I can remember. I remember, however, coming home from school when I was about in the first or second grade and throwing a book on the kitchen table and using the name of Deity in a vain manner that I had picked up somewhere and expressed thanks that that was over, that day's school. It offended her. She said, "We don't talk that way. That's the name of the Lord. We don't talk that way." She marched me into the bathroom. She got a clean washcloth. She got a new bar of soap. She turned on the water in the basin. She rubbed that washcloth on that soap, and she told me to open my mouth, and she washed out my mouth with soap. I can still taste it. I think it was Palmolive. But I have never forgotten that instance. And I think, and I hope, that in all of these years, now 75 years at least, and more, I have never used the name of Deity in vain. To think of the impressions of that one experience in terms of my life is tremendous to me.

She died while I was a student at the university. I went on a mission after that. It was in the bottom of the Depression. Money was terribly scarce. My father had a lot of property, but all that he was getting out of it was tax notices—no income from it. We discovered that my mother had established a savings account with the nickels and the dimes and the quarters she got in change when she bought groceries, and that spelled the difference that made it possible to cover my expenses in what was then the most costly mission in all the world. I am grateful for that.

I think I can share this with you. As I sat in the Tabernacle at the last conference and was sustained by the people of this Church, there came before me in my mind's eye the picture of my mother when I was a little boy. And I'm sure she must have thought then that I wouldn't amount to much, because I was not an easy little boy to deal with. I am grateful that I have the opportunity in my old age to bring honor to her name.

I like this little piece of poetry that I included in a talk that I gave previously, which I see has been published by Deseret Book. It comes from Rosemary and Stephen Benét.

> *If Nancy Hanks*
> *Came back as a ghost,*
> *Seeking news*
> *Of what she loved most,*
> *She'd ask first,*
> *"Where's my son?*
> *What's happened to Abe?*
> *What's he done?*
>
> *"Poor little Abe,*
> *Left all alone*

*Except for Tom,*
*Who's a rolling stone;*
*He was only nine*
*The year I died.*
*I remember still*
*How hard he cried.*

*"Scraping along*
*In a little shack,*
*With hardly a shirt*
*To cover his back,*
*And a prairie wind*
*To blow him down,*
*Or pinching times*
*If he went to town.*

*"You wouldn't know*
*About my son?*
*Did he grow tall?*
*Did he have fun?*
*Did he learn to read?*
*Did he get to town?*
*Do you know his name?*
*Did he get on?"*
    *[In Gordon B. Hinckley,*
    Motherhood: A Heritage of
    Faith *(1995), 3–4.]*

I think those authors caught the feeling of what Nancy Hanks might have said. I hope that every boy and girl in this vast congregation will have stirred within his or her heart this day the desire to live in such a way as to bring honor to the name of your mother. I've said to missionaries many times, in a rather joking way, as I have met with them, "Are you the kind of missionary your mother thinks you are? Are you the kind of son or daughter your mother thinks you are?" You know, if we would be the kind of boys and girls, sons and daughters, our mothers think we are, we'd all be pretty good. We'd be pretty good, we really would. We'd be pretty good.

How grateful I am for mothers. Fathers are all right, barely tolerated and prayed for and helped. But it is mothers who mold children. How true that is. I think it's been the mothers who have been the great carriers and purveyors of faith throughout the history of this Church. I believe that with all my heart.

There is included in this same talk a little account that I first told in general conference years ago, and since then it's been talked of a good deal all over the Church. It's the story of my wife's grandmother, who at the age of 13 left England with her parents. They had joined the Church in Brighton. They were fairly prosperous. They traveled across the ocean, a six-week journey. They traveled by steam train from Boston to Iowa City to be fitted out. They were assigned to travel with one of the handcart companies—the Martin handcart company—so that if the handcarts had trouble the wagon trains could help them. They had two yoke of oxen, one yoke of cows, a wagon, and a tent. It was at Iowa City that their first tragedy occurred. Their youngest child, less than two years of age, suffering from exposure, died and was buried in a grave never again visited by a member of the family. Mary went on to write in her journal:

> We traveled from 15 to 25 miles a day . . . till we got to the Platte River. . . . We caught up with the Handcart companies that day. We watched them cross the river. There were great lumps of ice floating down the river. It was bitter cold. The next morning there were fourteen dead. . . . We went back to camp and went to prayers. We sang. . . . I wondered what made my mother cry. . . . The next morning my little sister was born. It was the 23rd of September. We named her Edith and she lived six weeks and died. . . . [She] was buried at the last crossing of the Sweet Water.

When we arrived at Devil's Gate it was bitter cold. We left lots of our things there. . . . My brother James . . . was as well as he ever was when he went to bed. In the morning he was dead.

My feet were frozen [also my brother's and sister's]. It was nothing but snow. We could not drive the pegs . . . for our tents. . . . We did not know what would become of us. One night a man came to our camp and told us . . . [Brigham] Young had sent men and teams to help us. . . . We sang songs; some danced and some cried. . . .

My mother never got well. . . . She died between the Little and Big Mountain. . . . She was 43 years old. . . .

We arrived in Salt Lake City at nine o'clock at night the 11th of December 1856. Three out of the four that were living were frozen. My mother was dead in the wagon. . . . Early next morning . . . Brigham Young . . . came. . . . When he saw our condition—our feet frozen and our mother dead—tears rolled down his cheeks.

The doctor amputated my toes . . . [while] the sisters were dressing mother [for her grave]. . . . That afternoon she was buried. [In *Motherhood*, 5–6.]

Why did she come to Zion? Because she wanted her children to follow in the true Church.

That's where the strength of this work has lain, my brothers and sisters, in very large measure with women who taught their children faith and prayer and virtue and goodness and truth. God be thanked for the mothers of Zion. On this day when our nation honors mothers, we also pay tribute to these women who have been so very, very important in our lives and who, as a matter of fact, gave us life itself.

To the husbands who are here, I want to say, each of us can do a little better. You know it, as husbands and fathers. I am concerned that of all of the letters we get, many letters that come to the office of the President of the Church are from women who cry out in pain because of what they endure at the hands of abusive husbands.

Brethren, watch yourselves. Control your temper. Don't get angry. Be the kind of men you ought to be as the husbands of good women and the fathers of good children. I mean that. I read this letter to the priesthood yesterday, and I'm going to take the opportunity of reading it again. It came the other day to me.

> My husband is a righteous priesthood holder. That is the highest compliment I can pay him. When he is around it is as though the Savior Himself is directing us. He is kind and gentle, always finding ways to help me and our children. He is always the one who gets up with the children during the night if they have problems. He has never raised his voice or hand against us. Although we have had our differences of opinion we've never had an argument, and I know it is because he is so careful in the way he communicates with me. He guides us through personal Book of Mormon study and prayers, family study and prayers, and has now instigated a few moments of gospel study together in the evenings after the children are in bed. He is the best man I can think of. I feel it is a great honor to be married in the temple to such a man. We are happy and in love, and life is good.

Would that every woman could write words of that kind concerning her husband.

Now, in conclusion, I'd like to say a few words to the young people who are here. I see all these wonderful boys and girls here. I want to tell you something, an experience we had two weeks ago. We were in Boston for a regional conference of this kind. The stake president of one of the stakes had written and said that there were two young men in the hospital, Massachusetts General Hospital, in very serious condition and would we come and administer to them. And so, on Saturday morning, we went to the Massachusetts General Hospital. I can't say enough of good for the people who run that hospital. They were so gracious in arranging things for us. They brought those two young men from different parts of the hospital into the same room with all of the equipment that they had on them—tubes and pumps and everything else you can imagine. And we laid our hands upon those two boys and gave them a blessing.

Each of them is seriously paralyzed, one more so than the other, from the head down. They are bright, wonderful young men, one 17, one 16. They were driving home the other night from a Church function, driving a van with other young people. There were eight or nine in the van, and they were going too fast, and there was a curve in the road, a country road, and they rolled over the van. It's a miracle that both of them were not killed. One was the driver; the other was sitting next to him. Those in the back of the van were injured but were all right. But I thought as I looked at that tragic situation, those two boys unable to breathe on their own—fine-looking, handsome young men, faithful in the Church— I thought of the terrible consequences of a moment's carelessness. The terrible consequences of a moment's carelessness. They were having a good time, they were singing and driving along, careless in the fun they were having.

I called the stake president the other night to see how they are getting along. He said one is doing reasonably well; the other is still having terrible problems.

I just want to remind you, you boys and girls who are here today: It only takes one little careless slip, one villain, one mistake to blight our lives forever after.

I grew up on a farm. We lived on the farm in the summer (we lived in town in winter). We had about 35 acres and a lot of work. We had gates. We had a 10-foot gate, a 12-foot gate, a 16-foot gate. A little motion at the hinge has a tremendous effect out at the perimeter. Just a little motion at the hinge has a tremendous effect out at the end of the railings. It's the same with our lives. A little immorality, a little smoking, a little drinking of beer, a little pornography, a little profane language, a little thing, but it can have such a tremendous effect out here, where things really happen. I hope you will never forget that.

Years ago I worked for the railroad. I was in charge of what is called head-end traffic in the home office in Denver, and one day I received a phone call from my counterpart in another railroad in New Jersey to say that a train had arrived without its baggage car—where was it? Here was a train full of passengers angry because their baggage was missing, a whole carload of it. I immediately picked up the phone and called Oakland, California, and found that that car had been properly loaded and trained and delivered to us in Salt Lake City and we had carried it to Denver, where it was delivered to the Missouri Pacific and taken to St. Louis for delivery to the Baltimore and Ohio. But a careless switchman in the St. Louis railroad yards, misreading his instructions and not paying attention, had moved a piece of steel about three inches—a switch point in the St. Louis yards—and we discovered that the car that was supposed to be in Newark, New Jersey, was in New Orleans, Louisiana, 1,400 miles from its programmed destination. Now, that's the way with our lives. The little things we do make such a tremendous difference. Choose the right. A lot of children in the Church wear little CTR rings. I don't have one, but many of you do. Choose the right. Live the gospel. That's where happiness lies.

I read last night the conversation of Alma with his son Corianton. Corianton was a good boy in the beginning, and then he got a little wild, the way a lot of boys do—became a little arrogant, a little headstrong in his own way and caused a lot of trouble and embarrassment to his father and heartache for his mother. And his father sat him down and talked to him and said, "Corianton, wickedness never was happiness" (see Alma 41:10). Sin never was happiness and never will be. If you want to be happy in this life, you live the gospel. It's the Lord's way of happiness.

I leave you my testimony of the truth of these things, my brothers and sisters. God bless you that you will have cause to get on your knees and thank the Lord for His goodness to you. In the name of Jesus Christ, amen.

# London, England

# Missionary Meeting

## August 26, 1995

I'M NOT GOING TO BE HERE TALKING to you too long because we must go to another meeting. That's the story of my life—there's another meeting. President Kimball said to me once, "I just don't know how I can keep it up. Everywhere I go people expect me to speak, and they shake my hand until my arm aches, and I don't know how I can keep it up."

It's good to be with this choice and wonderful group. What a power you are, really. What tremendous capacity you have, actually, to change the lives of people. You do your very best. You work every day. You get up in the morning, and you keep at it, and when night falls you may say to yourself, "What in the world have I accomplished for all of this day?" But you keep going. And one here and another there listens to you, and lives are turned around. You never can foretell the consequences of that which you do when you teach somebody the gospel of Jesus Christ. It's marvelous and wonderful what happens.

I want to do my best, and I want you to do your best, whatever your calling or opportunity or challenge might be. When I say that you never can tell the consequences of your work, I think of when I was here. The Church was small and weak then. There wasn't a stake in all of Britain. There was not a ward in all of

Britain. There were 16 little districts with a handful of branches meeting in little run-down places.

I always remember the first Sunday that I was here. In those days we did the speaking in many of the meetings, and we went around circuits. I was in Preston, Lancashire, and I was sent to Accrington, I guess, or Burnley, I don't remember which, and I finally found the place. I don't know how I did it; I was a total stranger here. I went alone. We didn't always have to travel in pairs then. You do now, and that's good. But I found my way to the little branch meeting hall. It was an upstairs rented place. It was a lodge hall, and they cleaned up the cigarette butts and the beer bottles in the morning and had their meetings. The paper on the walls was peeling down where the roof leaked, and there we went to meetings. The branch president was a wonderful little man named Brother Dawson. He had a little black mustache, black hair, black beady eyes. I can still see him after all these 62 years. And he said this: "Brethren and sisters, I know this gospel's true. If I didn't know that, I wouldn't be here tonight. I'd be out enjoying myself."

That was my introduction as a missionary in England, although I arrived on a Thursday, I think, and went out to hold a street meeting that first evening. And that was a fearsome experience. But you get over those things. You get so you lay your fears aside and do what's expected of you.

It was tough. These were tough times—the bottom of the Depression. Men didn't wear white shirts in Lancashire in those days; they couldn't afford them, they were so terribly poor. They wore an old jacket with a kind of a wraparound thing that tied in a knot like a necktie, only it was about eight times as wide, and that's the way they came. They looked so mean and so tough, and they sounded so rough and mean also, but I soon came to know that they were great people with wonderful hearts. I couldn't understand their language in those days; they spoke the Lancashire dialect, just as strange as if it were French. But, as I say, we came to know their hearts. We were not there as tourists. We were in their homes, where we realized their goodness and their strength and their great intrinsic value. And we came to know something of the price that many of them paid in joining the Church, and we loved them for it.

I am going up to Lancashire on this trip to see how the temple is coming. Again, I'd like to take a little detour and go to Nelson and see old Bob Pickles again. He is as old as I am. He was in the branch in Nelson, a little struggling branch, and we went out together, working together. He is still alive. When I saw him at the temple groundbreaking, in a wheelchair, I went down into the congregation and took his hand. He cried, and I cried because of my great love for that man and his family, who through all of these 60 years and more have kept the faith. Wonderful, wonderful people I came to know. How thankful I am.

I hope you are grateful that you are in England. I hope that you feel that you have come to the best mission in all the world, because for you it is the best mission in all the world. I hope that you feel that you were called by inspiration, because you were. I hope that you know that the Lord called you. I hope that you know that people are praying for you. Every day throughout the world, wherever Latter-day Saints live, they remember the missionaries in their prayers. You can't do anything wrong, you can't do anything bad, you can't violate your trust, you can't let down your standards when you know that people all over the world are praying for you. I hope you never forget that—that wherever the sun rises and wherever the sun sets, people are praying for you. You must keep your standards high and keep the trust which is reposed in you. Otherwise, you disappoint not only yourselves, not only your parents, not only the Lord, you disappoint the whole Church; and I hope, therefore, that there isn't one here who isn't committed every day to doing his or her very best as you serve as a missionary in this great land among these good people.

In those days it was all one mission, and at one time the number of missionaries got down to 65 in all the British Isles. There are now about 1,300 of you scattered through eight missions.

Brother Charles A. Callis, who was a member of the Council of the Twelve years ago and who presided over the Southern States Mission for 25 years, told me that he had a missionary who came in to get his release, his last day's interview, and President Callis said, "What have you accomplished?"

And he said, "I haven't accomplished anything."

He said, "Haven't you baptized anyone while you've been here two years?"

And he said, "Just one boy, a 12-year-old boy in the back hollows of Tennessee who was so poor he didn't wear shoes or a tie or a shirt. Just a poor little tenant farmer boy in the back hollows of Tennessee."

Brother Callis said, "I was so intrigued by that missionary's feeling of failure that I decided to look that boy up the next time I went up into that area, and I found him. By then he had put on shoes. Something had happened. He came in a shirt and a tie. He was the clerk or secretary of the little branch Sunday School. I watched him through the years. He became the superintendent of the Sunday School. He became the president of the branch. He moved off that little tenant farm on which he and his parents and grandparents had lived and got a piece of ground of his own and made it productive. He became the district president. He finally sold his farm in Tennessee and bought a farm on the Snake River in Idaho and became a prosperous farmer. He married. He had children—sons. Those children married and had sons."

Brother Callis said, "I have just spent a week up in Idaho meeting with all the members of that family that I can find, and I have discovered that as a result of that one baptism by that missionary who came home thinking he had failed, more than 1,100 people have come into the Church."

289

Now, that's the effect of this thing. You baptize one here, another one there. Some of them drift away, unfortunately, and that's the greatest tragedy we have in the Church—the loss of those with whom you have worked so hard. But some stay, and they are active and strong and faithful, and the generations come after them, and miracles happen, and you're part of the beginning of the miracle in all of those odysseys of individuals and families who can be found across the world in this work.

I think I'd like to just take you through a little scripture. I'm going to read to you from some missionary letters, I think the two greatest missionary letters that I have ever read. They were written by Paul, who was probably the greatest missionary in testifying of the Lord Jesus Christ who walked the earth.

I'm going to start with 1 Timothy, the 4th chapter, the 14th verse: "Neglect not the gift that is in thee, which was given thee by prophecy, with the laying on of the hands of the presbytery." That's the way Timothy was called. He was called by the spirit of inspiration—prophecy—with the laying on of the hands of the presbytery. That's just the way you were called, my brethren and sisters, each of you—by prophecy, by inspiration, and then you were set apart by the laying on of hands. Who are the presbytery? The elders. Your stake president, in most cases, set you apart. You were called just as Timothy was called. As it was then, so is it now. Think of it. "Neglect not the gift that is in thee," which came with that call— the gift to teach the gospel of Jesus Christ as one ordained to that purpose. It's no small thing; it's a wonderful thing. "Meditate upon these things," said Paul to Timothy. "Give thyself wholly to them." You don't hold back; you give yourself entirely to this work. "Take heed unto thyself, and unto the doctrine; continue in them: for in doing this thou shalt both save thyself, and them that hear thee" (1 Timothy 4:15–16). Take heed unto thyself; look at yourself; meditate upon yourself. What are you doing with this time as a servant of the Lord?

Continuing, let there be constancy in all that you do. "In doing this thou shalt both save thyself, and them that hear thee." That's what happens. I could add a line to that: "and those who sent you," your families. I believe that every missionary who is diligent and faithful saves himself. Something happens to him. He's different when he goes home from when he comes out, not only physically but spiritually and mentally. "Thou shalt both save thyself, and them that hear thee"—those whom you teach, who will listen, and they may be few and far between, but they are precious, and we have to find them. And as I say, we could include your families who sent you. There are thousands upon thousands of cases in this Church where fathers have become active, where mothers' prayers have been heard concerning their husbands as a result of a missionary going into the field.

Years ago, when we didn't have as many cars in the states as missionaries have now, or in England, some parents were permitted to furnish cars to their sons. I was then in charge of the Missionary Department, and a man came in, a contractor, road builder, and said, "I have a son in California riding a bicycle, and he's going to get killed if he isn't careful. I'd like to take a car to him." And so permission was granted for him to take a car. He came back a week later, and he said, "Can I tell you what happened?"

He said, "I drove all the way to Los Angeles and found the place where he lived. It was about five or six in the afternoon. I knocked on the door. He came to the door, and he said, 'Gee, Dad, is that the car? Thanks. Can I have the keys?' " And his father handed him the keys, and he said, "We've got to go to a baptism. Why don't you go around the corner; there's a little restaurant. Get something to eat, and then come to the such and such meeting-house, and we'll have a baptismal service, and you can be there."

The father said, "This boy's mother died when he was a child. I married again. There was somehow a great chasm of difference that grew between us, and I said to myself as he took the keys, 'He's the same selfish boy he always was.' "

He said, "I thought I wouldn't go to the baptismal service; I'd go back home. And then I thought, 'Well, I'd better go.' So I went around and got something to eat and arrived at the service late. And they were having a testimony meeting, and those who had been baptized were giving their testimonies. And a man stood up and said, 'I am an old man, 75 years of age. I hold two university degrees. I have been a professional man. I've made good in the world. I thought I knew everything. And one day that young man and his companion knocked on my door. I invited them in because I didn't have anything else to do, and he told me things I had never heard before. Today I have literally been born again. I don't know who is responsible for his being in the mission field, but I'd like to thank whoever sent him. He has brought a new life to me.' And then he bore testimony of the gospel. And then a woman stood and bore her testimony similarly."

And the man who was telling me the story said, "They were talking about my son." He said, "I left there and threw away my cigarettes, and when I got home I threw out the coffeepot. I'm going to try to live worthy of my son." I saw that man in the Salt Lake Temple a year and a half later.

"Take heed unto thyself, and unto the doctrine; continue in them: for in doing this thou shalt both save thyself, and them that hear thee," and in so very many cases, those that sent thee. Think of it. Wonderful.

Chapter 6, 10th verse: "For the love of money is the root of all evil" (1 Timothy 6:10). That's kind of an interesting aside from Paul. We use that phrase a lot, and we don't know where it came from. "For the love of money is the root of all evil." It's the love of money. It's concentrating on that—or on things of the world while we are in the mission field instead of our work—that gives us problems. The Lord has said, "If your eye be single to my glory, your whole bodies shall be filled with light, and there shall be no darkness in you" (D&C 88:67). Think of it. "If your eye be single to my glory," you're not thinking of yourself, you're thinking of the Lord and His work, then "your whole body shall be filled with light, and there shall be no darkness in you." Gone will be the darkness of sin and temptation. Gone will be the darkness of laziness, and there will be a new light and a new life in your lives.

"The love of money is the root of all evil." The love of things. While you're on a mission, get them out of your minds. You don't need them. You don't need to take a lot of souvenirs home. They will cost less when you get there than they will here. Keep your mind on your work. I've seen missionaries go home loaded like Santa Claus. In fact, they could barely get on the plane, paying extra for the freight they carried home. Don't do it.

Twelfth verse: "Fight the good fight of faith, lay hold on eternal life" (1 Timothy 6:12).

The second epistle of Paul to Timothy, seventh verse of the first chapter: "For God hath not given us the spirit of fear; but of power, and of love, and of a sound mind. Be not thou therefore ashamed of the testimony of our Lord" (2 Timothy 1:7–8). Have you ever been frightened while you've been here? Dogs? People? Your companions? "For God hath not given us the spirit of fear." That comes from the adversary. That which comes from the Lord is power and love and a sound mind. Power—the power of your call, the power of your ministry, the power of the priesthood which you hold, the power of the message which you have to give. Love for the people, for the message, for the Lord. And of a sound mind. I think that refers simply to the simplicity of the gospel. It isn't all tangled up in mysteries. It's simple and straightforward and beautiful.

Sixteenth verse of the second chapter: "But shun profane and vain babblings: for they will increase unto more ungodliness" (2 Timothy 2:16). Don't be indulging in the kind of talk that tears you down. Be involved in the kind of talk that lifts and builds you up. It'll make all the difference in the world in the way you feel about the work. It's your attitude that makes the difference and the expression of that attitude.

Twenty-third verse: "But foolish and unlearned questions avoid, knowing that they do gender strifes" (2 Timothy 2:23). Don't get into arguments over doctrine.

And finally, these great words of Paul, fourth chapter, first verse: "I charge thee therefore before God, and the Lord Jesus Christ, . . . preach the word; be instant in season, out of season; reprove, rebuke, exhort with all longsuffering and doctrine" (2 Timothy 4:1–2). You just keep at it, and somehow, sometime there is a harvest that may be small but ever so important.

Paul concludes, "I am now ready to be offered." He knew that his death was coming. "And the time of my departure is at hand. I have fought a good fight, I have finished my course, I have kept the faith" (2 Timothy 4:6–7).

I hope that all of us, when the day of release comes from laboring in the London South Mission, can say, "I have fought a good fight, I have finished my course, I have kept the faith." If you do, you'll go on to fruitful lives. I have no question about that. Your future lies in the present, in the habits of work that you establish here, in your spirit of dedication, in your ambition to achieve something. As you do in the mission field, so you are likely to do all the rest of your lives.

I give you my testimony of this work. I know it's true. God is our Eternal Father. This is His plan that we are here to teach and explain. Jesus is the Christ, our Redeemer, our Example, whose gospel we are here to teach—the gospel of love and peace and forgiveness and kindness, of turning the other cheek, of lifting and helping and encouraging. The conversation which took place in the grove was as real and as intimate as is my conversation with you this day. I am sure of that. The priesthood is upon the earth, no question about it, with the sealing power, the only power on the face of the earth which reaches beyond the veil of death. The Lord is guiding this Church. I give you my testimony of that. I know it. I leave a blessing with you, my dear associates—a blessing that you will be happy, that you will see the fruits of your labors, that there will come into your hearts an unshakable witness of the truth. You'll have to keep feeding that all of your lives, but it will come here with an intensity that you have never known before. You will be able to say sometime, maybe, that that was not the easiest time of your life—no, it may have been the hardest, but it was the most fruitful time of your life.

I wish to tell you one story coming out of London, and then we'll go. We lived at 5 Gordon Square (the old building is gone) in London, and one night, one cold, rainy winter night, there came a knock on the door. I went to the door and let a young man in. I knew him. He was soaking wet. I invited him to come over to the fire. We had open fires then. He put his soggy hat down and sat down by the fire, and I said, "What's the matter? You're in trouble. What is the problem?" As I said, this was in the bottom of the Depression.

He said, "I'm licked. I don't know where to turn. I don't know what to do. When I joined the Church, my father told me to leave home and never come back as long as I was a Mormon. Then the athletic club of which I was a member, when they learned I was a Mormon, told me I was no longer welcome. And not long after that my boss fired me." And he said, "Last night the girl I love told me that she would never marry me because of my religion."

I said, "If this has cost you so much, why don't you leave? Why don't you go back to your father's home? Why don't you go back to your athletic club? Why don't you ask your boss for your old job? Why don't you marry that girl?"

He put his head down in his hands and sobbed and sobbed and sobbed. Finally he stood up, picked up his soggy old hat, looked me in the eye, and said, "I couldn't do that. I couldn't do it. I know it's true, and whatever it costs I'll know it's true."

He walked to the door. I walked behind him. He opened the door and stepped out into the rain. I watched him as he walked out under the gas lights and faded into the darkness. And I said to myself, "There is the strength of this Church. Not in buildings, not in the BYU campus, not in Temple Square, but in the hearts of the people, in the conviction that says it's true. It's true, come what may. It's true."

That's why people left England by the thousands and tens of thousands in the early days of the Church and went across the plains, some walking behind wagons and some towing carts. They paid a terrible, terrible price. I have dedicated four monuments in Wyoming where the Martin and Willie handcart companies were at various stations with terrible suffering and where hundreds literally died for this gospel. It's true. They knew it was true. You know it's true. I know it's true. May you be blessed of the Lord, I humbly pray, in the name of Jesus Christ, amen.

# VERACRUZ, MEXICO

# MISSIONARY MEETING

## JANUARY 27, 1996

YOU ARE SOMETHING TO LOOK AT. You're a miracle, you young men and young women who come out of the dusty towns of the United States and Mexico and go forth as ambassadors of the Lord Jesus Christ with authority to speak in His name, to call people to repentance, to teach the truths of the everlasting gospel, and to bring changes into their lives which will make them different from what they have ever been before. And as they listen to you and accept that which you have to offer, they set in motion a chain of events which goes on and on forever. You never can foretell the good you do when you teach the gospel to somebody as a missionary.

Let me tell you a little experience I had in Mexico some years ago. I came to speak at the graduation exercises at the school up out of Mexico City—Benemérito. And after the graduation exercise, all of the graduates were taken to a nice hotel, and most of those young men and women sat down in a beautiful dining room in a magnificent hotel for the first time in their lives. I was invited to be with them. I sat at a table with five of the graduates. Among those graduates was a young woman—a very fine, high-spirited girl. Then they had a dance that evening at the campus. I talked with the graduates who were there, and this young woman who had

been seated at our table brought to me her mother and her grandmother. There were three generations—the grandmother, the
mother, and the daughter—and I spoke with all three of them
because the young woman spoke English and she could interpret
for me.

The grandmother had been baptized many years earlier. She
had grown up in poverty—absolute, abject poverty. She was illiterate; she could neither read nor write, but she had come into the
Church, and others read to her the Book of Mormon, and she
loved its language. She joined the Church literally out in the bush.
Her daughter, the mother of this girl, was a little better educated.
She had gone to school for about three years, and then she had to
drop out to work to earn for the family. She could read and write a
little, but not very much. And then there was this daughter. Her
mother had done everything she could to help her daughter and
had shown her that education was the way of the future, and this
girl had gone to school and then come to Benemérito, where she
had graduated with honors.

I said, "What are you going to do now?"

She said, "I have received a scholarship, a full scholarship, to
the National University of Mexico medical school. I want to
become a doctor."

There I saw three women, and there I saw the miracle of
Mormonism in Mexico. It was a miracle, and we find it all over this
great land now. I don't know how long ago it was that I first came
to Mexico, but it was many years ago, and for the most part the
people were poor, with little opportunity for education, struggling,
really, to stay alive. And then I came down to dedicate the Mexico
City Temple, and the Saints had gathered from all over the nation.
I was inside the temple in the temple president's office, and I could
look out the window at the people who were lined up to come into
the temple, but they couldn't see me. Everyone was clean, bright-
looking, polished, a card in one hand and a handkerchief in the

other, to come to the house of the Lord and participate in the dedication of that sacred temple. That, to me, is the miracle of Mormonism in Mexico.

We had a priesthood leadership meeting earlier this afternoon. I was here in 1978 in Veracruz for a stake conference, and it was a small, struggling stake. Now, 18 years later, I saw every seat in this hall occupied by a man who holds the priesthood, who has been called to a position of leadership. That is the miracle of Mormonism in Mexico. It is as real as anything on this earth.

Now you are a part of it. You are a part of this great miracle. I want you to get excited about it. This is the greatest day of your lives. This is your time of rich and wonderful opportunity. For you sisters it will only last 18 months. For you brethren it will only last 24 months. Don't waste your opportunities. Put a smile on your face. Smile a little. You look so gloomy. Smile. You look better when you smile. Put a smile on your faces and a prayer in your hearts, and go out and stand tall and teach the gospel of Jesus Christ. There will never be another opportunity for you like this. There just never will! Some of you might become mission presidents at some time in the future, but that won't be the same.

Well, we're all in this together. I want you to know that. I have a responsibility, and you have a responsibility. We each have a responsibility, and I come back to this thought: you never can foretell the consequences of what you do as a missionary. I was riding a plane a few years ago from London to New York. I got into a conversation with a man and woman from England, and as a result of that little conversation, the mother and the three sons have joined the Church. Every one of those boys has been married in the temple. Those boys have now had sons of their own go on missions, and that conversation which I had on a plane will go on bearing fruit generation after generation after generation, like those three Mexican women of whom I have spoken to you—a grandmother, her daughter, her granddaughter. You never can foretell the good you do when you become the means of bringing into the heart of a man or woman a testimony of the living reality of the Lord Jesus Christ.

Now, I just want to leave you with a word or two of scripture from section 112 in the Doctrine and Covenants. This is a revelation which was given to Thomas B. Marsh, who was then the President of the Council of the Twelve Apostles. Brother Marsh, as some of you students of Church history may know, occupied that very high and wonderful responsibility as President of the Twelve, but his wife got in an argument with another woman over something of no consequence. He defended his wife, one thing led to another, and before long he had lost his faith and was out of the Church. But what the Lord said to Thomas B. Marsh in 1837 applies to you and me in 1996. Verse 5: "Contend thou, therefore, morning by morning; and day after day let thy warning voice go forth; and when the night cometh let not the inhabitants of the earth slumber, because of thy speech [or lack of speech]."

Verse 10: "Be thou humble; and the Lord thy God shall lead thee by the hand, and give thee answer to thy prayers." That's one of the great promises in this sacred book. It's one of the great promises in all sacred literature. "Be thou humble; and the Lord thy God shall lead thee by the hand, and give thee answer to thy prayers."

Well, verse 33: "Verily I say unto you, behold how great is your calling. Cleanse your hearts and your garments, lest the blood of this generation be required at your hands." What a great charge that is.

Let's go back to the 28th verse: "But purify your hearts before me; and then go ye into all the world, and preach my gospel unto every creature who has not received it."

"And he that believeth and is baptized shall be saved, and he that believeth not, and is not baptized, shall be damned" (v. 29).

That's the word of the Lord, my brethren and sisters, to you and to me.

Now, thank you, each of you. I mean that. Thank you for the faith to come here, for the willingness to go where you were called, for your obedience in accepting your call, for the effort you put into your preparation in the MTC, and for your devoted service.

One word in parting to you who are going home. Each of you is a part of the miracle that is Mormonism in Mexico. Never forget it. Never forget it. Keep the faith. Don't forget that "I was once a missionary in the Veracruz mission, where I was a servant of the Lord who bore testimony of His living reality." Remind yourselves of that periodically. Read the Book of Mormon the rest of your lives. Read it every two years, at least, in Spanish—in Spanish, the beautiful, musical language called Spanish. Read the Book of Mormon in Spanish the rest of your lives.

God bless you, my beloved associates. I do love you. I want you to know that. I know it isn't easy. It's discouraging at times, sure. Aren't you glad it isn't just all fun all the time? Those valleys of discouragement make more beautiful the peaks of achievement. We love you. God bless you, I pray, in the name of Jesus Christ, amen.

# Honolulu, Hawaii

# Missionary Meeting

FEBRUARY 17, 1996

How very nice to be with you. Wonderful to see these couples here. It is really good to be here, isn't it? Aren't you glad you are in Hawaii and not at home shoveling snow? Really, my compliments to you and my appreciation for what you are doing. I know it is not easy to pull up roots at your age and come to Hawaii and serve missions. Thank you for your faithful and devoted service and for your willingness to be here. You do so very, very much good—so very much good. Thank you again. Thanks to each of you. You look like missionaries look everywhere. You can tell how long a missionary has been in the field by his shirt collar—how often it has been washed by him, how long it has been since it has seen an iron with some starch on it. It is all right. You are not here to dress like a fashion plate. You are here to preach the gospel, and that is wonderful.

In 1960, that is 36 years ago, I was given the assignment of having responsibility for the work here in the Hawaiian Islands and all of Asia. I had that for eight years. And so I tramped over the back roads of this part of the world when there were fewer people living here on Oahu, Kauai, Molokai, and Maui, the big island, and even Lanai, and I knew this part of the world very well. And I was in Japan, from Hokkaido on the north to Fukuoka on the south;

302

and in Korea, from Seoul down to Pusan; and in Taiwan and Hong Kong; and in other places—Vietnam, India, Indonesia, Malaysia, Singapore, you name it. For eight years I tramped over that part of the earth. And then I had responsibility in South America when Brother Scott was a mission president there, and that is when I came to know and appreciate him. His daughter, who is with him today, was a little girl, and now she is the mother of five children. Then I had Europe and then back to Asia for another three years. So none of this part of the world looks strange to me.

Oh, how we worked in those days. I remember coming and dedicating two buildings in Japan and a building in Hawaii all on the same Sunday because of crossing the date line, and we were so tired that I was sitting on the stand trying to make a note of what to talk about and I was awakened by the noise of my pen dropping on the floor. But those are days past. But I have not lost my love for the missionaries of this Church.

You are such an asset to this Church. Think of what it would be without the missionary program. It would stagnate, I think. It is your work and the infusion of new blood that constantly goes on that adds strength to the work and brings cultural diversity to it and brings into it new life. You are part of that wonderful process of bringing people into the Church. There were 304,000 convert baptisms last year in the Church. That is the equivalent of 100 new stakes of 3,000 members each in a single year. Think of it. Think of what you are a part of—this great process of bringing in new blood, converts to The Church of Jesus Christ of Latter-day Saints, blessing their lives as you bless your own in this service.

I am not too worried about how many baptisms you have, whether it is 1 or 100. My only concern is that you give your very best effort to the work. And whether it be 1 or 100, it is wonderful. Every one is precious in the eyes of the Lord, and every one is precious as a new member of this Church. Thank you for your work, for your service. What a tremendous job you do. This is one of the great miracles of the earth, really, when all is said and done, this missionary program, with nearly 50,000 of you out giving your full time to the work of the Lord—every one called by the spirit of revelation and prophecy and set apart with the laying on of hands to go out and serve as an ambassador of the Lord Jesus Christ, bearing testimony of His divinity and reality to an unbelieving world. God bless you, my dear associates, in this great and sacred work.

I know you get tired. I know you get discouraged sometimes. I know you once in a while get sick. In the early days I went down to Pusan. We were to have a big conference in Pusan, and we had a little hall there where the man who is now president of the temple was district president. We set all the chairs out on Saturday night, and when we got there Sunday morning they were all gone. Some thief had stolen all the chairs in the night. There we were without a place to sit, with a meeting called. That is one of my experiences in Pusan. I could tell you some others, but I better not.

Well, anyway, I love this part of the world. It is a part of my life. I love Asia. It is part of my life. I am going there again in May to dedicate the Hong Kong Temple, and we are going also to hold meetings in Japan and Korea and Taiwan and maybe go to the Philippines. I hope it will all be in the missionary spirit.

This is the only time of your lives, unless you become a mission president, when you will be able to give all your time without reservation of any kind to the work of the Lord. Never again will you have such an opportunity as you have now to give without selfishness your total time. You do not have any family to worry about. You do not have money to worry about. You do not have girlfriends to worry about or boyfriends to worry about—no romancing in the mission field. You did not come to get a husband or to get a wife; you came to serve the Lord. Eat it up. Live it. Love it. Make the most of it. It is a tremendous opportunity for you.

I agreed to an interview with Mike Wallace of CBS's *60 Minutes*. He came to Salt Lake City. We went out to a gathering of missionaries such as this. He has been at this job for 39 years. He sat right on the front row, with a camera crew taking note of everything. Sister Hinckley spoke, and then I spoke. We had a closing song; I think it was "Called to Serve" (*Hymns*, no. 249). The missionary next to Mike Wallace handed him the hymnbook. And there he was, singing "Called to Serve" with the rest of the missionaries—this Jewish man sitting on the front row between missionaries, singing "Called to Serve." I don't suppose they will show that footage on the air, but nevertheless it was taken.

And then after that, he wanted to meet with half a dozen missionaries in a quiet setting. So we went out of the chapel, and he talked with them. He said to one of the elders, "Why are you here?" And the young man said, "I am here to teach the gospel of Jesus Christ." And Mike is a Jew, as I say, and the missionary said that without any hesitation or equivocation. Then he asked a young man why he had interrupted his schooling for two years to go out and knock on doors in Salt Lake City—he came from some other place in the country. And this young man said, "I am here to bring happiness into the lives of people, to help them turn around their lives and bring some happiness into their lives through learning the beautiful gospel of Jesus Christ." I think that says it all. I do not know what Mike's feelings are, but he did say this to me: "The whole world should know about this." He was tremendously impressed when he met with that group of missionaries, which had in its membership some people from Asia, three or four from Europe and from other parts of the world.

Well, brothers and sisters, it is just nice to see you. You look so good—wholesome, wonderful young men and women and these good older couples. Thanks for your effort. Thanks for your faith. Thanks for your devotion. You are making a sacrifice, but it is not a sacrifice, because you will get more than you give up. You will gain more than you give, and it will prove to be an investment with tremendous returns. It will prove to be a blessing instead of a sacrifice. No one who ever served in this work as a missionary who gave his or her best efforts need worry about making a sacrifice, because there will come blessings into the life of that individual for as long as he or she lives. I have not the slightest doubt about that. You belong to this great Church, which you are teaching the world to honor and respect and accept. It is the work of the Lord. There is nothing like it on the face of the whole earth.

We had a meeting this afternoon with about 700 priesthood leaders over in the Cannon Center of the university. What an inspiration to look into their faces, many of them converts to the Church, and see what it does for people. We were in Mexico three weeks ago, in Veracruz, and to look into the faces of those wonderful people there was an inspiration. And as you know, you can go to Korea and see the wonderful Saints there. You can go to Taiwan, and there are wonderful Saints there. The Church is moving out across the earth. Fifty years ago most of the membership of the Church lived in Utah—55 percent I think the figure is. Today only 17 percent live in Utah. We are crossing this month the line dividing Church membership in the United States and other parts of the world. After this month there will be more Latter-day Saints outside the United States than in the United States. It says something. We are in more than 150 nations.

The spread of the Book of Mormon is a miracle. When you think of what Joseph Smith and Martin Harris must have thought when they saw that first edition of the Book of Mormon coming off the press, to think that someday, in our time, the distribution of that book will have reached a figure of 70 to 80 million. Things are happening. You walk your little trail each day, and you do not have the great vision of this work, perhaps, because you are a small part of it—but a very important part of it. When you see the overall picture of what is happening, 100 new stakes created last year through the efforts of such as you, it is a miracle.

The Lord bless you. I leave my blessing on you that you may be happy and effective in your work, that you may serve with love and appreciation and respect for your companions with whom you are called to serve. Gain strength from your companions. Look for the virtues in their lives, and bring them into your own life, and you will be enriched and blessed. May you be happy in your work. May you go forward in faith. May you be watched over and protected by the power of the Lord from accident or harm or trouble, which you may be if you are discreet and careful and prudent. May you enjoy life, and may you in your letters to your loved ones impart faith and enthusiasm for the work, that those at home may share in the great things that happen to you here in the field. Whenever you get a favorable response, whenever you get a convert, those at home rejoice over it as well as do you.

The Lord bless you. This is a very cosmopolitan group. You come from all over, from many parts of the world, and that in itself is an expression of the depth and the breadth and the wonder of this great work. God bless you. Please know that we love you. We pray for you. We know that you pray for us, and we appreciate that. We pray for you. I do not think there is ever a prayer that we have as the Presidency and the Twelve in the temple that the missionaries are not remembered. People all over the Church are remembering you and praying for you. Do not ever forget that. And if you are ever tempted to move off into any evil path, just remember there are thousands upon thousands of people who are praying for you that you might be safeguarded and looked after.

How blessed you are to have this great mission president and his beloved companion. These are good people. I have known them for a long time. They love the Lord and His work, and they love you; and you can have total confidence in them, and you will appreciate them as long as you live if you will follow their counsel and advice.

God bless you. I know this work is true. You know it is true. I know that God lives. You know that He lives. I know that Jesus is the Christ, and you know that. I know that Joseph Smith was a prophet, and you know that. I know the Book of Mormon is true, and you know that, and we share our testimonies one with another. Out of that comes a great strength, for which I pray in your behalf in the name of Jesus Christ, amen.

# YOUNG ADULT FIRESIDE

MARCH 24, 1996

W ELL, HOW NICE TO BE WITH YOU; how wonderful to be with you. You're quite a picture, really, 1,350 of you here this evening—think of that—gathered from all over this San Diego area. Last night we had 1,100 in this hall—young people younger than you—and before that we were in the Vista stake center, where there were some 2,000 young people. We didn't come here to hold these meetings; we are here on another assignment, but I said, "Let's speak with the young people. Let's have a meeting with those great young people down in San Diego."

How many of you are returned missionaries? Look at that! Isn't that wonderful! All of these returned missionaries. How many of you are in school? Wonderful! You're smart; you're bright; you're good. You're better than you think you are, really. Do you know that? Yes, you are. You're great.

You're sons and daughters of God. You have such a tremendous potential for good. You have your heads on straight, and so many people in this world don't have their heads on straight. You know what life is for, what it's about—that you're part of an eternal plan, that you lived with purpose before you came to this life, that this life is a mission and not just a career, and that you will step over the veil someday and keep on going and growing. I don't know of

309

anybody in the world who has the concept of the meaning of life that we have as a result of the Restoration of the gospel of Jesus Christ.

I think I'd like to speak to a theme for a few minutes. I take it from the Gospel of John. You remember that when the resurrected Lord appeared to the Twelve, Thomas was absent. When the others told Thomas that the Lord had appeared to them, he said, "Except I shall see in his hands the print of the nails, . . . and thrust my hand into his side, I will not believe." Eight days later the Twelve were assembled again, and Thomas was present. And the Lord said to Thomas, "Reach hither thy finger, and behold my hands; and reach hither thy hand, and thrust it into my side: and be not faithless, but believing." And Thomas stepped forward and felt, and he said, "My Lord and my God." And Jesus said, "Because thou hast seen me, thou hast believed: blessed are they that have not seen, and yet have believed" (see John 20:25–29).

"Be not faithless, but believing." I'd like to leave that one line with you tonight. "Be not faithless, but believing." Believe in yourselves. Believe in your capacity to do some good in this world. God sent us here for a purpose, and that was to improve the world in which we live. The wonderful thing is that we can do it. That brings with it the opportunity and the challenge to educate our minds and our hands. I congratulate you—every one of you who is trying to do that. I know of your problems as young people. I know you worry. I know you're concerned. You worry what kind of a job you're going to get. You worry what your major should be in school. You worry whether you're going to make it. You're worried about who you're going to marry, where you're going to live, all of those things. You worry about money and nearly everything else, don't you? These are days of worry and concern for you. But they are days of such tremendous opportunity.

"Be not faithless, but believing." Trust in the Lord. Pray about it. Ask for His help and His direction. He has said, "Ask, and it shall be given you; seek, and ye shall find; knock, and it shall be opened unto you" (Matthew 7:7). I believe that! With all my heart, I believe that. "Be not faithless, but believing" in your capacity to do good things.

I met today a woman who is a cousin of Rex Lee. Rex Lee, as some of you know, was president of Brigham Young University. He died, and I spoke at his funeral a week ago Friday. He came out of a little rural town in Arizona—St. Johns. He went on a mission to Mexico and walked among the poor of that land and learned to appreciate them. He went to BYU, then to law school at the University of Chicago. He had a brilliant mind. He was appointed solicitor general of the United States—that is in some respects the top lawyer of the nation—and argued 59 cases before the Supreme Court, more than any other lawyer in the land—a little, thin, scrawny, sort of a pale-faced kid out of St. Johns, Arizona. You have it in your capacity to do great and good things. Seek the Lord. Live according to His pattern.

People ask me what is my favorite scripture. I tell them I have a number of them. One of them is this great statement found in the 50th section of the Doctrine and Covenants: "That which is of God is light; and he that receiveth light, and continueth in God, receiveth more light; and that light groweth brighter and brighter until the perfect day" (D&C 50:24). That, to me, is a great, basic, marvelous, wonderful truth. "That which is of God is light; and he that receiveth light, and continueth in God, receiveth more light; and that light groweth brighter and brighter until the perfect day." "Be not faithless, but believing" in your capacity to grow and grow and grow. What wonderful potential you have. Do it in the right way.

Some of you are in love. Most of you ought to be, at your age. We've been to the San Diego Temple today, as Brother Haight has said. What a magnificently beautiful building that is. But with all the beauty of that building, that structure is only a means to an end

311

and not an end in itself. That facility was erected and dedicated for the performance of the sacred ordinances which the Lord has revealed in this time, and among those sacred ordinances is that of marriage for time and all eternity. There is nothing like it elsewhere in all the world. And I hope, as you look to marriage, you'll make a decision in your lives from which you will not deviate: that you will be married in the house of the Lord. And I hope you young men who are married will treat your wives as companions. You are equals. We do not believe that the man walks ahead of the woman nor behind her but that they walk side by side as equals.

The saddest duty I have, really, when all is said and done, is judging the cases that come before us of people who want a cancellation of their temple sealings because they haven't made it. Do you know why? In nearly every case it's selfishness. It's thinking only of themselves instead of the well-being of their companions. Marriage, I've concluded, isn't so much a matter of romance as it is a matter of an anxious concern for the comfort and well-being of one's companion. When you plan on marriage, you plan on putting your companion's comfort and well-being first, ahead of yours; and if you do, you'll be happy. If you don't, you'll wish you had done it. I just want to say that to you. Believe in yourselves, in your capacity to make people happy and do the right thing.

Believe in your associates. Believe in your companions. Believe in others. Don't go around tearing people down. The Lord doesn't want that. He doesn't want us to spend our time destroying others. He expects us to build and sustain and cultivate and nurture and strengthen our associates. Wonderful things happen when you go forth with that kind of attitude.

Believe in the Church. Cling to the Church. We have a few people in the Church who wear out their lives trying to find some fault with it. There are a few of them, at least, and the media pay attention to them. I have had interviews with Mike Wallace, who is regarded as the meanest reporter on the air. I asked him what kind of a coach he had to make himself look so mean. He said when he got through interviewing me he went to talk to the dissidents, and then he talked again with me. I said, "Mike, look at them. How many are there, in this Church of 9 million plus? I could name a half-dozen. Suppose there are 100; suppose there are 500. That's still a very small statistical percentage. Get the big picture. Look at what this Church is doing across the world. Look at what it's accomplishing in touching the lives of people for good. Miracles are happening. Fifty thousand missionaries are out lifting people, helping them to become all that they can possibly be as sons and daughters of God." Get the big picture. "Be not faithless, but believing" in The Church of Jesus Christ of Latter-day Saints.

I want to make you a promise. I know it's true. The Lord will never let the General Authorities of this Church lead it astray. It won't happen. The President of the Church will not be permitted by the Lord to lead this people astray. This is the Lord's Church, and He has the capacity and the power and the right and the authority to lift any of us out of the way. It won't happen. We have a Presidency of three; we have a Council of Twelve Apostles. We meet together in the temple every Thursday. We pray together. We discuss together. We seek the inspiration of the Almighty, and it's my testimony that it comes. Somebody said to Brother Widtsoe once, years ago, "When will we have more revelation in the Church? It's been a long time since we've had a revelation. How long has it been?" And Brother Widtsoe replied, "Oh, about last Thursday." Now, you won't find it in the Doctrine and Covenants, but it's there. I want to give you that assurance, my dear young friends: the Church will not be led astray, nor will its people be led astray. The Lord has said that He has set up His work for the last time. This is the great winding-up period, as it were. I do not know when the windup is going to happen. I have no idea. I do know this—that the Lord is guiding this Church.

"Be not faithless, but believing," my dearly beloved friends. Believe in God as your Eternal Father in Heaven, to whom you can go in prayer. Now, as Sister Hinckley said, He will answer you. Maybe not the way you wish Him to, but He will answer in His time and in His way. "If any of you lack wisdom, let him ask of God, that giveth to all men liberally, and upbraideth not; and it shall be given him. But let him ask in faith, nothing wavering. For he that wavereth is like a wave of the sea driven with the wind and tossed" (James 1:5–6). God hears and answers prayers. I want you to know that. I know it. And I believe that you know. I am confident that you know it.

"Be not faithless, but believing." Believe in the Lord Jesus Christ, the Savior and the Redeemer of the world. We wouldn't be here tonight but for Him. Of course we wouldn't. He is the cornerstone of our faith. He is the keystone in the structure of our faith. He is the Son of the living God—the living Son of the living God. He is our Redeemer, who gave His life on Calvary's hill for each of us. None of us fully understands the Atonement. I think it's beyond the comprehension of any man, but we know something of it, and we know that as a result of it, all will be resurrected from the grave and those who walk in obedience to His commandments will be given the opportunity of going on to eternal exaltation. Nothing can compare with that, when all is said and done. All of us are going to die someday, but that won't be the end. We'll go on living because Christ broke the bands of death for each of us.

"Be not faithless, but believing." Believe in the innate goodness of people. There are wonderful people everywhere. There are other good lands. You know that, and I know that—wonderful people, wonderful members of this Church. In May we are going to dedicate the temple in Hong Kong. Before we get to Hong Kong we are going to Tokyo for some meetings and then to Kyoto; and then to Fukuoka; and then down to Naha, Okinawa; and then over to Pusan, Korea; and then up to Seoul; and then down to Taipei,

Taiwan; and then to Hong Kong; and then to Hanoi; and then to Ho Chi Minh City; and then to Manila and Cebu City in the Philippines—18 very busy days, one after another in a row, with meetings every day. I am going to meet with the people I love in that part of the world. I had responsibility for the work in Asia for 11 years altogether. I have in my heart a great feeling of appreciation and respect and love for the people of Japan and Korea and Taiwan and the Philippines and Hong Kong and Malaysia and Vietnam and Singapore and Jakarta, Indonesia. There are good people everywhere. I spent a lot of time in that part of the world, and I love the members of the Church in that part of the world.

I had two letters a day or two ago, one from a young woman about 20 years of age whose parents have left the Church and split up in a divorce. She wrote a very plaintive, sad letter saying, "What am I to do? I love the Lord. I love the Church. I know it's true, but I am just torn apart. I don't know what to do." My heart wept for her as I read that letter. And another one from a man who said, "We're off in a little branch way out in the wilderness, as it were, and we're poor, and we're broke, and conditions are hard and difficult. Won't you come and visit us and cheer us up a little?" And my heart reached out to those people. I love the people of this Church.

I love, in a particular way, the young people of this Church. You beautiful young women, you are beautiful. Cultivate that beauty, and be happy with that which the Lord has given you. And you handsome, strong young men, thank you for your faith. Go forward with your lives. Do the right thing. Live the gospel. "Choose the right when a choice is placed before you" (*Hymns*, no. 239).

You believe in prayer—pray. Another of my favorite scriptures is in the 112th section of the Doctrine and Covenants, the 10th verse, in a revelation which the Lord gave to Thomas B. Marsh, the President of the Twelve. What He said to the Twelve in those days applies to us—you and me. Said He, "Be thou humble; and the

Lord thy God shall lead thee by the hand, and give thee answer to thy prayers."

You can't make it alone. You can't do it with arrogance. You can't do it with egotism. You need a higher power. "Be thou humble; and the Lord thy God shall lead thee by the hand, and give thee answer to thy prayers."

"Be not faithless, but believing." When I went on a mission, a long time ago—62 years ago—my father said, "I want to give you just one verse of scripture to take with you." And he sat down and wrote out on a card these words from the book of Mark: "Be not afraid, only believe" (Mark 5:36).

God bless you. We do love you. We leave our testimony with you. Thank you for your faith. Thank you for your virtue. If you have stumbled somewhere along the line, I want to say this to you: don't quit; don't give up. Look to the Lord for forgiveness. Go to your bishop if it's serious. Talk with him in confidence. He will keep your confidence. Straighten up, and go forward with your life, basking in the light of the gospel. "Be not afraid, only believe." "Be not faithless, but believing."

I pray for you. I leave my blessing with you in the name of Jesus Christ, amen.

# DENVER, COLORADO

# STAKE YOUTH MEETING

### APRIL 14, 1996

T HIS MORNING WE FLEW TO Colorado Springs and there met in a chapel filled with young people. Then we came up here to Denver and had another meeting with other people, and now we are here meeting with you. And we will finish here, and then at 7:00 we will be in another meeting in the Willow Creek stake building. It is just that I like to be with you. We are not talking to your parents here on this occasion.

How many of you have "Choose the Right" rings? How many of you wear them? Some of you do. CTR—choose the right. Have you ever watched a big farm gate on one of these Colorado ranches when it opens? If you look at the hinge, you can scarcely see any movement. But if you look out at the perimeter, there is a great deal of movement. That is the way it is with our lives. A little thing that we do here has tremendous influence out here. "Choose the right when a choice is placed before you" (*Hymns,* no. 239). That is the way people become alcoholics. They start with one little drink that they say will not hurt them—a can of beer, maybe—or go on a beer bust at high school graduation. Every man who became an alcoholic, every man who became a drunkard started with a first drink. First drink—that little bit of imperceptible movement that had its effect later.

It is the same with drugs. I hope nobody here is on drugs. I hope no one here takes illegal drugs. How foolish can you be to take illegal drugs, really? They do not help you in any way. They hurt you. They make the dealers rich. They make you poor and weak. They shorten your life. They take away your control of yourself. What a crazy thing to do, really, when all is said and done. I hope never, never, never would one of you participate in partaking of illegal drugs, not one of you. Now, if you have done it, get hold of yourself, get control of yourself. Stop it, and seek help. Get them behind you. You must do so; it is so very, very important that you do so.

The Lord has blessed us with these wonderful bodies, these wonderful minds, these things with which we think. What a marvelous thing is a human mind. How wonderful it is. I put a record on my phonograph the other evening—one of Beethoven's concertos. I do not know anything about Beethoven—how big he was, how tall he was, how fat he was, how thin he was. But I know that out of the genius of that mind came something really tremendous and wonderful. The human mind—what it can do! Your minds—don't cloud them with drugs. It is tragic to see people who get themselves in that kind of situation.

The Lord makes a great statement to your parents; it is given in the words of Isaiah and was repeated by the Savior when He was on the American continent. Said Isaiah, "All thy children shall be taught of the Lord." That is the commandment, and this is the promise: "And great shall be the peace of thy children" (Isaiah 54:13; 3 Nephi 22:13). Now, you are in high school. You see those who use illegal drugs. You know they do not have any peace, do they? They are torn. Where they are going to get the next shot is what they worry about. It takes all their money, and before long they are stealing and doing this, that, and the other to try to satisfy their terrible appetite.

You are members of The Church of Jesus Christ of Latter-day Saints. You are children of a noble birthright. You have a special place in the plan of the Lord because you have accepted the gospel, you have been baptized, you partake of the sacrament. You impose upon yourselves each Sunday a renewal of your pledge and covenant to take upon yourselves the name of the Lord Jesus Christ. Did you ever think of that, of how important that is, of what it means to take upon yourselves the name of the Lord Jesus Christ with a pledge and a promise to keep His commandments? And He makes a pledge and a promise to you that He will give you His Spirit to be with you. What a wonderful thing that is.

You are in school. I guess you are all A students, every one of you. Good. I am going to give you some B's. We will let your teachers give you A's, and I am going to give you some B's tonight. Be grateful. Be smart. Be true. Be clean. Be humble. Be prayerful.

Be grateful and thankful. Sister Hinckley spoke to you about how grateful she is. This is what the Lord says to you: "Thou shalt thank the Lord thy God in all things. . . . And in nothing doth man offend God, or against none is his wrath kindled, save those who confess not his hand in all things" (D&C 59:7, 21). Have you ever stopped to think of the wonderful time in which you live and the wonderful land in which you live? This is a good land of which you are a part. How thankful you ought to be for this land, my dear brothers and sisters, and how thankful you ought to feel that you are born in this time. There never was a time like this time. You may think things are tough, and they are, but they are not anything like as tough as they once were. Think of all the blessings that you have. When we pulled up here tonight, I looked at all the automobiles parked around this building. Many of you drove here and have cars to drive. Think of that.

Think of the blessings you have in the way of medicine, health, and strength. When I was born, the average life expectancy in America was 50 years. Today it is more than 75 years. In the brief time that I have been upon the earth, the life of man in this country and western Europe has been extended from 50 years to 75 years. Think of it. What a marvelous age in which we live. We are free from diseases, so many of them. I have a list of all of those who died and are buried in one of the old cemeteries in Nauvoo. I spent a day looking through that list, and I found that so many children died of pertussis, of whooping cough. That does not happen now. Little Johnny—pertussis. Little Mary died such and such a day from a terrible cough. How blessed we are. I read an article just yesterday concerning smallpox. Once smallpox raged over the earth. You do not know what it is today; you do not hear about it. People died. Most of the people who did not die were left with terribly disfigured faces. Now smallpox has been eradicated from the earth. It is a miracle.

This is a great age. Be thankful for the age in which you live, and above all be thankful for this precious thing that you have, which is The Church of Jesus Christ of Latter-day Saints, of which you are members. The friends you have with you tonight, your associates, your Church friends—isn't it wonderful? Think of the blessings of the gospel. Think of the understanding you have. I read last night an article entitled "Who Is Jesus?" in a national magazine, and there various learned men, all ministers and priests, spoke concerning their interpretation of Jesus, trying to rationalize this and this and this. Was He real? Did He actually live? Did the miracles occur? They were rationalizing this, that, and the other. You do not have to worry about that. You have the testimony of the Bible, yes, and you have the testimony of the Book of Mormon, and you have the testimony of the Prophet Joseph Smith, and you have a testimony which comes into your hearts by the power of the Holy Ghost.

You know that Christ lived, don't you, every one of you? Is there anyone here who doesn't know that? Of course you know, and what a marvelous blessing to know that He died for us. He was the greatest of all. No other man who ever walked the earth was perfect except the Son of God, and we hold Him up as our great example. We learn about Him in Sunday School and in seminary and in family home evening and in all of the other opportunities that you have. Be thankful for that testimony which you carry in your hearts.

Be smart. You are all in school. Do not waste your time. This is a time of great opportunity that you will never have again as long as you live. Make the most of it right now. It is wonderfully challenging. It is hard, it is tough, isn't it? But what a wonderful thing to go and learn of all the accumulated knowledge of all of the centuries of time. Go on to college or whatever school, vocational school, whatever your choice is, but take advantage of every opportunity that you have because the Lord has laid upon you a mandate through revelation to the Prophet Joseph Smith concerning not only spiritual learning but secular learning. Yours is the responsibility, and you can't afford to waste your time. There is so much to learn. Be smart. Give it the very best that you have.

Be true. Be true to the promise that you make every Sunday when you go to sacrament meeting and partake of the sacrament. Do you know that when the priest who is at the sacrament table pronounces that prayer which was given by revelation, he places all of the congregation under covenant with the Lord? That is so very, very important. Think of the meaning of the sacrament every time you partake of the sacrament, and be true—true to the faith. You have sung this song: "True to the faith that our parents have cherished, true to the truth for which martyrs have perished" (*Hymns*, no. 254). People have died for the faith that is yours. Their graves are scattered all the way from the Mississippi on the east to the valley of the Great Salt Lake on the west as testimonies of their conviction concerning this work, that they actually regarded this sacred work as of greater importance than their very lives.

Be clean. Be clean in thought. Do not use filthy language. There is so much filthy language that is used by high school students, isn't there? Everywhere you run into it, isn't that so? Filthy, dirty language. Do not use it. You are members of The Church of Jesus Christ of Latter-day Saints. You cannot afford to use filthy language. The Lord expects something more of you than that. Stand above it. When you use filthy language, it says that you do not have vocabulary enough to express yourself without reaching down into the gutter for words. Do not use filthy language. The Lord does not like that, and whatever you do, do not use His name in vain. He said, when Jehovah's finger wrote upon the tablets of stone: "Thou shalt not take the name of the Lord thy God in vain; for the Lord will not hold him guiltless that taketh his name in vain" (Exodus 20:7). Do not take the name of the Lord in vain. Never, never, never.

I have told this story before, which I heard from President Kimball. When he was very sick he was coming out of an operation, and they placed him on a gurney to take him to the intensive care room. The young man who was wheeling the gurney hit the corner of the elevator and let out an oath, using the Lord's name in vain. President Kimball, who was barely conscious, said, "Please, please, you are talking of my friend." The young man said, "I'm sorry." Do not take the name of the Lord in vain.

You boys hold the priesthood. You girls have obligations likewise as members of this Church. Be clean in thought and in word and in deed. Now, I know that there is a lot of immorality that goes on in high schools also. You cannot afford to get mixed up in that. Do not ever get the idea, you girls, that it would be fun to have a baby without a husband. It won't be. It will not be fun. It will be a burden difficult to carry. The Lord has set forth the right plan concerning marriage in His holy house. Live for that so that you will be worthy of it, so that someday you can go to your bishop and look him in the eye when he asks you questions and tell him that you are clean and worthy to go to the house of the Lord. You will be happy all the days of your lives if you will do that.

Now, I want to add a postscript to that. If any of you have slipped, repent. Talk to your parents if you can. Talk to your mother; she is your best friend. She is the one who gave you life. She is the one who has cared for you, prayed about you. Talk to your bishop. He will keep confidential what you say. There is a way back so that you can get straight again. You do not need to hesitate to do it. You can start over, as it were. It may not be quite the same as it would have been otherwise, but it can be wonderful.

Be clean. "Let virtue garnish thy thoughts unceasingly," said the Lord (see D&C 121:45). You will not have trouble if you do not think of those things. Be clean. I cannot emphasize that enough. Be clean. It is so very, very important, and you at your age are in such temptation all the time. It is thrown at you on television. It is thrown at you in books and magazines and videos. You do not have to rent them. Don't do it. Just don't do it. Don't look at them. If somebody proposes that you sit around all night watching some of that sleazy stuff, you say, "It's not for me." Stay away from that which is designed to make a few conspiring men rich at the expense of those who spend their money to watch that kind of material.

Be humble. Let me review this great statement from the 112th section of the Doctrine and Covenants where the Lord says, "Be thou humble; and the Lord thy God shall lead thee by the hand, and give thee answer to thy prayers" (D&C 112:10). Nobody likes one who is arrogant, who is conceited, who is egocentric, who is thinking only of himself. There is no place for arrogance on the part of any of us, not one. Be humble before the Lord, and be prayerful.

Be prayerful. I know that every one of you here prays. I believe that with all my heart, or you would not be here tonight. You are LDS youth, and you pray. You pray every morning, I hope. You pray every night, I hope. You ask the Lord for direction in your lives. Pray about your dreams, your hopes, about your schoolwork, about your ambition, about your friends, about all who should be remembered before the Lord. Prayer is such a marvelous and mighty and wonderful power. You are a child of God. Was there ever a father who wouldn't listen to his child? I don't believe so, certainly not a loving father. Pray to your Father in Heaven in the name of the Lord Jesus Christ. The Lord Jesus has said, "Ask, and it shall be given you; seek, and ye shall find; knock, and it shall be opened unto you" (Matthew 7:7).

We just finished a great conference of the Church. It was a wonderful conference. Do you know why it was wonderful? Because there were so many prayers that went into it. There wasn't a man or woman who spoke there who didn't pray about it—not one. I am confident of that. Moreover, there were thousands and thousands and tens of thousands of members across the Church who were praying for the Brethren during the time of conference. You pray for us, and I want you to know that we appreciate it. We love you, my dear friends; we do love you. The Lord loves you, and our great interest is you.

Well, you get the A's; I gave you the B's. Be grateful, be smart, be true, be clean, be humble, be prayerful. "Choose the right when a choice is placed before you." Don't get on the wrong track. It only takes one little thing to put you there. It won't happen if you will follow the counsel of your parents and the Church leaders, your bishop, your stake president, and the General Authorities of the Church. God bless you. The whole future is yours. You are young in this great age, and everything is ahead of you. What a bright future you have if you will walk with faith and faithfulness, doing the right things.

I want to tell you that I know that God lives. You write it in your book, if you will, that you heard Gordon Hinckley say that he knows that God lives; and that he knows that Jesus is the Son of God, the Savior and Redeemer of the world, in whose name we pray to our Father in Heaven; and that you heard me say that Joseph Smith was a prophet and that which took place in the grove was as real and as personal and as intimate as is my conversation with you this afternoon; that the priesthood is upon the earth; and that the power of revelation is among us. Is the Church guided by revelation? Of course it is. I know it is.

There is a beautiful temple not far from here. It is the house of the Lord. Stay worthy to go to the temple. Choose the right. Keep on the right track. Be prayerful, and follow the counsel of those who love you most dearly—your parents—and those I think who love you second most dearly, and that is the officers of this Church. The Lord loves you better than that, more than anyone.

God bless you. Please know how much we love you, how much we count on you. You are so very precious to us. Take care of yourselves. You are precious to this work. The whole Church is the weaker if you stumble. The whole Church is the stronger if you remain true and faithful. I leave you my love and my blessing and my testimony and thank you for coming tonight, in the name of Jesus Christ, amen.

# Hong Kong

# Missionary Meeting

MAY 25, 1996

MY BRETHREN AND SISTERS, it is nice to be with you. I feel as if I have come home. Thank you very, very much. This has been a wonderful journey we have made to get here to dedicate the new Hong Kong Temple. The creation of this temple represents one of the great dreams of my life, at least for the last 35 years of my life. I first came here 36 years ago. Hong Kong was a different place then from what it is now. It is a miracle every time I come here. I do not know of another city in the world where I can see so much of magnificent architecture as I do here in this great and interesting and fascinating area. I have been captivated by Hong Kong ever since I first came here. I have had a great love in my heart for it. I have had a greater love in my heart for the missionaries who have labored here. There are thousands now who have come and gone over the years.

We have been meeting with missionaries in many places. They all look just like you. Oh, their name tags are a little different. Some of them are Japanese. Some of them are Korean. But they all look alike wherever we go. It is wonderful to be here and to have the tremendous opportunity of working among these marvelous Chinese people—these people who are the sons and daughters of God, who are hard to reach at times; but when the gospel message touches their hearts, something happens to them. They change. They turn around. They become remarkable and wonderful people. As I look at these Chinese missionaries here today, I see the fruits of this great work. God bless you, my dear brethren and sisters, for your devoted and faithful service.

We have held meetings of this kind with missionaries in Tokyo, Osaka, and Fukuoka, Japan; Naha, Okinawa; Pusan and Seoul, Korea; and yesterday in Taipei and today in Hong Kong. We have held great meetings with gatherings of the Saints. It has been an emotional experience for me to see the thousands and thousands of people who have turned out. We have spoken to more than 27,000 Latter-day Saints and their investigators in the last few days, gathered in the largest halls that could be found in the places where we have been, and those halls have been filled to capacity. I never could have dreamed, back in those early days when the work was just struggling along here, that the time would come when we would have Latter-day Saints gathered together in such numbers as we have seen.

David O. McKay, as an Apostle, came to Beijing in 1921, and he and his companion found a quiet place in the Forbidden City of Beijing. I have been there, and I think we have found the area where he offered the dedicatory prayer. He pleaded with the Lord to touch the great Chinese realm by the power of His Holy Spirit. He prayed in a particular plea that the Lord might touch the lives of the young men and the young women, that they would shake off the shackles of superstition of the past and take upon themselves the enlightenment of the gospel of Jesus Christ and change their lives and become a wonderful people. It has been a long time since he offered that dedicatory prayer, and not very much has happened during that time. But it is happening slowly and marvelously and wonderfully, and it will go on happening because these are the sons and daughters of God, our Eternal Father, and they are as entitled to receive the true gospel as are people of any nation on the face of the earth. As they accept it, their lives are blessed in the same way. Miracles happen.

We have with us today the Area President, Elder Kwok Yuen Tai. He joined the Church in about 1959 or '60. His wife was the daughter of a Christian minister in Taiwan. She came here, and she joined the Church, which was a great offense to her family. Her father got after her. She told me today that he took from the wall a picture of her family and tore her face off that picture and said, "That is what will happen to you if you join this Church." He felt so strongly this way. She married Brother Tai, and they went on to Sydney, Australia, where he studied chemistry and then to London, where he lived and worked. Then they came back here and then went to the States. They have a wonderful family. They are marvelous people. The night before last, her father was in the meeting in Taipei and said to his daughter and son-in-law things of a very complimentary and warm nature concerning this Church and our work.

Things happen. They do not happen very fast in China. China has been around a long time. But if we will be patient and keep at it, the Lord will bring about the harvest. I am satisfied of that. We do not need to be impatient. It has been said of China that she has been conquered many times but has absorbed all of her conquerors. That is what we do as a Church. We have had a lot of enemies. They may come after us, but we end up absorbing them.

There was never a better time to be here than right now. This is a moment of history in this great crown colony, which will become next year part of the Republic of China. You are here in this time of transition. Everybody here is a little jittery not knowing what will happen. I feel a peace in my heart concerning that time. I do not know what will happen. I pray with all my heart that Beijing will permit us to continue to come here and move forward our work and will not interfere with it in any way. I have that confidence; I have that faith. I pray that it may be so. I believe it will be so. It has been my vision of this work for a long time that we will not do much in opening the work in the mainland of China in a direct way, but there will be a gradual move in on the part of our people who are from Hong Kong and Taiwan—the Mandarin-speaking people of Taiwan and the Cantonese-speaking people of Hong Kong. Gradually there will be an infusion of our work into the mainland. And the virtue of their lives—the lives of our people, as the officials of the government see that virtue in our people—will be the door-opener for us in the years to come. I think it will be a natural evolution, and the Lord will lead the way. His will be the timetable. We will need responsive hearts and ears to hear His words and message concerning what we shall do, and I am satisfied that we will be made aware of what we should do.

I learned as a 12-year-old boy the Boy Scout Oath: "On my honor I will do my best to do my duty to God and my country and to obey the Scout Law; to help other people at all times; to keep myself physically strong, mentally awake, and morally straight" (*Boy Scout Handbook,* 10th ed. [1990], 5). Now, that great opening statement, "On my honor, I will do my best"—that is all you have to worry about in missionary service. Do your very best, and the Lord will take care of the fruit of your service.

You have to know that every time you bring a convert into this Church you bless a life—not one life, if he or she remains faithful, but many lives, for that which you do becomes the fruit of generations yet to come. All of us here are the fruit of missionary work—our fathers, our grandfathers, our great-grandfathers who accepted the testimony of missionaries and came into the Church. We are the beneficiaries. I never look at missionaries that I do not feel inclined to say that you never can foretell the consequences of that which you do in this service.

I remember so vividly going over to Aberdeen on the far side of the island. We were establishing a little branch in Aberdeen. We rented a small apartment. It was upstairs, and it was difficult to get up the stairs because refugees from China, who had no place to live and were new to these settlements, were sleeping on the stairs. We had to ask them to move in order to get up there to our meetings. We found a little handful of Saints, maybe 10 people. We created a branch of the Church and called a branch president—a poor Chinese man. The missionaries had met him at a fish market. They talked to him, and there developed the opportunity to teach him the gospel. I ordained this man an elder on that occasion and set him apart as president of the Aberdeen Branch. He subsequently left here and went to New York, where he worked in a Chinese restaurant. And, as the Chinese do, he worked very hard and saved very carefully. Soon he was independently operating a Chinese restaurant.

There came to call on me last year some of his family. They were bringing a son out to the MTC to go on a mission somewhere in this part of the world. He was of the third generation. Every one of this man's six or seven children are active and faithful in the Church. He had been president of the Chinese branch in New York. He has sons who are able and fine people. He has a daughter who has a top executive position with the AT&T office in New York. They have children who are able and fine and going on missions. That is the wonder of the work. The generations pass, and the numbers increase in a marvelous way. So you never can foretell the consequences of your work, and that knock on the door which may lead to an opportunity to teach—which may eventually lead to a conversion—will have eternal and everlasting consequences in the lives of those you teach.

Enjoy it here. Missionaries used to complain that they were cooped up in Hong Kong. That is so. You are right here in this limited area, and you cannot be transferred anywhere else. You have to spend all of your 18 months or two years here. Wonderful, isn't it? It is great. You do not have to go off to some forlorn place. You are right here in the middle of these millions of people all the time.

When you go home, you will wonder where the people are. You will miss the people. You will miss the Chinese chatter.

Matthew Cowley came here with Henry Aki, a Chinese man, in 1949. They went up on the peak, and there they offered prayer. It was not a dedicatory prayer, evidently. They considered President McKay's dedicatory prayer of the Chinese realm as the dedication of all of China. They offered prayer, and Henry Aki pleaded with the Lord to touch the hearts of his people that they might be responsive to the gospel message. Brother Cowley likewise pleaded with the Lord. Those prayers have been answered. We have done very well. We now have wards and stakes. We now have good meeting halls all over the territory. Now we have a temple. That is the kind of thing that says that the Church has reached full maturity here—wards, stakes, missions, and a temple of the Lord. How wonderful it is.

The Lord said concerning the reasons for the opening of this work in this, the dispensation of the fulness of times, as set forth in the first section of the Doctrine and Covenants, beginning with the 20th verse, "that every man might speak in the name of God the Lord, even the Savior of the world." What a marvelous thing that is. This is not a priesthood restricted to a few trained men, but "that every man might speak in the name of God the Lord, even the Savior of the world."

Two: "That faith also might increase in the earth" (v. 21). It is evident. It is here. When I see some of these old-timers here who have kept the faith, I see the power of faith. Brother Ng, for instance, has been here longer than I have been coming here. He was a translator when I first came here in that little group of people. He now serves as president of the Hong Kong Temple of The Church of Jesus Christ of Latter-day Saints.

I have on my wall a painting that was given to me by a woman here in Hong Kong. On the back it says, "To Elder Gordon B. Hinckley, with gratitude for the restoration of my eyesight," and then her name is signed. I did not restore her eyesight; the Lord did. But she says that that administration saved her eyesight, and the doctors could not believe what happened to her. She was going blind, and they told her she would be blind in a matter of a few months. It was faith in the power of the priesthood and, most important of all, the goodness of the Lord which made possible that miracle.

President Jay Quealy, whom some of you may know, was seriously injured while he was presiding here. One morning he went over to see the missionaries on the island. He foolishly rode a scooter, which they were permitted to do in those days. He was on a road where there was some pea gravel and skidded right into a police van. Of all the vehicles to hit, he picked the worst he could have. He was thrown right up over the hood and into the windshield. He broke both legs, an arm, and some ribs. I came over here to look after the mission for a time. He says—I do not say this—that when I administered to him I said that he would walk again on his natural legs and be unimpaired in his work. The doctors said he had gangrene in his legs and they would have to take them off. He said, "No, I won't let you take them off. I was given a promise by a servant of the Lord that I would walk again with my natural legs." The nurses, wonderful Chinese nurses, massaged his legs, and the gangrene miraculously cleared, and until the time of his death he walked on his natural legs. I have seen miracles here by the power of this priesthood, which the Lord here mentions, and by the power of faith, which is also mentioned here.

Three: "That mine everlasting covenant might be established" (D&C 1:22). Now, I want to talk about covenants. "That mine everlasting covenant might be established." What is that covenant? It is the covenant between Jehovah and Abraham—and subsequently with Isaac and Jacob, but primarily with Abraham—that through him and his seed all nations of the earth might be blessed and that Jehovah would be their God and they would be His people. That was the everlasting covenant that was established. And one of the purposes of the Restoration of this gospel is that this covenant might be reaffirmed in this, the dispensation of the fulness of times. People used to argue here as to whether the Chinese were literal descendants of Israel. I said that I do not worry about that. Whether they get their blessings by inherited birthright or whether they receive them by adoption, the end result is the same: they become partakers of the everlasting covenant between Jehovah and Abraham, which extends to all of his posterity and beneficiaries, whether they be by literal descent or whether they might come into that great family by adoption.

Now then, every baptism that you perform places someone under covenant—again this eternal and everlasting covenant, a special relationship with God, our Eternal Father, and the risen Lord Jesus Christ. Every time we partake of the sacrament, we renew that covenant, we take upon ourselves the name of Jesus Christ and contract, as it were, with Him to keep His commandments. He in turn says that His Spirit will be with us. That is a covenant, a two-party contract. Now, we have built this temple and are dedicating it tomorrow. That is a place of covenants also. We are a covenant people in a special relationship with God, our Eternal Father—eternal and everlasting if we live worthy of it. In that house of the Lord, as all of you know who have been to a temple, we take upon ourselves covenants and obligations regarding lives of purity and virtue and goodness and truth and unselfishness to others. This is a glorious day when you are here. You each will have the opportunity of participating in the wonderful dedicatory services.

Four: "That the fulness of my gospel might be proclaimed by the weak and the simple unto the ends of the world, and before kings and rulers . . . that they might come to understanding" (vv. 23–24). That is what you are—the weak and the simple. It is all right; we are all that way. We are missionaries.

Carry on. Carry on. In the old days, I used to interview the missionaries, every one, every time I came, and I came at least every six months and sometimes three times a year. I have now spent, I think, in accumulated time, more than three and a half years in Asia among the wonderful people of this part of the world, whom I love and honor and respect. I cannot interview all of you. I would love to interview you, every one of you—just sit down and talk. I wish we could hold a testimony meeting and hear from every one of you.

I hope every one of you is the kind of missionary your mother thinks you are. If you are that kind of missionary, you are all right. I hope every one of you has a great feeling of respect and love for your companion, that you work harmoniously together, because in that companionship there is strength that never can be found when you are alone. Great is the program of having missionaries work in pairs. They not only double their effectiveness, they triple their effectiveness when there are two working harmoniously together. "In the mouths of two or more witnesses shall all things be established," said the Lord (see Matthew 18:16; 2 Corinthians 13:1; D&C 6:28).

God bless you, my beloved co-workers. The burden is on your narrow shoulders, and it is going to occur in the spirit of love. Go forward in faith. Sister Hinckley likes to tell the story of a missionary sister who stood up in one of our testimony meetings here and said, "I am from New Zealand. When I left for my mission, at my farewell the people sang, 'I'll go where you want me to go, dear Lord . . . ; I'll be what you want me to be' " (*Hymns*, no. 270). She said, "That never crossed my mind again, that song, until one day, when we had been tracting in the rain all day long and were soaking wet, we came to another resettlement flat where refugees lived. My companion said, 'We are soaking wet. Let's go home.' " She said, "We started for home, and the words of that song came into my mind: 'I'll go where you want me to go, dear Lord; I'll say what you want me to say . . . ; I'll be what you want me to be.' " She pulled the arm of her companion's slicker and said, "We have to go back. I don't know why, but we have to go back." They went back, and there was a light up on the fifth or sixth or seventh floor. They climbed the stairs and knocked on the door. There was a family who subsequently were baptized—a father, a mother, and three children. "I'll go where you want me to go, dear Lord . . . ; I'll say what you want me to say . . . ; I'll be what you want me to be."

Sister Hinckley has been tracting in Hong Kong with the sister missionaries in the resettlement flats. She said to the beautiful young woman with whom she was tracting, "Wouldn't you rather be back at BYU dancing with the boys?" And this young sister said, "Sister Hinckley, I would rather be doing this than any other thing in all this world."

We bring you the love of all of the General Authorities of the Church. We bring you the love of the entire Church. Everybody in this Church loves the missionaries. Everyone prays for you. As President Monson said, we pray for you in our temple meetings, we pray for you everywhere we go. You, above all people, are prayed for in this Church. If you are ever tempted to do something wrong, do not do it. You are in the world here. It is all around you. Do not stumble. Do not look in the direction of those things. Hold your heads high. Cultivate cleanliness and virtue in your thoughts and your words and your lives. You can do it. People are praying for you—your fathers, your mothers, your brothers, your sisters, your bishops, the people in your wards, the General Authorities—all are praying for the missionaries. Never forget it.

To the older brothers and sisters who are here I want to express a word of thanks to you for coming here at this time of your lives. Thank you for all the good that you do. Thank you so very, very much.

I leave my blessing upon you as a servant of the Lord that you may be happy, that you may enjoy His Holy Spirit as you labor with love and faith, that you may be prayerful and humble, and that when the time comes for you to go home you will shed more tears over leaving Hong Kong than you shed when you left home to come here. I humbly pray for you, as I leave you my witness and testimony of the divinity of this work, in the name of Jesus Christ, amen.

# HANOI, VIETNAM

# BRANCH FIRESIDE

## MAY 29, 1996

W HEN WE DETERMINED TO come and dedicate the Hong Kong Temple, I said I'd like to do something else also while we were here. For a long time I had responsibility for the work in Asia. Beginning in 1960 I tramped over this part of the world, back and forth; stood in the long lines; endured customs and immigration— the man with the rubber stamp, who is everywhere. We started this trip in Tokyo—had a big meeting there with more than 3,000 in attendance—and then went to Osaka, where there was another large meeting, and then Fukuoka and Naha, Okinawa; then over to Pusan, Korea; up to Seoul, Korea; down to Taipei, Taiwan; to Hong Kong for the dedication; and then over to Phnom Penh in Cambodia yesterday and this morning in Ho Chi Minh City and Hanoi this afternoon. Tonight we will be in Manila, where we will have a big meeting tomorrow. They say there will be 20,000 in that meeting, and I don't doubt it. Then we'll go down to Cebu, and then we'll fly to Honolulu and do some work there before we fly home, arriving Sunday night. This is 18 days going about as fast as an old man can go, but it's been wonderful.

I have seen the miracle of Asia, of the Church in Asia. I have seen the kind of thing we saw last night. We had 439 people at a meeting in Phnom Penh, and just to look at them—they have not been in the Church for long; they're just learning. I saw the same thing in the Philippines in the early years. The Saints in Phnom Penh look just like the people once did in the Philippines. I saw the same thing in Korea. I saw the same thing in other places. Great things are happening in this part of the world. This is a wonderful place, this great area where most of the people of the world live. This is part of that vast horde of millions upon millions. More than a billion in China alone—a billion and 250 million. In India, 60 million. In Indonesia, 180 million. They are everywhere by the millions and millions.

I met Dr. Phan this morning and had a very pleasant and delightful visit with him in which he expressed his great appreciation for what you are doing, you wonderful people, and what a great blessing the Church has brought to his country by reason of your service and the humanitarian aid we have given. He said, "I know this is the first time you've been to Vietnam." Well, I didn't say anything; I haven't been to Hanoi before, but I have been to Ho Chi Minh City—Saigon, while the war was on—quite a number of times. I got as far north as Da Nang. I have held meetings in Da Nang, Nha Trang, and up and down Cam Ranh Bay and that area and all over this part of the world—Asahikawa, in northern Japan; down to Coimbatore, in India; Burma; Thailand—everywhere, it seems to me, in these hot, sweaty lands.

I used to come over here for two months at a time and tour through all of these areas, interview every missionary—and I'd do that twice a year. I can't do it anymore. I don't have the energy or the strength. I don't move as fast as I once moved; but nevertheless, I feel in my heart a great love for the people of Asia. The suffering in this part of the world has been terrible, unimaginable— the suffering of the people of this part of the world through centuries of wars, famine, trouble, stress, terrible animosity one nation toward another, the days of colonialism, when they were at times abused, although what the colonial powers did here—Britain and

France—in this part of the world left a great mark for good on these lands. I think nobody can question that. But they are all free now and on their own, and they are going their own way under their individual governments.

I hope that the time will come when we can have missionary work here. It will come. I dedicated South Vietnam for the preaching of the restored gospel in 1966. We had no place to go to do it. We couldn't go in a park because of gun emplacements. We couldn't do it on a mountain because of war. We were staying at that time at the Caravalle Hotel in Saigon, and we went up on the roof of the hotel and there dedicated South Vietnam for the preaching of the restored gospel. Lance Wickman, who is now of the Seventy, was an army officer and on that occasion was there with us, along with others whom I have met from time to time.

When we were in Ho Chi Minh City this morning, we went to the old Caravalle Hotel, which will be shut down for a total renovation. The day after tomorrow it will be closed. But it was open today, and we went there and went back up on the roof where we had held that meeting in 1966 with some 200 men in uniform.

On that trip, we flew from Saigon up to Da Nang, and I remember when we landed at Tan Son Nhut, Colonel Rosa put a piece of paper in front of me and said, "Sign this."

I said, "What is it?" He said, "It's a release relieving the United States government of any responsibility for you while you are in Vietnam." I signed the release, and we climbed aboard an old "goony bird" and went down the runway, and the sergeant had left the door open. When we got up in the air I said, "Aren't you going to close the door?" And he said, "It's too hot." And so we flew up to Da Nang, and I'll never forget that meeting as long as I live. Men came in from the battle areas, stacked their M-16 rifles at the door of the building; three of them had been killed that previous week, and we held a memorial service for them and had a meeting and then a subsequent meeting. The Jews were to have the building that night—it was Saturday—and when they saw how many of us there were and there were only about a half-dozen of them, they generously said, "You go back in and use the building."

When the meeting was over, we were loaded into an army ambulance and taken to a field hospital that was not finished. It was made of components that were being bolted together—produced in the States and shipped here—but the air-conditioning wasn't working, and so it was like an oven; the windows were all sealed. To take a shower we had a big barrel of water with a dipper. All through the night F-14 aircraft were flying north, and we wondered how many of them would come back.

We went down to Nha Trang on the Sunday morning and held a wonderful meeting there and had the sacrament with men who hadn't had the sacrament in months.

Well, I can't get started on that or we could stay here all night and talk about these things. I've had so many remarkable and, I think, wonderful experiences in this part of the world.

When Saigon fell in 1975, I said, "How will that blessing ever be fulfilled that I pronounced on this land? We fled South Vietnam. How will the restored gospel ever be taught there?" Well, some years passed, and I went to a conference of Vietnamese and Hmong converts to the Church in Utah, and there were young men who were being ordained to the priesthood and a half-dozen who were approved to receive the Melchizedek Priesthood, and I said, "That's the way it will be fulfilled. The time will come when the sons and grandsons of those who have left here will come back and preach the gospel in the land of their forebears." I feel satisfied that that day will come. I just feel confident. And you who are here now are the pioneers. You're building a wonderful reputation here with the government officials. They speak so highly of you and of the work you are doing and are so appreciative. And somehow, in the providence of the Lord, the hearts of the leaders of the government will be touched for good, and things will open.

I once gave a talk at the BYU taken from my journals over here which I titled "A Silver Thread in the Dark Tapestry of War." And I have seen that silver thread woven in this part of the world where our service people, in many areas—Japan, Philippines, Korea, Taiwan—were the pioneers and planted the gospel. Sometimes the seeds they planted didn't amount to any more than tiny little sprouts, but now there are great things there. We never owned a building in all of Asia when I began coming here—never a building anywhere. We rented little, smelly places. And see what we have now—a beautiful temple in Tokyo, another one in Seoul, another one in Taipei, another one in Manila, now one in Hong Kong. It's marvelous to see what's happened with meetinghouses, stakes of Zion, scores of missionaries from these lands who are teaching their own people. It's a miracle to behold.

Well, I believe the Lord loves these people and is anxious for us to help them, and you are helping them. "Inasmuch as ye have done it unto one of the least of these my brethren, ye have done it unto me" (Matthew 25:40); and that's what you are doing—working among these people, teaching language skills, medicine, medical practice, medical knowledge to these people to ease the suffering of those in this land where there has been so very, very much of suffering.

Well, somebody asked, "When you dedicated South Vietnam, did that include North Vietnam?" It was specifically pointed to South Vietnam. I think as we conclude this meeting I'd like to add an addendum to that prayer of dedication, here, which will include the whole nation of Vietnam, north and south, and all of its people. And so, if you'd like to bow your heads and join in that prayer, I think we'd like to do it.

# MANILA, PHILIPPINES

# MISSIONARY MEETING

### MAY 31, 1996

WELL, WHAT A PLEASANT SIGHT. You'd be more pleasant if you were a little cooler, but you're accustomed to the heat, I know. You just don't escape it in this part of the world. We have been on a very long journey in which we have met many, many thousands of people. Before we met last night, we had met nearly 30,000 in other parts of Asia. Last night was a great capstone to all of that. I suppose it was the largest congregation of Latter-day Saints that has ever assembled in one place, under one roof, at one time. I don't know, but I think that's probably right.

At general conference I announced that we were considering building a very large building. The Tabernacle only seats 6,000. People sit out on the lawn by the thousands because there is not a place in the Tabernacle. We have television, it's true. We have access to cable, it's true. We have a satellite system, it's true. But there is nothing like being there—right there—so we have architects and engineers now working on the possibility of building a very large meeting hall in Salt Lake City. When we can get 30,000 in the Araneta Coliseum with people standing outside, it says something. However, we can't see them. It was either my bifocals or the time of night or the lighting. I looked at those people up in the rafters, and I could scarcely see them.

Yesterday was a great day in my life. Every day is a great day in my life. I hope every day is a great day in your lives—every one of you. I hope you can get ready to go in the morning and shake the hand of your companion and say, "Brother (Sister), life is good. Let's go out and have a good day." And when you come in at night, I hope you can say to one another, "It's been a good day. We've had a good time. We've helped somebody along the way. Remember so-and-so and so-and-so and so-and-so we met today. We'll follow up with them and pray and hope that they will come into the Church." Every day ought to be a good day in the mission field. There aren't very many days for you—two years; that's 365 times twice. For you sisters, 18 months—365 plus a half of 365. That comes out with an odd half. I don't know what you're going to do about that.

We were out to the American military cemetery yesterday. I think that is probably the most hallowed piece of ground in all of the Philippines, made so because of the sacrifice of those who are remembered there, who gave their lives for the freedom of this land and other lands in the great war that engulfed this part of the world. It was there that we invoked the Spirit of the Lord to brood over this land, to touch the hearts of the people, to open the minds of the officials who would make it possible for us to come here and begin missionary work.

We did not meet with a friendly reception when we came here. I remember sitting in the hot outer room of the office of the commissioner of immigration, as he was then. Finally, we got in to see him—the mission president, Brother Robert Taylor, and I—and he was very curt with us and offered us no help whatever. He grudgingly said they couldn't keep us from bringing missionaries here for six months, but they'd have to leave after six months. It was not a very happy experience. It was a poor start, and the interesting thing is, when he ran for reelection he was defeated and the door began to open for us.

Now, we've had ups and downs since then. I can't blame the Philippines government for worrying about you—there are a lot of you. The problem is they simply do not understand that we are here not to take from the people but to add to what they have, to bring happiness into their lives, to bring the blessings of the Almighty down upon their heads, to bring peace and love in their hearts and kindness. They have known so much of suffering over the years. All of this part of the world has known so much of terrible suffering as a result of wars and jealousies, civil wars, international wars—all of those things.

These are great and good people. Their hearts are good. There is much of kindness in them. There is integrity in them.

The Lord has said, "If your eye be single to my glory, your whole bodies shall be filled with light, and there shall be no darkness in you" (D&C 88:67). What a wonderful promise that is. If you are working with an eye single to the glory of God, if your mind is on the objective of teaching the gospel to these people, if you are not thinking of other things, if you are putting the world out of the way and behind you, gone will be the darkness of selfishness. Gone will be the darkness of sin. Gone will be the darkness that clouds your minds, and there shall be light and understanding and faith. Live for that. Work for that, I humbly pray.

Brother Wirthlin mentioned keeping away from temptation. It's everywhere in this world. There are those who would like to entrap you if they could. Each of you has a companion. Why? Well, for one reason because the Savior said, "In the mouth of two or three witnesses [shall all things] be established" (Matthew 18:16). Another is for your mutual protection—so that you can protect one another. When you are together, it isn't likely that both of you will go wrong. One of you might be tempted to. The other will pull him up and straighten him out and give him strength to resist. Subtle are the ways of the world. Clever are the designs of the adversary. Be careful. You want to go home in honor. You must go home in honor, having completed your missions. Don't step into tragedy. Transgression never was happiness. Sin never was happiness. Evil never was happiness. The violation of mission rules never was happiness.

There is an interesting account in Proverbs; I'll read it. I am going to skip some verses:

"For at the window of my house I looked through my casement,

". . . I discerned among the youths, a young man void of understanding,

"Passing through the street near her corner; and he went the way to her house,

"In the twilight, in the evening, in the black and dark night:

"And, behold, there met him a woman . . . subtil of heart. . . .

"So she caught him, and kissed him, and with an impudent face [spoke] unto him."

And that led to evil, and "with her much fair speech" she flattereth him, and he succumbed to her flattery (see Proverbs 7:6–27).

I have paraphrased much of that, but it describes the greatest tragedy that can happen to a missionary. It happens to relatively few, but now and again it happens. We were in Taiwan not long ago, and I thought of a missionary I knew there who, in the middle of the night, climbed over the roof and got into trouble and was excommunicated from the Church. That was 35 years ago. I have tried to find him. I have never been able to find him. I think he has remained out of the Church, and the generations after him may be out—all because of yielding to a foolish, sinful influence. "Be ye clean, that bear the vessels of the Lord" (Isaiah 52:11; see also 3 Nephi 20:41; D&C 38:42; 133:5). Keep your lives clean while you are here. Work at it. Resist evil, my brethren and sisters. "If your eye be single to my glory, your whole bodies shall be filled with light, and there shall be no darkness in you."

God bless you. You are the instruments of the Lord to bring to pass His purposes in the Philippines. On your narrow shoulders rests the responsibility of the Church in this part of the world. Don't ever let the Lord down. You are His ambassadors. You have, as it were, plenary powers to teach, to bring about conversions, to baptize.

I regard you as my companions in this work. Go forward in faith, without fear.

To the Filipino missionaries who are here, I want to say to you *mabuhay* for your presence. This will be a great and marvelous blessing in your lives. This will bring blessings to you that will grow through the years because of the service you have given here in this cause. Be faithful and true. To each of you my love and my blessing, my testimony, my faith, in the name of Jesus Christ, amen.

# MISSIONARY MEETING

JUNE 13, 1996

I T IS NICE TO BE HERE WITH YOU. I mean that very sincerely. We came to break ground for a temple in Madrid, Spain. That's a remarkable thing in and of itself, that in two years' time we will have a house of the Lord on Spanish soil. That is tremendously significant in my mind. We have a regional conference this coming Saturday and Sunday in Berlin. That left a few days in between. I said, "Let's go to Brussels and Holland—Rotterdam or The Hague or Amsterdam, wherever a meeting might be held—and to Copenhagen. Let's go to those places and spread the word and give our testimonies and our love and leave our blessings."

I'm glad we came. I love this part of the world. I like Holland and Belgium. There is a certain cleanliness and a brightness about these lands, and we are here on this beautiful day. I don't know how you could have a more beautiful day in the entire year than we have experienced here today. We plant tulips every fall that come from Holland. They are reminders of this good land. What a choice and wonderful place it is. I first came here in 1935—that's a long time ago, 61 years ago—as a missionary released from my mission in England, with two of my companions. At that time the idea was to take a little travel after your mission. We don't encourage it anymore, but in those days we were doing what was usually done. We visited around here and caught the flavor of this land.

I received a patriarchal blessing when I was a boy. In that blessing it said that I would lift my voice in testimony of the truth in the nations of the earth. I had labored in London for a long time and given my testimony many times there. We came here, and I had opportunity in a meeting to say a few words and offer my testimony. We then went to Berlin, where I had a similar opportunity. We then went to Paris, where I had a similar opportunity. We then went to the United States, to Washington, D.C., and on a Sunday there I had a similar opportunity. When I arrived home, I was tired. My father said, "We're taking a trip to Yellowstone. Wouldn't you like to go to Yellowstone?" I said, "I never want to travel again. I have traveled as far as I ever want to travel. I have completed the phase of my blessing. I have lifted my voice in the great capitals of the world—in London, Berlin, Paris, and Washington." And I really felt that way. But somehow, under the providence of the Lord, I have been blessed to lift my voice in scores of nations and lands where the word of the Lord, the restored gospel, has been carried forth. I am grateful for the marvelous blessings of the Lord.

I came here again in 1962 with Henry D. Moyle of the First Presidency, and we held a meeting like this all day long—here in this chapel. In the morning I spoke for four hours and went through a course of procedures on missionary work, and he spoke for two hours in the afternoon. Then we had something to eat and moved on to the next city. In 23 days we went into every mission in Europe. When we were all through, he said, "I'm going home on the boat; I want to rest. Why don't you come home on the boat?" And I said, "I'm flying home to take a vacation." And I did.

And I have been here for a stake conference. So I am not a stranger in this beautiful land. I have been to Antwerp. I have been to Rotterdam and The Hague and these other cities, Utrecht and such historic places. This morning we went to Delft to see that historic and beautiful and attractive city, the place of the many, many canals. It was very interesting to go to Delft and visit those two old churches there that go way back through the centuries. One's called the Old Church, one's called the New Church. They both looked old.

It was interesting to reflect there, to stand in those buildings and think of the meaning of the Restoration of the gospel of Jesus Christ. Said the Lord to the boy prophet, "Having a form of godliness, but they deny the power thereof" (Joseph Smith—History 1:19). That's exactly what I was thinking about as we were in those old churches—a form of godliness but no life in their worship. I know why the Lord restored this gospel in this great dispensation: because the time had come when, along with all the other enlightening influences which were taking place in the world—the great leap forward of science—there should be a leap forward of eternal truths, the word of God, a renewal of our acquaintance with our Father in Heaven and the Redeemer of the world. And that's the essence of our message—that God has spoken again from the heavens to declare the everlasting truth, the word of salvation and exaltation to all who will accept the message we have come to teach. That's why we are here. It isn't easy. People don't want it. They are satisfied with what they have, but they need it—how urgently they need the gospel in this land of Holland and Belgium, where you have the opportunity of serving.

I don't know why it's so difficult. It's been difficult so very, very long. I've had a feeling sometimes that the Lord has said to the people of western Europe, "I've tried and tried and tried to get through, and you won't accept me, and so I'm going to lift my hand and bless other nations." That's what has happened to a marked degree. But we have to keep going; we have to keep working at it. We know the blood of Israel is in this land among these good people, who are sons and daughters of God and worthy of the very best that He has to offer, and that best is His everlasting gospel with all that goes with it. And so we keep trying, we keep working, and we find a soul here and another soul there, and they become very, very precious. Out of it all, eventually, comes strength. We have four stakes here now. Isn't that wonderful? I wish that we could build a temple here. I wish we could. I hope and pray and I believe that the time will come when there will be a house of the Lord on this soil. But it isn't now, and it won't be for some time, until there are more who are worthy of that great blessing. But we go forward in faith and do the work of the Lord, and He brings about His reward in His way.

President Peck spoke of the disappointments that you have had. I know that, but when it's all over you'll forget those, and you will remember the sweet and wonderful days that you spent in this land of tulips and wonderful people. You learned the language. That's a miracle in and of itself. LeGrand Richards used to say that when he came here as a young man—that was before there was any language training mission—he couldn't learn the language. He liked to hear the dogs bark because he could understand them. They barked the same way here as they did in his hometown.

I had an uncle come here, Alonzo A. Hinckley, way back in the early days. He later became a member of the Council of the Twelve. He spoke of the miracle—the great difficulty in learning this language and of his pleas with the Lord to help him, to loosen his tongue so that he could speak to the people words of testimony and truth. And suddenly, just out of the clear blue, he sat in a meeting and understood what was being said and then was called upon to speak and spoke with clarity to the people. A miracle. This is a land of miracles, and as has been said, this is a work of miracles.

You are part of it, my beloved friends. Thank you for being here. Thank you for accepting the calls you received to come here. Thank you for your faithful service as missionaries here. Thank you for your faith. Thank you for your prayers. Thank you for the love which you have cultivated in your hearts. I wish to pay special tribute to the older couples who are here. The Lord bless you for coming here and serving as missionaries in this good land. This will be a marvelous blessing in your lives, one that you will never forget, nor will the people forget you for the service which you have given.

I want to express my deep appreciation to the stake missionaries and those associated with them, who can do so much in bringing to the full-time missionaries those men and women who are willing to be taught the gospel of Jesus Christ.

I want to take a few more minutes, if I may. Some of you are going home. I was in South America on one occasion with some missionaries who were going home. They were out shopping to buy things to take home—souvenirs—and I thought of the souvenirs that we ought to take home with us from our missions. There are 10 of these:

1. A testimony of the living reality of God, our Eternal Father, and His Son, Jesus Christ. "This is life eternal, that they might know thee the only true God, and Jesus Christ, whom thou hast sent" (John 17:3). This is life eternal, to know the Father and the Son. Every missionary ought to take home, as the number-one gift that has come to him in the field, a living, vibrant testimony and conviction and knowledge of the living reality of God, our Eternal Father, and His Son, the Redeemer of the world.

2. A greatly enlarged understanding of the gospel. This is a marvelous season, perhaps the greatest of your lives, to enlarge your understanding of the gospel, to grow in knowledge concerning things divine, and to have showered upon your minds the light of eternal truth. What is it that is said in the 50th section of the Doctrine and Covenants? "That which is of God is light; and he that receiveth light, and continueth in God, receiveth more light; and that light groweth brighter and brighter until the perfect day" (D&C 50:24). That's one of my favorite verses of scripture. That says something that speaks of the whole eternal plan of this work.

This is the time to plant and nurture the seed of knowledge of the gospel of Jesus Christ.

3. A love for the people among whom you labor. If you don't love the people here, it isn't because there is something wrong with them. It is because there is something wrong with you. I hope and pray that for as long as you live you will never lose your love for the people among whom you served as a missionary. I have a son here who, as has been indicated, is a stake president of a large stake in Salt Lake City. He served among the German people. He thinks there is no one like the Germans. I served as a young man in England. I came to know the British. I came to know their hearts. I love them because I worked among them—not as a tourist, but at their firesides. I developed a great love which has never left me. I hope that you, each of you, will have developed that love and take it home with you.

4. A greater love and appreciation for your parents. Somehow, selfish, arrogant, conceited young men, when they get into the mission field, begin no longer to take their parents for granted but have come into their hearts a greater love for them. I hope you are not ashamed to write and tell your mother that you love her. And I hope you are not embarrassed even to tell your father that you love him. He might faint when he reads it, but he will appreciate it.

5. An understanding of the meaning of hard work. If there is anything that's needed in this world, it's more work, and you are learning how to work here, to get up every morning, to get out and work in the face of discouragement. The harder you work, the more you love the work. That's the wonderful thing about missionary service, and this will bless your lives all of your days—this habit of work which you cultivate as a missionary in the field.

6. An enlarged understanding of the meaning and true worth and value of personal virtue. There is no substitute for it under the heavens, and you live in a world where it is fading and being lost sight of. Said the Lord through the Prophet Joseph Smith, "Let

virtue garnish thy thoughts unceasingly" (D&C 121:45). And then He says the Holy Ghost shall distill upon you as the dews from heaven. That is a commandment with a promise. You ought to develop while you are on a mission—you must develop and take with you—an increased understanding of the true worth of personal virtue. Said the Lord in the opening of this missionary work, "Be ye clean" (D&C 38:42). Be ye clean.

7. Increased poise, the ability to meet people, to converse with them, to talk with them. It begins to shine in your faces. You develop a wonderful radiance. You take on cleanliness and orderliness and neatness. I hope you won't go home and revert to the grubby ways of your lives that some of you knew before you came, but that you will take back with you that refinement which comes of service to the Lord in the mission field.

8. The courage to act. My, the courage that missionaries develop. Oh, you do. When I finished my mission, I wasn't afraid to go talk to anybody.

9. The faith to do. The faith to try.

10. And finally, the humility to pray. The humility to pray.

Those are 10 gifts which I'd like to suggest to each of you to take home with you from the mission field.

The Lord is with us. It is His work. Let us stand tall, each of us, and go forward with love and confidence and prayer and faith to do that which is expected of us and to know the sweet rewards that shall come therefrom, I humbly pray in the name of Jesus Christ, amen.

# Nauvoo, Illinois

# Member Fireside

JULY 11, 1996

My BELOVED BRETHREN AND SISTERS, what a great pleasure it is to be with you. I like to come to Nauvoo. I have been here many times. I first came in 1935, on my way home from my mission. In those days missionaries were permitted to pick up a new car for their fathers and drive home from Detroit. One of my companions and I picked up cars for our fathers and drove home. We came this way. Nauvoo was not what it is today, I want to say that. It was a run-down, forsaken place. We went from here to Carthage and to other places, and to see today the transformation that has been made has been most wonderful and most remarkable.

I never come here that I do not think of the circumstances under which Nauvoo came to be established. I wonder tonight what Joseph Smith and his associates would think, as they walked across the boggy ground that went from here down to the river, if they knew that 150 years later there would be 9.5 million people scattered through more than 150 nations across the world who would remember them with respect, almost with reverence, for their tremendous accomplishments.

Nauvoo became the fair city on the Mississippi back in those days. It did not grow in ragtag fashion, as so many cities in early America did. It rose like the sunrise, planned from the beginning. It faded like the sunset after a short day. The season of its glory lasted only from 1839 to 1846.

Nauvoo always does something for me, and out of that feeling I speak tonight as one who has an appreciation for this remarkable city, which for one brief, shining moment was the home of our people, the fulfillment of their dreams, and then the shattering of their hopes.

In February of 1839, while they were refugees in Quincy and their prophet was a prisoner in Liberty, they first received the friendly attention of Dr. Galland, who owned considerable property at Commerce and from whom they later made significant purchases, including the land on which we meet. Seven years from that February, the first group of their people abandoned Nauvoo and began the long journey which would bring them to the mountain valleys of the West.

Ever since the Prophet named the place, we have spoken of it as Nauvoo the Beautiful.

It is beautiful. May I mention several aspects of that beauty.

First, Nauvoo is beautiful in its location. One day we drove from St. Louis to Carthage, there to dedicate the improvements on the block where stands the jail. We then took the river road up here to Nauvoo. We noted again the great sweeping bend of the Mississippi, with this city standing as it were on a peninsula, eagerly reaching out, pointing to the west, where the people who lived here would go. It was swampy in 1839, but the Prophet had a vision that the lands could be drained and a city created reaching from the waterfront up to the higher ground to the east.

There is something majestic and tremendous about the great river which flows around the Nauvoo point. "Ol' Man River" is beautiful and awesome.

There is something magnificent about the water as it rolls south to New Orleans and the Gulf. There is something inspiring about the great farmlands that reach from the river to the east and to the west where the corn grows "as high as an elephant's eye," and soybeans and other crops are cultivated for the markets of the world. Nauvoo, I remind you, is beautiful in its setting.

Secondly, for me Nauvoo is beautiful in its beginnings. This was a place of asylum, a refuge, a safe harbor in a terrible storm. Jackson County, Missouri, was to have been Zion, the home of the Saints of God. It became a place of bitterness and hatred. Clay County and Daviess and Caldwell Counties provided peace for a short season. Far West was a place of dreams and hopes, Adam-ondi-Ahman a place of prophecy. Then came the terrible order of extermination issued by Governor Boggs. Missouri is wide to drive across even in a comfortable automobile today. It was a very long distance from Far West to Quincy for the fleeing Mormon exiles.

Eternal will be our gratitude to the people of Quincy who provided shelter to the homeless. But these thousands could not stay there. They had to find a place of their own. Commerce became the site, and Nauvoo became the city. Again there were dreams and the peace to pursue them. How inviting is the port—any port—that is reached in a storm. How lovely is a place of refuge when there has been oppression and pursuit. How beautiful to the homeless is a home. Commerce may have seemed a dismal prospect back in those days, but something could be done and something was done about it. Nauvoo was beautiful in its beginnings as a place of refuge.

Thirdly, it was beautiful in its creation. There is no music like the music of industry. This place fairly rang with the cutting and shaping of timber, with the chiseling of stone, with the hammering of hot iron on the anvil, with the surveying and building of streets, the plowing of farmland, the planting and tilling of the soil, the gathering of the harvest. The homes of Nauvoo were beautiful, with their salmon-colored brick and their interesting, stepped walls. The Seventies Hall was a structure of graceful lines and a place of learning. The printing plant was an expression of a desire to know what was going on, the temple an expression of faith, even of conviction, concerning the eternity of life and the power of the priesthood of God to reach beyond the veil of death.

I marvel at what those people built during those few short years. There was nothing temporary about it. They built as if they were going to live here for generations. Nauvoo, I submit, was beautiful in its creation.

It was beautiful even in its suffering. There can be beauty in suffering when there is faith. Tragedy, yes; sorrow, of course, but there is something sublime in suffering for a great cause. I am not saying that the Saints enjoyed it. It was terrible. But there was something magnificent about the way they held up their heads and kept on going notwithstanding the travail through which they passed. Much of that suffering was painful and personal. Some of it was similar to the suffering of other peoples on the frontier. I have read the lists of names of those buried in the old Nauvoo cemetery up here, which we now have and have again made beautiful. So many of them were children who died of illness now quickly cured through the miracles of modern medicine. Such diseases as whooping cough took a terrible toll. One can only sense in some small degree the sorrow in the loss of a beautiful child after there had already been so many other painful losses. A bronze monument now stands in the old cemetery. It represents a father and a mother who have buried a child. The monument is beautiful in the sorrow it represents.

Finally, looking back a century and a half, Nauvoo is beautiful in its death. Notwithstanding tragedy there is beauty in heroism, there is beauty in faith, there is beauty in devotion to an ideal and a principle. All of these are exemplified in the exodus from Nauvoo. The suffering was indescribable, the disillusionment terribly difficult to bear, the hopelessness overpowering. It is difficult to imagine the emotions that must have been felt when for the last time, men, women, and children walked out of these beautiful homes, pulled shut the door, looked upon the fields they had culti-vated and the stature of the trees they had planted, climbed aboard their wagons, and drove down to the river, there to cross and move slowly over the soil of Iowa, looking back now and again at what they had left and would never see again. Most desperate were the circumstances of the sick, the aged, and the poor who were late in leaving. All of you know of the miracle of the quail that came as food when there was no food. But with all of that suffering, there was a certain beauty in the solemnity of it, in the sublimity of their faith, in their resolution to leave Nauvoo behind and re-create it on a grander scale somewhere in the West.

Sunrise and sunset on the Mississippi, with a brief day in between—such is the capsulated story of Nauvoo the Beautiful.

I am happy for all that has been done to rebuild a portion of it as a tremendous reminder that more than a century and a half ago a homeless people came to this ground and found a refuge even for only a short season. I am grateful that they built not shacks for tem-porary shelter but homes and other structures of beauty and per-manence and that as the crowning flower of their creation they constructed a temple as a witness of their faith in the eternal purposes of God.

I am grateful to Dr. Roy Kimball, who passed away a few years ago, for all that he did originally in connection with the organiza-tion and direction of Nauvoo Restoration Incorporated, because it was his vision that led to what we have today. I am grateful to all who have taken over the leadership of that organization. I am grateful that Nauvoo today stands remembered and restored, reaching up from the Mississippi with planned streets, with homes that are beautiful now as they were then, with the place of the temple properly fenced and protected, deserving of our looking upon it and meditating on its purposes. I am grateful, my brethren and sisters, for what Nauvoo does for me in giving to me a sense of gratitude, a sense of respect, a sense of worship, a sense of love for those who loved the Lord and served Him through sunshine and storm.

My own grandfather was 18 years of age in 1846. He and his brother had lost their parents. They were orphaned boys. At the age of 18 he was doing the work of a man as a blacksmith and wagon builder. He built a sturdy wagon for his uncle right here, and that wagon was among those that rolled down Parley Street to the river, crossed the Mississippi, and ponderously crossed Iowa—a small part in that vast caravan that left here to find a refuge somewhere in the West. His brother was among those who enlisted in the Mormon Battalion. My grandfather, as a young married man with his bride and 11-month-old child, left with the Saints to go west, up the Elkhorn to the Platte, and along the Platte to the Sweetwater, in search of their dream in the West. She died when they reached the Sweetwater. His half-brother also died on the same day. He dug the graves in which both were interred and laid them tenderly away in a place the exact location of which we do not know.

My father was president of the Northern States Mission, which included this area, back in 1939, the 100th anniversary of the founding of Nauvoo. He staged here the first great celebration held here by our people to commemorate the centennial of the founding of Nauvoo.

And so there is an affinity within me for this soil, for these old homes, for the foundation stones of the temple, and for Carthage, where the Prophet and Hyrum were murdered on June 27, 1844, for their testimony of the truth.

May the Lord keep ever green in the memories of our generation and succeeding generations a recognition of the miracle that was performed in the city by the river which was known as Nauvoo the Beautiful, I humbly pray as I leave you my witness and testimony of the integrity of those who once lived here, of the strength of their faith, of the power of their resolution, of their absolute loyalty and fidelity to the principles which they embraced and which have become for each of us a heritage of value beyond measure, in the name of Jesus Christ, amen.

# SANTIAGO, CHILE

# MEMBER FIRESIDE

## NOVEMBER 11, 1996

MY BELOVED BRETHREN AND SISTERS, what a tremendous picture you present—thousands upon thousands of you here. You have come from great distances, and we thank you for the effort you have made to be here. God bless you for your great faith and faithfulness.

I remember the time when I first came to Santiago. We had only a very few members of the Church here. We had a little school of poor little boys and girls, who met in a toolshed. We kept working and created the Ñuñoa Branch. We had the Ñuñoa chapel then. And as the years passed, we thought we were ready to have a stake of Zion. I came here to organize the stake, but when I interviewed all of the brethren, I discovered they were not paying their tithing. I worried very much about what to do. The next morning we met in the Ñuñoa chapel and I said to the people, "You are not ready to have a stake. You are not paying your tithing." I said, "I will be back in six months, and I will give you that time to start paying your tithing." I came back in six months. We organized the first stake in all of Chile. Since that time the work has rolled along in majesty and power until today we have some 400,000 Latter-day Saints in this land of Chile. We have 94 stakes of Zion. Brother Hammond tells me that by early next year we will be ready to organize the 100th stake of Zion. What a glorious blessing that will be.

I make of that occasion a challenge for each of you this day to put your lives in order, to be worthy to go to the house of the Lord and there to partake of the blessings that are peculiarly yours. Could there be a greater blessing in all the world than the sealing of husbands and wives, than the sealing of children to parents? My brethren and sisters, please do not pass up this great opportunity. It is worth everything. Please take advantage of it. Please get yourselves ready to go to the house of the Lord and there be sealed together as families. There is that beautiful temple which is waiting for you. Please take advantage of it, and God will bless you with happiness in your hearts and lives. There is no other place in all of Chile which can equal the house of the Lord. No other church has anything like it. But it is your privilege, my beloved brethren and sisters, to take advantage of that holy house. That means that we keep the Word of Wisdom. That means that we pay our tithing. That means that we have a testimony of the truth and divinity of this work. That means that we treat our wives and our children with kindness and love and respect. Great are the requirements, but greater still are the blessings, and I hope, therefore, that you will take advantage of these.

Now, I want to touch on something else. I want to go to the first section of the Doctrine and Covenants, wherein the Lord tells of why He has restored this work. First He says, "That every man might speak in the name of God the Lord, even the Savior of the world" (v. 20). Think of what that means, my brethren and sisters. "That every man might speak in the name of God the Lord, even the Savior of the world." What a marvelous and wonderful thing that is—that you and I can speak in God's holy name, can bless in His holy name, can hold positions of governance in His holy name, can live the doctrine of the priesthood. If there is any man here who has not partaken of the blessings of baptism, let him make up his mind forthwith to be baptized. Let him be true and faithful and active. Then let him receive the holy priesthood, that he may "speak in the name of God the Lord, even the Savior of the world." What a different world this would be if that were so. There would be no cheating. There would be no living below a high level of responsibility. But every man would conduct himself in such a way that the blessings that he gives as a servant of the Lord will be answered upon the heads of those whom he blesses.

Two: "That faith also might increase in the earth" (v. 21). What a wonderful thing that is. This next year we will commemorate the 150th anniversary of the arrival of the Mormon pioneers in the Salt Lake Valley. That was a great act of faith. And there are other acts of faith, and you are part of them. "That faith also might increase in the earth." What a marvelous and wonderful blessing that is.

Three: "That mine everlasting covenant might be established" (v. 22). Said Jehovah, "I . . . will be your God, and ye shall be my people" (Leviticus 26:12). We are a covenant people, my brethren and sisters. We make covenants in the house of the Lord. We make a covenant with God when we are baptized. We make a covenant with God when we partake of the sacrament, and we renew this ancient covenant that we will be the children of God and He will be our Father and we will do His will.

Finally, "That the fulness of my gospel might be proclaimed by the weak and the simple unto the ends of the world, and before kings and rulers" (D&C 1:23). We have about 1,800 missionaries in Chile. Think of that. Most of them are young men and young women. They are the weak and the simple of the earth. But see what miracles they perform in bringing into the waters of baptism such wonderful people as you.

Those are the four great reasons:

"That every man might speak in the name of God the Lord, even the Savior of the world;

"That faith also might increase in the earth;

"That mine everlasting covenant might be established;

"That the fulness of my gospel might be proclaimed by the weak and the simple unto the ends of the world, and before kings and rulers."

There is another one. I go back to the matter of temples—the eternal nature of the obligations we undertake in the house of the Lord and the great sealing ordinances which take place there. Some years ago there was a man who came to the Salt Lake Temple. It was when the Vietnam War was on. He had joined the Church while he was in the Air Force. He was being sent to Vietnam to serve as pilot of a spotter plane. That was a plane which would go over enemy territory and attract their fire. Then the artillery would pour in where that fire came from. He was sealed in the house of the Lord—he and his wife and their three children. After that sacred ceremony he took his wife in his arms, and they took their children in their arms, and he said, "I am not afraid to go, for I am yours and you are mine for all time and all eternity." That is what it means.

Now, my beloved brethren and sisters, please let me express my great love for you. We love you. We honor you. We respect you. We admire you. God bless you, every one. I would like to reach out and give you each an *abrazo* [hug]. There are so many here that I cannot do that. But please know of our great love and respect for you. I pray that when you return to your homes this day, you may carry with you that love.

I bear my testimony of the truth of this work. I hope that everyone here will remember this: that you heard Gordon B. Hinckley say that he knows that God lives and that Jesus is the Christ and that Joseph Smith was a true prophet, all of which I do humbly and gratefully, in the name of the Lord Jesus Christ, amen.

# São Paulo, Brazil

# Member Fireside— Second Session

### November 14, 1996

GOOD EVENING. GOOD EVENING, all you people out there. How wonderful it is to meet with you. It's difficult to see your faces; there are so many of you, but every one of you is an individual, a distinctive person, and we greet you as such. I thank all who have worked so hard to make this conference a great success. I thank the wonderful choir. They have sung magnificently. Their music has been beautiful. I see all of these flowers here at the stand; they are beautiful. I thank all who have brought them here and arranged them so beautifully.

I first came to São Paulo many years ago. There was one mission in all of Brazil—150 missionaries to cover all of Brazil. There was one small stake in São Paulo. It was presided over by Brother Spat, who was a wonderful man, and he did a wonderful work. Now the work has grown. There are missions all up and down this land, from Porto Alegre in the south to Manaus up in the north. What a marvelous and wonderful thing is happening, that the few hundred who were members of the Church then have become many thousands today.

I thank you for your faith and faithfulness. I pray that the Lord will bless you. I thank you for the way you go to the temple. You are crowding the temple, and that is a great blessing. On Friday night the temple is open all night long—from early Friday morning all through the day, all through the night, and all through Saturday. It is a great and marvelous thing. Tomorrow we go to Recife, where we will break ground for a new temple up north so that the lives of those people may be blessed as your lives are blessed.

Well, my dear, dear, wonderful friends, thank you for the goodness of your lives. God bless you for your faith and faithfulness. You are here tonight by the thousands and tens of thousands. Now, this Church expects great things of you. You are members of The Church of Jesus Christ of Latter-day Saints. You have a tremendous obligation. We expect great things of you. What do we expect of the Latter-day Saints?

1. That they will have a testimony of the gospel, a testimony of the living reality of God, a testimony of the living reality of the Savior of the world, even the Lord Jesus Christ. When He was upon the earth, He fed the 5,000. They enjoyed that, and they lingered and came back. And He taught them the doctrine of the kingdom, and some said, "This is an hard saying; who can hear it?" (John 6:60), and they left. Their hunger had been satisfied, but they had no faith. And the Lord said to the Twelve, "Will ye also go away?"

"Then Simon Peter answered him, Lord, to whom shall we go? thou hast the words of eternal life.

"And we believe and are sure that thou art that Christ, the Son of the living God" (John 6:67–69).

It is expected that every member of this Church will have a testimony of the Father and the Son. If you do not have it, now is the time to get it. And the Lord gave the method by which to get it. He said, "If any man will do his will, he shall know of the doctrine" (John 7:17). If you have any question concerning the truth of this work, you do the will of God, and you will know that it is true.

2. Loyalty to the priesthood. No General Authority of this Church ever served because he wanted to serve. He was called of God. It was not an easy thing for most of the Brethren, but they responded, and we are all trying to do our very best. There must be, in the Church, unity and respect, and that comes of loyalty to leadership—loyalty to the priesthood.

3. The Word of Wisdom. What a marvelous and wonderful blessing that is. It has guided this Church since 1833. No tobacco. No alcohol. No tea and coffee. Those who remember and do these things, said the Lord, shall run and not be weary and walk and not faint, and the Lord will give unto them knowledge, even hidden treasures of knowledge (see D&C 89:18–20). What a marvelous blessing this is. How wonderful a blessing—the Word of Wisdom, a guide to health.

4. The payment of tithing. The Lord has made a great promise. He asks:

"Will a man rob God? Yet ye have robbed me. But ye say, Wherein have we robbed thee? In tithes and offerings.

"Ye are cursed with a curse: for ye have robbed me, even this whole nation.

"Bring ye all the tithes into the storehouse, . . . and prove me now herewith, . . . if I will not open you the windows of heaven, and pour you out a blessing, that there shall not be room enough to receive it.

"And I will rebuke the devourer for your sakes. . . .

"And all nations shall call you blessed: for ye shall be a delightsome land, saith the Lord of hosts" (Malachi 3:8–12).

That is the word of the Lord, my brothers and sisters. That is not the word of Gordon Hinckley. That is the word of the great Jehovah. He is in a position to keep His promise, and it is my testimony to you that He does so.

5. Sacrament meeting attendance. You go to sacrament meeting to partake of the sacrament, the emblems of the suffering and

the Atonement of the Lord Jesus Christ, as a renewal of our covenant with Him. You will not go wrong if you go to your weekly sacrament meetings and there partake of the sacrament.

6. Family home evening—the marvelous program of gathering our children around us and teaching them the ways of the Lord. What a glorious program that is. "All thy children shall be taught of the Lord," said Isaiah, and then he gives this promise of the Lord: "And great shall be the peace of thy children" (Isaiah 54:13).

7. Prayer. Prayer. Bless the food that you eat. Thank the Lord for it, and bless it. Have your private prayers, and have family prayers, and great blessings will come of that.

8. And finally, family relationships. Fathers, are you the kind of men you ought to be? Do you treat your wives with kindness and respect? You are not lord and master. The woman you married is a daughter of God, and if you abuse her, you offend her Father in Heaven. Treat your wives with respect and honor. Wives, treat your husbands kindly, and magnify them in their priesthood callings. And parents, your children are sons and daughters of God. You don't need to whip them; you don't need to beat them. You do need to love them and rear them in love. What a different world this would be if there were love and kindness and appreciation in the homes of the people.

My brothers and sisters, these are some of the things which we expect of you as Latter-day Saints. May you be blessed to make these a part of your lives, and if you do so, you will be a happy people.

Now, in conclusion, I just want to tell you again that I love you. You are here in large numbers, but you are all sons and daughters of our Father in Heaven. I love you; please know that. I leave my blessing with you. I bless you in the authority of the holy apostleship that if you will be true and faithful you will enjoy the smiling favor of God, and you will have bread on your tables and clothing on your backs and a shelter over your heads, and the destroying angels shall pass by you as the children of Israel and not slay you. I leave you this blessing. I leave my testimony of the truth of this work, and I say, God be with you till we meet again, in the name of Jesus Christ, amen.

# Ogden, Utah

# Institute of Religion Devotional

### April 15, 1997

Good morning. It is nice to be with you this beautiful morning when you would rather be here than in class. Now, I am not here to preach to you this morning. I invited Brother Hall to invite you to submit some questions, and you did so, and he has collated all of them and put them in good order, and now he expects me to answer them.

First let me say that I am glad you are here at this great university. I am glad you are here to expand your minds and increase your understanding, to get an education, to equip yourselves to move out into the society of which you will become a part. I congratulate you, every one of you, and wish you good fortune in your studies. I hope you will look upon the educational opportunity that you have as a great blessing. I know it is a grind. I know it is difficult. I know you get discouraged at times. I know you wonder why you are doing it at times. But keep on, keep hammering away, and keep learning. You will never regret it as long as you live but will count it as a great blessing—the education you receive here at Weber State. The Lord bless you. Now I am going to get at these questions.

"Should girls go on a mission?" That is something on the minds of the girls. That does not bother the boys very much, but it is on the minds of the girls. Let me say this concerning this matter:

The Church will think as highly of you, regard you with the same respect, honor you, and appreciate you whether you go on a mission or whether you do not go on a mission. Girls should not feel a pressing obligation to go on a mission. Missionary work is primarily a priesthood responsibility, and every able young man is expected to go. With girls it is a little different. If we had all girls in the mission field, think of where we would be. If we had more girls than elders, think of where we would be. If we had the same number of girls as we have elders, think of where we would be. Well, if you really want to go on a mission, you talk with your bishop. You will have to wait until you are 21. We have not changed the age. But do not worry about it. Go forward with your schooling.

Next question: "Should girls finish their schooling first? What do you think of professional women?" Well, I regard them very highly. I think every girl should get an education to equip herself to take care of herself. Whether she is married or single, the time may come when she may need the skills that she acquires. If she is not married, and you have to assume that not everybody will be married, she is equipping herself to go out and take care of herself out in the world.

Now, I repeat, the Church will respect you and honor you and think the same of you whether you go on a mission or do not. But if that is the desire of your heart, if you feel within yourself that you cannot meet your full program unless you do so, then you talk with your bishop and do not worry much more about it. Answer to questions one and two.

"How should girls prepare themselves for missions?" Well, attend institute. Work at it. Keep yourselves clean and good and decent, and be worthy to go out and represent the Lord. Whether you go on a mission or not, you ought to do that; you ought to be deporting yourself in a manner that becomes those who are members of The Church of Jesus Christ of Latter-day Saints.

Next question: "What is your most important accomplishment in life?" Oh, I do not know. We have had failures and accomplishments. We are like you. We are just garden-variety people who go along trying to do what is expected of us and do it in a way that the Lord would have us do it. I do not know that there is one great accomplishment that stands out in my life. I have just tried to do what I felt was right and give my strength and energy to moving forward the work of the Lord and try along the way to bless the lives of other people.

"What one experience had the greatest effect upon your spiritual life?" I do not know. Well, maybe, when I was on a mission. I went way back in the days of the Depression. Very few missionaries were going out, because there was not any money. Money was the scarcest item in the world. It was terrible then. If a man had a job at $50 a month, he considered himself fortunate, with the result that very few missionaries went into the field. I was one of the fortunate ones who went to England. I was assigned to a place where things had not gone well with the two previous elders. I was not well, and I became a little discouraged. I wrote home to my father and said, "I am wasting your money and my time. I think I might as well come home and do vicarious baptisms." He wrote back to me a very short letter in which he said, "I have your letter of [such and such a date]. I have only one suggestion—forget yourself and go to work." About the same day I received that letter, we were reading in the scriptures, and I read these great words: "He that findeth his life shall lose it: and he that loseth his life for my sake shall find it" (Matthew 10:39). And between my father's letter and that statement, I made a resolution which changed my whole attitude and outlook on life, and everything that has happened to me since then that is good I can trace back to that decision. It had a very marked effect upon my life.

I was in England a little while ago—it was three or four years ago, I guess, but it seems like yesterday. I went to the old house in which we lived in Preston, Lancashire, where I had that experience. Of course, there were photographers taking pictures of me in front of that house, and an elderly English woman came out. She said, "Here, here, what's going on?"

I said, "I have come home."

"You've come home? What do you mean you've come home?"

"This is where I once lived many, many years ago."

"You lived here?"

"Yes."

"What were you doing here?"

"I was a Mormon missionary."

"You were?"

I said, "Yes. Could we come in the house and take a look at it?" So she said it was all right, and she led us in the front room, and it looked so small. I said, "Could we go upstairs to the bedroom we once rented?" And she said, "Well, don't get in bed." So we went up to the bedroom where I had that experience way back in 1933 and reflected on that great decision day of my life.

Next question: "What are the qualities you admire most about your wife?" I guess number one is endurance. She has been with me for 60 years. We celebrate our 60th anniversary next week. We have been at it through thick and thin through all these years. We have 5 children, 25 grandchildren, and 18 great-grandchildren. And we still love and honor and respect one another and enjoy one another. My, it has been a long time. When we were married we were poor, and the Lord has blessed us with such an abundance we do not know how really to take care of it; we are so blessed, so richly blessed. The Lord has been so very, very kind to us. And now in our old age we still have one another. I hope we will have one another for a good while and then that we can both die on the same day.

Next question: "What counsel would you give to married couples just starting out?" First, respect one another. Respect and honor one another. That takes a good deal of effort sometimes. You come out of different backgrounds, different homes, different ways of doing things. You have to respect one another and honor one another and build one another and encourage one another, and do not look for all of the faults in one another. If you do, you will find them, because none of us is perfect. But if you will respect one another and build one another and uphold and sustain one another and regard your companion as your equal or a little better, you will get along all right. The Lord bless you as you embark on this great thing which we call marriage, and may your days be happy, and may there be very, very many of them, and may there be no divorce in your lives is my prayer in your behalf.

"How does the Lord bless the single person who is doing everything possible to be righteous but marriage seems out of the picture for her?" Well, you have to face life. You have to face it. You have to take what comes. You can bend it some, yes. You can do a few things that would be very helpful, and the first is do not dwell on it, do not become obsessed with it. You will be more attractive to somebody else if you do not become obsessed with it. Go along and build your lives and get your education and cut out your niche in the world and go about doing good and being helpful. If you are not popular, do something exceptionally well. Make something good and great and wonderful of your lives.

My, what a great time it is in which you live. What a wonderful day in which to be alive, even if you are single; what a wonderful day to be alive. This is the greatest season in the history of the earth. This is your great day of opportunity. There has been more of invention and discovery during my short lifetime than during all of the previous centuries of human history. Do you know that? I was born in 1910—that is 87 years ago in June. That is a long time for an old man with thin hair. What a marvelous time it is to be alive. What a marvelous time it is to be preparing yourselves. What a marvelous time it is to be stepping out into the world with skills to do something good and worthwhile. Employment is available to you, and you can do well at it. The Lord bless you. Now, you get discouraged, I know, but buck up and put a smile on your face and go to work and get yourselves ready for the great competitive world that lies ahead of you.

"How do you prepare for the Second Coming?" Well, you do not worry about it. You just live the kind of life that if the Second Coming were to be tomorrow you would be ready. Nobody knows when it is going to happen. No one knows when the Savior is coming—not even the angels in heaven. Our job, our responsibility, is to prepare ourselves, to live worthy of the association of the Savior, to deport ourselves in such a way that we would not be embarrassed if He were to come among us. That is a challenge in this day and age. It is not easy. It is difficult. You have all this sleazy rot around you—pornography and all kinds of filth. You have to stand above it. You have to live above it. You have to keep it out of your lives. It will destroy you. You cannot afford to take drugs—any of you, not one of you. They will destroy you; they will literally destroy you. You must keep yourselves clean and bright and strong and wise and able and not succumb to these things. Now, that is a challenge, and it is not easy. But every young man and young woman in this hall today knows that you are capable of doing it. God bless you so to live your lives.

"How do you keep faith when promised blessings never seem to come?" It is not easy. It is not easy for any of us. The Lord is wiser than we are. You make that assumption first. He will answer our prayers—maybe not the way we wish them answered, but He is aware of us. He desires to help us. We are His sons and daughters. He loves us and appreciates us and respects us and will help us if we will live worthy of His help.

There were many questions pertaining to discouragement. Well, you are discouraged at times, aren't you? It gets a little tough at times—end of the quarter, test week. It reminds me of the student who had been wasting his time during the quarter, and the teacher went up to the board and wrote out a question. He looked at that question and looked at his book and said, "Lord of Hosts, be with us yet, lest we forget, lest we forget." He sat there the entire hour, and finally when the last question was written on the board, he said, "Lord of Hosts, forsake us not; we have forgot, we have forgot."

"I feel like I am the only woman not going to the temple, yet my bishop thinks I am too young." So what? Don't go. Wait until your bishop thinks you are mature enough to go. You rely on your bishop's good judgment. He will understand. I do not know why you need to rush to the temple. Every young man and woman in this Church ought to have as an objective in his or her life going to the temple, being married in the temple, going repeatedly to the temple. But you do not have to get in a great hurry to go to the temple unless you are going on a mission. So do not worry about that. It is all right. The time will come that will be the proper time for you to go to the house of the Lord, and don't you worry about it.

"What does the Church feel about cloning?" Who would we clone? Any of you been accepted for cloning? I do not suppose anyone is going to clone me. Well, we believe in the doctrine of marriage—a man and a woman. We believe that the powers of procreation should be exercised in the proper way under the proper circumstances for the proper purpose for the begetting of children to come into the world the way the Lord ordained they should come and not as a sheep who is cloned in Scotland.

"If I get active, my parents say they would disown me. How should I handle this?" I do not know your parents. They ought to wish that you were active in the Church. I think my advice to you would be to be active. Do not be offensive to your parents. You do not need to be offensive. You just be active, and let the light of the gospel shine in your life, and let there be kindness and love and respect towards your parents, and I feel satisfied the time will come when they will reach out to you and express their appreciation for you.

"Some people are afraid to confess to the bishop for some reason or another. If they have stopped doing the sin and are not going to do it again, what will happen to them?" I think you can trust your bishop; I hope you can. Your bishop has been set apart and blessed and given the spirit of discernment and understanding to help those of his ward. That is his peculiar responsibility—to be of help to those who reside in his ward, to give counsel and respect and honor to those who come to him. I would hope with all my heart that there would never be any disclosure on his part, that it would be absolutely confidential between you and him. That is the way to get it out of your system, to get rid of it, to dispose of it, to put it behind you. The Lord stands willing to forgive and help. He said, "I will forgive your sins and remember them no more against you" (see D&C 58:42). What a marvelous and wonderful promise that is. "I will forgive your sins and remember them no more against you." He said, "I, the Lord, will forgive whom I will forgive, but of you it is required to forgive all men" (D&C 64:10). That is our duty, our responsibility—to extend forgiveness.

Now, in the first place, do not do anything that you would have to confess. In the second place, if you do, do not feel that all is lost. It is not. There is a way to set things straight and get on with your lives and go forward without having a great chain around you— pulling you down all the time—of worry and concern about the things that you may have done. Put them behind you. Talk to your bishop in confidence. Pray to the Lord about it, and rely on His mercy and goodness and kindness, and He will bless you. There will come into your heart—maybe slowly and gradually—a feeling that all is well. He has said, "Be still, and know that I am God" (Psalm 46:10). I believe that.

"How do you keep the Spirit of the Lord with you at all times?" Well, you live worthy of it; you live worthy of the Spirit of the Lord. That is what you do. And you will have it. Now, young people are very idealistic. We all know that, and we bless you for it. Just live right. Stay away from the sleaze. Stay away from pornography. Stay away from these things that pull you down. The books you read, the magazines you read, the videos you look at, the television programs you look at, the shows you go to, all have an effect on you and will do if you subject yourself to the influence of those titillating kinds of things which are designed to make you poor and somebody else rich. Stay away from them.

"How can I know that the messages I am receiving are from my Heavenly Father and not just my thinking?" That is a good question. This is what Mormon says: "But behold, that which is of God inviteth and enticeth to do good continually; wherefore, every thing which inviteth and enticeth to do good, and to love God, and to serve him, is inspired of God" (Moroni 7:13). If it entices you, if it inspires you, if it helps you to do good and look to God, then you may be sure that it is of Him. "For behold, the Spirit of Christ is given to every man, that he may know good from evil; wherefore, I show unto you the way to judge; for every thing which inviteth to do good, and to persuade to believe in Christ, is sent forth by the power and gift of Christ; wherefore ye may know with a perfect knowledge it is of God. But whatsoever thing persuadeth men to do evil, and believe not in Christ, and deny him, and serve not God, then ye may know with a perfect knowledge it is of the devil" (Moroni 7:16–17).

I think that pretty well answers that question, but I am going to a related matter in the 50th section of the Doctrine and Covenants. People ask me what is my favorite verse of scripture. I say that I have many of them, but this is one of them, and it is pertinent to this question: "That which is of God is light; and he that receiveth light, and continueth in God, receiveth more light; and that light groweth brighter and brighter until the perfect day" (D&C 50:24). That is a marvelous statement, my dear young friends. "That which is of God is light; and he that receiveth light, and continueth in God, receiveth more light; and that light groweth brighter and brighter until the perfect day."

People ask me every now and again if I believe in evolution. I tell them I am not concerned with organic evolution. I do not worry about it. I passed through that argument long ago. But I believe in this kind of evolution—this marvelous statement that speaks of the growth of the human soul: "That which is of God is light; and he that receiveth light, and continueth in God, receiveth more light; and that light groweth brighter and brighter until the perfect day." What a remarkable statement that is. "How can I know that the messages I am receiving are from my Heavenly Father?" If they lead to growth, if they lead to righteousness, if they lead to faith, if they lead to good works, you may be assured they are from the Lord. If they lead to evil, if they tear you down, if they make things dark for you, you can be sure they are of the adversary. And that is the answer to that question.

I think I have answered all but one of your questions. Have I answered all of them? I am coming to the last one.

"I just want to hear your testimony of the gospel and the Lord Jesus Christ." This is my opportunity to leave you my testimony of the gospel and the Lord Jesus Christ and God, my Eternal Father. Do I know that They live? Of course I do, and I think most of you do. I hope you do. I know with a certainty that God is my Eternal Father; He who is the Governor of the universe is my Father. I can pray to Him. I am His child. I do not know how He hears all of our prayers; I don't know that. I just know He does, because I have my prayers answered. So do you, I think. When you think about it, I think you would say that you have had yours answered. He is my Eternal Father, and I know also that the day will come when I will have to make an accounting to Him of my life and what I have done with it, how I have used it, what I have accomplished, what good I have done in this world. The books will be opened, and the record will be clear, and we will be judged out of the record of our lives—of that I know. I know He is merciful. I know that He is kind. I know that He loves His sons and daughters. I know that He wants us all to be happy. I know that He wants us to make something good of our lives. I am confident of that. I am sure of that. I know that.

I know that His Only Begotten in the flesh, His Beloved Son, is my Redeemer and my Savior and my Lord—Jesus Christ, the Son of God, once the great Jehovah, who came to earth, born in a manger in a vassal state among a people where there was so much of hatred and meanness. He was the great Prince of Peace, who taught love and kindness and forbearance, who went about doing good, healing the sick, raising the dead, causing the blind to see. He is my Savior, who bled at every pore as He spoke to His Father in Gethsemane and died upon the cross for each of us and then came forth again the third day to become the firstfruits of them that slept. He is my Savior and my Redeemer.

God the Father and the risen Lord appeared to the boy Joseph Smith in the grove of his father's farm and there told him to join none of the churches, for none of them was true, and to be patient and that the Lord would use him according to His way to accomplish His purposes. Then came the Book of Mormon under the hands of Moroni, a resurrected being. Then came the Aaronic Priesthood under the hands of John the Baptist. Then the Melchizedek Priesthood under the hands of Peter, James, and John. Other keys of the priesthood were restored under the hands of Moses, Elias, and Elijah. These things are true. They are true. God bless us to be faithful to the great knowledge that we have, to cultivate within our hearts a spirit of testimony, and to shape our lives accordingly and draw from our lives that great happiness which will be the blessing of each of us is my humble prayer, in the name of Jesus Christ, amen.

# Potomac, Virginia

# Regional Conference— Priesthood Leadership Session

### April 26, 1997

THIS IS A TREMENDOUS PICTURE, with this great hall filled with men on a Saturday afternoon. Thank you for coming this afternoon. It's a pleasure and an honor to be with you, to be one of you.

It's a great thing to belong to The Church of Jesus Christ of Latter-day Saints. It's a great thing to hold the priesthood of God, brethren. Don't ever forget that. That places upon each of us a very sacred and demanding responsibility to live the gospel and do what we can to improve the world in which we live. We have a great mandate laid upon us by the Lord to teach the gospel and save the people, and we cannot run from it. We have to face up to it, and that's a privilege and an honor and a sobering responsibility, really, when all is said and done.

I appreciated the music of this wonderful men's chorus singing that song of Charles W. Penrose:

> *School thy feelings, O my brother;*
> *Train thy warm, impulsive soul.*
> *Do not its emotions smother,*
> *But let wisdom's voice control.*
> *["School Thy Feelings," Hymns, no. 336]*

381

Do you know how that came to be written? He had been presiding in England. He was there for 11 years. He had never been to America, had never really known the organization of the Church. He thought they had forgotten him. He was presiding in Liverpool, and finally when he got his release, he was getting ready to move. During those 11 years he had accumulated a few sticks of furniture, besides that which the Church furnished. He had called the shipping agent and was bringing his things out of the house and putting them in the wagon, and some of the Saints came along and said, "Look. President Penrose is taking the Church's furniture."

He was a fiery Englishman. He had a temper, and he flared up when he heard that kind of remark. He then thought better and went up into his room and wrote those words and put them to a popular tune. "School thy feelings, O my brother; train thy warm, impulsive soul." That's the story of the song they've sung. It's a great hymn, and there is a message for each of us in that—each of us. So many people get so angry over such little things. We lose our tempers. We don't know how to control our emotions. Men come home tired at night after a long day and take it out on their wives and children. "School thy feelings, O my brother." Please, watch your temper. Whatever you do, watch your temper.

Now, I'd like to submit to you that when all is said and done, the work and the mission of this Church is to save. It's just that simple and just that profound, brethren—to save people. That's the whole purpose of what we are doing. That's why we have home teachers. That's why we have visiting teachers. That's why we have classes. That's why we have sacrament meeting. That's why we build temples—to save the living and the dead. That's our work. "This is my work and my glory—to bring to pass the immortality and eternal life of man" (Moses 1:39). And that's what it is all about, and we're not saving people as we should do. We are losing people.

It's simply a matter of neglect. I don't think it has to happen. I'm convinced it does not have to happen. I'm absolutely converted to the fact that it need not happen and that it must not happen. We can do better than what we have been doing, my brethren. We can do a lot better than what we have been doing.

I feel so strongly about this. I think it's so important. It is hard to join this Church. It's a different thing from what they have known. They need somebody to take them by the arm and say, "Come on, let me show you what it's all about. This is wonderful, this Church. I want to help you experience the beauties and the wonders of this Church."

Well, brethren, I repeat, we can do better than we have been doing in this matter. And this is a responsibility of the Melchizedek Priesthood. It's a responsibility of the Relief Society. It's a responsibility of the Aaronic Priesthood. It's a responsibility of the Young Women. It's a responsibility of the Primary even—to see that that comes to pass.

Years ago I was in a stake conference up in Wyoming, and it was in the days when we used to have not only a session in the morning but a session in the afternoon. The brethren have been improving; they can say all in the morning that they used to say in two sessions. But in the afternoon session—it was a winter day, snow outside, and everybody was sleepy. In fact, they were asleep. It was my turn to speak, and I saw right in the congregation a young man and his wife and three children. I'd asked all who were converts to the Church to raise their hands, and their hands had gone up. I said, "Brother whoever-you-are, come up here, and tell us about your experience in coming into this Church." And so he very sheepishly came up. He said, "I'll tell you what happened."

He said, "I'm a graduate chemical engineer. I came here to work in this big plant that's been built out here on the desert. I have a chemical engineering doctorate from Stanford. My wife has a degree in English. I know all about engineering; she knows all about English. But we don't know anything about getting along together. Our marriage was on the rocks. We were in trouble. We were ready to get a divorce. And my wife said, 'Why don't we join a church?' And I said, 'Okay, what church do you want to join?' And she said, 'the Mormon Church,' because she had worked for a man in San Francisco who was a member of the Church and for whom she had developed a great regard." And he said, "All right."

And so the first Sunday they drove around the block to see what time church started. And the next Sunday they came through that back door, and a man greeted them there and said, "I'm Brother so-and-so," and he said, "I'm so-and-so." He said, "What ward are you from? I haven't seen you before." He said, "Ward? What do you mean 'ward'?"

Well, anyway, the man at the door finally sensed that this was an investigator so he invited him in and sat with him on the back row. "It was Sunday School, and when it was time to go to class, he said, 'I'll go to class with you so you won't feel uncomfortable.' And he went and took our children to their respective classes and introduced them to their teachers, and then we went to the Gospel Doctrine class, and he sat with us."

Well, he said, "It was a nice experience, and the man said, 'Now, we have a meeting this evening, sacrament meeting' "—this was before the block plan. And they took him to sacrament meeting, and then he said, "Why don't you come to our home for dinner on Wednesday night? We'll invite the missionaries there—they can teach you better than we can teach you—and they'll teach you the gospel."

"And so we went to their home for dinner, and then the missionaries taught us. And three weeks later we were baptized, and the bishop was at our baptism. And as soon as we were baptized, we were confirmed members of the Church. And then the bishop said, 'Brother so-and-so, we have a job for you. We're putting you in charge of the hymnbooks. We sing in this church, as you know, and we are going to ask you to be at Sunday School and sacrament meeting 15 minutes early to see that all the books are in place. And Sister so-and-so, we're calling you to be assistant secretary in the Primary. Sister Smith, who presides over the Primary, will get in touch with you and talk about your duties.' "

And he said, "There we were. I was in charge of the hymnbooks, and she was to be assistant secretary in the Primary. Well, we felt pretty well about that. We said to ourselves, 'This is different, but it's good.' And so every Sunday morning I was there 15 minutes early. One Sunday it was snowing a terrible blizzard, and I said to my little boy, 'Let's go over and set out the hymnbooks.' And he said, 'Do we have to go in this storm?' And I said, 'Yes,' but then I stopped and said to myself, 'Jones, what's the matter with you? Here you hold a PhD in chemical engineering, and you are walking through this blizzard to go over there to hand out some hymnbooks.' Well, I went, and I handed out the hymnbooks. I tried to do what I'd been asked to do, and the bishop thanked me—before all of the brethren who came to the meeting that morning—for getting the books out. He thanked me again."

And he said, "Two weeks later, they gave me a different job, another job, and that's why we are here in this stake conference this afternoon. We are members of this Church. We've been baptized. We've been confirmed. We received the priesthood, and next month we're going to the temple in Salt Lake to be sealed together. We've fallen in love with one another again." And he thanked everybody who had been so helpful to them and then took his seat.

Now, it's just that simple. It just takes a little kindness and courtesy—love. That's all. Interest and concern.

Now, you have missionaries out from these stakes. The parents, some of them, are here—the fathers. They are writing them letters. They are praying for them. They are asking the Lord to lead them to the honest in heart, and yet you are neglecting those right here at home.

Brethren, the time has come to be "convert conscious" in this Church, for everyone to become convert conscious and hold on to these people who make that great, fearsome step of baptism into The Church of Jesus Christ of Latter-day Saints. Will you do it?

*Congregation:* Yes.

Thank you very, very much. Thank you ever so much. I am going to keep lifting my voice in this cause. If there is only one thing that I hope will happen during the time that I am where I am, it will be building an interest in, and a love for, those who come into the Church.

The Lord bless you, each one of you, in your tremendous responsibility for the converts who come into the Church.

# Adelaide, Australia

# Member Meeting

MAY 13, 1997

$\mathbf{M}$Y, YOU LOOK GOOD. You look good for having traveled so far. Many of you have come long distances. Are any of you here from Darwin—way up north? My, that is a long way. Is anybody here from Owl Springs? I don't see anybody from Owl Springs.

It is wonderful to be with you. It is wonderful to worship the Lord together as members of The Church of Jesus Christ of Latter-day Saints. I was here 20 years ago, back in 1977. There weren't as many then. You were much smaller. The Church has grown in this land in a marvelous and wonderful way. The Spirit of the gospel is among you. The Spirit of the Lord is with you. We thank you for who you are and what you do, for your faith and your faithfulness. We thank you for the love of the Lord, which you carry in your hearts—you people who strive to do the right thing, who rear your families in righteousness, who get on your knees and pray. That isn't a common thing anymore, to actually get on your knees and pray. Thank you for all that you do, my beloved brothers and sisters.

We received at the office the other day an interesting letter, and I would like to read a few words of it. I guess I can take that privilege, and the people who are here are those of whom it is written. I hope you draw some strength from it. This man who is in Arizona in the United States now writes as follows:

My parents, Mavis and Lloyd Edwards, live in Port Pirie, South Australia, and they tell me you will be visiting Adelaide in May. They joined the Church 34 years ago on December 29, 1962. When I was about eight, my mother was carrying her fifth child and was experiencing severe depression over bringing another child into this unstable world. We were active members of the Methodist religion, and mother went to her minister with her questions and found no answers. She investigated other religions but to no avail. She prayed often and was in a state of total hopelessness.

One night she went to bed quite troubled and had a dream. She was in a church that she had never seen before, and the feeling of total peace came over her. [She told other details that I won't go into now.] But when she woke the next morning, this peace remained with her and continued with her until my sister, Kay, was born. The change in her was greatly noticeable to my father and others. Two missionaries knocked on our door, but they didn't come back. Mother found a copy of the Book of Mormon, read it, and pondered it and didn't know what to do. Then, several months later, Elders Michael Jeppsen and Joseph Collett knocked on our door and found a woman explaining that she had been waiting for them. She received all of the discussions in a week and studied continually.

My father wanted nothing to do with what she had found and threatened divorce. My mother's parents and my father's father were in an uproar. One night they barged into our home and bodily removed the elders. They then set about trying to dissuade my mother from joining the Church. When all else failed, they told my father to divorce her and take the children, as she had gone crazy. That is the kind of estimate they had of the Church. They said they thought that the Mormons would take their daughters off to America. My grandparents, from whom my parents were buying our house, said that they would require immediate and complete payment or throw us out in the street. My mother, who until this time in her life had been a quiet, unassuming woman, just cried, saying over and over, "I can't say it is not true." After a long, unsuccessful time, my grandparents left. They did not return to our home for almost 15 years. My father, seeing that my mother had uncharacteristic strength, consented to listening to the missionaries. My parents, my brother, and myself were baptized two weeks later. My father in a short time was made president of the branch. We sent our children on missions; they taught the gospel wherever they were sent.

My parents are now old. My father has had a stroke. My mother is not well. They have seven active Church-member children, however, to bless their lives. Six married in the temple and one married, may I say, to a future member. Thirty-three active grandchildren, and the oldest grandson, my son, is now serving a mission. If one was to ask them, "Was it worth it?" I know that they would say, undoubtedly, with tears in their eyes, how grateful they are for the gospel that came into their lives.

There is a story of faith, my brothers and sisters—a story of love and devotion to the work of the Lord. There is faith among you. I know that. Great faith. You believe in the gospel of Jesus Christ. You love your Father in Heaven. You love your Savior and your Redeemer. You have faith in your lives.

Now, we are glad to be here. We were coming to Australia, and I said, "We don't have much time, but we must go to Adelaide. Somehow we have got to stop at Adelaide." We are here, and you are here. Again, my deep appreciation for your being here.

You've been told that we have been interviewed by a newspaper reporter this morning—two the day before. So it goes. They want to know what makes us tick. They want to know why this Church is growing. They want to know why we are a peculiar people. We are large in our membership. My answer: "We are different. We are unique. We're not like the rest of the world. We don't disparage other religions. We think they all do great good. We simply say to people, 'Take all the goodness you have, and come and bring it, and see if we can add to it.' " Now, that is, in the last analysis, the very essence of our work. Bring the good you have, and let us see if we can add to it.

We are a peculiar people. We are different. Can you imagine anybody in Australia not drinking tea? We don't drink tea. We don't drink coffee. We don't drink alcohol. We don't smoke cigarettes. Since 1833, when the Word of Wisdom was given, we have tried to abstain from these things. Now there is coming to light a great thought, as it were, on the part of the tobacco companies in America, acknowledging that they have known that cigarettes are addictive, that they have known that they are a causal factor in cancer and other matters. The Lord used the words "evils" and "conspiring men in the last days" (D&C 89:4). Now, as we have listened to the news in America, I had heard those same words—"conspiring men"—in these great companies which produce the cigarettes that we consume in America and ship across the world.

A study of the University of California at Los Angeles, recently issued, indicates that because of the Word of Wisdom, Mormon people, actuarially speaking, live 10 years longer than their peers in comparable groups. What a marvelous thing that is—10 years of life. Believe me, when you get to my age, 10 years of life means something. I am so grateful for the blessings of the Lord that come of the Word of Wisdom. We are expected to abide this, but it does not carry with it anything of constraint; it carries with it a blessing for those who will observe it. They "shall run and not be weary." They "shall walk and not faint." And "the destroying angel shall pass them by, as the children of Israel, and not slay them." And they shall have knowledge, "great treasures of knowledge, even hidden treasures" of the things of the kingdom of God. (See D&C

89:19–21.) My brothers and sisters, if nothing else came of the gospel except that precious Word of Wisdom, it would be a marvelous and wonderful thing for all who subscribe to it.

Now, that is only a very small part of it, as you know. Every principle of the gospel, my brethren and sisters, carries with it a conviction of its truth and divine origin. I said to these reporters that we finance the Church with tithing. You don't have to teach tithing to a man who pays his tithing. He has the conviction in his heart of the truth and the promise of the Almighty that those who are honest with Him in the payment of tithes and offerings, to them the windows of heaven will be opened and blessings will be poured down upon their heads that there shall not be room enough to receive them (see Malachi 3:10). I believe that with all my heart. That is not my promise. That is the promise of the Almighty. I give you my testimony that He keeps His promise.

My brothers and sisters, we have the marvelous blessings of the temple. I know you have a long ways to go to the temple in Sydney—a very long ways and a very costly journey—but you are trying to get there now and again. And the Lord blesses you for your faith and faithfulness. I hope that every man in this congregation has taken his wife to the house of the Lord, so that she might be sealed to him for time and all eternity—and their children. I was at the New Zealand Temple at the time of the dedication—1958. I went to a testimony meeting of Australian Saints before the temple was dedicated. I heard a man say this: "I was a young man with a young family. I had very little. We had an old car. We rented a house. We had a few sticks of furniture. We had a few dishes. I had a job, and that is all we had. I said, 'We can't go. As much as we'd like to go to the temple, we simply cannot afford to go.' " And then he said, "I looked across the table at my beautiful wife and at our three beautiful children, and I said, 'We cannot afford not to go. We must go.' You can sell your furniture. You can sell your dishes. You can sell your car and have enough to get there, and the Lord will somehow bless you to replace those valuables. But if you should ever lose these, your companion and your children, you would be poor indeed." So, he said to that little group, "We are here. After the temple is dedicated, we are going into that sacred house, and we will be married for time and for all eternity." There is nothing like it anywhere in the world. We are a peculiar people in our belief in that salutary doctrine. It is wonderful.

I was at the London Temple when it was built. Before it was dedicated, it was open for public showing. People lined up in long lines. The policeman said, "This is the first time I have ever seen people in a queue in England to go to church." They actually lined up to get into that beautiful temple. And I went over there for the missionaries in the evening. A young couple came out of the temple. I asked them, "Is there anything that I can do to help you? Do you have any questions?"

And the girl, who was holding her husband's hand, said, "Yes, what about this thing of eternal marriage that we saw a sign concerning in one of those rooms in the temple?"

I said, "I suppose you were married by the vicar."

She said, "Yes."

I said, "I suppose he said something like this: 'In sickness and in health, for richer or poorer, for better or for worse, till death do ye part.' " I said, "Did you realize that when the vicar pronounced your marriage, he also decreed your divorce?"

She said, "What do you mean?"

I said, "He didn't say anything beyond life. In fact he said, specifically, 'Till death do ye part.' Can you imagine heaven without the companionship of this young man whose hand you are holding here tonight?"

And she said, "No."

They walked out, hand in hand. I don't know what came of it. But I do know that as surely as the vicar married them, he also pronounced their separation. There is nothing anywhere in the entire world like the great sealing ordinance of the house of the Lord.

Brethren, if you haven't been to the temple, if you have not been sealed in the temple, work for it. Get a temple recommend. Carry it in your pocket. Save to go. Take your companion, your children, if you can, and go up to Sydney to the house of God, and there be joined under a covenant which time cannot destroy and death cannot break. We are a peculiar people. Thank heaven we are a peculiar people.

What about families? We believe in the eternity of the family. We believe that our children are the most precious things we have. Thank the Lord for children. I hope we treat them with kindness. Brethren, I hope that you don't abuse your wives, that you are not unkind to them. I hope that you love them and that you let them know that you love them. God designed that it should be so.

I hope that you are having your family home evenings. I said to a reporter who interviewed me today, "The family is falling apart all over the world. We see it everywhere. Children are turning to drugs and all of these other vicious things." This is what Isaiah said: "And all thy children shall be taught of the Lord; and great shall be the peace of thy children" (Isaiah 54:13). Have you seen children who didn't know peace? I have—children on drugs, children in jail, children in gangs, things of that kind. There is no peace in their lives. None whatever. "All thy children shall be taught of the Lord; and great shall be the peace of thy children." I don't know of a more wonderful blessing in all of this world than to have children who have peace in their hearts. "In righteousness shalt thou be established: thou shalt be far from oppression; for thou shalt not fear: and from terror; for it shall not come near thee. . . . No weapon that is formed against thee shall prosper; and every tongue that shall rise against thee in judgment thou shalt condemn. This is the heritage of the servants of the Lord, and their righteousness [is] of me, saith the Lord" (Isaiah 54:14, 17). We are a peculiar people.

We believe in that principle, that "all thy children shall be taught of the Lord; and great shall be the peace of thy children."

We believe that the Lord's law of finance in His Church is the law of tithing. I am happy for that. Wherever I go I see meeting-houses across this world. I see beautiful temples. You have contributed to make all of this possible. There are temples up and down the earth now, in South America, in Central America, in Mexico, in Europe, in Australia, in New Zealand, in Korea, in Japan, in Taiwan, in Hong Kong, in the islands of the sea, to bless the people.

Well, the time is about up. I can't say any more about that, except to compliment you on your faith. The Lord bless you, my dear associates in this great work. May He bless you with growing faith. May you, in love one to another, give peace and strength. May you help one another, lift one another. We are Latter-day Saints. We belong to the family of God. We have an obligation to help one another. We have an obligation to help the missionaries in their great undertaking. Their work is our work, and we must be about it.

You know that God lives, just as I do. You know that Jesus is the Christ, just as I do. You know that the priesthood is upon the earth, just as I do. You know that the Book of Mormon stands as another witness for Jesus Christ, just as I do. We have all of these blessings through the gospel of Jesus Christ. We are a peculiar people, yes, but how happy we are and how grateful.

Let us go forward now in faith and with love for the Lord and do what is expected of us and build the kingdom of God in this great and good land, working together, I humbly pray. We leave our blessings upon you and our love with you as we bear solemn witness and testimony of the truth of this work in the name of Jesus Christ, amen.

# Nuku'alofa, Tonga

# Member Meeting

OCTOBER 14, 1997

I SUPPOSE THAT THIS IS THE largest gathering of members of the Church ever held in Tonga. There are thousands of you here today. I have been to Tonga on a number of occasions in the past, but I have never seen so many people, and I am very deeply grateful to you. We had the opportunity earlier today of meeting with the king, and we had a very pleasant visit with him. We are grateful for the presence of these government officials today and thank them for coming. We are grateful for this wonderful campus. You people here have all of the blessings of the Church. You have meeting-houses all over these islands. You have this wonderful school [Liahona High School] with this great campus, and you have the house of the Lord. You are so richly blessed, and these blessings are yours because of your faithfulness and your love of the Lord and the manner in which you live the gospel.

God bless you, my dearly beloved brothers and sisters. I bring you the love of the entire Church throughout the world. How thankful I am for the faith of the Saints of Tonga. Through long years of history you have been faithful. First there were very few of you, and now the number has grown, and you have become an impressive body of Saints in this kingdom. Thank you again for being the kind of people that you are.

Now I pray that the Lord will bless me to say something that will be of benefit to you. We do not have much time left, and I think you must be tired of sitting for this long time. God bless you.

Live the gospel. My message to you today is to live the gospel. Cultivate in your hearts a testimony and a love for God your Eternal Father. We sing, "I am a child of God" (*Hymns,* no. 301). That isn't just a figment, a poetic figment—that is the living truth. There is something of divinity within each of us, my brothers and sisters, that needs cultivation, that needs to come to the surface, that needs to find expression. You fathers and mothers, teach your children that they are, in a very literal way, sons and daughters of God. There is no greater truth in all the world than that—to think that we have something of divinity in us.

Let every man or woman here have in his or her heart a conviction that Jesus is the Christ, the living Son of the living God, who gave His life on Calvary's hill for each of us. Let that become part of the very fabric of our lives. It is the duty, it is the responsibility, it is the opportunity of every Latter-day Saint to have a conviction concerning this great truth. Jesus said, "He that doeth the will of the Father shall know of the doctrine" (see John 7:17). That is the promise of the Lord Himself to each of us.

Let there be in our hearts an unshakable faith that God the Eternal Father and the risen Lord appeared to the boy Joseph Smith and spoke to him just as I am speaking to you this day. Let there be a conviction in the hearts of every one of us that this Book of Mormon is verily the word of God come to earth in our generation that we may have another witness of His living reality, for in the mouths of two or more witnesses shall all things be established (see Matthew 18:16; D&C 6:28).

Let there be a conviction in the heart of every member of this Church that the holy priesthood is upon the earth—the power to bless in the name of the Lord, the power to govern in the affairs of the Church, the power to be exercised in the name of God. This is a great and marvelous blessing which is among us. Let every man here—every man who has received the holy priesthood—live worthy of it, be as a true husband and father in his home, treating his wife with kindness and love and respect and treating his children as sons and daughters of God with love and respect and understanding and, above all, with great kindness. Let every man here who holds the priesthood know that that priesthood carries with it the power to bless and the power to heal. You have seen miracles in this land in the exercise of the holy priesthood. The sick have been raised up, and the blessings of the Lord have rested mightily upon them.

Let every man and woman in this congregation this day know that as members of this Church, he and she have an obligation to live the law, to bend their lives into conformity with the law of the land in which you live, to be good citizens—honest and upright and true in every respect, my brothers and sisters.

Let every woman who is here who is a member of this Church cultivate in her life those great virtues which are of the very essence of the gospel of Jesus Christ, to reach out in kindness and love and helpfulness to those who are in distress. May you be good mothers. As Sister Hinckley has suggested, read to your children; read from these great books. Your children may not understand all that you read, but they will feel something that will be sweet and good to them, and as the years pass they will grow in holiness before the Lord.

Let every boy here resolve within his heart that someday he will go on a mission and live for it and prepare for it and make a determination to have it come to pass. You will bless your lives. We have here today the missionaries now serving here. Everyone who serves in faithfulness will be magnified, will be strengthened, will be blessed throughout his life by reason of the service which he gives.

Let every man and woman here, and every boy and girl, resolve to attend his or her sacrament meetings, there to partake of the sacrament, the emblems of the Supper of the Lord, in remembrance of Him who is our Redeemer and there grow in faith and faithfulness as the gospel is taught.

Let man and woman take advantage of the great opportunities of the house of the Lord to be married for eternity, to live worthy of that blessing. There is no greater gift of God than the assurance that the most beautiful of all relationships will continue into the eternities. And let you who are able to go to the temple go there and labor in behalf of the dead in that great and unselfish work.

God bless you. I simply urge you to live the gospel. I promise you that if you will do so, you will be blessed in your homes, you will be blessed in your families, you will be blessed in your employment and in whatever else you do.

Now, my dear friends, you have been here for a long time. I have no desire to continue to preach for a long time. I want to tell you how much I love you. You are my people, and I am your servant, and there exists in our hearts a great love one for another. I don't know of any better people on the face of the whole earth than you people who are assembled here today. We pray for you. We want you to know that. We know that you pray for us, and we thank you for your prayers.

I leave with you my testimony of this great work. It is the work of God. It is the work of the Savior, whose name this Church bears and in whose name we carry forward all of the ordinances.

Let us resolve as of this day—every one of us—that we will be a little kinder, a little more helpful, a little more patient, a little more full of love one to another.

God bless you. God be with you till we meet again. I don't know whether we will come to Tonga again. I am now an old man, and it isn't as easy to travel as it once was. But I am here to express unto you my love and to leave my blessing upon you, and this I do as your friend and as your servant, in the name of Him whom we all serve, even the Lord Jesus Christ, amen.

# Brigham Young University

# Devotional

NOVEMBER 4, 1997

Tʜᴀɴᴋ ʏᴏᴜ, Bʀᴏᴛʜᴇʀ Wɪʟʙᴇʀɢ, for that very stirring music. It was wonderful. I think I would like to be the drummer. Thank you, Rhee Ho Nam; it is nice to hear from you again. I first met Rhee Ho Nam in 1960. That would be 37 years ago, when he was a little fellow in Korea. Now he is a little fellow in Provo. We had many interesting times together over there in the Land of the Morning Calm. I have a great regard for this, my dear friend Rhee Ho Nam.

My beloved brethren and sisters, what a wonderful thing it is to look into your faces—the thousands and thousands of you who are here this morning. Thank you for coming. You do us great honor by your presence. We are grateful for your lives, for your faith, for your love of the Lord, for your desire to walk His way and be the kind of men and women that the Lord expects you to be. Thank you for the goodness of your lives.

What a wonderful time it is to be alive. What a wonderful time to be a student at this great university. There is peace in the world. We are closing the bloodiest century in the history of all mankind, and there is peace—a few little skirmishes here and there, but no great, cataclysmic wars. How thankful you ought to be for that fact so that you are free to go forward with your lives. You live in a time when perhaps there are greater career opportunities than at any other time in the history of the world.

In a recent meeting of the board of trustees, members of the administration of the university spoke of ways to give a larger number of young people a taste of "the BYU experience."

I thought of that much after the meeting. The BYU experience—what is it? What is unique about attending this university in contrast with another?

I recently spoke on the campus of a sister institution in this state. The paper reported there were 20,000 in attendance. I think that figure is exaggerated, but the fact is there was a huge crowd. Most of them were institute students. They looked just the way you look. They were clean, well groomed, and neatly dressed. They were eager and attentive. As high a percentage of them will be married in the temple as there will be of you.

Returning from my experience on this other campus, I asked myself, "What does the BYU have to offer that this school does not?" Perhaps we need to go beyond our neighbor universities with their strong institutes. We need to reach out across the nation and beyond and take note of what is happening on the campuses of America. We have some truly great institutions of learning in this nation, but in so many cases are found circumstances which are seriously disquieting. Many of you, I am sure, read of the student who recently died of overdrinking—binge drinking, as they called it. There have been other cases of this. We have coeducational dormitories on some campuses. There are many faculty members who, perhaps even boastfully, speak of a lack of belief in God as if that were the mark of a great scholar. There are other problems, so very many of them.

I have reflected much of late on the unique features of this Church university. I am not surprised that students from far and wide are trying to get in here. It is a tragedy that so many must be turned away. Sometimes I wish we could support a dozen institutions such as

400

this. But we cannot, and the problem becomes more serious every year as we have in the Church an increasing number of young people.

What do you have here that, for the most part, is not found elsewhere? Is there any substance to this so-called BYU experience?

Well, I think so. For instance, you have student wards and stakes. I do not know how many of you really appreciate the meaning of this. There is no competition to get into social fraternities, and yet there is every opportunity for sociality. Here every student stands on an equal footing in belonging to a student ward. That ward is presided over by a bishop, a man called by the spirit of prophecy and revelation, with all the keys and the authority of a bishop in The Church of Jesus Christ of Latter-day Saints. He stands ready to listen to your problems, and you seem to have so very many of them. He stands ready to advise and counsel under the inspiration and guidance of the Holy Spirit. Your bishop, I submit, is your friend. He prays about you. He worries about you. He stands ready to help you at all times and in all circumstances. Further, you have elders quorums comprised of young men of dedicated purpose. They stand ready to help and to assist in any way they can.

In a severe recent storm, lightning struck the house next to my daughter's place. Windows were blown out of some 23 homes in the neighborhood. It was not 30 minutes, with the rain still falling, before an elders quorum was going from house to house boarding up the shattered windows so that there could be some measure of comfort in each home.

One of those neighbors was not a member of the Church. She had come from Europe. She was of a different faith. Her windows were boarded up along with the others. She said to my daughter, "I cannot understand your Church. Those young men were here immediately after I needed them. They seemed to come out of nowhere. No money was asked for or expected. I do not belong to your Church, but I was treated as though I did."

You young women have a Relief Society, a remarkable organization of your own.

The Sunday before last I attended a stake conference where a young woman, president of the Relief Society of a singles ward, spoke of service and the great opportunity afforded the young women in her ward. You have all of this. You have your own organization. You have able leaders to counsel you. You have those who will reach out to you to help you in your times of trouble and distress.

I believe you belong to the greatest brotherhood and sisterhood in the world. You are bound together by an endowment of one faith, one Lord, one baptism. You work together with appreciation and respect one for another. This is all part of the BYU experience.

You of this great institution have just to the east of you the house of the Lord, the beautiful Provo Temple. Many of you go there on a frequent basis. You go again and again. You go very early in the morning before your classes start. You have this great and remarkable opportunity to work unselfishly in the interest of others while growing spiritually yourselves. This is another aspect of the singular BYU experience.

I wish to add parenthetically that we do not encourage our young sisters necessarily to go to the temple unless they are being married or going on missions. This is a matter of choice which they must make after prayer and much deliberation, as well as discussion with their bishops and stake presidents.

You have the proscriptions and the prescriptions of the Word of Wisdom. Hence, drinking is not one of your problems. What a wonderful thing it is to have pleasant and happy associations without any inclination whatever to indulge in drinking or any related practice. And beyond this is the wondrous promise that you will receive "treasures of knowledge, even hidden treasures" (D&C 89:19). This does not mean that you will necessarily be smarter in your normal studies. It does mean that the power of the Holy Ghost may distill upon you and bring to you an increased knowledge and understanding of the sweet and marvelous things of the Lord. This is another phase of the BYU experience.

You have a unique and dedicated faculty to teach you. They bring to this great responsibility the learning of all the ages of man in a vast variety of fields of knowledge. They are, for the most part, dedicated Latter-day Saints—men and women who feel as much at home in the house of the Lord as they feel in the classrooms of this university. When all is said and done, it is not this elaborate campus that really counts. It is the faculty who teach you, who lead you, who encourage you, who help you find your way as you go forward with your studies. This, again, is an element of the unique and singular BYU experience.

Your studies will qualify you for your vocations. Time here will pass quickly, and you will soon be out in the world of work. You have a great variety of job opportunities from which to choose. I hope that you will be inspired in your choice, that you will be happy in the work you will undertake for the remainder of your lives. I hope you will make a great contribution in the fields in which you serve. I hope you will distinguish yourselves as leaders, as workers with a great sense of loyalty and dedication. I hope your training at this university will endow you with an increasing and powerful sense of responsibility toward the world of which you will be a part. Your performance will reflect honor on your alma mater.

I hope that the BYU experience will cause you to take on those qualities which will make of you a true disciple of Jesus.

All of you are taking religion classes while here. I hope that you are gaining much more than a knowledge of the organization of the scriptures and such matters as that. I hope that you are receiving a great desire to walk in the footsteps of the Master, to reach out to those in distress, to serve the Church with great faithfulness, and to serve your fellowmen in a spirit of love and consecration.

I hope the lessons of the second mile, of the prodigal son, of the good Samaritan, of the Son of God, who gave His life in a great offering of Atonement, will motivate you and never leave you.

I hope that this university will give to you a great sense of tolerance and respect for those not of your faith. The true gospel of Jesus Christ never led to bigotry. It never led to self-righteousness. It never led to arrogance. The true gospel of Jesus Christ leads to brotherhood, to friendship, to appreciation of others, to respect and kindness and love.

Mr. Shimon Peres called on us last Wednesday in the Church Administration Building. He is one of the elder statesmen of the world, the former prime minister of Israel. He has seen much of conflict and trouble in his time. He is a wise and able man who speaks with the spirit of a sage.

I asked him whether there was any solution to the great problems which constantly seem to divide the people of Israel and the Palestinians. He replied that of course there is. He said an interesting thing. As I recall, he said, "When we were Adam and Eve, we were all one. Is there any need for us to be divided into segments with hatred in our hearts one for another?"

He told a beautiful story that he said he got from a Muslim. The Muslim told of a Jewish rabbi who was conversing with two of his friends. The rabbi asked one of the men, "How do you know when the night is over and the day has begun?"

His friend replied, "When you look into the distance and can distinguish a sheep from a goat, then you know the night is over and the day has begun."

The second was asked the same question. He replied, "When you look into the distance and can distinguish an olive tree from a fig tree, that is how you know."

They then asked the rabbi how he could tell when the night is over and the day begins. He thought for a time and then said, "When you look into the distance and see the face of a woman and you can say, 'She is my sister.' And when you look into the distance and see the face of a man and can say, 'He is my brother.' Then you will know the light has come."

Think about that story for a minute. What a wonderful thing it says.

Not long ago I was asked to speak at a convention of the Religion Newswriters of America. Following my talk I invited questions. I was asked, "What are you going to do when 15,000 or 20,000 Baptists visit you in Salt Lake City next summer and try to proselytize you?"

I replied, "We are going to welcome them. We are going to do everything we can to make them feel at home. These are our brethren and sisters. They accuse us of not being Christian. I hope that our people will try to show them, by the very manner in which they act, that we are truly disciples of the Lord."

I said to these professional journalists, "As all of you know, we carry on a vast missionary program in this Church. But it is not argumentative. We do not debate. We, in effect, simply say to others, 'Bring all the good that you have and let us see if we can add to it.' "

We have no worry about the strength of our doctrinal position. We need only explain it—not with vociferous argument but in a quiet and friendly manner.

I hope that you will take from this university the habit of seeking knowledge and that this habit will never leave you for as long as you live. A truly educated man never ceases to learn. He never ceases to grow. I hope you young women, as you take upon yourselves the burden of rearing families, will never set aside your desire to acquire knowledge. I hope that you will read to your children. They will be blessed and you will be blessed if you do so. I hope that you will even read to your husbands. They need to be read to. I hope that you will read to yourselves.

Will you pardon me if I tell you about my father? When he was about the age that I am now, he was fully retired. But he was active. He lived in a rather simple but comfortable home in a rural area. He had an orchard around him and enjoyed giving away the fruit. The yard of his home included lawns and shrubs and trees.

It had a rock wall about two feet high separating one level from another. Whenever the weather was good he would sit on the wall, an old hat on his head to shade his eyes from the summer sun. When we went to visit him, I would sit at his side. With a little prompting he would talk of his life—of the time when as a boy he lived in Cove Fort. He would smile as he told of the time that his brother found a loaded pistol in the telegrapher's office. The boys began fooling around, the pistol fired, and his brother shot my father in the leg.

His father sent to Beaver for the doctor. The doctor arrived hours later and tried to remove the ball with a darning needle. He only made the pain worse. Father, sitting on his wall, would lift his pant leg, feel the flesh of his leg, and say that the ball was still there.

The family moved from Cove Fort to Fillmore, and when father was in his late teens he came here to Provo and enrolled in the Brigham Young Academy. He was a student of Karl G. Maeser, whom he came to know well. From here he went east to school. He then came back and taught here until the First Presidency of the Church asked him to move to Salt Lake City and preside over the business college, for which the Church had some great plans.

He was an educator. He was a successful business man. He presided over the largest stake in the Church with more than 15,000 members. He served as a mission president and in many other capacities. And now he was retired, and he sat on the wall. He was a great reader with a wonderful library. He was an excellent speaker and writer. Almost to the time he died, just short of the age of 94, he read and wrote and contemplated the knowledge that had come to him.

I discovered that when he sat on the wall, hours at a time on a warm day, he would reflect on the things he had read from his library.

I think he grew old gracefully and wonderfully. He had his books with the precious treasures they contained of the thoughts of great men and women of all the ages of time. He never ceased to learn, and as he sat on the wall he thought deeply of what he had read the night before. He acquired the habit while a student here under Dr. Maeser. It was part of his BYU experience.

At times I almost envy him. Time to read and time to ponder—what a blessing. He reminded me of leaves on the trees. When autumn comes with killing frost, the leaves change their color, and they give off a new beauty until they eventually drop to form a carpet on the ground.

Now, my friends, you are young, and why am I telling you of an old man and the wall on which he sat? I am telling you because I think it has a lesson for each of us. We must never cease to learn. We believe in eternal progression and that this life is a part of eternity to be profitably lived until the very end.

I have talked with you about the BYU experience as I sense it. I have spoken of a few of the many things which are a part of it. It has or will become a part of each of you. You are involved in it. You are going through it. It should, it must, leave an everlasting impression upon you. It is scarcely perceptible most of the time. But it is nonetheless real. It should become an inseparable part of your very nature, something almost intangible but of great substance.

You might have gone to another school and received an excellent education. But you came here and were fortunate enough to be accepted. You came because you wanted the BYU experience, although perhaps you could not define it. Having gained it, never lose it. Cultivate it in your lives, and hold its very essence until you grow old and gray. Even then you can sit on the wall on a warm summer day and think of the things you are still learning in light of the great experience you had as a young man or woman in this institution.

God bless you. I leave my love and blessing upon you, and my testimony of this great work, in the name of Jesus Christ, amen.

# CHRISTMAS DEVOTIONAL

## DECEMBER 7, 1997

M Y BROTHERS AND SISTERS, Merry Christmas to each of you, wherever you may be. May there be peace in your hearts, food on your table, and love in your homes at this wondrous season of the year.

This is a time, a season, of great significance. In a few days it will be the time of the winter solstice. In the Northern Hemisphere it is the time of year when the sun has reached its southernmost position. For six months it has been moving south. The days have grown progressively shorter and the nights longer. It is winter. It is cold. Now comes the promise that spring will come again and summer will return, as it has through all the millennia that men have been upon the earth.

It is no wonder that in ancient times Christmas, commemorating the birth of the Christ child, was celebrated at this solstice season. Men had no knowledge of the time of His birth, and so they came to bond the celebration of Christmas with the celebration of the return of the sun.

While we now know through revelation the time of the Savior's birth, we observe the 25th of December with the rest of the Christian world.

This month also marks the 192nd anniversary of the birth of the Prophet Joseph Smith. His birthday will grow in recognition and in importance as the years pass and the Church continues to grow. He was the great prophet of this, the dispensation of the fulness of times. It was to him that the God of the universe and the Redeemer of the world appeared to part the curtain and open the way to the restoration of eternal truth and divine authority. That incomparable visitation marked the beginning of a new day for all mankind, for the work that was to spring from that singular event would eventually affect all the sons and daughters of God who are willing to listen and obey, both the living and the dead.

That First Vision became the ultimate consequence of the atoning sacrifice of the Lord Jesus Christ. What He did for all mankind cannot reach its highest benefit without acceptance of gospel ordinances on the part of those who become the beneficiaries of His redemption.

Born in humble circumstances, reared largely without benefit of formal education, Joseph became the leader of this the cause of Christ whose influence will yet be felt throughout the earth.

It was the Prophet Joseph who received and held the keys of the eternal priesthood, "the fulness of the priesthood" (D&C 124:28), whose powers reach beyond the veil of death. He it was who translated and brought forth a second witness of the divinity and reality of the Lord. He it is who stands at the head of this dispensation as prophet and apostle, as seer and revelator.

At this season of his birth, it is well that we pause to remember him as we determine within ourselves to follow his teachings that came of revelation from the Almighty.

And now, most importantly, we honor the birth of our Lord, the Son of God, who condescended to come to earth because He loved us. He came to do for us that which we could not do for ourselves. Without His Atonement we would be helpless before the unrelenting grasp of death. Our destiny would be that dark and

410

dismal "country from whose bourn no traveler returns" (William Shakespeare, *Hamlet*, act 3, scene 1). We would stand hopeless and helpless in our sins, going nowhere, making no progress.

But because of Him—and of Him alone—there is hope, there is peace, there is light and understanding. Through His great act of redemption, through His atoning sacrifice, came eternal life. The gift of the resurrection is afforded all, and the opportunity for eternal progress and eventual exaltation is granted those who will listen to Him and obey Him.

There is nothing to compare with it in all of earth's history. The great political empires have come and gone. But the lonely figure of the Son of God, hanging on the cross on Calvary's hill to die a mortal death and to rise again in immortality, has become the realization of the eternal hope of the world. "O death, where is thy sting? O grave, where is thy victory?" (1 Corinthians 15:55).

It is the miracle of the Resurrection that gives wonder to His birth.

And so at this Christmastime we not only honor the birth of the Babe of Bethlehem but also the crucified Lord who died for each of us and rose the third day to become "the firstfruits of them that slept" (1 Corinthians 15:20).

> *I stand all amazed at the love Jesus offers me,*
> *Confused at the grace that so fully he proffers me.*
> *I tremble to know that for me he was crucified,*
> *That for me, a sinner, he suffered, he bled and died.*
> *Oh, it is wonderful that he should care for me*
> *Enough to die for me!*
> *Oh, it is wonderful, wonderful to me!*
> *["I Stand All Amazed," Hymns, no. 193]*

How thankful we ought to be. How grateful we must be for this gift that is greater than all other gifts.

At this season we offer presents one to another in a shoddy similitude of His great gift to all mankind. We empty the stores of vast inventories of merchandise. It almost becomes a travesty of the true spirit of Christmas. But possibly the effort is not all lost. At least there comes into our lives a touch of generosity toward others. Our hearts are opened, our thoughts are lifted as at no other season of the year. We greatly overdo it, but perhaps it is not all bad. We think of others, and what a blessing that is.

And now, my brothers and sisters, may I, as His servant, leave with you my testimony of the Redeemer of the world, He who was born in Bethlehem of Judea and of whose birth we sing this night.

He was and is the Son of God, the Firstborn of our Eternal Father and His Only Begotten in the flesh. He was the Creator of the heavens and the earth under His Father's direction, for as John says, "Without him was not any thing made that was made" (John 1:3).

He was Prince in His Father's royal household, who stood at His Father's side. He was of the lineage of the Gods. And yet He condescended to come to earth, to be born in the humblest of circumstances of Mary, His mother. She was mortal, and thus He took upon Himself mortality. His Father was immortal, and thus He took upon Himself immortality.

"For unto us a child is born, unto us a son is given: and the government shall be upon his shoulder: and his name shall be called Wonderful, Counsellor, The mighty God, The everlasting Father, The Prince of Peace" (Isaiah 9:6).

"And the spirit of the Lord shall rest upon him, the spirit of wisdom and understanding, the spirit of counsel and might, the spirit of knowledge and of the fear of the Lord" (Isaiah 11:2).

He grew as a child in Nazareth. But He must have had some sense of His great mission, for when He was lost and Mary and Joseph found Him with the learned men in the temple, He said,

"Wist ye not that I must be about my Father's business?" (Luke 2:49).

He was baptized of John in Jordan "to fulfil all righteousness" (Matthew 3:15). He suffered temptation, fasting in the wilderness to gain the power to rebuke Satan and overcome the world. In His brief ministry He walked the roads of Palestine, teaching by example and precept the simple and sublime ways of the Lord. He fulfilled the law of Moses and gave to the world a new testament. He healed the sick, caused the blind to see, the crippled to walk, and the dead to rise again. He rebuked the scribes and Pharisees as hypocrites, and they conspired to take His life.

He was arrested and brought before Pilate, who found no fault in Him but succumbed to their cries that He be crucified. In mockery they placed a crown of thorns upon His head and a robe of royal purple upon His shoulders. He carried the instrument of His death to the place of crucifixion. There the nails pierced the quivering flesh of His hands and feet.

As He was dying, He cried out, "Father, forgive them; for they know not what they do" (Luke 23:34). He was buried in the tomb of Joseph of Arimathea.

He rose from the grave the third day as the Redeemer of the world, the Savior of mankind, triumphant over death and hell. He was seen by many in both the Old World and the New. He ascended to His Father on high and there He stands as King of Kings and Lord of Lords. He has come to earth again in a glorious vision to usher in this last and final dispensation in which we live. He presides over this great latter-day work as head of the Church which bears His name.

We, you and I, are His disciples. We have taken upon ourselves His holy name. We worship Him. We love Him. We look to Him as our truest friend, as our incomparable leader, as the promised Messiah, the living Son of the living God.

413

*Joy to the world, the Lord is come;*
*Let earth receive her King!*
*Let ev'ry heart prepare him room,*
*And Saints and angels sing.*
*["Joy to the World," Hymns, no. 201]*

In His holy name, even the name of Jesus Christ, I so testify. Amen.

# ACCRA, GHANA

# MEMBER MEETING

FEBRUARY 16, 1998

$M$Y DEAR FRIENDS, MY BELOVED brethren and sisters, what a wonderful picture you are. My, you look great! You look just wonderful! All of you seem so happy. You ought to be. You have found the pearl of great price. You have found the gospel of Jesus Christ. It has come into your lives. You ought to be very, very happy, and I think you are. I want to bring to you the love and the blessings of all my associates among the General Authorities of the Church—my counselors in the First Presidency, the Council of the Twelve, the Seventy, and the Presiding Bishopric—and all who have responsibility to lead this program throughout the world. They would have me convey their love to each of you as I convey my own. I am so glad we have come to Africa to meet you people, to marvel at the wonderful people—you Latter-day Saints of great faith and strong testimony who are trying to live the gospel in your lives. You are a testimony of this work.

I remember back in the days before we ever came here. A handful of men and women—before there was ever a Church here—organized what they called The Church of Jesus Christ of Latter-day Saints and tried to move the program forward. Now it is here in full glory, and the blessings are yours. You have so very many blessings in the Church. We are trying to see that you have

415

everything the Latter-day Saints have everywhere in the world. You have meetinghouses. We will build more. You have stake centers. We will build more. And before I get through I might communicate to you a secret concerning something else—if I don't forget it, and maybe if I do, it will be providential.

It is so good to be with you—wonderful to be with you. We love you. We have had the opportunity of traveling across the world in many parts of the earth—all up and down South America and Central America and Mexico and Asia, New Zealand, and Australia. And I said to my secretary, who is here today, "I think we ought to go to Africa. We should go to Africa and meet those wonderful people there." And so we are with you today.

Coming here we stopped in Halifax, Canada, for a meeting like this. We had to sleep overnight there, so we stopped and held a meeting. We had to sleep another night, and so we stopped in the Canary Islands and held a wonderful meeting there. Latter-day Saints are everywhere. And then we held a meeting yesterday in Port Harcourt—a wonderful meeting, with more than 12,000 people in attendance. It was remarkable and wonderful. And now we are here today meeting with you in this historic place— Independence Square. There is a great gate down there that says "1957—Freedom and Justice." That commemorates the British leaving here and allowing Ghana to govern itself. It speaks of freedom. It speaks of justice. It speaks of independence. It speaks of opportunity. And I commend you most warmly.

As Brother Holland said, we had the very great privilege today of meeting your president, His Excellency, President Jerry Rawlings. We had a very delightful visit with him. We found him to be a good man, a man of foresight, a man of vision, a man who understands where he would like to lead this nation as it moves forward among the nations of the earth. We gave him the assurance that the Latter-day Saints of Ghana are loyal to this nation. They uphold this nation. They strengthen this nation by the goodness of their lives. I want to call on everyone who is here this day to make that apparent to all who see you and know you in your daily activities, to be men and women of loyalty to the nation of which you are a part. Love of country is a great thing. It is a good thing. If we want to change the world, we begin with ourselves, and then we move out to include our fellow citizens and build goodness among the people. That is what you have been doing and I hope that you will continue to do. This is a good land of which you are part. It is getting better all the time. I was here a few years ago, and I have noticed a great difference—the improvements which have been made. You are in a good land, and you ought to be very proud of it and grateful for it, for the Lord has blessed you with citizenship in this nation of Ghana.

I would like to commend the missionaries who are here. They are all right here at the front. They all look very sober. Now, smile a little, you missionaries! That looks better. You are preaching the gospel of good news. The things you have to teach are good. They are designed to make people happy and live a better life. You ought to put a smile on your face and go forth to do the work which the Lord has outlined for you, and He will bless you. And the missionary's experiences which you have will become a great part of your lives, a great period in your lives to which you will look back all of your days with appreciation and gratitude. You are only on missions for a short time; make the most of it. I know that those who have just arrived think that it is a very long time. It will look like a long time for the first three months, and then suddenly it will get very short and look very brief, so enjoy it, and live it up, and be happy in the great opportunity that is yours.

Now, I want to base my remarks on the great statement of Peter. My son has read one statement; I want to read another—a great statement of Peter which he wrote to the people of his time but which I believe he also wrote to us in this day and time in the work of the Lord. Said he—and I am reading from the second chapter and the ninth verse of 1 Peter—"But ye are a chosen generation, a royal priesthood, an holy nation, a peculiar people; that ye should shew forth the praises of him who hath called you out of darkness into his marvellous light" (1 Peter 2:9).

Those are wonderful words, my brothers and sisters, in which Peter reminds us that we are "a chosen generation." Of all the people who have lived upon the earth, we are most fortunate, most blessed in the great time in which we have come forth in the history of the world. This is a period of great enlightenment, a period of great understanding, a period when scientists have discovered things which will prolong life. There has been more scientific discovery during the period of my life than during all of the previous time of the history of the earth. What a glorious season this is to be alive. And with all this, and most important of all, we have the gospel of Jesus Christ restored to the earth through a great opening vision experienced by the Prophet Joseph in which he witnessed and spoke with the Father and the Son. There had been nothing like that in centuries and centuries of time. That, in my judgment, is the greatest event that has occurred in the history of the modern world—that the Father of us all, the God of the universe, would speak to a young boy words of instruction, introducing His Beloved Son and telling him to hear what His Beloved Son had to say.

I listened to a videotape the other night prepared by the Baptists. They are coming to Salt Lake to hold a convention, and they want to convert us all. But they say, among other things in that videotape, that we are not mainstream Christians. As I understand it, they believe that God the Father and the Son, Jesus Christ, and the Holy Ghost are one being. The scriptures tell a different story. Jesus prayed to His Father in Heaven. His Father in Heaven spoke at the time of His baptism. There was a vision of His Father at the time of Transfiguration. And in that great, classic prayer, He said, "Our Father which art in heaven, Hallowed be thy name"

(Matthew 6:9). He said, "I will be your access to the Father" (see John 14:6). They are two beings, entirely separate. And He promised the Holy Ghost as the Comforter when He should leave them. They are separate beings. Joseph Smith, I would like to submit, learned more about the nature of Deity as a 14-year-old boy in the grove of his father's farm than the acts of all the ministers and priests and the divines who have long argued that question.

Do we have a testimony of the God of heaven? You do. I do. God, our Eternal Father, lives, and what a marvelous thing. We know that He lives. He who rules the universe is our individual Father, to whom we may speak as a son speaks to his father. Jesus is the Christ, the great Jehovah of the Old Testament, the promised Messiah of the New Testament, our King, our Lord, our Savior, our Redeemer, who gave His life for each of us. And the Holy Ghost bears testimony in our hearts concerning the Father and the Son.

Ye are a chosen generation, my brothers and sisters, who have been blessed with light and knowledge and understanding of these eternal truths of the gospel of Jesus Christ.

Ye are a royal priesthood, a royal priesthood. Do you men here know that you have in the priesthood that has been bestowed upon you the authority and the gift to speak in the name of God, to act in His stead in moving forward His work, in blessing others, in standing as watchmen on the tower? Ye are a royal priesthood. Never forget that, my brethren. Don't ever do anything—never do anything which would sully the wonderful power which you hold. Don't you ever abuse your wives, you men. No man who abuses his wife is worthy of the priesthood of God. I want to say that very plainly. No man who abuses his children is worthy of the priesthood of God. No man who is dishonest with his neighbors, with those with whom he does business, is worthy of a royal priesthood. That is your great and marvelous blessing. No one else has it. "We believe that a man must be called of God, [through] the laying on of hands by those [having] authority to preach the Gospel and administer in the ordinances thereof" (Articles of Faith 1:5). That is your privilege, and that is your opportunity. That came to you through a prophet of God in 1978, who received a revelation that all worthy men would be worthy of every privilege the Church has to offer. I was in that meeting. I was a personal witness to that which happened 20 years ago this coming June.

Now, what a blessing that has been to this nation. What a blessing that has been to all of Africa. You and I are brethren and sisters. We are of the same family. God is our Eternal Father. We have love one for another and respect and honor and appreciation one for another. God bless you good men to be faithful, to be true, to live up to your covenants and be the kind of men which God, our Eternal Father, expects you to be—men of a great, royal priesthood.

An holy nation—I don't think that description applies to a political nation. I think it applies to a congregation of Saints, of men and women who have taken upon themselves the name of the Lord Jesus Christ and become part of an holy nation, of a great body reaching across the earth. We have become that. We are now 10 million strong in more than 160 nations, and we are growing faster than we have ever grown in the history of the Church. And we shall continue to spread and multiply, and no force under the heavens will be able to stop the growth of this cause, because it is the cause of Christ, it is the cause of God, our Eternal Father. And They are They who rule in the heavens above and outlined the destiny of those who live here upon the earth.

Ye are an holy nation—I repeat, 10 million strong—and yet we are concerned with the individual. We don't bring in masses of people. We don't deal in masses of people; we deal with individuals. All of us are just alike. We get sick. We have pain. We worry about our affairs. We worry about our children. We worry about all of these things which are individual problems, and the Church stands ready to help us. It points the way that we should go if we would have happiness in this life. And so to each of you who is a member of this great and holy nation of which Peter spoke, I give words of encouragement to carry on, to do what is expected of you. Be prayerful. Rely on the Lord. Look to Him, and you will be blessed. It is imperative that you bless one another with acts of kindness and outreach, to assist all who are in distress, to assist all who are in need and reach out to those in trouble and sorrow and sickness and pain who need our help.

"A peculiar people," said Peter. We are a peculiar people. We are a little different. I tried to tell President Rawlings that today. He spoke of all the Christian religions here in this nation, how they can become a force for good or a force for evil. I think that is true. We must stand forth as a force for good to bless this nation with our very presence and our very way of living. We are a peculiar people. We don't smoke—no cigarettes. No, I should say not! We don't drink—no alcohol. No, of course not! Not even tea or coffee. Of course not. We don't take these things into our bodies. We believe that the body is the temple of the spirit, that the body is sacred, that it is a creation of the Almighty, that we were formed in His image to do His work and do it in a way acceptable unto Him. We are a peculiar people in the manner of our living. We observe the Word of Wisdom. What a wonderful blessing that is. It isn't a burden. It is a blessing. It has been shown by a professor at the University of California at Los Angeles, whom I have met, that those who observe the Word of Wisdom live longer, much longer— 10 years longer than their class, actuarially speaking, who do not observe it. What is 10 years of life worth, I ask you? What is it worth? Is that a burden? It is a marvelous and wonderful blessing. We are a peculiar people in the things we teach. No drugs. There are young people here today. I want to tell you: Avoid drugs. Stay away from them. They will utterly destroy you if you let them get possession of you. Avoid them as you would a plague. Stay away from pornography. It will destroy you if you let it take possession of your life. Avoid it. You don't need these things.

We are a peculiar people in our love of the Lord and our obedience to His mind and will. God bless you, my beloved friends. You are loved by all of us more than I can say. I feel a great outreach of love toward you.

Now I would like to read to you the words of Alma to his son Helaman. Alma, speaking to his son Helaman, who was going out among people like you, said this: "Teach them an everlasting hatred against sin and iniquity." What a remarkable statement that is.

"Teach them an everlasting hatred against sin and iniquity.

"Preach unto them repentance, and faith on the Lord Jesus Christ; teach them to humble themselves and to be meek and lowly in heart; teach them to withstand every temptation of the devil, with their faith on the Lord Jesus Christ.

"Teach them to never be weary of good works, but to be meek and lowly in heart, for such shall find rest to their souls.

"O, remember, my son, and learn wisdom in thy youth; yea, learn in thy youth to keep the commandments of God" (Alma 37:32–35).

I commend those words from the 37th chapter of Alma to each of you and urge you, when you return to your homes, to read them and to study them.

Now, brethren and sisters, we are glad the Church is growing in Ghana. It is growing in a remarkable way. We are grateful for each of you. We hope, we pray, we plead with you that every one of you will reach out to those who become converts to this Church and put your arms around them and make them feel at home, to teach them the doctrine of the kingdom, to befriend them and help them in every way possible. When they come into this Church, they are strangers. They don't know quite what to do. I ask you, with all the fervor of my heart, to reach out to save every convert who comes into this Church. You will be blessed if you do so. The

Church will be blessed. The kingdom of God will grow here to bless the people. They have made a great move.

I told President Rawlings today that we do not argue and fight with other churches. We do not. We simply go forward preaching, in a positive way, our doctrine. We say to people, in effect, "You bring with you all the good that you have, and then you come and let us see if we can add to it." Now, that is our purpose, and that is our mission.

Brethren and sisters, will you make a special effort, will each of you make a special effort—let's see thousands of your hands to make a special effort to reach out to every convert who comes into this Church that the Church may grow in a marvelous and remarkable way. And I make you a promise that if you will do it, you will be blessed with a temple in your midst.

Now, you have gone a long time without a temple. When I was here five years ago, we tried to find a place that we could build a temple. We didn't find anything, and we didn't say anything to anybody. But—I'm breaking new ground here, and I know the media is here, so it will get back to Salt Lake very quickly—this morning we approved the purchase of a beautiful piece of ground on which we propose to build a temple in Accra, Ghana. When it is completed you won't have to travel all the way to London or all the way to Johannesburg to have the blessings of the Lord, the greatest blessings He has to give. Don't expect it all in a day. It will take two or three years to build it. We have to get authorizations from the various bodies of government to make that possible, but it will come as a great blessing, my brothers and sisters.

And now is the time to get ready for that day when it will be dedicated. Now is the time to get a temple recommend. Even if you have no temple you can go to now, get a recommend, and treasure it, and live for the great privilege of going to the house of the Lord for your own endowment and to be sealed with that sealing the like of which there is nothing else anywhere on this earth. I am happy to bring you that good word and hope that it is fulfilled as quickly as possible, because I would like to see the faithful Saints of this land able to go to a house of the Lord for their sacred covenants—those covenants which we make with God concerning the nature of our lives and our faith. For you are "a chosen generation, a royal priesthood, an holy nation, a peculiar people, that [you might] shew forth the praises of him who hath [led] you out of darkness into his marvellous light" (1 Peter 2:9).

God bless you, my good friends. I love you. I leave my testimony, I leave my blessings, I leave my love with you and do it as your fellow servant, in the name of Jesus Christ, amen.

# Geneva, Switzerland

# Member Meeting

### June 6, 1998

Y OU HAVE COME HERE THIS Saturday afternoon, and I pray that the Spirit of the Lord may be with us. I pray that it may guide me in what I say, that I may bring to you a remembrance of those sacred and wonderful things which constitute our testimonies of this work.

I have been thinking as I have been sitting here of a great meeting that was held 25 years ago in Munich, Germany. It was a European conference of the Church—a great area conference. It was held in the Olympics facility in Munich. People came from all over Europe—from way up in Scandinavia, from Italy, from Spain, from all of the closer countries, France, Switzerland, Austria—in a great conference. I was there, and to me it is an absolute miracle what has happened in this Church during those 25 years. At that time we had about as many people as we have here today.

Last night we were in Frankfurt, and there were 6,200 people in a meeting. Before that we were in Paris with a great crowd like this. Today this hall is filled with faithful Latter-day Saints.

I love this part of the world, this beautiful land of Switzerland. I love to get over among the mountains and look at those tremendous Alps, which rise from the valleys of Germany and Switzerland, Austria, France, and Italy; the great rivers that flow to the sea from the melting snows in these vast mountains; the crystal lakes that lace the landscape; the dark and beautiful forests; the quaint villages; the well-kept farms; the architecture in these marvelous cities of Europe. And I feel particularly blessed to be in this great city of Geneva—*Genève*—this wonderful city which through the centuries has harbored the dissenters, the reformers, and given asylum to those who spoke with a different voice—brave and bold men who spoke out words of truth as they understood them.

I have looked at all of these beautiful things in this part of Europe as through the years I have come here. But the most beautiful thing I have seen is not the mountains; it is not the rivers; it is not the lakes; it is not the architecture. It is you, my brethren and sisters of great faith. You are here gathered today giving strength one to another, the faithful of the Church in this area. Many of you have come long distances to be here, and it feels good to have Latter-day Saints around you in large numbers. Most of you are converts to the Church, and in your lives you have felt a great loneliness, the lonely experience of joining this Church, of leaving the past behind you and coming into the present. How you must have appreciated those who befriended you and showed love to you.

I want to make a plea. I want to plead with every one of you who is here today to reach out in love, to reach out in friendship, to reach out in companionship to the new converts to the Church. Let them feel that they have in you an anchor in the stormy world in which they find themselves—an anchor of faith and truth and friendship. All of us, I think, in some measure, have experienced this loneliness. With all the numbers that we have, we are still a very small group, a very small body in the midst of the population of this part of the earth. We need one another's companionship. We need to befriend and build one another, to extend love and kindness one to another.

We occupy a special position, you and I. We are members of The Church of Jesus Christ of Latter-day Saints. We stand in a

426

position of leadership before the world, and there is a loneliness in that leadership. . . . "Uneasy [rests] the head that wears a crown" (William Shakespeare, *King Henry IV, Part 2,* act 3, scene 1). The crown of the gospel of Jesus Christ rests upon our heads. When in this dispensation the Lord declared that this is "the only true and living church upon the face of the whole earth" (D&C 1:30), we were immediately put in a position of loneliness—the loneliness of leadership, from which we cannot shrink nor run away. Every true member of this Church who lives and breathes the Spirit of the gospel knows something about that loneliness. But once having gained a testimony, once knowing that this work is true, we have to live with our conscience. We have to live with our faith. We have to live with our testimony. The price of adherence to conscience is loneliness. The price of living with principle is loneliness.

The Savior of the world was one who walked alone much of the time. I know of no statement more underlined with the pathos of loneliness than His statement: "The foxes have holes, and the birds of the air have nests; but the Son of man hath not where to lay his head" (Matthew 8:20). There is no lonelier picture in all of history than that of Jesus upon the cross alone, the Redeemer of mankind, the Savior of the world, bringing to pass the Atonement—the Son of God suffering for the sins of mankind. Some of you may have visited the Garden of Gethsemane in Jerusalem. If so, you sensed in your minds the terrible struggle through which He passed there, pleading with His Father in Heaven, wrestling within Himself until blood came from every pore of His body, and then being led away and nailed to the cross and crying out, "My God, my God, why hast thou forsaken me?" (Matthew 27:46).

When the tyranny of religious oppression was smothering Europe, there arose a man here and a man there who stood above the crowd and spoke up in defense of truth. I believe that the reformers were inspired of God to lay the foundation for another time when an angel would fly through the midst of heaven, "having the everlasting gospel to preach unto them that dwell on the earth, and to every nation, and kindred, and tongue, and people" (Revelation 14:6).

I salute Hesse and Zwingli, Luther and Tyndale, who knew the meaning of loneliness as they stood out in testimony of the truth against the powers of the government and the powers of the church in their day. Some of them gave their lives for the stand which they took.

Joseph Smith was a man of loneliness. The 14-year-old boy who came out of the woods on his father's farm was hated and persecuted. Can you sense something of his loneliness as reflected in these words: "While they were persecuting me, reviling me, and speaking all manner of evil against me falsely for so saying, I was led to say in my heart: Why persecute me for telling the truth? I have actually seen a vision; and who am I that I can withstand God, or why does the world think to make me deny what I have actually seen? For I had seen a vision; I knew it, and I knew that God knew it, and I could not deny it" (Joseph Smith—History 1:25).

There are few more sorrowful pictures, my brothers and sisters, than of the Prophet Joseph being rowed across the Mississippi River to get away from his enemies. Then there were some of his own people who accused him of running away. Under these circumstances he said, "If my life is of no value to my friends it is of none to myself" (*History of the Church,* 6:549). He returned and was taken to Carthage, where on June 27, 1844, he was killed as a martyr for the truth.

In your hearts you carry a testimony of the truth of this work. It is a gift of God which has come to you by the power of the Holy Ghost. It is more precious than all else. It puts you in a position of loneliness, but you have no alternative but to go forward and live the gospel. Live the Word of Wisdom. Pay your tithes and offerings. Be faithful and true. Go to the temple. And you young men and women, there comes upon you the responsibility, inescapable, under which you must live up to the knowledge which you carry in your hearts. Prepare for a mission. Prepare for marriage in the temple. Go out with those in the Church so that you will marry someone in the Church. You will be happier if you do so.

My brothers and sisters, I remind you that when you have embraced the gospel you must stand up—if it means loneliness, yes—for the truth. Proclaim it. Live it. Teach it. Practice it. You must observe the practices of the Church. The Word of Wisdom becomes the word of the Lord to you when you have that testimony in your hearts. You may feel lonely at times. That is the price of membership in The Church of Jesus Christ of Latter-day Saints. God help you and bless you, every one, to be faithful, to be true. The world may scoff. Your friends may belittle you, but that testimony must shine through in your lives. May you be true and faithful. You great Saints in this chosen part of Switzerland and in this chosen part of France, walk boldly. Quietly, yes, but with confidence and assurance in your hearts. And when all is said and done, you and I must carry in our hearts that testimony and that conviction of the everlasting truth.

God help us to be faithful, I humbly pray, in the name of Jesus Christ, amen.

# Provo Missionary Training Center

# Friday Night Devotional

JUNE 26, 1998

$I$T IS SO VERY, VERY NICE TO BE with you. I scarcely know what to say. I haven't a prepared talk. I'm just going to speak out of my heart, and if I ramble around a little, I hope that will be all right.

First, I want to congratulate you, every one of you who is here, on having the confidence of your bishop and your stake president to recommend you to serve a mission for The Church of Jesus Christ of Latter-day Saints. That isn't a built-in right in this Church; that is a privilege that is extended to those who receive a call. I congratulate you most warmly on having received the call to the mission to which you are going. I want to thank you for the great service which you will give. You've come to the MTC, and this is quite a thing, in and of itself, to be here as long as you will be here and to be subject to the regimen and the pressures of this great institution which we call the MTC. Thank you for your faith. Thank you for your desire to go. Thank you for your will and your wish to serve the Lord.

Wherever you are called and whatever your duty might be, may the Lord bless you, and may you find joy therein. You will start as a junior companion. I hope you have a good senior companion. I hope you will look for the good in him. I hope that you will find a great deal of virtue in him. I remember interviewing some missionaries in Asia at one time, and I said to one of the missionaries, "What do you see in your companion's life that you'd like to put into your own?" He was dumbstruck. He didn't say a word. He'd never seen any virtue in his companion. He said, "I don't know." I said, "Well, you think about it." He began to think, and then he began to talk a little. He said, "He's a hard worker. He gets up in the morning and gets out on the street. He does what is expected of him." I said, "Do you?" He said, "No, I'm not quite as good as that." I said, "You adopt into your life the virtues of your companion." Every missionary has a companion. In the mouths of two or more witnesses shall all things be established (see Matthew 18:16; D&C 6:28). You stand as witnesses one with another in this great work of bearing testimony of the restored gospel of Jesus Christ.

In the early days of the Church, missionaries worked independently; and, until relatively recent times, missionaries would go into a city, and one would go down one side of the street and one down the other side of the street. We don't do that now. We work together so that one may stand as a witness of the other should there be troubles, should there be difficulty, or should there be an opportunity to bear testimony of the truth of this work.

You will have companions all during your mission. I hope you will appreciate them. I hope you look for the good in them. You will find it if you look for it. You won't find it if you don't look for it. I will be forever grateful for my missionary companions of long ago. I listened to a missionary the other night say that he had 15 companions during the 2 years that he was in the field. I had 4 companions, one of them for 15 months—the same companion for 15 months. I'll always be grateful for that young man. He was a wonderful young man. I went through the university with him, but I didn't get to know him there. But I got to know him as my missionary companion. We worked together, we prayed together, we learned to love and appreciate and respect one another. He has now passed on. He married out of the Church and was not active, I'm sorry to say, for many of the years after he returned. The day that he died, his wife called me and said, "I'd like you to give him a funeral." That was her way of expressing it. "You knew him better than anybody else." I think I did know him better than anybody else. We had worked together for 15 months in the great city of London, England.

He was a precious and wonderful young man. He was a gifted young man. He was a young man of culture and refinement. He was a young man to whom I will always be grateful. We had a wonderful time together. We worked together, we served together, and I still feel a great, overflowing sense of gratitude for that young man and will always be grateful to him.

I organized his funeral. Homer Durham—who has passed away and was a member of the First Quorum of the Seventy—and I constituted the program. We sang the old hymns of England, "Abide with Me" and "God Moves in a Mysterious Way," and things of that kind. Each of us spoke of his virtues. I want to say to you that good companions can be very, very precious people. If you will cultivate a good companion relationship, that appreciation and respect for one another will remain with you throughout your lives.

I belong to what we call the Windsor Club. It is a group of missionaries who served together in England way back more than 60 years ago. We've been meeting together the last Sunday of each month for all these 60-plus years. We call ourselves the Windsor Club, after the ruling house of Britain, and our wives are known as the Merry Wives of Windsor. We have a wonderful time. I don't get with them very often these days, but it is a wonderful group of those who served together. We have remained friends, good friends, all these years. What a precious thing is a good companion. He becomes your protector in times of trouble or in times of temptation. He becomes, if he is your senior, your guide, your helper, your introduction to the work.

When I went to England 65 years ago, I was sent up to Preston. I went up on the train. My companion met me at the train station. We walked back to where we lived. He said, "Now, brother, you and I will get along very well if we observe one rule, and that rule is this: everything that I have is mine, and everything that you have is mine." Then he said, "We are going down to hold a street meeting tonight." Well, I said, "You've got the wrong man." He said, "Come along, we are going down to hold a street meeting." So we went down to the marketplace, put down our little stand, sang a song first, and had prayer; then he stood up and introduced me. That was the first gospel sermon I think I ever preached in my life—on the Market Square of Preston, England.

I look back on those days as being very, very precious. I said to the mission presidents previously, we dedicated the Preston Temple the other day, and for me it was a very inspirational and emotional time, because it was exactly 65 years ago this month that I landed in Preston, England, my first field of labor; and to go back now to dedicate that beautiful house of the Lord, with its surrounding buildings, including a large missionary training center, was indeed a remarkable and much appreciated blessing.

There is something about a mission that is different from all the other experiences of our lives. We have all kinds of experiences as we go through life, but a mission occupies a particular niche. You grow so fast, for one thing, in the mission field. You go out green as grass, and in about three months you mature in a miraculous and wonderful way. Your fears leave you. You're not afraid to go up and knock on a door. That is a terrible thing the first time you try it, but your fears leave you. You are able to stand in a street meeting, if that is the practice of the mission to which you go. There comes into your heart a new assurance and a new boldness to do that which you ought to do.

Well, that's what lies ahead of you. Now you are here being trained. What a great blessing this is. We haven't had a missionary training center for too many years. For a long time we had what was called a Missionary Home. When I went on a mission in 1933, that home was an old house on State Street in Salt Lake City over behind the Church Administration Building. The Church had purchased that home and one next to it, and there we slept. There weren't very many of us. I suppose there might have been altogether 25 or 30 of us from all the Church. It was the bottom of the Depression. People didn't have any money. They literally didn't have any money. Missionaries were very, very scarce. We send out more in a week now than, in those days, we sent out in a year.

The course of training was a little different, quite different, from what you go through now. There was no language training of any kind. Missionaries who went to foreign-language-speaking missions simply went and learned the language when they got there. They had no training before they left. The rest of us, who spoke English, simply went there for a week, and then we were on our way. We traveled on the train in non–air conditioned coaches, traveled by ship to wherever we were going if we were going overseas. I will always be grateful for that missionary training program that we had. It was simple. But I remember President David O. McKay so very vividly. He came over and was our instructor for two or three hours. He was a counselor in the First Presidency at that time, and he spoke to the subject of what it means to be a missionary. I've never forgotten some of the things of which he spoke.

Each of us was required to write a paper on what it means to be a missionary. We did so. He then read those papers. Missionaries' handwriting was much easier to read then than it is now, let me tell you that. The handwriting that you have is absolutely undecipherable, except by your mothers, and they have grown up with it. For others, it is terrible. Well, that's an aside on that. But it is a true aside.

Now times have changed, and we have this wonderful facility through which you go, and 11 or 12 or 13 or 14—or whatever it is—other facilities in various parts of the world, so that nearly every missionary now has the opportunity of going through a missionary training center. You go out much better prepared. I think you do a better job than we did. You know more about it. I'm grateful for that. I hope this improvement will continue until we have learned how to really speak to the world. I'm satisfied that if we knew how to convey our message, at least twice as many people would come into the Church. We have not learned the ability to really tell people about the Church. Someday we will be better at it than we are today. In the meantime, we do the very best that we can. I wish for each of you the power and the capacity to testify of the truth of this work to those you can get to listen to you. That is the big problem—getting somebody to listen to you. But you'll find people here and there. You'll find them on the streets. You'll find them on the trains. You'll find them on the trams. You'll find them in various places.

I was in Tokyo one day, and we had to go from Tokyo South to Tokyo East to Tokyo North to Tokyo West and back to Tokyo South. We were looking at building sites. In those days we had the power to buy building sites, and the mission president had scouted out these sites, and he was taking me around to see them. Two missionaries traveled with us. The trains were crowded, and as we were riding the trains, they took out little cards from their pockets on which they had the Japanese characters. Then they began to mumble to themselves, saying words from the Japanese characters: *konnichiwa, konnichiwa, konnichiwa*. By that time the Japanese on the train were all looking over to them, curious at these two American young men who were trying to say *konnichiwa*. Well, before we had finished those train rides, they had lined up seven cottage meetings, discussion groups, families—just with that simple little thing. It is wonderful what we can do if we practice a little ingenuity.

Missionary work need not be all tracting. It can be street contacting; it can be other things. You ought to take advantage of

435

every opportunity in the world to speak with people about why we are there and what we are doing and give them some taste of a gospel message. You never can tell that, while they may not join the Church at that time, a later missionary may bump into them, and he will remind them of a time when they met a former missionary, and that may lead to conversion and baptism.

I know of a family exactly like that in Germany. My son tracted him out, and it wasn't until seven years later that he joined the Church. But he still harks back to that first contact that he had so long before. So we just work at it. We don't get discouraged. That is easy to say, but you don't get discouraged in the mission field. You don't get offended. Brother Sterling Sill, who was an insurance man, once said, "I've been spit on. I've been sworn at. I've been kicked out the front door and right onto the ground. But I've never been insulted." That's the kind of attitude that we use when we are in the mission field. We may be spit on. We may be sworn at. We may be kicked off the front porch. But we'll never be insulted. I hope that will obtain with reference to each of you.

Now, I've set apart, while I've been down here this afternoon, a mission president to go to Taejon, Korea. I spent altogether 11 years in Asia supervising the work there and had many, many wonderful experiences. I set apart this mission president this afternoon. It was an emotional experience for me—and for him. We threw our arms around one another and shed a tear or two, going back to those pioneer days in Korea, back to 1960 when the work was beginning there. It was tough—so difficult. Korea was very poor then. It had come through the war and been left devastated. People had nothing, and thieves were everywhere. I remember the time when the thieves stole a piano out of the Seoul Central Branch. They hoisted it up over the wall and put it down onto the shoulders of eight men and ran off with it. The piano! Another time they stole 150 chairs that we had set up on Saturday night to hold a meeting on Sunday morning, a Pusan District meeting. During the night the thieves stole all of those chairs. We had to stand the next morning.

But my thoughts go back to those marvelous and wonderful days when we had little more than our testimonies, really. We had an old house. There was a little room there, in which I slept. The rats would run across in the ceiling above. It was the same on Okinawa. We were in a straw-thatched little house with rats in the ceiling. Those were the days.

I went to Okinawa on one occasion and out to a place called Futemma, where the missionaries lived in a Quonset hut. I looked up, and there was a big piece of paper on the wall with five rats drawn on it. I said, "What is that for? What does that mean?" They said, "That's this week's kill." I said, "Well, we're going to do something about this." The next day was preparation day, and I bought some cement, and they got some sand and gravel, and we mixed concrete all day and poured it around the base of that Quonset hut to make it rat-proof.

I want to urge you missionaries to guard your health. Be careful of what you eat and what you do. Live in a sanitary, hygienic way. In those days, I would visit every missionary apartment, and what I saw would have curled your hair. I'm sure the mothers of the young men who were there at the time—there were no sisters there then—would have almost dropped dead if they had seen the way their sons were living. Cockroaches on the toothbrushes, and things of that kind.

Now, missionaries are careless. My, you are careless. You are just terribly careless. Your mothers have taken care of you all your lives now, and you are going out to care for yourselves, and you don't know how to do it. Be careful. Guard your health. Eat good food—not rich food but good food. Observe good hygiene, good sanitation. Stay away from sickness. Keep your apartments tidy. Clean them up. Make your beds. It is amazing how many beds are made when, at a missionary meeting, the mission president says, "I'm going to visit your digs tonight." Everybody runs home and makes the bed that hasn't been made for two months. Make the bed, every day, and live orderly lives. I plead with you to do that. We have altogether too much sickness in the mission field—too much of it. It is terribly costly in money and in time. Live lives that will preserve your health as much as it is possible to do so, because a sick missionary becomes a handicap. His companion can't work alone, and he can't go out. The result is that everything stops. Guard your health, and be very careful and clean in your ways of doing things.

Now, the next thing I'd like to say is keep the rules. Every mission has some rules. The other day, in the office of one of the missions, I noted a big bulletin that says, "Rules of This Mission: one, two, three, four, five." I don't particularly care for that kind of thing, but you know that there are rules in the mission field. Observe them. There is safety in observing those rules. Be careful. Be wise.

We have a missionary killed in the field every now and again, sometimes because of carelessness. The other day a missionary riding a bike in a foreign country grabbed hold of a truck to pull him up the hill. He hit some gravel, and the bicycle wheel spun beneath him, and he was thrown under the wheel of the truck and killed. We don't want that. We don't like that. We want to avoid it. Take care of yourselves. Protect yourselves against physical danger, and keep your tempers. People will swear at you a little. Don't swear back. Return good for evil. Don't be like that missionary who was walking down the street and a man was sprinkling his lawn. As the missionary came along, the man turned the hose on him and said, "I understand you believe in baptism." The missionaries turned around and grabbed him and said, "Yes, and we also believe in the laying on of hands." Don't get involved in that kind of thing. Today they will sue you if you do that. And we have too many of those lawsuits in the mission field.

I want to plead with you to keep your thoughts clean—the things you think about, the things you dwell on. Get out of the gutter, and stand tall and clean, and keep yourselves aloof from those things. They will only destroy you. They are just like a terrible poison. They will tear you down and utterly ruin your lives. Stay above them. If you are busy with your missionary work, you won't be troubled with those things. If you are not busy, you're likely to be troubled with those things. Keep your thoughts clean, and speak clean words.

Do what ought to be done by servants of the Lord. You go out; you've been set apart. You go out to teach the world, to teach the people repentance, and to baptize them in the name of the Savior— the Father, the Son, and the Holy Ghost. Be worthy of the great and tremendous commission which you have as a missionary of The Church of Jesus Christ of Latter-day Saints.

I want to make another suggestion, and that is that you write regularly to your parents. They feast on your letters. I think your mother will be able to read your writing. I don't know that your father will, but I think your mother will, and she can read it to others. But write regularly. A woman called me one day when I was managing the missionary department and said, "I haven't heard from my son in three months. What am I going to do?" I said, "Don't send him any money, and you'll hear from him." Well, in those days, the remittances went directly from the parents to the missionary. She didn't send any money, and she heard immediately from him. Write to your parents. Your letters need not be long, but they ought to be informative. Tell them of what is going on, of what you are doing, of your work as a missionary, of your companion, of the ward or branch in which you are laboring, and of the great happiness that you find in the work. They will appreciate it. They are praying for you. They are sacrificing for you. They are doing everything they know how to do to back you up at home, and they are deserving of a letter at least once a week.

Well, the Lord bless you, my dear young friends. I want to read to you a little from the Doctrine and Covenants, section 112. This is a revelation given to Thomas B. Marsh, who was President of the Twelve, who did missionary work in those days on their own. But these words apply, I believe, to every missionary in the world. The Lord says, "Let thy heart be of good cheer before my face" (v. 4). Be happy, the Lord is saying. You can't bring anybody into the Church while you are scowling. Have a smile on your face. You look better with a smile on your face. It doesn't cost you a thing. Be happy about it. Let that happiness shine through you as a radiance from your countenance. "Let thy heart be of good cheer before my face; and thou shalt bear record of my name. . . . Contend thou, therefore, morning by morning; and day after day let thy warning voice go forth; and when the night cometh let not the inhabitants of the earth slumber, because of thy speech [or lack of speech]" (vv. 4–5). That is a tremendous mandate laid upon you, my brothers and sisters, a tremendous mandate. "Contend thou, therefore, morning by morning; and day after day let thy warning voice go forth; and when the night cometh let not the inhabitants of the earth slumber" because you failed to speak to them. "Be thou humble; and the Lord thy God shall lead thee by the hand, and give thee answer to thy prayers" (v. 10).

Listen to the promptings of the Spirit. Be humble. You may be led to someone by the hand of the Lord because of your spirit, your attitude, your feeling, your humility.

I remember a missionary sharing an experience he had one day while tracting. He said, "We knocked on a door, and a woman came to the door. It was evident that she had been crying. I said to her, 'Madam, you are troubled. Is there anything we can do to help you?' And she said: 'I need help so badly. My little daughter died, three years of age. I've been talking with a priest. She was not baptized as an infant, and he tells me that she has gone to hell.' She burst into tears." [The missionary] said, "We were moved by the

Spirit to tell that woman that her little daughter had not gone to hell, but through the mercy, the Atonement of Jesus Christ, she was saved, free of sin, and we were moved to open the pages of the Book of Mormon and read to her the words of Mormon concerning that matter" (see Moroni 8).

Keep yourselves open to the inspiration of the Lord. Listen to the whisperings of the Spirit. I remember when Brother Lee set me apart as a stake president. He said, "Listen for the whisperings of the Spirit in the stillness of the night." Now, I believe in that. I have seen that in my experience, and I think I can testify that the Lord has spoken quietly. I didn't hear any words, but in the middle of the night ideas have come into my head which, I think, have been prophetic in their nature.

Says the Lord, "But purify your hearts before me." He doesn't give a lot of reasons. He simply says, "Purify your hearts before me; and then go ye into all the world, and preach my gospel unto every creature who has not received it" (D&C 112:28). Well now, brethren and sisters, that is an injunction to you.

Now let me take you to the 84th section, which I read to the brothers and sisters in the previous meeting. This, to me, is a wonderful statement of the Lord to you and to each of us: "Any man that shall go and preach this gospel of the kingdom, and fail not to continue faithful in all things, shall not be weary in mind, neither darkened, neither in body, limb, nor joint; and a hair of his head shall not fall to the ground unnoticed. And they shall not go hungry, neither athirst" (v. 80). What a promise that is. If you will work at it, keep at it, the Lord will bless you, and you will fail not.

"Behold, I send you out to reprove the world of all their unrighteous deeds, and to teach them of a judgment which is to come.

"And whoso receiveth you, there I will be also"—you won't be there alone; the Lord will be with you—"for I will go before your face. I will be on your right hand and on your left, and my Spirit shall be in your hearts, and mine angels round about you, to bear you up.

"Whoso receiveth you receiveth me; and the same will feed you, and clothe you, and give you money.

"And he who feeds you, or clothes you, or gives you money, shall in nowise lose his reward" (vv. 87–90).

I'd just like to say, parenthetically, that anyone who befriends a missionary of this Church throughout the world will not lose because of what he does for him or her. The Lord will bless those who are generous toward the missionaries of this Church.

Now, you occupy a position different from any that you'll occupy at any other time in your lives. Never again will you be able to devote your full time to the work of the Lord. For most of you, almost all of you, that will never happen again. You don't need to worry about money; that is all taken care of. You don't need to worry about girlfriends; they are all well taken care of. You don't need to worry about boyfriends; that's taken care of. You are not going to the mission to fall in love. You're not going on a mission to find a wife or a husband. You are going on a mission to serve the Lord—no other consideration in your lives. What a privilege. What an opportunity. What a blessing. And what, when all is said and done, a very small gift to give—the payment of a tithe of your life to the advancement of the work of God in all the world.

It doesn't matter where you are called to serve. The circumstances are largely the same. Love the Lord, and seek to do His will, and I promise you that you will be happy. I say further that you will never be able to judge the consequences of that which you do as a missionary—never. If you bring someone into the Church and that individual stays in the Church, that harvest will go on growing and growing through the years and through generations of time.

Well, I have spoken to you long enough. I have rambled, I know. But I hope that I have conveyed to you some feeling that we place tremendous confidence in you. We count on you to do a superb job, to do your very best. No less than your best will do. You must do your very, very best. We have every confidence in you. We know that if you are prayerful, if you are obedient, if you do what is expected of you, if you get up and go to work, if you are not lazy, the Lord will bless you and bring to you some measure of harvest for which you will be grateful all the days of your lives.

We will be praying for you. You are the only people in all the world who are constantly prayed for by the membership of this Church. If you are ever tempted to do something wrong, just remember, there are hundreds of thousands of people across this Church who are kneeling at home and offering their prayers and speaking of you, the missionaries, who are serving across the world.

As the Presidency and the Twelve meet together in the temple, we pray for you, because we love you and we know you are on the front lines of the world doing a thing that is tremendous and wonderful and of great consequence. Please know of our love. We love you. I have been with your kind now in the last three years, hundreds and hundreds—thousands of them, all the way from Cambodia to Scandinavia, across this world, from the tip of Africa up into Canada, where we are going next month.

God bless you. Our prayers will be with you. The Lord's Spirit will attend you. You will grow in faith and knowledge and understanding, and the memories of a sweet and wonderful experience as a missionary will remain with you throughout your days. For this I humbly pray as I leave my love and my blessing with you in the name of Jesus Christ, amen.

# Hamilton, Canada

# Member Meeting

AUGUST 8, 1998

Once Sister Hinckley and I were growing taller; now we are growing smaller. That is the way life is. You are young, and you grow up, and you grow up, and suddenly you find yourselves old, and you go down and down. I am glad all of you look so young. You are still growing. It is wonderful to be here with you this very delightful day, Saturday. And you have been off work and come here from near and far. You greatly honor us with your presence. Thank you for the effort you have made to come.

I pray for the direction of the Holy Spirit. I would like to say something that would be faith promoting.

Well, this is the end of a long and wonderful journey. This is the 16th meeting in which we have participated during the last few days. We started in Victoria, British Columbia; we went from there to Vancouver and then to Prince George and then across the mighty Rockies. There is no experience quite like riding an airplane over those tremendous Rockies of the West. How magnificent they are, with the alpine lakes that are to be seen there and the glaciers that are never without snow. We went to Edmonton and Lethbridge, then out onto the prairie and Regina and Winnipeg. They are really out on the prairie. The land out there is just as flat as the Canadian dollar. Then we went to Sudbury, that great

444

mining town; then over to Ottawa and Montreal and Quebec, where they speak French; and then here.

When I was in Quebec I thought of the story of a Frenchman who came to the United States and made a long tour across the country. This was many years ago, and when he got home his friends said, "How are the roads? How did you find the roads over there?" "Well," he said, "those highways that were named for the American presidents Washington and Lincoln are wonderful, but you should have seen the highway that was named for that Frenchman named De Tour."

Now, there are about 12,000 of you here. Who would have ever dreamed a few short years ago that we could fill a hall of this kind to this extent with faithful Latter-day Saints? How marvelous and wonderful it is that you should be here, all of you, in such numbers. As we sang this song, I thought of the truth of it:

> *As children of Zion,*
> *Good tidings for us.*
> *The tokens already appear.*
> *Fear not, and be just,*
> *For the kingdom is ours.*
> *The hour of redemption is near.*
> *["Redeemer of Israel,"*
> Hymns, *no. 6]*

We are living, my brothers and sisters, in the day of prophecy fulfilled. This is the greatest season in the history of the Church. There never before was a time like this. We are larger in numbers— a great family of 10 million people scattered through 160 nations. The media treat us honestly and generously and right. We have a good reputation among most people—perhaps not in the small places of the world, but in the great cities we have come to be recognized for what we are and the good we do. This is a wonderful time to be alive. It is a wonderful time to be a member of this

Church. I envy these young people who are here today. Their lives are ahead of them. They will see marvelous things in the years that lie ahead. I have no doubt of it whatever. The Church will grow and grow and grow, and no force under the heavens can stop it.

I copied down these words from Joseph Smith one day: "Hell may pour forth its rage like the burning lava of Mount Vesuvius, . . . and yet shall 'Mormonism' stand. . . . Truth is 'Mormonism.' God is the author of it. He is our shield. It is by Him we received our birth. It was by His voice that we were called to a dispensation of His Gospel in the beginning of the fullness of times. It was by Him we received the Book of Mormon; and it is by Him that we remain unto this day; and by Him we shall remain, if it shall be for our glory; and in His Almighty name we are determined to endure tribulation as good soldiers unto the end" (*Teachings of the Prophet Joseph Smith*, sel. Joseph Fielding Smith [1976], 139).

I see nothing but a bright future for this great work. It will go on and grow across the earth and fill the world. I am satisfied of that. What a glorious thing it is to be a part of it, my brothers and sisters—the Church and kingdom of God in the earth. We have nearly 60,000 missionaries out. We had a meeting before this one with the missionaries from two missions. My, they looked wonderful—able, handsome young men and beautiful young women and some older, devoted couples among them who are doing such a glorious and wonderful work. God bless His Church and kingdom. The Lord bless us that we may play a part in its advancement over the earth, I humbly pray with gratitude and thanksgiving in my heart. I just have one regret. I am so old, I don't know how much longer I have to go, but I am going to stay as long as I can and see as much as I am permitted to see of these glorious and wonderful times.

I have had a great experience on this trip. When we were in Ottawa, a counselor in the stake presidency said that he had found the place where my grandfather was born. My grandfather was born in Leeds County, province of Ontario. I don't know how his father got there. They lived down in Connecticut and Massachusetts. But in any event, he came up here, and he was baptized in the early missionary work that spread across upper Canada, as it was called. He died from a smallpox epidemic that raged through that part of the country. Two or three days ago, I stood at what we presume to be his grave in that part of the country. I walked out through a cow pasture to get to it, to find it. It is a little fenced-in cemetery there, and I had feelings of reverence and respect and gratitude and thanksgiving. His widow left there eventually, crossed the St. Lawrence River on the ice, moved to Springfield, Ohio, and then to Springfield, Illinois. She died, and the two boys, my grandfather and his brother, walked to Nauvoo and there met the Prophet Joseph and were baptized. My grandfather later, with the exodus of the Saints, started west, and somewhere in what is now western Nebraska or Wyoming, his wife died and his half-brother died, both on the same day. He made coffins for them, rude coffins, and buried them with his own hands. Then he picked up his 11-month-old infant and carried her to the Salt Lake Valley. I am grateful for that faith and that devotion which was so abundant then.

And I see that same faith and that same devotion among the Latter-day Saints wherever we go. Men and women who try to do the right thing as they understand it. Men and women who love the Lord. Men and women who can bear testimony of His reality and of the reality of His Son, the Redeemer. Men and women who know that Joseph Smith had a vision in which he saw God, the Eternal Father, and the risen Son, the Lord Jesus Christ. Men and women who have taken upon themselves in solemn covenant the name of the Lord and who try to live up to that covenant. Men and women who pay their tithes and offerings that the work might be moved forward across the world. Men and women who live the Word of Wisdom. Men and women who go to the temple and do their own work and also ordinances in behalf of the dead. You are great people, my brothers and sisters; you are great people who get on your knees and pray, and that is a very significant thing. The Lord bless you.

We have those, of course, who belittle us, who see no good in us, who say we are not biblical. I would like to point out two or three things this afternoon. This is the only Church, in my judgment, which recognizes and lives up to the teachings of the Holy Bible on things that the others don't seem to understand. Now, I have no argument with other churches. I recognize the good that comes of every church and want to say to the whole world, "Bring all the truth that you have, all the goodness that you have, and come and let us see if we can add to those things in the spirit of missionary work."

"And I saw another angel fly in the midst of heaven, having the everlasting gospel to preach unto them that dwell on the earth, and to every nation, and kindred, and tongue, and people" (Revelation 14:6). How do our friends of other churches interpret that? They pass over it. They don't have the explanation of it. Everyone who looks up to a temple on which stands the figure of Moroni recognizes the fulfillment of those great words of prophecy spoken by John the Revelator. "Another angel fly in the midst of heaven, having the everlasting gospel to preach unto them that dwell on the earth" and bringing with him the words of truth and light and understanding, the words of a second witness of the Lord Jesus Christ to the world.

"And other sheep I have, which are not of this fold: them also I must bring, and they shall hear my voice; and there shall be one fold, and one shepherd" (John 10:16). "What is the explanation of that?" I say to my friends of other churches. I have never heard one give an explanation of it. To us it is prophetic, wonderfully so, of the people described in the Book of Mormon, who came to this Western Hemisphere and here wrote this testament of the New World, which stands side by side with the Bible as the word of God.

"The word of the Lord," says Ezekiel, "came again unto me, saying, Moreover, thou son of man, take thee one stick, and write upon it, For Judah, and for the children of Israel his companions: then take another stick, and write upon it, For Joseph, the stick of Ephraim, and for all the house of Israel his companions: And join them one to another into one stick; and they shall become one in thine hand" (Ezekiel 37:15–17). Now, various scholars have spent a lot of time talking about the interpretation of that word *stick*. But the fact remains firmly in my mind that—whatever the description of the instrument—this Holy Bible stands as the stick of Judah and this [Book of Mormon] stands as the stick of Joseph and they have become one in the hands of the Lord.

"Moreover," the Lord said, "I will make a covenant of peace with [my people]; . . . and I will place them, and multiply them, and will set my sanctuary in the midst of them for evermore. . . . I will be their God, and they shall be my people" (Ezekiel 37:26–27). This is a great covenant which the Lord promised would come forth when He revealed the words which have become the first section of the Doctrine and Covenants, that His everlasting covenants might be restored to the earth (see D&C 1:22)—the words spoken by Jehovah that He would be Israel's God and they would be His people. And we, my brothers and sisters, partake of that solemn and sacred covenant.

"Let no man deceive you by any means: for that day shall not come, except there come a falling away first" (2 Thessalonians 2:3)—those words of Paul, prophetic in their statement which declare that there should be a falling away before there should be a restoration.

"Repent ye therefore," said Peter, "and be converted, that your sins may be blotted out, when the times of refreshing shall come from the presence of the Lord; And he shall send Jesus Christ, which before was preached unto you: Whom the heaven must receive until the times of restitution of all things, which God hath

449

spoken [of] by the mouth of all his holy prophets since the world began" (Acts 3:19–21). These are the days of restitution. These are the days of restoration spoken of in the Holy Bible plainly and forcefully by Peter the Apostle and by Paul. I repeat, you and I are a part of prophecy fulfilled, a part of the divine plan of the God of heaven that there should be a falling away and that there must be a restoration.

"Else what shall they do which are baptized for the dead, if the dead rise not at all? why are they then baptized for the dead?" (1 Corinthians 15:29)—the great doctrine of baptism for the dead, which was pronounced as a revelation to the Prophet Joseph. When Jesus was upon the earth, He declared that man should be born of the water and of the spirit and unless he was so born he could not enter into the kingdom of God. Did He exempt anyone? In His conversation with Nicodemus, did He leave anybody out in that requirement that we should be born of the water and of the spirit? No! (See John 3:1–5.) But only in this Church, my brothers and sisters, is there the realization of the fact of fulfillment of those words of Paul indicating they had baptism for the dead in his time. Under the interpretation which we inevitably are led to in the statement to Nicodemus, baptism must apply to everyone—every man and woman. How is it going to happen? It can happen only through vicarious work for the dead. It is so important. The dead cannot go forward without this saving ordinance, and these boys and girls who are here today—12 years of age and older—can go to Brampton, into the house of the Lord, specially recommended by their bishops, to be baptized for someone. You are young—you are only a child, as it were—and yet you may stand in the place of someone who perhaps was once of great fame and note.

Yesterday, in Quebec City, I looked over the Plains of Abraham where the tremendous battle took place between the English, led by General Wolfe, and the French, led by General Montcalm. There Montcalm was defeated by the English army, which was much stronger. Many were killed in that place. And I thought to myself, "Has their work been done? Have those who died here on the Plains of Abraham had their work done for them?" The work is so large, my brothers and sisters. There is so much to be done that I hope we are not neglecting it. President Wilmott is here, who is president of the temple. I am sure that if he were to speak he would invite you to come and be more faithful in attending the temple.

Now, we are going to build more temples in Canada, because Brampton is so far away for so very many people and Cardston is so far away for so very many people. This is a land of great distances. We are going to build a temple in Halifax. We are going to build a temple in Regina. We are going to build a temple in Montreal. I hope I have the right place. Maybe one more. These will be smaller temples, but each will have a wonderful baptistry— a beautiful font into which you may go and be baptized for the dead. That is the interpretation we make on this statement of Paul, and it is an interpretation which is based on the revealed word of the Lord.

"And it shall come to pass," said Isaiah, "in the last days, that the mountain of the Lord's house shall be established in the top of the mountains, and shall be exalted above the hills; and all nations shall flow unto it. And many people shall go and say, Come ye, and let us go up to the mountain of the Lord, to the house of the God of Jacob; and he will teach us of his ways, and we will walk in his paths: for out of Zion shall go forth the law, and the word of the Lord from Jerusalem" (Isaiah 2:2–3). The magnificent temple in Salt Lake City is the only one of which I know which answers that description of these words of Isaiah. It is found in the mountains, in the top of the mountains, as it were. There is a constant procession of people who come seeking to learn of us. I don't think there is a week, scarcely, that passes that we don't have somebody of note call on the First Presidency. They come to pay tribute to us. They come to learn. They are respectful and kind and good to us, and we are grateful for their visits.

Well now, these are a few verses of scripture that I have read simply to point out that we are a biblical church based on the great basic doctrines taught in the Bible and confirmed and strengthened with those found in the Book of Mormon and the Doctrine and Covenants, the Book of Mormon containing the confirmatory word of the Bible and the Doctrine and Covenants speaking with words of modern revelation, with truths—the pattern, the doctrine on which we should go forward.

God bless you. We are all in this together as part of the great family of the Lord. This is His work. This is His work in this, the dispensation of the fulness of times. The Lord God of heaven has spoken in parting the curtains to open the restoration of His mighty work. This is no small thing. Every one of us ought to be better than we are. We could be better if we would watch ourselves just a little.

I want to say to the fathers here, you men who hold the priesthood of God, live worthy of it. Live worthy of the priesthood which you hold, my brethren. That priesthood came under the hands of Peter, James, and John, Apostles of the Lord who held it anciently, for it was He who gave it to them, saying to them, "And I will give unto thee the keys of the kingdom of heaven: and whatsoever thou shalt bind on earth shall be bound in heaven" (Matthew 16:19). Live worthy of the priesthood. There is no room among you—any of you—for spouse abuse. There is no room among any of you for child abuse. You ought to be the best husbands in the world and the very best fathers. God help you to do so.

You mothers, live up to the great potential that is yours. You precious women, you belong to the greatest women's organization on earth, three million strong, the Relief Society of The Church of Jesus Christ of Latter-day Saints.

You boys and girls, you be careful. Watch yourselves. You belong to this Church. You boys hold the priesthood of Aaron, which carries with it the promise of the ministering of angels. Think of that! Now, look, no pornography in your lives. Don't let it touch you. It will only injure you. It can destroy you. No drugs in your lives. They will destroy you if you partake of them. No profanity in your lives. Where you go to school, there are so many who use foul and sleazy language. You can't afford to do that; you are members of this great Church. None of that filthy language. Never take the name of the Lord in vain, for God will hold him responsible who taketh His name in vain. Be better than those around you.

I talked with a policeman last night in Quebec. He said when he first joined the police force he was the only member of the Church on a force of 1,000 men, and did they have a good time with him. They made life hard and difficult for him. I said, "Do they still do it?" He said, "No. Now they respect me. They look up to me." So it will be with you, my dear young friends.

Well, I leave my testimony with you. I know, just as you know, that God, our Eternal Father, lives. I know, just as you know, that Jesus is the Christ. I know, just as you know, that the Book of Mormon is true, that Joseph spoke to the Father and the Son, that the priesthood is here and all of the doctrine and teachings which will save us if we will live up to them.

Well, it is so wonderful to be with you. We go home now, and we will feast on the experience we had in being with you. Elder Coleman is right. I would like to throw my arms around every one of you. But that would take all day today and all day tomorrow. We have other appointments to keep. Please know, if we can't shake your hands, if we can't throw our arms around you, that we still love you. We are all together in this thing. God bless you temporally and spiritually. May you have food on your tables, clothing on your backs, a shelter over your heads, and above all, the sweet, wonderful Spirit of the Lord, the Holy Spirit to bless you, the Holy

Ghost to prompt you and lead you, is my humble prayer as I say, God be with you till we meet again.

Thanks, and every good wish and every happiness, is my humble prayer in the name of Jesus Christ, amen.

# MISSIONARY SATELLITE BROADCAST

## FEBRUARY 21, 1999

M Y BELOVED BRETHREN AND SISTERS, it is a wonderful and serious responsibility to speak to you. Speculation has been going about that President Hinckley is going to announce some new and glamorous program. I assure you that this is not so. My Brethren of the Twelve, who are deeply concerned about our missionary work throughout the world, have asked that I share with you some feelings that I have on this most important matter.

In terms of the eventual audience, this is probably the largest gathering ever convened in the cause of missionary work. The Tabernacle is filled. The proceedings of this meeting will be seen by almost all of the nearly 59,000 full-time missionaries laboring throughout the world. Additionally, the thousands—the hundreds of thousands of Church officers who have an interest and responsibility in this matter are gathered with us, or the proceedings of this hour will be taken to them.

I forewarn you, this will be a rather long talk. I am an old man. I do not know how much longer I will live, and so I want to say what I have to say while I have the strength to say it. I do not know when I will give a talk this long again. I shall give two speeches interrupted by the singing of a hymn. Altogether, I will take about

40 minutes. Having been warned, some of you will wish to get comfortable. Pleasant dreams.

I spoke the other day with one of the most enthusiastic converts I have ever met. We were in Chicago for a big meeting which brought together some 20,000 members of the Church in the United Center, where the Chicago Bulls play basketball. Randy Chiostri, a new member of the Church, drove us about while we were there. All during those long rides in the Chicago traffic he was talking about missionary work, praising the Church as the most wonderful institution in the world, talking of the gospel and the plan of salvation as the greatest thing that had ever come into his life. Randy's introduction to the Church came when he dated Nancy. He took her to dinner. On the first date she said she drank no liquor. She would not take wine. "How curious," he thought. She said it was against her faith. Smoking was also against her faith. Her faith became the subject of their conversations.

He married her on the one-year anniversary of that first date. But he could not accept her religion. It took him almost eight years to overcome his doubts. One pair of missionaries after another taught him. Finally he was touched by the Spirit. He was baptized last March.

He visited the Hill Cumorah. He visited Nauvoo. He said, "I visited 17 temples. I visited them on the outside but not on the inside." He went to every temple he could get to. He now looks forward to the day that he will visit them on the inside. That first inside visit, in Chicago, will be in April. He will receive his endowment, and then the next day he and Nancy will be sealed.

After his baptism, Randy was immediately put to work. He was ordained to the Aaronic Priesthood. After being a member for about nine months, he was ordained an elder in the Melchizedek Priesthood. He loves the Church. He is consumed with his love of the gospel. It has become the major interest of his life. He cannot stop talking about it. Each night and morning he gets on his knees and thanks the Lord for the wondrous thing that has come into his life.

I learned a few things from Randy as I listened to him. The first is the tremendous power of the example of a member of the Church. It was Nancy's firm but quiet stance on that first date concerning no liquor and no wine which caught his attention. The missionaries worked on him through the years, but she was the key that unlocked his heart to a love for the Lord and his mind to an understanding of the plan of salvation.

The second thing I learned is that you never give up when there is the slightest spark of interest. It took him nearly eight years to come into the Church. His mind was open, but there was a lurking fear over taking so bold a step. He was setting aside the traditions of his forebears and stepping into something new and strange and difficult to understand.

Thirdly, he was put to work immediately following his baptism. His bishop saw that he had something challenging to do. Was he qualified to handle the assignment? The bishop gave that question very little attention. He saw an eager new convert, and he gave him a responsibility on which to grow.

The bishop saw that he had friends in the Church. The first, of course, was his wife, Nancy; and there were a few more able people who could answer his questions and listen patiently when he did not understand. He was not left friendless, to grope through the dark. He had those who were willing to take the time to talk with him.

Does he know all there is to know about the Church? No, of course not. He is constantly learning, and with that learning is a growing enthusiasm.

He is excited about what he has found. He is eager to receive the higher blessings of the temple. His testimony has become strong and secure within less than a year's time. He is a 100 percent convert, and his enthusiasm is contagious. We need more of this kind, and we need many more to work with them.

From the beginning of this work, missionary service has been a four-step process:

1. Finding the investigator.
2. Teaching the investigator.
3. Baptizing the worthy convert.
4. Fellowshipping and strengthening the new member.

Last year there were approximately 300,000 convert baptisms throughout the Church. This is tremendously significant. This is the equivalent of 120 new stakes of 2,500 members each. Think of that—120 new stakes in a single year! It is wonderful. But it is not enough. I am not being unrealistic when I say that with concerted effort, with recognition of the duty which falls upon each of us as members of the Church, and with sincere prayer to the Lord for help, we could double this number.

The big initial task is first to find interested investigators. So many of us look upon missionary work as simply tracting. Everyone who is familiar with this work knows there is a better way. That way is through the members of the Church. Whenever there is a member who introduces an investigator, there is an immediate support system. The member bears testimony of the truth of the work. He is anxious for the happiness of his investigator friend. He becomes excited as that friend makes progress in learning the gospel.

The full-time missionaries may do the actual teaching, but the member, wherever possible, will back up that teaching with the offering of his home to carry on this missionary service. He will bear sincere testimony of the divinity of the work. He will be there to answer questions when the missionaries are not around. He will be a friend to the convert, who is making a big and often difficult change.

The gospel is nothing to be ashamed of. It is something to be proud of. "Be not thou therefore ashamed of the testimony of our

Lord," wrote Paul to Timothy (2 Timothy 1:8). Opportunities for sharing the gospel are everywhere.

Dr. William Ghormley served as president of the stake in Corpus Christi, Texas. He bought his gasoline at a particular station. Each time he filled his tank he would leave a piece of Church literature with the station owner. It might have been a tract or a Church magazine or the *Church News,* but he never went there without leaving something. The man who ran the station was converted by the power of the Spirit as he read that literature. When last I checked, he was serving as a bishop.

The process of bringing new people into the Church is not the responsibility alone of the missionaries. They succeed best when members become the source from which new investigators are found.

I would like to suggest that every bishop in the Church give as a motto to his people, "Let's all work to grow the ward." I am not sure the grammar is correct, but the idea is right.

Let there be cultivated an awareness in every member's heart of his own potential for bringing others to a knowledge of the truth. Let him work at it. Let him pray with great earnestness about it. Let each member pray, as did Alma of old:

"O Lord, wilt thou grant unto us that we may have success in bringing [others] again unto thee in Christ.

"Behold, O Lord, their souls are precious, and many of them are our brethren; therefore, give unto us, O Lord, power and wisdom that we may bring these, our brethren, again unto thee" (Alma 31:34–35).

My heart reaches out to you missionaries. You simply cannot do it alone and do it well. You must have the help of others. The power to help lies within each of us. But you must do all you can. You must be anxiously engaged. When you are not working on referrals of members, you must be developing those referrals yourselves through tracting and related means.

I spoke at the funeral of a dear friend the other day. Some years ago he served as a mission president. He felt totally inadequate when he arrived in the field. He was sent to succeed a very good man—a man of great ability, an excellent leader, and a very able president.

When this new man took over the mission and made his first tour of meetings with missionaries, he said, "I never served a mission as a young man, and so I don't know what you are going through. But do your best—your very, very best. Say your prayers, and work hard, and leave the harvest to the Lord."

With that kind of spirit and that outreach of love, a whole new attitude spread through the mission. Members got behind the missionaries. Within a year the number of converts had doubled.

And now this word from Moroni, both to the missionaries and to the converts: "See that ye are not baptized unworthily; see that ye partake not of the sacrament of Christ unworthily; but see that ye do all things in worthiness, and do it in the name of Jesus Christ, the Son of the living God; and if ye do this, and endure to the end, ye will in nowise be cast out" (Mormon 9:29).

Speaking of worthiness in coming into the Church, President Joseph F. Smith once wrote:

> People must be taught before they are fit candidates for baptism. Now, what shall they be taught? Why, faith in God, in Jesus Christ, and in the Holy Ghost; faith in the efficacy of prayer, and in the ordinances and principles of the gospel which Jesus taught; faith in the restoration of this gospel and all its powers, to the Prophet Joseph Smith; faith in the Church which he was instrumental in establishing; faith in the priesthood, as authorized servants of the living God; faith in the revelations received in modern times; faith in the performance of the works required of a Latter-day Saint; faith in the principle of tithing, and in all other requirements, temporal and spiritual, mentioned in the law of God; and, finally, faith

to live lives of righteousness before the Lord. ["Baptism," *Improvement Era*, Jan. 1911, 267–68]

Now, my brethren and sisters, we can let the missionaries try to do it alone, or we can help them. If they do it alone, they will knock on doors day after day, and the harvest will be meager. Or as members we can assist them in finding and teaching investigators.

Whose responsibility is it? I begin with the stake presidents and their councils. A stake mission with a mission president is found in each stake. It is their responsibility, working under the general direction of the stake president, to work constantly at the task of finding and encouraging investigators. Those finders include every member of the Church.

Let there develop in every stake of the Church an awareness of the opportunity to find those who will listen to the gospel message. In this process we need not be offensive. We need not be arrogant. The most effective tract we will carry will be the goodness of our own lives. And as we engage in this service, our lives will improve, for we shall be alert to see that we do not do or say anything which might impede the progress of those we are trying to lead toward the truth.

I request each stake and district president to accept full responsibility and accountability for the finding and friendshipping of investigators within your stake or district. I request each bishop and branch president to accept the same responsibility within your ward or branch. You brethren have a sacred obligation before the Lord for this effort. You set the example for what others may do under your inspired leadership. We have full confidence in your capacity and willingness to do it.

There needs to be an infusion of enthusiasm at every level in the Church. Let this subject be dealt with occasionally in sacrament meeting. Let it be discussed by the priesthood and the Relief Society in their weekly meetings. Let the Young Men and the Young Women talk about and plan ways to help in this most important undertaking. Let even the Primary children think of ways to assist. Many a parent has come into the Church because of a child who was invited to Primary. I have a granddaughter who has a little nonmember friend. She takes her to Church. The girl's mother, without malice, said to her the other day, "You say grace just like the Mormons."

Ward and stake council meetings should have on the agenda the status of investigators developed by the ward members and every convert who has recently come into the Church.

If this happens, then the missionaries will be busy. They will be happy. They will be productive. The revelation says to them:

"Ye shall go forth in the power of my Spirit, preaching my gospel, two by two, in my name, lifting up your voices as with the sound of a trump, declaring my word like unto angels of God.

"And ye shall go forth baptizing with water, saying: Repent ye, . . . for the kingdom of heaven is at hand" (D&C 42:6–7).

The Lord further said: "And any man that shall go and preach this gospel of the kingdom, and fail not to continue faithful in all things, shall not be weary in mind, . . . neither in body, limb, nor joint; and a hair of his head shall not fall to the ground unnoticed. And they shall not go hungry, neither athirst" (D&C 84:80).

He continues: "Whoso receiveth you, there I will be also, for I will go before your face. I will be on your right hand and on your left, and my Spirit shall be in your hearts, and mine angels round about you, to bear you up" (D&C 84:88).

Missionaries may appropriately ask the members for referrals. We know that missionaries who ask for referrals are far more likely to receive them. The number of member referrals has declined in many areas because the matter does not receive attention. For instance, in the United States and Canada 42 percent of investigators came from member referrals in 1987. By 1997 that number had dropped to 20 percent. A similar decline is found across the world.

Brothers and sisters, this downward trend must be reversed. We need again to give this important matter its proper priority. The Lord will bless those who assist in this all-important work.

"And if it so be that you should labor all your days in crying repentance unto this people, and bring, save it be one soul unto me, how great shall be your joy with him in the kingdom of my Father!

"And now, if your joy will be great with one soul that you have brought unto me into the kingdom of my Father, how great will be your joy if you should bring many souls unto me!" (D&C 18:15–16).

Joseph Smith declared, "After all that has been said, the greatest and most important duty is to preach the Gospel" (*Teachings of the Prophet Joseph Smith*, sel. Joseph Fielding Smith [1976], 113).

And again, "Let the Saints remember that great things depend on their individual exertion, and that they are called to be co-workers with us and the Holy Spirit in accomplishing the great work of the last days" (*Teachings*, 178).

Every one of the Presidents of the Church has spoken on this important matter.

Great is our work, tremendous is our responsibility in helping to find those to teach. The Lord has laid upon us a mandate to teach the gospel to every creature. This will take the very best efforts of every missionary—full time and stake. It will take the very best efforts of every bishop, of every bishop's counselor, of every member of the ward council. It will take the very best interests of every stake president and his council. . . .

God bless you, my beloved brethren and sisters, in meeting the tremendous challenge that is ours. We cannot evade it. We cannot escape it. We must face up to it. The opportunities are tremendous. We are equal to it, and the Lord will bless us as we try.

Now let us sing together, and then we shall talk about retaining and strengthening the convert.

*[Congregational hymn.]*

Now I come to the second half of my talk, which will not be as long as the first. Having found and baptized a new convert, we have the challenge of fellowshipping him and strengthening his testimony of the truth of this work. We cannot have him walking in the front door and out the back. Joining the Church is a very serious thing. Each convert takes upon himself or herself the name of Christ, with an implied promise to keep His commandments. But coming into the Church can be a perilous experience. Unless there are warm and strong hands to greet the convert, unless there is an outreach of love and concern, he will begin to wonder about the step he has taken. Unless there are friendly hands and welcome hearts to greet him and lead him along the way, he may drop by the side.

There is no point in doing missionary work unless we hold on to the fruits of that effort. The two must be inseparable. These converts are precious. Every convert is a son or daughter of God. Every convert is a great and serious responsibility. It is an absolute imperative that we look after those who have become part of us. To paraphrase the Savior, what shall it profit a missionary if he baptize the whole world unless those baptized remain in the Church? (see Mark 8:36).

I received the other day a very interesting letter. It was written by a woman who joined the Church a year ago. She writes:

"My journey into the Church was unique and quite challenging. This past year has been the hardest year that I have ever lived in my life. It has also been the most rewarding. As a new member, I continue to be challenged every day."

She goes on to say that when she joined the Church she did not feel support from the leadership in her ward. Her bishop seemed indifferent to her as a new member. Rebuffed, as she felt, she turned back to her mission president, who opened opportunities for her.

She states that "Church members don't know what it is like to be a new member of the Church. Therefore, it's almost impossible for them to know how to support us."

I challenge you, my brothers and sisters, that if you do not know what it is like, you try to imagine what it is like. It can be terribly lonely. It can be disappointing. It can be frightening. We of this Church are far more different from the world than we are prone to think we are. This woman writes, "When we as investigators become members of the Church, we are surprised to discover that we have entered into a completely foreign world, a world that has its own traditions, culture, and language. We discover that there is no one person or no one place of reference that we can turn to for guidance in our trip into this new world. At first the trip is exciting, our mistakes even amusing, then it becomes frustrating, and eventually the frustration turns into anger. And it's at these stages of frustration and anger that we leave. We go back to the world from which we came, where we knew who we were, where we knew our role, where we contributed, and where we could speak the language."

I have said before—and I repeat it—that every new convert needs three things:

*One:* a friend in the Church to whom he can constantly turn, who will walk beside him, who will answer his questions, who will understand his problems.

*Two:* an assignment. Activity is the genius of this Church. It is the process by which we grow. Faith and love for the Lord are like the muscles of my arm. If I use them, they grow stronger. If I put them in a sling, they become weaker. Every convert deserves a responsibility. The bishop may feel that he is not qualified for responsibility. Take a chance on him. Think of the risk the Lord took when He called you.

Of course the new convert will not know everything. He likely will make some mistakes. So what? We all make mistakes. The important thing is the growth that will come of activity.

As a part of this process of giving responsibility, it is proper and very important that the new convert, if he be a man, is ordained to the Aaronic Priesthood. Then before too many months, he may be ordained to the Melchizedek Priesthood. He will have the fellowship of the elders quorum. He will become one of a vast body of priesthood throughout the world—men of integrity and faith who love the Lord and seek to move forward His work.

*Thirdly,* every convert must be "nourished by the good word of God" (Moroni 6:4). It is imperative that he or she become affiliated with a priesthood quorum or the Relief Society, the Young Women, the Young Men, the Sunday School, or the Primary. He or she must be encouraged to come to sacrament meeting to partake of the sacrament, to renew the covenants made at the time of baptism.

Not long ago I listened to a man and woman who spoke in my home ward. This man had served in many capacities in the Church, including that of bishop. Their most recent assignment was to fellowship a single mother and her children. He stated that it was the most joyful of all his Church experiences.

This young woman was full of questions. She was filled with fear and anxiety. She did not wish to make a mistake, to say anything that was out of line that might embarrass her or cause others to laugh. Patiently this man and his wife brought the family to Church, sat with them, put a shield around them, as it were, against anything that might happen to embarrass them. They spent one evening a week with them at their home, teaching them further concerning the gospel and answering their many questions. They led that little family along as a shepherd leads his sheep. Eventually, circumstances dictated that they move to another city. "But," he stated, "we still correspond with that woman. We feel a great appreciation for her. She is now firmly grounded in the Church, and we have no fear concerning her. What a joy it has been to work with her."

I am convinced that we will lose but very, very few of those who come into the Church if we take care of them. They may not be thoroughly converted. How can they be, having had only six lessons? They may not meet all of the desirable qualifications. But they have been awakened to a new sense of values and opportunities. They have been taught that they are sons and daughters of God. They have been baptized in the name of the Father and the Son and the Holy Ghost. They have been confirmed members of the Church and received the gift of the Holy Ghost.

I was recently in Canada, where I visited, among other cities, the city of Regina. There we were hosted by President D. Lawrence Penner, president of the Saskatoon Saskatchewan Stake. He is a wonderful man, an excellent executive. At 20 years of age, he was baptized. It was a huge step for him. He had been referred to the missionaries by members of the Church. They immediately looked him up. They talked to him. They taught him. They baptized him. They encouraged him, as did his local Church officers. He was ordained to the priesthood. He was given things to do. A year later he was called on a mission and served in Japan. He returned the stronger for that experience. With the encouragement of many people who have helped him along the way, he today stands as the presiding high priest of this great stake of Zion. He is the husband and father of a good family, all of whom are active. He is an example of the kind of man who should be coming into the Church as a convert and remaining to become a leader.

Now, you missionaries, you are part of this responsibility of binding your converts to the Church. You may not be able to continue to visit them, but you can write them occasionally and give them encouragement. I hope that every one of you will make a record in your scriptures of every man, woman, and child whom you baptize, together with their home addresses. Your penmanship may be terrible, but an occasional note from you will give reassurance and comfort and a rekindling of joy. When you go home, do not forget them. At all times live worthy of their trust. Write to them occasionally, assuring them of your love.

To the missionaries, I repeat, it will do no good for you to baptize someone and have that individual fall away from the Church shortly thereafter. What have you accomplished? You may have labored long and hard; you may have fasted and prayed as you taught a particular individual the gospel. But if he does not remain active in the Church, all of your labor has been in vain. The whole process counts for nothing. *Any investigator worthy of baptism becomes a convert worthy of saving.*

Elder Bruce Porter of the Seventy recounts this experience:

As a missionary in Germany nearly 25 years ago, I arrived in the city of Wuppertal as a new zone leader shortly after the missionaries who preceded me had had phenomenal success in baptizing several families and individuals. Their baptisms represented a substantial addition to that branch, which had nearly 100 members. We decided as missionaries to concentrate a great deal of effort on integrating and fellowshipping these new members so that they would remain active members of the branch for the rest of their lives. We taught them all of the new member lessons, as well as additional lessons of our own making; we enrolled them in a yearlong Gospel Essentials class taught by the missionaries; we worked with the branch leadership to ensure that they received callings and were integrated into the branch through socials and fellowshipping by members; we arranged for them to meet one another and help teach other investigators so that they would form bonds among themselves that would help them as a group remain active in the future. In short, we spent more than six months after their baptism doing what we could to ensure that their testimonies were strong and that they were integrated into the Church.

Today, 25 years later, almost all of those families and individuals are still active and faithful. Many of their children have served missions and have been married in the temple. We now have a second and even a third generation of activity in the Church. The one couple who did go inactive had a daughter who remained active and has since been married in the temple. Although this is only one case, my experience then persuaded me that time spent by missionaries working with members to integrate new members into the Church will pay off richly in the long term. [Letter to Elder Richard G. Scott]

That is a powerful testimony of what can be done. However, missionaries do not need to neglect proselyting to assist in fellowshipping the members. The two efforts can go hand in hand. You have the Saints to help—all of them. You have bishops and their ward councils. You have stake presidents and their stake councils. . . .

To you bishops who hold your ward council meetings, a discussion of the status of converts in that meeting may be the most important business you will conduct. You are not bound by rigid rules. You have unlimited flexibility. You are entitled to answers to your prayers, to inspiration and revelation from the Lord in dealing with this matter. I am appalled when I hear that a bishop is indifferent toward those who come into the Church. At that time, they may not be very attractive people. But if they are treated right, the gospel will refine them. Their very dress, their demeanor, their deportment will improve. All of us have seen miracles occur. How great is our opportunity, how tremendous our challenge.

My beloved brethren and sisters, it is our responsibility, the responsibility of each of us—of the stake presidency, of the high council, of the bishopric, of the Sunday School presidency, of the Primary presidency, of the Young Men presidency, of the Young Women presidency, of the Relief Society presidency, and of the priesthood quorum officers—to see that everyone who is baptized is encouraged and made to feel the wondrous warmth of this gospel of our Lord. I am pleased to report that we are making progress, but there is so very much more that remains to be done.

How glorious is this work. It is filled with miracles. We could talk about them all evening as we have witnessed them.

Brothers and sisters, all of you out in the wards and stakes and in the districts and branches, I invite you to become a vast army with enthusiasm for this work and a great, overarching desire to assist the missionaries in the tremendous responsibility they have to carry the gospel to every nation, kindred, tongue, and people. "The field is white [and ready] to harvest" (D&C 4:4). The Lord has repeatedly declared this. Shall we not take Him at His word?

Before the Church was organized, there was missionary work. It has continued ever since, notwithstanding the difficulties of many of the seasons through which our people have passed. Let us, every one, resolve within ourselves to arise to a new opportunity, a new sense of responsibility, a new shouldering of obligation to assist our Father in Heaven in His glorious work of bringing to pass the immortality and eternal life of His sons and daughters throughout the earth.

This is God's holy work. This is His Church and kingdom. The vision that occurred in the Sacred Grove was just as Joseph said it was. We are building a new temple overlooking this hallowed ground to further testify to the reality of this most sacred event. As I recently stood in the snow to determine the spot where this new temple will stand, there came into my heart a new understanding of what happened in the Sacred Grove. The Book of Mormon is true. It testifies of the Lord Jesus Christ. His priesthood has been restored and is among us. The keys of that priesthood, which have come from heavenly beings, are exercised for our eternal blessing. Such is our testimony—a testimony which we must share with others. I leave this testimony and my blessing and my love with each of you, in the name of Jesus Christ, amen.

470

# Ricks College

# Devotional

I'VE TAKEN NOTE OF THAT CLOCK up on the scoreboard. It's hard to see from here, but where you are seated you can see it. So if I go over the allotted time, give me a signal. I'll try to stop.

It is wonderful to be with you, you great young people. My, you look good—you beautiful girls, you handsome young men. Actually, you put on white shirts today. How come? You look so good. I'm grateful for your presence and for all that you stand for—for decency and goodness and scholarship and work. Thank you for being what you are, my dear young friends. Thank you for being a credit to this great Church, of which you are members. God bless you as you go forward with your lives.

I'm grateful for the presence here of members of the Kimball family—two of President Kimball's sons. I value them highly as friends. We appreciate the effort they have made to be here.

We have dedicated this morning the beautiful new building on this campus as the Kimball Building, the administrative hub of this great and beautiful campus. And now having done that and being appreciative of the fact that it will carry his name—this great and good and wonderful friend who stood as a leader of this Church over a very long period of time and gave of his very best to the work of moving this cause forward in all the earth—God bless his

471

memory, and may we keep ever green in our memories an appreciation and respect for this dear man.

Now we have the opportunity of meeting with you and speaking to you, and that is a great challenge. As Brother Eyring has indicated, whether you realize it or not, you are a very fortunate group. It is your opportunity to attend this college, which is operated by the Church of which most of you are members. You are proving to the entire world that faith in the Lord Jesus Christ can walk hand in hand with secular learning. May the Lord bless you in your pursuit of knowledge. May the friendships you establish here warm your hearts throughout your lives. May this always remain in your memories a pleasant and delightful season.

Last Saturday and Sunday we were in Columbus, Ohio, dedicating a new and beautiful temple. The temple and the nearby ward chapel were filled for all of the six sessions. The Spirit of the Lord was present, and it was a great and significant occasion to dedicate the second temple in the history of the Church in the great state of Ohio.

With me were my wife and my daughter, who was there to assist her mother. To our delight, a granddaughter and two of her children, our great-grandchildren, drove in from St. Louis, where they live.

As I sat in the celestial room, I thought of my great-grandfather. He lived in Canada for a part of his life, but I did not know where until a year ago when I was in Ottawa and a counselor in the stake presidency told me he thought he had located my great-grandfather's burial place. We traveled about 50 miles south to a rural area near the U.S. border. There we visited a little burial place. There was a headstone which now cannot be read. There were other stones in a straight row.

My great-grandfather died of smallpox when an epidemic raged through that part of the country. He had been baptized into this

Church by the early missionaries who went into Canada. He had two little boys—my grandfather and his brother.

Upon his death, their mother decided to move south to Ohio. They crossed the St. Lawrence River when it was frozen. From Ohio they later moved to Springfield, Illinois. The mother died, and the boys were left orphans. They had been too young to be baptized. Now they were grown to young manhood. They walked from Springfield, Illinois, to Nauvoo. Here they met the Prophet Joseph. They were baptized. They cast their lot with this Church for the remainder of their lives. My grandfather, as a young man, started the long journey across the plains with his young wife, their baby daughter, and his half-brother. Somewhere out in the wilderness of that long journey his wife sickened and died. His half-brother died the same day. He made crude coffins and buried them in a place of which we do not know. He picked up his baby and brought her to the valley of the Great Salt Lake.

He became a man of some prominence. Brigham Young called him to go down and build Cove Fort. More than a century later that fort still stands, now a popular tourist attraction. For us of his family it is a memorial.

He became the first president of the stake in Fillmore, Millard County. He gave most of his fortune to the establishment of the Millard Academy, a Church school which once existed there.

Then came my father. He taught at BYU and then was asked by the Brethren to come to Salt Lake and establish what is today the LDS Business College. He too became a stake president and for years presided over the largest stake in the Church, with more than 15,000 members.

I came along. I too was once a stake president. Sister Hinckley and I have a son who is now a stake president. So we have had four in succession in our family who have served as stake presidents. We have 5 children. We have 25 grandchildren. We have 23 great-grandchildren.

As I sat in the temple in Columbus, Ohio, the other day, looking at my great-grandchildren, a peculiar thing happened. I suddenly realized that I stood midway, with three generations with which I am familiar behind me and three generations ahead of me. My heart literally turned to my fathers. My heart also turned to my posterity.

I envisioned a chain of the generations. That chain goes back a very long way into the distant past, of which we know so very little. It now reaches for three generations beyond me. I pictured that chain in my mind's eye, to date unbroken and shining and strong.

I thought of the time when I was a boy and we lived on a farm in the summer. We had horses and plows and harrows and mowers and rakes—and chains. We were familiar with chains. Later on we got a tractor, and I recalled the day when I put the chain around a tree that we wished to remove, with the other end fastened to the tractor. I started slowly. The tree scarcely moved. I turned up the gas. The wheels ground into the earth. Then suddenly the chain snapped. I had not pulled the tree, but I had broken the chain. It had a weak link. I undid the two pieces from the tree and the tractor. I went to a hardware store and bought a repair link. With that link I joined the two pieces of the chain together. We used that chain for years and years after that. But it was never the same where the repair link was. The link never quite fit. The adjoining links were crowded where the repair was made. It was always a misfit. It never looked right. Whenever I pulled with that chain after that, I watched the repair link. It never was what it should have been.

Now I thought, as I sat in the temple, that I am a link joining all of the generations of the past and all of the generations of the future. All that I have of mind and body, of tissue and limb and joint and brain have come as an inheritance from those who were before me. And all that my posterity have has passed through me to them. I cannot afford to break that chain. My posterity cannot

474

afford to break that chain. If that should happen, we could obtain a repair link, but it would never be quite the same.

I wish I had the eloquence of language to convey to you young people here today the feeling I had in the temple—the great, overwhelming desire that neither I nor my posterity should ever break the chain of the generations of our family.

To you I say with all of the energy of which I am capable, do not become a weak link in your chain of generations. You come to this world with a marvelous inheritance. You come of great men and women, of men of bravery and courage, of women of accomplishment and of tremendous faith. Never let them down. Never do anything which would weaken the chain of which you are a fundamental part. Should that happen, through repentance there might be repairs. But there will also be scars. There will still be regret. There will still be sorrow.

You are loved by your parents, your grandparents, your great-grandparents. You have an obligation toward them. Their hearts yearn to see you succeed, to see you move forward in the world doing your part to improve the society in which you live.

My thoughts today go back to Absalom, the son of King David. He was a gifted young man, a very able young man. The scripture records that "in all Israel there was none to be so much praised as Absalom for his beauty: from the sole of his foot even to the crown of his head there was no blemish in him" (2 Samuel 14:25).

But Absalom became ambitious. His pride got the best of him. He stepped over the line; he did foolish things. He even plotted to kill his father, King David. While following his ambition, he was riding one day upon a mule, "and the mule went under the thick boughs of a great oak, and his head caught hold of the oak, and he was taken up between the heaven and the earth; and the mule that was under him went away" (2 Samuel 18:9).

This was reported to Joab, the king's officer—that Absalom was hanging in the tree. Joab, aware that the young man conspired to kill his father, "took three darts in his hand, and thrust them through the heart of Absalom, while he was yet alive in the midst of the oak" (v. 14). Joab thought he was doing a favor to the king by saving him from the threats of his own son. "And they took Absalom," according to the scripture, "and cast him into a great pit in the wood, and laid a very great heap of stones upon him" (v. 17).

Joab thought he had pleased the king. But when David heard of the death of his son, the scripture records that "the king was much moved, and went up to the chamber over the gate, and wept: and as he went, thus he said, O my son Absalom, my son, my son Absalom! would God I had died for thee, O Absalom, my son, my son!" (v. 33).

I can sense the overwhelming sorrow of King David as he grieved over the loss of the boy who had broken the link of the chain of his generations. "O my son Absalom, my son, my son Absalom! would God I had died for thee, O Absalom, my son, my son!"

I knew well a man of great prominence, a man whose forebears were men and women of faith and great integrity. I heard him frequently pray that among his future generations there would be no empty chairs. I know today the grandson of that man. He became prideful and arrogant. He apostatized from the Church. He took his children with him into apostasy. He had broken the chain that his grandfather counted on with such great hope.

It is interesting to read the first chapter of Matthew. It begins with this verse: "The book of the generation of Jesus Christ" (v. 1). It then gives the names of those who were links in the chain of generations from Abraham to the Savior of the world. It then states that "all the generations from Abraham to David are fourteen generations; and from David until the carrying away into Babylon are fourteen generations; and from the carrying away into Babylon unto Christ are fourteen generations" (v. 17).

These count up to 42 generations, and insofar as I know, they constituted an unbroken chain that became the mortal foundation for the Son of God. He who was the Only Begotten of the Father in the flesh came through a lustrous line of great people.

To you young women who will marry and become mothers and pass on the qualities of your generations, to you young men who will become fathers and pass on the lineage which is your greatest possession, I say, be true. Be true to the faith. Be true to the faith that your parents have cherished. Be true to the faith for which martyrs have perished. (See *Hymns*, no. 254.) Be loyal to your great inheritance. Pass on in an unblemished fashion to those who come after you the great virtues of those who have preceded you. All of your heritage of body and mind have come from your forebears. Pass to those who will follow an unblemished inheritance, and thus continue bright and strong the links of your generations.

For this I humbly pray in the name of Jesus Christ, amen.

# SECTION 3

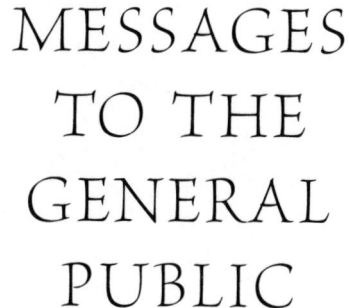

# MESSAGES
# TO THE
# GENERAL
# PUBLIC

# STATEMENT TO THE MEDIA

MARCH 13, 1995

*President Hinckley delivered this statement at a press conference
in the Joseph Smith Memorial Building one day after being ordained
and set apart as the 15th President of the Church.*

THANK YOU FOR YOUR PRESENCE this morning, and thank you for
the manner in which you handled the passing of our beloved friend
and leader, Howard W. Hunter. His death has deeply affected all of
us. The memories of his great virtues will long linger with us.

One cannot come to this sacred office without almost overwhelming feelings of inadequacy. Strengthened resolution to go
forward comes from the knowledge that this is the work of God,
that He is watching over it, that He will direct us in our efforts if
we will be true and faithful, and that our accountability is to Him.

With that assurance we reach out to our own people and to
those of goodwill throughout the world, in that spirit of love and
brotherhood which comes from the Lord Jesus Christ.

I am grateful for these two men of faith and ability who serve
with me as counselors and to my stalwart and able brethren of the
Council of the Twelve Apostles. There is total harmony among us,
as there must be in this sacred work if it is to prosper.

As the Church moves forward on its divinely appointed
mission, I do not anticipate any dramatic change in course.
Procedures and programs may be altered from time to time, but
the doctrine remains constant. We are dedicated, as have been those
before us, to teaching the gospel of peace, to the promotion of

civility and mutual respect among people everywhere, to bearing witness to the living reality of our Lord Jesus Christ, and to the practice of His teachings in our daily lives.

We are concerned with the quality of family life within so many homes. The home is the seedbed of all true virtue. If proper values are not learned in the home, they are not likely to be learned anywhere.

We are grateful for the faith and the strength of the people of this Church. They now number some 9 million in approximately 150 nations and political entities. The membership is growing consistently and solidly. We are confident that this will continue as the Church stands as an anchor of truth in a world of shifting values and standards. We are particularly proud of our youth. I think we have never had a stronger generation of young men and women than we have today. For the most part they are true to the faith of their forebears. Surrounded by forces that would pull them down and tremendous pressures to pull them away from time-tested virtues, they are going forward with constructive lives, nurturing themselves both intellectually and spiritually. We have no fears or doubts concerning the future of this work.

If we have offended any, we apologize. Our only desire is to cultivate a spirit of mercy and kindness, of understanding and healing. We seek to follow the practice of our Lord, who "went about doing good" (Acts 10:38).

Thank you very much.

# Excerpts from an Interview with Mike Wallace of *60 Minutes*

## December 18, 1995

*On November 13, 1995, President Hinckley spoke at the Harvard Club in New York City. While there he met Mike Wallace, who asked if he could do a profile of President Hinckley for the television news program* 60 Minutes. *This interview is the result.*

**Mike Wallace:** Mr. President, why did you agree to give us this rare interview?

**President Hinckley:** Because I felt it was an opportunity to tell the people of America something about this great cause in which I have such a keen interest.

**Mike Wallace:** But that is not traditional with Mormons.

**President Hinckley:** Oh, I don't know. I don't know. We have—

**Mike Wallace:** Can you tell me the last President of the Mormon Church who went on nationwide television to do an interview with no questions ahead of time so that you know what is coming?

**President Hinckley:** No, I don't remember one.

**Mike Wallace:** So, Gordon Hinckley decided, apparently, that there is a message that the Mormon Church has for America and, for that matter, the world.

**President Hinckley:** Yes, indeed.

**Mike Wallace:** And that message is?

**President Hinckley:** That message is that there is a way to greater peace. There is a way to greater harmony in our living. There is a way to revive the values that have made America strong. There is a way to improve things. That is what I would like to say.

*Mike Wallace:* And you have even retained a public relations agency.

*President Hinckley:* Yes, to assist us in this effort.

*Mike Wallace:* And you have been advertising on television.

*President Hinckley:* Yes, we've done advertising on television. We've done a great deal of work on television over a period of many years. We produce what are called Homefront spots that have been running for many years on television stations and radio stations across the nation and the world.

*Mike Wallace:* Is that to proselytize? Is that to get people to join the Mormon Church or to tell the rest of us heathens what we are missing?

*President Hinckley:* It is to tell the rest of you what you are missing, yes.

*Mike Wallace:* And what is it that we are missing?

*President Hinckley:* You are missing the lift that comes of living close to the Lord, walking with faith and with purpose, with a feeling that life is really purposeful—that it is a mission rather than just a career. There is something wonderful about having some concept of who you are as a son of God with a divine destiny and that you can make more of your life than you may have been making of it.

*Mike Wallace:* But that's not the way I believe; that's not the way the world has been going.

*President Hinckley:* No, it isn't.

*Mike Wallace:* Certainly not in the last half century, and especially in the last quarter century. Why?

*President Hinckley:* Well, the world has been going its own way. There isn't any question. Anyone who looks at what's happening in America knows that there has been a tremendous loss. Our value system has deteriorated; it's crumbled in many areas with millions of people. It is time to get hold of ourselves, to stop this downward slide and turn around and come back and live more up to our potential—and particularly for young people to do that, to get some vision of what they might make of their lives.

*Mike Wallace:* All of this is developing to be worse. The question is, what happened? We were together—when I say "we," we Americans were together—I believe, during the Second World War. Did you serve in the war?

*President Hinckley:* No. No, I didn't. I applied but was washed out.

*Mike Wallace:* Really?

*President Hinckley:* Yes.

*Mike Wallace:* You were 4-F?

*President Hinckley:* I applied for a Navy commission, and because of a series of allergies with some asthma, they just cut me out. It was a great disappointment to me.

*Mike Wallace:* I spent three years in the Navy, and they were three of the best years—the most useful years—of my life. But since the war, since World War II, we seem to be splintering; we seem to be becoming, since World War II, perhaps more selfish, more self-absorbed, less community minded. Families don't seem to mean so much. Morality, forgive me, has gone to hell in a hand-basket. Why?

*President Hinckley:* Well, for one thing, the basic factor is failure in our homes. Parents haven't measured up to their responsibilities. It is evident. A nation will rise no higher than the strength of its homes. If you want to reform a nation, you begin with families, with parents who teach their children principles and values that are positive and affirmative and will lead them to worthwhile endeavors. That is the basic failure that has taken place in America, I think: a failure in our homes. And we are trying to make a tremendous effort—we *are* making a tremendous effort—to bring about greater solidarity in families. We have programs. For instance, among our people, every Monday night is dedicated as family home evening, when father, mother, and children sit down together—

*Mike Wallace:* And read scriptures—

*President Hinckley:* Pray together, read the scriptures together, talk about family plans, about family problems, discuss matters that affect each of them, and come to some unity on what they are trying to do. It gets tremendous results.

*Mike Wallace:* Yes, but Mr. President, your competition is *Monday Night Football.*

*President Hinckley:* Yes, I know, but there is football all during the week too. You can certainly dedicate one evening a week to this kind of process that will bring blessings to your children. Look, when all is said and done, you as a parent have no greater responsibility in this world than the bringing up of your children in the right way, and you will have no greater satisfaction as the years pass than to see those children growing in integrity and honesty and making something of their lives, adding to society because they are a part of it.

*Mike Wallace:* You are eight years older than I.

*President Hinckley:* I never dreamed of it. I thought we were the same age.

*Mike Wallace:* You are eight years older than I. The point is this: that is the way that you were brought up, and that's—I guess to a certain degree—the way that I was brought up. And I have tried to understand why parents today apparently don't feel the way that our parents felt.

*President Hinckley:* I don't understand it either. I wish I did. We are trying to help. We recognize the phenomenon. I can't tell all the causes of it. But I think I can do something to assist with the problem, and that is exactly what we are trying to do.

*Mike Wallace:* In the Mormon Church?

*President Hinckley:* Yes.

*Mike Wallace:* And you seem to be more successful than some other churches.

*President Hinckley:* I hope we are achieving something worthwhile, yes.

*Mike Wallace:* Do you have any idea what it is in Mormonism—

*President Hinckley:* Well, first there is the basic premise that each of us is a child of God—a son or daughter of God—that we come with a divine inheritance, that we have an opportunity to do something, that God is our Father and that He loves us and that He will bless us as we make efforts to live after His pattern. That is basic. The second thing is that fathers and mothers are custodians of our Father's children. They have responsibility, and there will be a time of accountability concerning what they do in their role as parents. That is a tremendously important premise.

*Mike Wallace:* Accountability when? Where? How?

*President Hinckley:* Accountability in this life when they face the futures of their children and, someday, accountability before God.

*Mike Wallace:* You believe in an afterlife?

*President Hinckley:* I certainly do. I think life after this life is as certain as life here. I believe we lived before we came here, that we live here for a purpose—

*Mike Wallace:* Wait. Wait. You believe we lived before we came here.

*President Hinckley:* Oh, absolutely—as intelligences. Yes. As spirits—

*Mike Wallace:* Not as bodies.

*President Hinckley:* As sons and daughters of God. No, with mortal bodies, no.

*Mike Wallace:* But there was—

*President Hinckley:* There was entity.

*Mike Wallace:* There was a spirit of Gordon Hinckley.

*President Hinckley:* Absolutely. And Mike Wallace.

*Mike Wallace:* I hope not.

*President Hinckley:* Life is an eternal thing, Mike. It is part of an eternal plan, our Father's plan for His sons and daughters, whom He loves. His work and His glory is to bring about the immortality and eternal life of His sons and daughters. It's purposeful. It's meaningful. It is something that we may look up to, to be useful.

*Mike Wallace:* Your Church has a very strict health code.

*President Hinckley:* Yes.

*Mike Wallace:* Why is that a part of religion?

*President Hinckley:* Well, because the body is the temple of the Spirit. The body is sacred. This body which I have is sacred. It was created in the image of God. It is something to be cared for and used for good purposes. It ought to be taken care of, and this thing which we call the Word of Wisdom, which is a code of health, is most helpful in doing that. It proscribes certain things.

*Mike Wallace:* Yes, it does proscribe certain things.

*President Hinckley:* Alcohol.

*Mike Wallace:* No alcohol. No tobacco. No coffee. No tea. Not even caffeinated soft drinks. Eat meat sparingly. Exercise. Get plenty of sleep.

*President Hinckley:* That's right. It's wonderful.

*Mike Wallace:* You don't have to be a man of God to do all of those things.

*President Hinckley:* No, you don't, but it is wonderful to have that kind of motivation—wonderful.

*Mike Wallace:* And how do you enforce that, or is it a question of persuasion?

*President Hinckley:* We teach people. We teach people correct principles, and they govern themselves.

*Mike Wallace:* Is there a difference between the Mormon Church and the Mormon culture?

*President Hinckley:* Oh, I don't think you can separate one from the other, no. I don't see how you can. The Mormon Church is the agency through which the culture is taught, cultivated, brought about. Culture becomes the expression of the teachings of the Church.

*Mike Wallace:* And for some, particularly those who are not Mormons, that makes for conformity, rigidity. Those are the complaints one hears.

*President Hinckley:* Oh, yes, you may hear those complaints. I don't think it is so. I don't think there is substance to it. Our people have tremendous liberty. They are free to live their lives as they please.

*Mike Wallace:* Are they?

*President Hinckley:* Oh, absolutely. Surely. They have to make choices. It is the old, eternal battle that has been going on since the War in Heaven, spoken of in the book of Revelation—the forces of evil against the forces of good. Choices that we all make. The agency we exercise as individuals in the choices we make which determine our behavior. All of these matters of living.

*Mike Wallace:* The result of the health code, if you want to call it that, in the Mormon Church: longer lives, lower rates of cancer, less cirrhosis of the liver, fewer low-weight babies. As a group, it is my understanding that Mormons live longer and are healthier.

*President Hinckley:* Studies have shown that to be the case, yes.

*Mike Wallace:* And you think it is a direct result of the health code of your religion?

*President Hinckley:* I think it is traceable to that. I think so.

*Mike Wallace:* All right. Beyond the health code, you have a moral code.

*President Hinckley:* Right.

*Mike Wallace:* Do you want to list—

*President Hinckley:* We believe in chastity before marriage and total fidelity after marriage. That sums it up. That is the way to happiness in living. That is the way to satisfaction; you can obtain satisfaction in your life. It brings peace in the heart and peace in the home.

*Mike Wallace:* Some of the students that we've talked to, Mr. President, say that the health code is easy compared to the no premarital sex. And that does not mean necessarily intercourse. They say that not smoking or not drinking is a clear line but that the sexual line is somewhere way before intercourse, and they are confused, some of them anyway, about where that line is.

*President Hinckley:* Oh, I think they know. Look, any young man or young woman who has grown up in this Church knows where that line is. When you see yourself slipping, begin to exercise some self-discipline. And if it is a serious problem, take it to the Lord. Talk with God about it. Share your burden with Him. He will give you strength. He will help you. They know that. I am confident they know that.

*Mike Wallace:* So if a young couple—I don't want to go on and on about this, but—so if a young couple are attracted one to the other, a kiss is okay, but not much more beyond that.

*President Hinckley:* I'm not going to get clinical and draw straight, hard lines, no. I simply say, if you see yourself slipping, feel yourself slipping, get hold of yourself. Exercise some discipline. You can do it.

*Mike Wallace:* Well that's easy for an 85- or a 77-year-old man to say, but it's—

*President Hinckley:* I know it.

*Mike Wallace:* It's not so easy when you are 21.

*President Hinckley:* Here is an interesting thing, Mike. A survey has shown that the higher the level of education among our people, the more active they are, the more faithful they are. That's an interesting phenomenon. For instance, this survey indicated that those with high-school education or below had an average attendance record at their meetings of about 34 percent. Those with postgraduate work, 80 percent. The greater the level of education, the higher the level of activity. Now, that says something.

*Mike Wallace:* Now, when you say "activity," you mean—

*President Hinckley:* Attendance at meetings, participating in the programs of the Church, observing the teachings of the Church.

*Mike Wallace:* Observing a health code and a moral code?

*President Hinckley:* Yes, but the primary barometer is attendance at meetings, because if they come to meeting, they are doing the other things as well.

*Mike Wallace:* Why must only men run the Church?

*President Hinckley:* "Only men" do not run the Church. Men have their place in the Church. Men hold the priesthood offices of the Church. But women have a tremendous place in this Church. They have their own organization. It was started in 1842 by the Prophet Joseph Smith and called the Relief Society because its initial purpose was to administer help to those in need. It has grown to be, I think, the largest women's organization in the world, with a membership of more than three million. They have their own officers, their own presidency, their own board. That reaches down to the smallest unit of the Church everywhere in the world.

*Mike Wallace:* But they don't have the power.

*President Hinckley:* They have office. They have responsibility. They have control of their organization.

*Mike Wallace:* But you run it. The men run it. Look, I'm not being—

*President Hinckley:* The men hold the priesthood, yes. And the women have their organization. And it works.

*Mike Wallace:* You sound like the pope.

*President Hinckley:* Well, if the pope looks at it that way, I may sound like the pope.

*Mike Wallace:* I mean, he suggests the same thing. But churches evolve, churches change.

*President Hinckley:* Oh, sure. We hope they do.

*Mike Wallace:* The point that I guess that I am making is that there is a whole crowd now in the Catholic Church that is saying, "Look, we are equal, we women are equal; we are still not equal in the Mormon Church." You, men, run it.

*President Hinckley:* You ask my wife who makes those decisions.

*Mike Wallace:* But you are the head of the household.

*President Hinckley:* She is my companion. In this Church the man neither walks ahead of his wife nor behind his wife but at her side. They are coequals in this life in a great enterprise.

*Mike Wallace:* The emphasis on family—does that perhaps have a tendency to make a single Mormon or a divorced Mormon feel a little out of it?

*President Hinckley:* It may have that effect, I am sorry to say. Our hearts reach out to those people. We try to do everything we can to try to assist them. We have a great program for singles in the Church, where they can mingle one with another and socialize together and meet companions. And that happens— not infrequently. It is a working program that accomplishes that result. But we know that some people will never marry, and I am sure they feel the effects of that. Every normal man, every normal woman, I am confident, would like to be married to a good companion and be part of a good, strong family.

*Mike Wallace:* Why do Mormons have so many children? You have five. You have a picture of your family up there. My, with grandchildren and great-grandchildren—

*President Hinckley:* Twenty-five grandchildren, fourteen great-grandchildren. Wonderful family.

*Mike Wallace:* Why is it that you Mormons apparently have so many children?

*President Hinckley:* We don't dictate family size. That is left to the father and the mother, the husband and wife. And we expect them to make of this the most serious business of their lives, the rearing of the family.

*Mike Wallace:* Mormon values—your value system apparently works. Compared with national averages, Mormons have fewer illegitimate children, less premarital sex, less adultery, more marriage, less divorce.

*President Hinckley:* We are trying to strengthen these values in our people. They are fundamental. We can't have a strong nation without a nation based on values. They are the very core of our civilization.

*Mike Wallace:* You have said that you have the most demanding religion in the country.

*President Hinckley:* I don't know that I have said that, but I am sure people feel that we have a demanding religion. We have great expectations concerning our people. We have standards that we expect them to live by and to uphold. It is demanding. And that is one of the things that attracts people to this Church. It stands as an anchor in a world of shifting values. They feel they have something solid that they are standing on while the ground is moving beneath them.

*Mike Wallace:* And if your Church is so demanding, one would think that perhaps, in this world in which values seem to be dissolving to a certain degree, that your Church would be growing smaller, instead of which it is growing larger.

*President Hinckley:* It is growing larger because people are looking for something of substance and strength and based on eternal truth and eternal values. The gospel of the Lord Jesus Christ. The law of the Golden Rule. The principles of the Beatitudes which Jesus taught of going the second mile, of helping people. The example of the good Samaritan. These are things of reality, I hope, with us. We teach them.

*Mike Wallace:* What is the relationship of the Mormon Church to Judaism, Islam?

*President Hinckley:* I think we have a very good relationship with our Jewish friends. We have many of them right here in this community. We have an excellent relationship with them, and that goes back through the years to the early years of this settlement, when some of them came here. We have had good relationships with Muslims insofar as we have had them. Recently a group of Muslims went into one of our welfare canneries and used those canneries to can food for their programs of humanitarian aid. We made our facilities open to them. We live together as neighbors here. I don't see much sign of stress or problems here among our neighbors. We get along well with the Catholics and with others, the Protestants.

*Mike Wallace:* There are those who say that Mormonism really began as a cult. You don't like to hear that.

*President Hinckley:* I don't know what it means, really. But if it has negative connotations, I don't accept it as applying to this Church. People may have applied it; they may have applied it in the early days. But look, here is a great Church now. There are only six churches in America with more members than this Church. We are the second church in membership in the state of California. We are reaching out across the world. We are in more than 150 nations. This is a great, strong, viable organization with a tremendous outreach across the world. I don't know how many could so describe it. We are not a weird people.

*Mike Wallace:* A weird people?

*President Hinckley:* Yes.

*Mike Wallace:* Some of the youngsters, Mormons, say, "Please tell them we are not weird."

*President Hinckley:* Well, we are not weird. We are people who work at the vocations of life. You find our people in business institutions, high in educational circles, in politics, in government, in whatever. We are ordinary people trying to do an extraordinary work.

*Mike Wallace:* Scandal?

*President Hinckley:* Scandal? What kind of scandal are you talking about? I don't know.

*Mike Wallace:* Money?

*President Hinckley:* I don't know. I don't know of any. Scandal?

*Mike Wallace:* People who have fallen away, people who have—believe me, we looked for it. We couldn't find it.

*President Hinckley:* Well, we have a few who fall away—of course we do. Every organization has its failures, regrettably.

*Mike Wallace:* What have been the failures, if any?

*President Hinckley:* We have a few people who fall away, yes—who don't seem to enjoy their membership in the Church.

*Mike Wallace:* Oh, no. They find you too rigid.

*President Hinckley:* Yes, a few.

*Mike Wallace:* They find it too conformist.

*President Hinckley:* A few.

*Mike Wallace:* That you are—that Mormons come off an assembly line, everybody with a white shirt, a dark suit, a prudent tie—

*President Hinckley:* Well, just let me take you to one of our recreational opportunities, one of our great facilities where our people have fun together. You will see all kinds of costumes there.

*Mike Wallace:* No, I'm sure you will see all kinds of costumes, but—

*President Hinckley:* With all kinds of personalities and a lot of wonderful, wholesome fun.

*Mike Wallace:* And it's expensive?

*President Hinckley:* What's expensive?

*Mike Wallace:* Being a Mormon.

*President Hinckley:* Oh, it isn't expensive. You are living by the law of the Lord—tithing.

*Mike Wallace:* Well, I know that. But 10 percent of your gross goes to the Church, and you have nothing to do with the way that money is spent. I say "you," the average Mormon.

*President Hinckley:* The average Mormon—yes, he has a good deal to do with it. He is a member of the Church. What is that money used for? It is used for Church purposes.

*Mike Wallace:* What are Church purposes exactly?

*President Hinckley:* Building chapels—about 375 a year. Think about that—new buildings each year to accommodate the needs of the growing membership. It is used for education. We maintain the largest private, church-sponsored university in the world.

*Mike Wallace:* Brigham Young.

*President Hinckley:* Brigham Young University, with 27,000 students on that campus, as well as other campuses. We maintain a tremendous institute of religion program, where we have off-campus but in connection with the major universities of America—nearly every university and college of any consequence—an institute of religion. You will find it at UCLA,

USC, Harvard, Yale, Princeton, the University of New York, the University of Massachusetts, Massachusetts Institute of Technology.

*Mike Wallace:* What about all these?

*President Hinckley:* These are where students in those universities can come together, can talk about their problems, can gather for instruction.

*Mike Wallace:* You mean Mormons in these various universities have a special place, a special chapel to go to?

*President Hinckley:* Yes, they have a special facility, an institute of religion, where students can come and, under an able director, a man of education and a man of faith, they study together and talk over their problems together; they reason together; they talk about the pros and the cons; and they grow in faith as they do so.

*Mike Wallace:* How about intermarriage? How does the Church feel about Mormons marrying out of the Church?

*President Hinckley:* We think that people are happy if they marry within their own church. I think our experience demonstrates that. We have no rule against that. We encourage marriage within the faith because we think the opportunities for happy family life are enhanced when that occurs.

*Mike Wallace:* Why?

*President Hinckley:* Because people see things together. They rear their children with the same objectives, with the same understanding.

*Mike Wallace:* You are going against, really—against the grain of so much that is going on in America today, right?

*President Hinckley:* I guess that's what makes us distinctive.

*Mike Wallace:* Uh-huh.

*President Hinckley:* But all I want to say is this: Judge us by our fruits. Good fruits come from good roots. Jesus said: "Do men gather grapes of thorns, or figs of thistles? . . . By their fruits ye shall know them" (Matthew 7:16, 20). That's the only standard by which we ask that we be judged.

*Mike Wallace:* And you are proud of your fruits?

*President Hinckley:* I am proud of our fruits. I wish that we were more successful.

*Mike Wallace:* How could you be more successful?

*President Hinckley:* Oh, we could be more successful. We lose some.

*Mike Wallace:* But you have nine million—nine million Mormons now worldwide. And I guess—for the first time, I guess, maybe within the next year, there are going to be more Mormons outside the United States than in?

*President Hinckley:* We think we are crossing that line this spring— that we will have more members of this Church outside the United States than in the United States. And that brings with it great challenges and great opportunities.

*Mike Wallace:* Where are these new Mormons? What countries, particularly—what parts of the world?

*President Hinckley:* Oh, all up and down South America—all the nations of South America—the nations of Asia, the nations of Europe, everywhere we go.

*Mike Wallace:* A practicing Mormon, Mr. President—how much time each week does he or she spend on religious activities?

*President Hinckley:* That would depend on his or her responsibilities—if he or she is an officer, for instance. A bishop in a local congregation—he would spend a good deal of time. He would spend perhaps three or four evenings a week as well as Sunday and possibly some time on Saturday. But I would hope that he would reserve Monday evening for his family home evening with his family and at least another evening when he and his wife or his children can get out and go somewhere and be together as a family and live as a good family. He isn't to rob his employer of his time, and he isn't to rob his family of their time. And with a careful budgeting of his time, he can make it work, and he does make it work, and we have **22,000** of them.

*Mike Wallace:* Twenty-two thousand?

*President Hinckley:* Local bishops across the world who do this, all serving on a volunteer basis. That's the genius of this thing. And that's one reason that we have the resources to do what we do. We don't have a paid clergy. These people give of their services.

*Mike Wallace:* And they make their own living at their own vocation?

*President Hinckley:* Oh, yes. I could tell you of executives who have very high responsibility in business organizations in this nation—

*Mike Wallace:* And still give—

*President Hinckley:* And carry heavy Church responsibility. Bill Marriott Jr., CEO of the Marriott Corporation; Jon Huntsman, here in Salt Lake, head of Huntsman Chemical Corporation.

*Mike Wallace:* How about Steve Young of the 49ers?

*President Hinckley:* Steve Young's a good boy, good young man. He isn't a bishop, but he's a good and faithful Latter-day Saint.

*Mike Wallace:* When you say "Latter-day Saint"—when I first heard "The Church of Jesus Christ of the Latter-day Saints," I thought, "Well, who are these 'Latter-day Saints'?"

*President Hinckley:* Well, just as the early Christians were known as Saints, so in these latter days we are known as Saints.

*Mike Wallace:* In other words—

*President Hinckley:* Followers of Christ. That's it.

*Mike Wallace:* All good Mormons are Latter-day Saints?

*President Hinckley:* They are members of The Church of Jesus Christ of Latter-day Saints. This Church carries the name of the Savior of the world. We are Christians in a very real sense.

Everything that we do is done in the name of Jesus Christ. He is the central figure of our religion.

*Mike Wallace:* And to get back to Steve Young—when he throws a touchdown pass, he's doing it for the 49ers or for Jesus?

*President Hinckley:* Steve Young's employed by the 49ers. Give unto Caesar that which is Caesar's and unto God that which is God's (see Mark 12:17).

*Mike Wallace:* Politics and the Church.

*President Hinckley:* Uh-huh.

*Mike Wallace:* Are you in it?

*President Hinckley:* No.

*Mike Wallace:* You are not for or agin, whether it's Dole or Clinton or Ross Perot?

*President Hinckley:* As a Church institutionally we take no position in favor of any candidate or any party. We do not make our Church facilities available for political purposes.

*Mike Wallace:* Wait—

*President Hinckley:* We urge our people to exercise their franchise as citizens of this nation. But we do not tell them how to vote and we do not tell the government how it should be run.

*Mike Wallace:* The reason I said "Wait" is that I was covering Richard Nixon back in 1968 when he was running for the presidency, and he came here to Salt Lake City. And I am under the impression, unless my memory is gone, that he did make a speech over at the Tabernacle.

*President Hinckley:* Yes. And so did John F. Kennedy on one occasion.

*Mike Wallace:* Yes. So it's not—

*President Hinckley:* We have opened the Tabernacle for public purposes, civic purposes, yes. When the president of the United States comes here, of course.

*Mike Wallace:* Well, when the president—but he was running for president at the time.

*President Hinckley:* That's right. The last election, who came here to visit us? George Bush. Three days later, Bill Clinton. Yes. We entertained both of them, talked with them, met with them, had a very pleasant visit with each of them.

*Mike Wallace:* Perhaps some people regard Mormonism, if you will—perhaps some people, Mr. President, regard the Mormon Church as a cult because so much has been secret. For instance, I could not go into one of your temples, could I?

*President Hinckley:* Yes.

*Mike Wallace:* Yes what?

*President Hinckley:* Oh, yes. Hundreds of thousands of people have been in our temples. When the San Diego Temple was opened, 900,000 people went through that temple. Before a temple is dedicated, it is open to the public.

*Mike Wallace:* Oh, before it is dedicated.

*President Hinckley:* Before it is dedicated, yes. They are free to go in, see anything that is there, to ask any questions they might have.

*Mike Wallace:* But what goes on—

*President Hinckley:* But when a temple is dedicated, it partakes of a particular sanctity. Things are sacred to us, and it becomes the house of God. And it is not a building just to be tramped through, as it were, but is a holy and sacred edifice, the house of the Lord, a place that we hold dear. Those who go there after that are expected to live up to the highest standards of the Church.

*Mike Wallace:* You have to be a really good Mormon to be admitted into the temple.

*President Hinckley:* You should be a good, faithful member of this Church to go into the temple after dedication.

*Mike Wallace:* And marriages take place there?

*President Hinckley:* Marriages take place there, indeed they do, under the wonderful, peaceful, beautiful atmosphere of that holy house. Marriage is not only for time but for eternity. When the Lord was with His Apostles anciently, He said, "And I will give unto thee the keys of the kingdom of heaven: and whatsoever thou shalt bind on earth shall be bound in heaven" (Matthew 16:19). We believe that that same priesthood has been restored in this day and time and is exercised in this holy house and that marriages and families can be forever.

*Mike Wallace:* Forever.

*President Hinckley:* Forever.

*Mike Wallace:* After you pass—

*President Hinckley:* Forever. It goes on. Can you conceive of the highest degree of happiness in a life beyond without the companionship of your wife, your family? Isn't it reasonable to believe that the God who loves us all would make it possible for us to continue those relationships in eternity?

*Mike Wallace:* Forgive my cynicism, and it's only partly a joke— there are some husbands or wives who are just waiting for their mate to depart so they will finally be rid of them.

*President Hinckley:* I know.

*Mike Wallace:* And they are going to have to meet them up there?

*President Hinckley:* Not very many of those who are married in the temple have those feelings.

*Mike Wallace:* I'm sure.

*President Hinckley:* That's right.

*Mike Wallace:* The Church is traditionally secret on the subject of money, about how much money it has, about how much money it collects.

*President Hinckley:* Well, why should it spread all of its figures before the world? These funds are all carefully audited. We have a corps of auditors who are qualified CPAs, who are independent from all other agencies of the Church, and who report only to the First Presidency of the Church. We try to be very careful. I keep on the credenza behind my desk a widow's mite that was given me in Jerusalem many years ago as a reminder, a constant reminder, of the sanctity of the funds which we have to deal with. They come from the widow; they are her offering as well as the tithe of the rich man, and they are to be used with care and discretion for the purposes of the Lord. We treat them carefully and safeguard them and try in every way that we can to see that they are used as we feel the Lord would have them used for the upbuilding of His work and the betterment of people.

*Mike Wallace:* With nine million Mormons now, and some of them very, very successful—I mean, Mormons generally speaking have the reputation for being very good businessmen—

*President Hinckley:* They ought to be, because they are high-principled men.

*Mike Wallace:* And so you must make—

*President Hinckley:* That isn't the word.

*Mike Wallace:* No, that's right. So you must collect from the tithes, the Church does, billions every year—five, eight, ten?

*President Hinckley:* You are way high. You are way high. You have to realize that our membership is not only in the United States, but it extends across the world, including in some Third World countries where people have very, very little. No, you are very high. But we have enough. Providentially, we have enough to take care of our needs. The payment of tithes isn't so much a matter of money as it is a matter of faith. It is a freewill offering. There is no coercion in the matter of tithing. A man isn't dropped from the membership rolls of the Church if he doesn't pay his tithing.

*Mike Wallace:* No?

*President Hinckley:* He pays it out of faith, out of appreciation for this Church, out of respect for a commandment of the Lord. Tithing isn't a new principle. It goes back into the times of the Old Testament. It's God's law of finance for the handling of His work. And it works. It works.

*Mike Wallace:* How did you get to be President?

*President Hinckley:* How did I get to be President?

*Mike Wallace:* You are now "the man." I know you have two counselors—it's a trinity, is it not?

*President Hinckley:* It's a triad arrangement, yes.

*Mike Wallace:* A triad.

*President Hinckley:* Yes. How did I get to be President? In 1961 I was called as a member of the Council of the Twelve Apostles, and through the years I moved up through the ranks of that circle until I became the senior Apostle. When the last President of the Church passed away, I was the senior Apostle, and the senior Apostle succeeds to the office of President of the Church. It's the smoothest kind of succession that you could see in this world. It takes place very quietly, without election, without fanfare, without campaigning, without anything of the kind. It works. By the time a man gets to be the President he has been trained; he has been refined, I hope; he has traveled around the world; he knows this Church inside and out; he knows the people of the world—their problems, their aspirations.

*Mike Wallace:* You began your work in the Church as a missionary, didn't you, back in the U.K.—way, way back?

*President Hinckley:* More than 60 years ago I served, like other young men of this Church, as a missionary in England, right. It was a tremendous experience. But like all other missionaries, I went at my own expense and the expense of my family and came back to resume my normal life.

*Mike Wallace:* And the young people of the Church, even today, do the same thing? They give, what, a couple of years?

*President Hinckley:* Two years. Young men give two years.

*Mike Wallace:* And women?

*President Hinckley:* Young women, 18 months—a year and a half. The work is strenuous; it is difficult. It isn't easy to go to New York, to go to London, to go to Tokyo, to knock on doors, to face people you have never met before.

*Mike Wallace:* To knock on doors?

*President Hinckley:* Yes.

*Mike Wallace:* To spread the word.

*President Hinckley:* Yes.

*Mike Wallace:* To proselytize.

*President Hinckley:* Yes. It does something for you. It does two or three things. It creates, in the first place, a feeling of reliance on the Lord. It isn't easy for a young man to do that. It builds within him something of strength and capacity, I believe. If he goes to a foreign land, he develops expertise in the language; he learns to speak the language of the people. Wherever he goes, he comes to know the people among whom he serves and brings back with him something of their culture, their way of doing things, with appreciation and respect for them and their conditions and circumstances. There is nothing like it—when you think we have nearly 50,000 out right now, and that number is constantly rotating so that it touches the lives of hundreds of thousands of these people. I can walk down the streets of Salt Lake City with you and meet people who speak fluently in Japanese and Chinese and Swedish and Norwegian and Finnish and Spanish and Portuguese and what have you and who have love in their hearts for the people among whom they served.

*Mike Wallace:* These are Americans who have—

*President Hinckley:* Returned missionaries, yes. And in addition to that, we have missionaries come here to the United States from Japan, from Europe, from South America, wherever.

*Mike Wallace:* Why are members of the Church expected to keep a year's supply of food, clothing, and fuel?

*President Hinckley:* We teach self-reliance as a principle of life— that we ought to provide for ourselves and take care of our own needs. And so we encourage our people to have something, to plan ahead, keep a little food on hand, to establish a savings account, if possible, against a rainy day. Catastrophes come to people sometimes when least expected—unemployment, sickness, things of that kind. The individual, as we teach, ought to do for himself all that he can do for himself. When he has exhausted his resources, he ought to turn to his family to assist him. When the family can't do it, the Church takes over. And when the Church takes over, our great desire is to first take care of his immediate needs and then to help him for so long as he needs to be helped, but in that process to assist him in training, in securing employment—some way of getting on his feet again. That's the whole objective of this great welfare program.

*Mike Wallace:* Well, this is a church welfare program. Are Mormons permitted to take government welfare checks?

*President Hinckley:* Mormons are free to do as they please. Mormons have their agency just as everyone else, and I suppose some do. I suppose some do. But the fact of the matter is we help very, very large numbers.

*Mike Wallace:* You have your own welfare program.

*President Hinckley:* We have our own welfare program, which is maintained as an effort to help people to help themselves. And through that welfare program we reach out to people in distress in many parts of the world. We have given millions and millions

and millions of dollars' worth of aid to people in distressed circumstances in Asia, in Africa, in Central and South America—

*Mike Wallace:* With no objection from the membership?

*President Hinckley:* With no objection. With encouragement.
When the terrible problems occurred in Africa a few years ago
and the networks were carrying these heartrending programs—

*Mike Wallace:* Ethiopia, the starvation?

*President Hinckley:* Ethiopia, the starvation there. We held a fast
day in this Church and asked our people in the United States
to refrain from two meals and give the value of those two meals
to assist the suffering Ethiopians. Within 10 days we had eight
million dollars, which was sent to assist the people in those
countries and distributed, not by us but through Catholic chari-
ties, the International Red Cross, the present organization, and
organizations of that kind. We are giving in humanitarian aid
about 30 million dollars a year.

*Mike Wallace:* Why is Salt Lake City so clean?

*President Hinckley:* Well, we hope it is a reflection of the people
who live here.

*Mike Wallace:* It is astonishing to walk down the streets of Salt
Lake City.

*President Hinckley:* We hope it will stay that way. I hope it reflects,
in some measure at least, some of the teachings of this Church.
Look at the beauties of Temple Square right here in the heart of
the city, the very core of the city. Look at the magnificent
temple and that great Tabernacle. They were built with vision
by people with culture, with refinement, with artistry. These are
not the work of charlatans. They are the work of people who
had a great vision to do beautiful things.

*Mike Wallace:* Many religions, Mr. President, are based on stories
that are taken on faith. But Mormons seem especially "dug in"
in taking everything in Church history as literally proven. Yes?

*President Hinckley:* Oh, I don't know that I would say that. Of course we accept much on faith, but we are scholars—we dig, we study. This Church has as its motto, if it has anything, "The glory of God is intelligence" (D&C 93:36). That comes from our scripture.

*Mike Wallace:* Your Church says God and Jesus spoke with your founder, Joseph Smith, back in 1820 and told him to start this Church. You believe that?

*President Hinckley:* Yes, sir.

*Mike Wallace:* He was 14 years old—

*President Hinckley:* Yes, sir.

*Mike Wallace:* A backwoods farm boy—

*President Hinckley:* Yes, sir.

*Mike Wallace:* In New York state.

*President Hinckley:* That's the miracle of it.

*Mike Wallace:* You believe it?

*President Hinckley:* Yes.

*Mike Wallace:* Do you talk to God and Jesus?

*President Hinckley:* I certainly pray, yes.

*Mike Wallace:* Do they talk back to you?

*President Hinckley:* I think I hear the whisperings of the Spirit. It's—let me explain this—it is like the case of Elijah as set forth in the Book of Kings, 1 Kings, where he inquired of the Lord, and there was a great wind, and the Lord was not in the wind. And there was an earthquake, and the Lord was not in the earthquake. And there was a fire, and the Lord was not in the fire. And after the fire a still, small voice. (See 1 Kings 19:9–12.) That's the voice of the Spirit, and I want to give you my testimony that it is real. It is real. And I—

*Mike Wallace:* You hear—

*President Hinckley:* I say that I don't necessarily hear words spoken, but there comes into my mind—I have experienced that—the voice of the Spirit, which is real, and I say out of experience and observation that the fruits of that become the test of its validity, and those fruits are good. You look at this Church; you look at what it is doing; you look at its influence for good among people; you look at its programs—you have to recognize that, in terms of the adversity through which it has come and the status to which it has grown and the work which it is now doing, there is something of a divine hand behind it. And that hand is made manifest in its affairs.

*Mike Wallace:* Some Mormon historians find it difficult to go along with that, as you know. They claim that at least part of the Church history is myth, not fact.

*President Hinckley:* Oh, well, now, let's look at that; let's look at that for a minute. This Church has critics—of course it does. It has some within its membership who become disaffected and wear out their lives looking for little things, nitpicking over this, that, and the other. We have had them from the beginning. They come. They go. The Church goes on. They don't trouble me. I don't worry about them. I feel sorry for them. I'd do anything in this world I could to help them.

*Mike Wallace:* Not everyone who is 85 has your mind, has your energy, your vitality. I mean, you know it's true, and there are those who say, "This is a gerontocracy. This is a church run by old men."

*President Hinckley:* Isn't it wonderful to have a man of maturity at the head—a man of judgment who isn't blown about by every wind of doctrine?

*Mike Wallace:* Absolutely, as long as he is not dotty.

*President Hinckley:* [*Laughs*] Thank you for the compliment. Thank you, Mike, for the compliment.

*Mike Wallace:* Why is your Church so aggressive about spreading the word, having missionaries knock on doors where they may not be welcome and where they're obviously not invited?

*President Hinckley:* Well, we believe that the Lord meant what He said when He said, "Go ye into all the world, and preach the gospel to every creature" (Mark 16:15). We believe in that mandate. We think it rests upon us to try to fulfill it. We are doing that with all of the energy and resources that we have.

*Mike Wallace:* How do you view non-Mormons?

*President Hinckley:* With love and respect. I have many non-Mormon friends. I respect them. I have the greatest of admiration for them.

*Mike Wallace:* Despite the fact that they haven't really seen the light yet?

*President Hinckley:* Yes. To anybody who is not of this Church, I say we recognize all of the virtues and the good that you have. Bring it with you, and see if we might add to it.

*Mike Wallace:* The Mormon Church traditionally has called Jews "Gentiles." What's that all about?

*President Hinckley:* Well, that's just a little catchphrase. There isn't any real substance to that. That simply comes of a fact that we are probably closer to the Jewish people than most people think we are. We believe in Israel. We believe in Israel's place in the plan of the Lord. We believe that we are of the house of Abraham and Isaac and Jacob, as are the Jewish people. We believe in those things. The Old Testament is a fundamental part of our scripture. We have, we treat, an affinity for them.

*Mike Wallace:* Therefore they are Gentiles?

*President Hinckley:* Well, they are not the same as we are, and that is simply a way of saying, "Look, you are on one side of the street, and we are on the other side of the street." There's nothing of a denigrating attitude in that statement.

*Mike Wallace:* I understand that you were almost as big as Chicago—back, way back.

*President Hinckley:* We were larger.

*Mike Wallace:* Larger than Chicago.

*President Hinckley:* Nauvoo was a larger city than Chicago.

*Mike Wallace:* Whatever happened to Nauvoo?

*President Hinckley:* Nauvoo—our people were evicted from Nauvoo by mobs, with guns at their backs, driven across the Mississippi in the winter of 1846. Left their city, left their beautiful temple. Marched their way across Iowa. Died along the way. Built a winter quarters on the Missouri. Gathered their strength, such as they had, and marched across the plains to this valley of the mountains. It was a bold undertaking to bring people here on the part of a man who had never been here, who knew nothing, really, about this part of the world.

*Mike Wallace:* Brigham Young.

*President Hinckley:* Brigham Young. He had a prophetic vision. Can anyone doubt it who looks here today, looks around here today? No. And that's the way it is with this Church. It has been led by revelation. "We believe all that God has revealed, all that He does now reveal, and . . . that He will yet reveal many great and important things pertaining to the Kingdom of God" for the blessing of His sons and daughters wherever they may be found (Articles of Faith 1:9).

*Mike Wallace:* As you know, some skeptics say that major changes in Church policy have come from political pressures, not necessarily as revelations from God. For example, the business of ending polygamy, say the skeptics, wasn't because it was revelation but because Utah wanted to become a state.

*President Hinckley:* One of the purposes of a prophet is to seek the wisdom and the will of the Lord and to teach his people accordingly. It was the case with Moses when he led the children of Israel out of Egypt. It was the case for the Old Testament prophets when people were faced with oppression and trouble and difficulty. That is the purpose of a prophet, to

511

give answers to people for the dilemmas in which they find themselves. That is what happens. That is what we see happen. Is it a matter of expediency, political expediency? No! Inspired guidance? Yes!

*Mike Wallace:* How big a problem, Mr. President, is child abuse in the Mormon Church?

*President Hinckley:* I hope it isn't a big problem. . . . This is a serious phenomenon that is finding expression all over the world. It is a terrible thing. It is a wicked thing. It is a reprehensible thing. It is a thing of which I have spoken time and again.

*Mike Wallace:* What are you doing to reduce it?

*President Hinckley:* We are doing everything we know how to reduce it. We are teaching our people. We are talking about it. We have set up a course of instruction for our bishops across the nation. All last year we carried on an educational program. We have set up a help-line for them where they can get professional counseling and help with these problems. We have issued a journal dealing with child abuse, spouse abuse, abuse of the elderly, the whole problem of abuse. We are concerned about it. I am deeply concerned about the victims. My heart reaches out to them. I want to do everything we can to ease the pain, to preclude the happening of this evil and wicked thing. . . . I know of no other organization in this world that has taken more exhaustive measures, tried harder, done more to tackle this problem, to work with it, to do something to make a change. We recognize the terrible nature of it, and we want to help our people, reach out to them, assist them.

*Mike Wallace:* One sociologist tells us that the root of the problem is the fact that men, in effect, in your Church have authority over women so that your clergymen tend to sympathize with the men being abusers instead of with the abused.

*President Hinckley:* That's one person's opinion. I don't think there is any substance to it. I think that the men of this Church, the bishops of this Church, the officers of this Church are as concerned with the welfare of the women of the Church as they are with the men of the Church and with the children of the Church. I wouldn't hesitate to say that for one minute. I am confident of that. I have been around a long time. I have known this Church from the ground up, inside and out, over a very, very long period of time. I am 85 years of age now, and I've lived with it all my life, and I think I know how it functions. I think I know the attitude of our people. Now, there will be a blip here, a blip there, a mistake here, a mistake there. But by and large the work is wonderful, and vast good is being accomplished, and the welfare of women and children is as seriously considered as is the welfare of the men in this Church, if not more so.

# WASHINGTON, D.C.

# MEDIA LUNCHEON

## DECEMBER 2, 1996

*This luncheon was arranged by the Public Affairs Department
of the Church. Approximately 20 media representatives and business and
government leaders attended, including Katherine Graham of the*
Washington Post *and filmmaker Jack Valenti.*

T HANK YOU, LADIES AND GENTLEMEN, for being here today. You have come back to your offices after the Thanksgiving holidays and found your desks piled high, and I know this is a very busy time for you. We hope that it will also be a time for a little relaxation.

Nineteen ninety-seven will be a great year of celebration for us. It will mark the 150th anniversary of the entrance of the Mormon pioneers into the Salt Lake Valley. All during this past year there has been a reenactment of history going on in Iowa. Wagon trains have left Nauvoo on the Mississippi to make their way across Iowa to Council Bluffs on the Missouri. Most of those who participated in this have been nonmembers of the Church.

A century and a half ago today, our people were constructing winter quarters on lands they leased from the Potawatomi Indians. They were building scores and scores of houses to provide shelter during that bitter 1846 winter. They had been evicted from their beautiful Nauvoo, Illinois, homes. They were the victims of uncontrolled mobs, who set fire to the houses, burned their fields, and made life absolutely intolerable for them. They determined to move west, tens of thousands of them, to go to a place where, as they say, "the devil cannot [come and] dig us out" (Joseph Smith, *Teachings of the Prophet Joseph Smith,* sel. Joseph Fielding Smith [1976], 332).

514

Next spring will mark the 150th anniversary of their departure from Council Bluffs and the Omaha area across the river en route to a place they had never before seen.

One hundred and twenty-one days were required for the move of the initial pioneer company. They arrived in the valley of the Great Salt Lake on July 24. It was hot and dry and barren.

They turned the waters of the mountain streams onto the sun-baked soil, plowed, and planted their crops to save their seed for another season.

Thousands followed them. Around 4,000 of them died on their journey to the Salt Lake Valley. I am only the third generation from those who made that trip. My grandfather came as a young man. He buried his wife and his half-brother, both of whom died on the same day, somewhere in what is now eastern Wyoming. He carried an infant daughter to the valley of the Great Salt Lake.

We have come a long way since those days of pioneering. Our forebears grubbed the sagebrush, irrigated their fields, and made the desert blossom as the rose. Ours is a different mission. We are trying to bring hope and peace and a sense of the meaning of life to people throughout the world. We are now established in more than 150 nations. Our membership will reach 10 million sometime later next year. We have become, in very deed, a mighty people in the midst of the Rocky Mountains. We have also become an important people throughout this nation and throughout the world.

During this past year I have visited with groups of our people across the United States; in Japan, Korea, Taiwan, Hong Kong, Cambodia, Vietnam, the Philippines; in various areas of Europe. And I have just returned from a trip to South America, holding large meetings in Bogotá, Colombia; in Lima, Peru; in Cochabamba, Bolivia; in Santiago, Chile; in Buenos Aires, Argentina; and in Porto Alegre, São Paulo, Recife, and Manaus, Brazil. Everywhere there were huge crowds—30,000, 40,000, 50,000 of them—gathered in football stadiums.

We have now passed the point where we have more members of the Church outside the United States than we have in the United States. This is no longer a Utah church or an American church. It has become a world church. This presents serious problems. It involves the training of local leaders. We do not have a paid clergy. All of our local congregations are presided over by men who go forward with their daily vocations while at the same time presiding over a body of anywhere from 200 to 500 members of the Church. They need training, and we are giving it to them. The other great problem we face is the construction of buildings. We are now building about 350 new buildings a year. But only this past week we were presented with a study which indicated that we must construct some 4,000 new buildings within the next five years in various international areas. That is 800 new buildings a year. I know of no other church that is carrying forward a building program of the magnitude of the one that we are engaged in.

We have more than 53,000 missionaries scattered across the earth. For the most part these are young men who interrupt their university studies to go wherever they are sent. They learn the languages of the people among whom they labor. They do not go as tourists. They live among the people. They meet in the homes of the people. They learn to know and appreciate the native cultures. They serve for two years in this capacity, entirely at their own expense and at the expense of their families. It does something for them. They learn to communicate. They learn to appreciate the people among whom they serve, and the lands where they serve. We also have some young women and older couples in this service. They never get over this experience for as long as they live.

I can walk down the streets of Salt Lake City and meet those who fluently speak Japanese; Korean; Chinese, both the Cantonese and Mandarin dialects; Thai; the languages of India; all of the languages of Europe; and Spanish and Portuguese, which are spoken in Mexico, Central America, and South America.

We maintain a language-training facility in connection with our missionary program, at Brigham Young University, which is unexcelled in all the world.

We are proud of our university—BYU. It is the largest private, church-owned university in America, with an enrollment of some 27,000. We have had to put a cap on the enrollment, and each year we turn away many thousands of applicants. We are demonstrating that it is possible to turn out first-class scholars in a variety of secular disciplines while at the same time maintaining and strengthening faith. The graduates of BYU now serve on the faculties of nearly every great educational institution in America.

This year we have a good football team, I am proud to say. We are currently rated seventh in the nation in the Associated Press and the *USA Today*–CNN college football polls. I notice by this morning's issue of the *USA Today* that we have moved to number six. Pretty good. In 1984 we won the national college football championship. I would like to see a repetition of that occur this year.

One of our deep concerns is how to meet the needs and desires of the very many who would like to attend BYU but who cannot because of a lack of facilities.

Additionally, through what we call our seminary and institute programs, we are giving spiritual training to some 610,000 young people of high school and university age, for the most part in facilities owned by the Church, built near educational facilities.

The Church operates more than 2,800 family history centers throughout the United States and in many countries of the world. You could find your pedigree there and very much about yourselves, and you are welcome to try. Approximately two billion microfilmed records containing information about several billions of persons have been gathered and preserved from more than 100 countries. These microfilmed records, along with many other important documents, form the largest collection of genealogical information in the world. Last year more than four and one-half million patrons, 70 percent of whom were not members of our Church, used these facilities free of charge. All are welcome, members and nonmembers alike. They are crowded with people anxiously seeking their roots.

We have a remarkable welfare program. We have sought to take care of our own. We operate large farms, canneries, dairies, grain mills, and other facilities for the production of food. We have large markets stocked with goods which cannot be bought but which are provided without cost to those in need. Those in need are given opportunity to work in a variety of situations according to their abilities so that they have the satisfaction of knowing that they have earned what they receive. The needs of those who are unable to work are, of course, taken care of. The average recipient receives help for about four months. Contrast that with generations of those on federal welfare. As the nation speaks of welfare reform, we believe something has been learned from our experience.

We have reached out in humanitarian efforts to the suffering and the needy across the earth. In the last five years we have provided $142 million in humanitarian aid involving hundreds of projects to the needy of Africa, of Asia, and of other parts of the world, including many in the United States, all not of our faith.

Our objective wherever we go is to lift people, to strengthen them, to bring purpose into their lives, to provide stability in a world of ever-changing values. Our purpose is to make bad men good and good men better. Today there are only six other religious bodies in the United States larger than this one. We are the second largest church in California. We are on the move, and we invite your suggestions to help us in this vast undertaking.

Perhaps the thing for which we are best known is our emphasis on the family. America faces a crisis. You need not be told of that. Much of the world is in serious trouble over the disintegration of the family. The family is the basic unit of society. No nation is stronger than the homes of its people.

If the current American divorce levels persist, about 50 percent of all marriages contracted in the past 15 years will end in divorce. Of all marriages contracted in 1995, it is expected that 60 percent will end in divorce.

Lawrence Stone, the noted Princeton University family historian, says: "The scale of marital breakdowns in the West since 1960 has no historical precedent that I know of, and seems unique. . . . There has been nothing like it for the last 2,000 years, and probably longer" (in David Popenoe, "A World Without Fathers," *The Wilson Quarterly,* spring 1996, 13). You are familiar with all of these matters. You are familiar with the fruits of broken homes. I think the home is the answer to most of our basic social problems, and if we can take care of things at that place, other things will take care of themselves.

We are trying to preserve the traditional family—father, mother, and children working together in love toward a common goal. In large measure we are succeeding against great odds. We advocate a family home evening, for instance—one night a week reserved for family activity together. Lessons from the scriptures are taught. Family business is discussed. Vacations are planned. We sing together. We pray together. It works!

Our forefathers gathered to their Zion in the West. Today, without neglecting that West, we are reaching out across the world. We go wherever we can go. We go in the front door, with the knowledge and approval of the governments involved. We carry a message that God lives, that He loves and is concerned with the welfare of His sons and daughters. We carry a message that Jesus is the Christ, the Redeemer of mankind, the Author of peace. We feel we are succeeding, but we need to do even better. We are in a contest with great forces that seem to be sweeping the world along.

All of you who drive the beltway know of our presence here, the beautiful temple out in Kensington. Included in our membership are members of Congress. But as an institution we are not involved in politics. We teach our people everywhere to exercise their franchise, to vote according to the dictates of conscience. But the Church as an institution becomes involved only in those issues which are moral in their nature or which have direct impact upon the Church. For the latter reason we were involved with RIFRA [the Religious Freedom Restoration Act]. We jealously guard the First Amendment to the Constitution, the Bill of Rights, guaranteeing the free exercise of religion and, as I may add, freedom of the press, freedom of speech. If we lose any one of these, we will all go down. I think it is so very important.

Our only objective is to do good in a world that has so very, very many problems. Our great hope is to bless mankind wherever we go.

Thank you for listening to me today. If you have any comments, questions, or anything of the kind, we would be pleased to entertain them. Thank you very, very much.

# Fort Douglas, Utah
# National Prayer Breakfast Ceremony

February 25, 1997

*This meeting was part of the National Prayer Breakfast program. It was sponsored by the 96th Army Reserve unit, General Richard Reeder, commanding officer.*

GENERAL REEDER, DISTINGUISHED members of the military, ladies and gentlemen, thank you for the invitation to be with you. I had no idea you could get so many people so early in the morning to come to a soldier's breakfast. When they put that plate in front of me, I wondered who they were feeding. Thank you ever so much. Thank you, Chaplain Ralston, for your prayer, and Chaplain Goldman for giving the national prayer. I am grateful to you. I express thanks to all who have sponsored this sacred service and have gathered here this morning.

We have on our currency and our coinage a national motto: "In God We Trust."

I know of no other nation that has such a motto. Others use the phrase "By the Grace of God." But none other categorically states, "In God We Trust."

When that statement was adopted, it was believed in. It came of our great Judeo-Christian inheritance. I think we were then a humbler people than perhaps we are today. The recognition of God, seeking His help in prayer, and giving honor and glory to Him, have been characteristic of our nation's history.

Long before we were a nation, our Pilgrim fathers, before they left the *Mayflower* to set foot on the soil of America, signed a compact which was to become the instrument of their governance. That compact begins with these words: "In the name of God, Amen." It goes on to state that the signers "by these presents, solemnly and mutually in the presence of God, and one of another, covenant and combine ourselves together into a civill body politick" (in Charles W. Eliot, comp., *Harvard Classics,* 50 vols. [1910], 43:59).

The first president of our nation, George Washington, in his inaugural address spoken April 30, 1789, said these words: "No people can be bound to acknowledge and adore the invisible hand, which conducts the affairs of men, more than the people of the United States. Every step, by which they have advanced to the character of an independent nation, seems to have been distinguished by some token of providential agency" (in *Harvard Classics,* 43:226).

Once, the people of our nation gathered their families together in daily prayer. They remembered before Deity this nation and its leaders. That practice is largely disappearing from our society. Are we forgetting the Almighty, who in times of last resort is our greatest strength?

We repeat the Pledge of Allegiance to the flag of the United States and "to the republic for which it stands." We say, "One nation under God, indivisible, with liberty and justice for all." I pray that we will never forget that we are in very deed a nation under God and that with the strength which comes from Him, we will remain "indivisible, with liberty and justice for all."

Many of our public gatherings are opened with the singing of the national anthem. This boys' chorus sang it this morning. However, we sing only the first verse. I remind you of the third verse, which we seldom now hear:

> *Oh, thus be it ever, when free men shall stand*
> *Between their loved homes and the war's desolation!*
> *Blest with vict'ry and peace, may the heav'n-rescued land*

*Praise the Pow'r that hath made and preserved us a nation!*
*Then conquer we must, when our cause it is just,*
*And this be our motto: "In God is our trust!"*
     *["The Star-Spangled Banner," Hymns, no. 340]*

In recent years the Boy Scouts of America have been challenged in the courts on the language of the Scout Oath: "On my honor I will do my best to do my duty to God and my country" (*Boy Scout Handbook,* 10th ed. [1990], 5).

Oaths of office and oaths in other legal procedures have concluded with the phrase "So help me God."

Now, according to the *Wall Street Journal,* the state of New Jersey has passed a law banishing the mention of God from state courtroom oaths. Following this action by the legislature, a county judge decided to ban the use of Bibles for such oaths "because you-know-Who is mentioned inside" the Bible ("Godless New Jersey," July 31, 1996, A14).

When we fail to acknowledge Deity, when we fail to recognize the Almighty as the ruling power of the universe, the all-important element of personal and national accountability shrivels and dies. I am confident that this is one of the reasons for the great host of social problems with which we deal these days. Teen pregnancy, abandoned families, failure to recognize the property and rights of others, general incivility, have resulted in large measure, I am satisfied, from failure to recognize that there is a God to whom someday each of us must give an accounting.

Can we doubt that there is a grave sickness in our society? We cannot build prisons fast enough to accommodate the need. We have in this nation well over a million people in prison. The number is growing. Our people are forsaking the Almighty, and I fear He may be forsaking us. We are closing the door against the God whose sons and daughters we are. We sing, "My country, 'tis of thee, sweet land of liberty." We need to sing again and again the fourth verse of that great hymn:

523

*Our fathers' God, to thee,*
*Author of liberty,*
*To thee we sing;*
*Long may our land be bright*
*With freedom's holy light.*
*Protect us by thy might,*
*Great God, our King!*
     *["My Country, 'Tis of Thee,"*
     Hymns, *no. 339]*

During a recent trip to Asia I revisited Vietnam. During the war years I went there a number of times in the interest of the large number of servicemen of our faith who were there.

We landed first at Ton Son Nhut, a name familiar to many of you. Today it is a quiet airport in contrast with what it was when some of you were there. We drove about the streets of Ho Chi Minh City, formerly Saigon. We paused in front of the abandoned American embassy, from whose roof that last historic helicopter flight was made in 1975.

We then flew to Hanoi, drove past what was called the Hanoi Hilton and other places which will be forever etched in the memory of those who were imprisoned there and who suffered so terribly.

No one can calculate the pain, the death incident to that conflict. This was the result of a system of government created under a philosophy that ruled out God and declared that religion is only the opiate of the people.

Returning to George Washington's first inaugural speech, he expressed the hope "that the foundations of our national policy will be laid in the pure and immutable principles of private morality." He continued, "There is no truth more thoroughly established, than that there exists . . . an indissoluble union between virtue and happiness, between duty and advantage, between the genuine maxims of an honest and magnanimous policy, and the solid rewards of public prosperity and felicity; since we ought to be no less persuaded that the propitious smiles of Heaven can never be expected on a nation that disregards the eternal rules of order and right, which Heaven itself has ordained" (in *Harvard Classics,* 43:227).

The Psalmist wrote, "The counsel of the Lord standeth for ever. . . . Blessed is the nation whose God is the Lord" (Psalm 33:11–12).

Paul of old declared: "Where the Spirit of the Lord is, there is liberty" (2 Corinthians 3:17).

One of the stirring pictures of our national heritage is that of General Washington kneeling in prayer at Valley Forge, pleading with the Almighty in behalf of his hungry, freezing, dying men of the Continental Army.

We are secularizing America. We are closing the door on the Almighty. I plead with each of you to add your strength to the enhancement of our trust in God. This is the foundation upon which our national strength is laid. We sing, "God bless America." I pray that America will always be worthy of His blessing. There is no place for arrogance among us. There is no place for egotism or conceit. As we look to God, we will grow in strength as well as in brotherhood. I invoke the peace of the Almighty upon our nation in the name of Him who is the Prince of Peace, even the Lord Jesus Christ, amen.

# EXCERPTS FROM AN INTERVIEW WITH DAVID BRIGGS, ASSOCIATED PRESS

SEPTEMBER 14, 1997

*President Hinckley was invited to speak at the conference of the*
*Religion Newswriters of America, held in Albuquerque, New Mexico.*
*David Briggs, religion writer for the Associated Press, was given*
*a one-on-one interview with the President.*

*David Briggs:* I guess you have a busy day ahead of you.

*President Hinckley:* Yes, we do. They are all busy. We were up in Denver. We've just come from a great celebration there. We had 23,000 people there last night in the McNichols Arena and outside as well. Tremendous celebration.

*David Briggs:* You have been more open to the media, talked with different publications, some—

*President Hinckley:* For good or ill.

*David Briggs:* For good or ill. I just wondered if I might ask what your experience has been.

*President Hinckley:* Oh, we've had a good experience. I think so. Wherever we go—South America, New Zealand, Australia recently, everywhere—people treat us well, and we like them.

*David Briggs:* Is this a decision you made just to be more accessible and open to interviews?

*President Hinckley:* I decided when I became President that I would try to get out among the people for as long as I could do it. And so we've been in all the countries of South America and all the countries of Central America. We'll be in Mexico later this year. We've been in Australia and New Zealand, and we're going to the Pacific Islands the end of October. We've been all over Asia, including Vietnam. Back during the war, I

526

was there a number of times, and I just wanted to go back and see what it looked like. We've been in Hong Kong, Cambodia, Japan, Korea, Taiwan, the Philippines, even Saipan—that little island out in the Pacific, meeting with our people—and in Europe, many parts of Europe.

*David Briggs:* There is somewhat limited time. I was wondering if I might ask what are some of the public policy issues that you believe Church members should be concerned with in the United States?

*President Hinckley:* Well, we follow this policy—that we would not be involved in politics, as such. We don't endorse any candidate. We don't endorse any party. We don't permit the use of our buildings for political purposes. But we do become involved in what we call moral issues and those things which directly affect the Church. We've been involved in opposition to horse racing, gambling, same-sex marriage, alcohol, those things. We try to work as part of a coalition. We try to join forces with other like-minded people and work together to accomplish our common purpose. The Catholic bishop who is responsible for these matters in Oregon, for instance, wrote us the other day asking for our assistance on a campaign against physician-assisted death. He said, "Our church and your church are the number-one and number-two constituencies in Oregon, and we'd like to invite your participation." Well, we were already in it, to a degree, on the part of our people. Now, the Church, institutionally, very seldom becomes involved in things, but we encourage our people as citizens to become a part of these coalitions and to work together with others to accomplish the purpose according to their feelings.

*David Briggs:* About a decade ago, the Church added a subtitle to the Book of Mormon, "Another Testament," and more recently it changed its logo to put a greater emphasis on Jesus Christ. What is the reasoning behind the theological emphasis, or is there a greater theological emphasis on Christ in the Church? Are people talking about it more in religious education classes?

*President Hinckley:* It's been a very interesting thing. I was a party to both of those changes. Really didn't think much about it. We just arrived at it and did it, but it stirred up quite a lot of interest. It was simply an attempt to affirm in a very open, straightforward way our belief in the Lord Jesus Christ as the Son of God and the Author of our faith and to give emphasis to that thought. That's the situation from which all else stems. That's the name of the Church. That's our whole effort. It stems from the fact that Jesus Christ is our leader, and we did what we did knowingly, but we didn't make a great stir over it. It was just to give a little more emphasis to that fact. But it seems to have been given a lot of emphasis out in the world.

*David Briggs:* As the Church has grown remarkably and distributed geographically throughout the United States, what are the issues now, as head of the Church, that that presents?

*President Hinckley:* Well, of course, our constant concern is with the growing secularism in the world. And we face it. Other churches face it. Humanism becomes more and more evident, stronger. It's a traditional thing that goes back a long, long time—that is a growing thing. Now, we feel very strongly that there's no conflict between religion and education. We maintain Brigham Young University, which is the largest church-sponsored university in America, perhaps in the world, with 27,000 students—a first-class, tip-top university—and other schools as well. This Church came out of intellectual dissent. That was its origin, and we feel that the education of the mind in secular matters is a very important thing, as is education of the spirit in religious matters, and we combine the two. We teach education, the importance of education. We foster it. We encourage our young people to get all the education they can, regardless of where they live in the world. I've been preaching it all up and down wherever I've gone these past two and a half years to our young people. It's the door to opportunity for them. But we foster that compatibility between education—secular education—and religious education. So very, very many people do not. There is a growing secularism in America—and I think across the world—of which we must all be cognizant and do what we can to overcome.

*David Briggs:* In your travels around the world, how do you think the Church in the United States has learned from the Church in other parts of the world?

*President Hinckley:* Oh, we learn many things. We've learned a universal love for people, a respect for people. People are good everywhere. You find wonderful people everywhere. People are able. One of our great concerns is the teaching of leadership, finding of leadership. All of our local congregations through the world, more than 24,000 of them, are presided over by local leaders. They have to be trained. They're able. They get on. They catch on. They do things very, very well, and I see the same strength in Argentina that I see in Denver. I see the same strength in Chile that I see in Los Angeles. They're people. We're training leaders everywhere, and they accept it and embrace it and make it a part of their lives, and not only does it bless them in their Church activity, but the interesting thing is that those leadership principles bless them in their daily vocational work.

*David Briggs:* Has it become an issue in native countries as to how you integrate local customs?

*President Hinckley:* It's a most interesting thing. Really, it is. People used to ask me, because I had responsibility for our work in Asia for a long time, "How do you talk to the Asians? They're not Christians. How do you talk to them?" I said, "You talk to them just the way you do everybody else." They're sons and daughters of God. Their hearts beat the same way. They respond to the same kind of teachings and the same kind of questions and the same kind of activities. People are essentially the same the world over, and really, I'm enthusiastic—I must say that. I feel a great enthusiasm about our people across the world.

*David Briggs:* I guess I've always been very interested in the subject of missions, going back to graduate school. Is there something the people in Denver can learn from the people in Argentina?

*President Hinckley:* Yes. They can learn to get along. They can learn to respect one another. That's so very important. Americans sometimes have a tendency to look down upon people elsewhere. There's no reason for it. There is no substance to it. There are good, strong people everywhere. And we've become a part in this search of a great international family. We're in 160 nations. I don't know of any place where we have to make great cultural adaptations. People just respond to the teachings we have. Today is Sunday. The same things will be taught in more than 24,000 congregations of this Church across the world, whether they're in Africa or Asia or Europe or the United States and Canada, and those teachings will be accepted, talked about, discussed in the same way.

*David Briggs:* In Africa, would the people dress differently or use different music?

*President Hinckley:* Yes. Sure. And they will in the Pacific Islands. They'll wear their lavalavas. Yes. That doesn't make any difference to the people in Denver if they wear a lavalava in Samoa. No. The Otavalo Indians down in Ecuador—they comb their hair straight back, that black hair, to a little ponytail, and they wear white trousers and a little blue jacket. That's their culture. But so what? They come and sit in the meetings, somebody else wearing these old, staid, blue suits, and we're all the same people. It isn't what we wear; it's who we are that matters.

*David Briggs:* We talked about issues of growth in the United States. What are the issues that confront the Church in terms of this phenomenal growth overseas?

*President Hinckley:* Well, we're growing here as well, of course. We're growing here as well. We're growing very substantially here, and it's an interesting thing to me that I don't think there's a city of any substance in the United States where there isn't a Mormon congregation today. Everywhere you go, in the small hamlets—but I don't think there is a city of any substance anywhere where you won't find Mormon congregations. That's a significant thing. We've come a long way since the Church was organized, and we're keeping it up. We're just moving ahead.

# NAACP Convention

*This address was given at the annual convention
of the western region of the NAACP.*

LADIES AND GENTLEMEN, I am grateful for the opportunity to be
with you. This is a new experience for me. It is one that I welcome.
The time has come when we need to talk with one another across
barriers of race, real and imagined.

I got over any prejudices I had while I was still a very young
boy. I grew up in a home with a large front porch. I have a confession to make. One day, when I was about five years of age, two or
three friends and I were seated on the front porch when a black
family walked down the street. I made some kind of disparaging
remark. I do not know that they heard me, but I know that my
mother, who was just inside the house, heard me. She called me in
with my friends and immediately proceeded to sit us down and talk
with us. She gave us to understand, in no uncertain terms, that
among the peoples of the earth there is neither inferiority nor superiority, that we are all sons and daughters of God, and that we have
an obligation to respect and help one another.

I have never forgotten that simple lesson. I have carried it with
me all my life and across the world.

I learned later that my mother, at about 14 or 15 years of age,
had stood up for and befriended a black boy in the school who had
been taunted by others. I learned this from the individual himself

when he was grown to manhood. He was Abner Howell, who served as sergeant at arms in the Utah legislature and who lived in our area and went to the same church that we attended.

In the course of my life I have mingled widely with people of all races, with those of Asia and Africa, Europe and Polynesia, with people in high station and low station, both good and bad. The world is my neighborhood, and its peoples, regardless of status, are my friends and neighbors. I include all within the compass of the mandate of the Savior, who said: "Thou shalt love the Lord thy God with all thy heart, and with all thy soul, and with all thy mind. This is the first and great commandment. And the second is like unto it, Thou shalt love thy neighbour as thyself" (Matthew 22:37–39).

I am deeply concerned about what is happening in America. All of us are now equal under the law. The provision is *de jure,* but the situation *de facto* is that there is still very much of prejudice. However, I am an optimist. I think matters are gradually getting better. I think there is more of tolerance, there is more of respect, there is more of acknowledgment of the good in each of us. The fight has been uphill, but it is being won. I meet men and women of great distinction, of tremendous capacity, even of brilliance in many professions, and they are of diverse ethnic and racial backgrounds.

I have recently been up and down Africa, where I have spoken to tens and tens of thousands of the good people of that continent. I find that when they are given opportunity, they respond. They have good minds worthy of training. They have a wonderful capacity to do things. They are kind and generous. They are good. They are beautiful people.

About a year ago the *Baltimore Sun* sent reporters to Africa—to the Sudan I think it was. There the *Sun* purchased two slaves for $1,000 each. They owned them—two young men. They returned them to their families, but the fact is, the slave trade is still operative in that part of the world.

But there is another slave trade going on much closer to home. It involves people of all races. For much less than $1,000, young men and women are being inducted into the slavery of drugs and other substances and practices which take hold of them until they lose all control of themselves. One thing leads to another, with miseries compounding themselves.

I need not go into detail on these matters. They are familiar to all of you. I speak of the scourge of teen pregnancy, which comes of ignorance, social irresponsibility, and lack of self-discipline. Every baby born has a father, and in so many, so very many cases, the young men who are responsible for fathering children simply do not step up to that responsibility.

Single mothers by the tens of thousands in this land, largely with little education, struggle throughout their lives to rear children, because a baby and responsibility for its life never seem to go away.

Babies born of drug-ridden mothers have become a social problem of terrible consequence. What a tragic thing it is to give birth to a child who will have absolutely no opportunity for a normal life through all the years that must follow.

The terrible plight of gangs affects our cities. They scheme, they roam, they destroy property, they fight, they murder one another and innocent victims who happen to get in their way. They are an ill-begotten lot of young people who drift in a mire of terror and whose lives lead in only one direction, if they survive, and that is to prison.

We cannot build jails and prisons in this nation fast enough to accommodate the hundreds of thousands of inmates, whose numbers are constantly increasing.

And so I might go on. All of this, and much more, becomes the great, tragic waste of America. As you know all too well, many, very many of these people, given the right motivation and the right opportunity, could do something useful with their lives. When I was a boy, my father read to us the story of George Washington Carver. What that lone man did with peanuts was an inspiration to us.

Now, among the things you will discuss in this conference will be the question of how to bring about corrections in this dismal picture. The NAACP is doing many things for which I commend you. I add two others that I think need doing.

Long ago, 40 years ago, back in 1958, I read an article in the *Reader's Digest* entitled "Put Father Back at the Head of the Family." It was written by a Judge Leibowitz of New York City. In his capacity as judge, he spent his days listening to evidence and handing down sentences. He traveled to Europe and discovered that the conditions among the youth there were much better than in America. He investigated and thought and pondered and out of a vast experience came to the conclusion that the easiest, most simple remedy in reducing delinquency among the young was to put the father back as head of the family.

I submit that the black family in this nation has been a tremendous institution. It has added much to our culture and to the strength of our people. But in far too many cases, families of all races have been denied leadership—the leadership of a good and devoted father who stands at the side of an able and kindly mother in quietly training, gently disciplining, and prayerfully helping the children for whom they both are responsible.

The God of heaven designed the family as the basic unit of society. He did not design that children should be begotten and left to a single—and often poor—mother to rear. He designed that a father should stand as the pillar of strength in every household.

I do not believe that women resent the strong leadership of a man in the home. He becomes the provider, the defender, the counselor, the friend who will listen and give support when needed.

How do we get him to take his place? It may be a slow process, but it is worth the effort. We begin with very young boys and teach them and motivate them and point them in this direction. It will not be easy. We will not save them all. But I believe we can save many more than we are now saving.

I believe that no one else other than a good and exemplary father can so effectively teach children the value of education; the dead-end nature of street gangs; the miracle of self-esteem, which can change their lives for good.

I remember reading in the *Wall Street Journal* four or five years ago of a lawyer in Ohio, a well-educated African American whose name was King. He spoke of his boyhood and told of his father taking the family for a ride on a Sunday afternoon in their old car. While they were going down the street, a fancy red Cadillac passed them.

The boy asked his father why some people had Cadillacs while theirs was an old jalopy. His father responded that everyone couldn't have the same, but that he, his son, had something that was of absolutely tremendous worth, which many others did not have, which was of greater worth than any Cadillac. He was a son of the King family and of the Jones family, and there flowed in his veins the best blood of each of those families. He taught his son that while all could not achieve temporal equality, everyone could cultivate that wonderful quality which we speak of as self-esteem. The boy grew to manhood, studied law, and became a successful practitioner.

I read this from Jenkins Lloyd Jones some years ago:

"The kid who isn't loved knows it. There is no trauma so excruciating as parental rejection. No other form of human cussedness can more efficiently wreck a human life. Yet there persists the superstition that 'advantages' are a substitute for affection. They aren't.

"The finest of the advantages a family can offer can't be found in a department store, a car dealer's show room or a prep school. The only priceless one is the sense of belonging. Otherwise, the family becomes a combination cafe and dormitory. There's no glue in it" ("Needed: Device To Point Out Unfit Parents," in *Deseret News*, July 13, 1968, 12A).

I think we must point out to our youth, white and black together, that there is a better way than the way so many are now going. It will take patience. It will take persuasion. I believe it will take prayer. And this brings me to the conclusion of my remarks.

This is a greater problem than any of us can solve with our own wisdom. It is a problem for which we need inspiration and spiritual guidance. The things of God are understood by the Spirit of God, and I submit that what is needed is that motivating and powerful spiritual inspiration which is real and which can come into the lives of those who seek it.

I put the father back as head of the family, but while doing so, I plead with him to institute and follow a practice which was commonplace in the homes of America a hundred years ago. We have largely lost sight of it. That is the practice of family prayer.

A father who will kneel with his wife and children will do wonders for them. The very act of getting on one's knees before a higher power becomes an acknowledgment of our need for help. To thank the Lord in the presence of one another for life, health and strength, and family carries with it a wonderfully salutary effect. Remembering the poor and the needy and the unfortunate before the Almighty has an inevitable effect upon children. It leads to unselfishness, to concern for others, to a desire to lift and bless those in distress. To pray for guidance in one's life, to offer an invocation for the blessings of heaven upon children has an inevitably positive effect.

In the Church which I have the honor to represent, we have a basic and fundamental teaching, and that is that each of us is a child of God. It matters not the race. It matters not the slant of our eyes or the color of our skin. We are sons and daughters of the Almighty, who loves us and who stands ready to listen to our pleadings and help us with our problems. When a child comes to realize that there is something of divinity within him, then something great begins to happen.

And so, am I asking too much? Am I getting into a field where I do not belong when I take the liberty of suggesting to you able and concerned people that the time has come for the citizens of this land to acknowledge our failures and our weaknesses in dealing with some of these terrible problems and to get on our knees and seek the wisdom of heaven?

The marvelous thing is that it works. I have seen it. I am the product of such a home, where our father called us together night and morning, inviting us to kneel around the table. Here we took turns—father, mother, and children, down to those who barely knew what they were saying—in offering prayer to the Almighty.

I am a churchman. You may expect this of me. But I wish to say that family prayer is still a basic and fundamental practice in the homes of millions of people across the world. They can and will testify that it has a salutary influence on rearing a family in the nurture and admonition of the Lord.

I believe there is no greater thing we could do.

God bless you, my dear friends, in your very serious work. Thank you.

# University of Utah

# Commencement Exercises

JUNE 12, 1998

*President Hinckley was invited to speak at this commencement*
*by Bernard Machen, president of the University of Utah. President*
*Hinckley's granddaughter Ann graduated this day.*

Members of the board of regents and trustees of the university, President Machen and members of the administration and faculty, to each of you graduates and your families and friends, I extend my warm congratulations and thank you for the opportunity of speaking to you.

I wish to take just a moment, my first public opportunity, to thank the Alumni Association for giving me the Distinguished Alumnus Award some years ago and to thank the university for bestowing upon me an honorary doctorate degree in 1992.

I feel very old this morning. It was an even 70 years ago, in 1928, that I timidly walked through the doors of the Park Building and registered as a freshman. At that time there was no computer or telephone registration. Everything was done by hand, and the lines were long and the experience frustrating.

I had an unmerciful dean who would sign my registration papers, then look intently at them through his half-moon glasses, cross out his signature, look up at me, and say, "Hinckley, you know you can't do that. You're not ready for that advanced course." He would wave me off, and I would start all over.

Back then, in 1928, America was rolling along in prosperity. This heady atmosphere continued for a year, and then came Black

Thursday of 1929. Suddenly the whole economy fell apart and nosedived into the worst depression this nation and the world have ever known. Men who were once rich found themselves penniless. At the time there was no unemployment insurance, no government welfare—nothing of the kind. Hunger became an ever-present reality. The unemployment rate in Utah exceeded 35 percent, almost all of whom were sole breadwinners.

They sold apples at five cents each. They chopped wood to feed their furnaces to keep warm. Churches stepped into the breach magnificently, and people helped one another in a very generous and neighborly way.

I do not recall what the tuition was here at the university, but I think it was $25 a quarter. Practically no one drove a car. There was no parking problem. Not even the faculty drove. We walked to school or rode the streetcar, which ran along 13th East. The fare was five cents, with transfer privileges anywhere the streetcars ran, and they ran almost everywhere. Most students carried lunch in a brown paper bag, or, if we could afford it, we could buy in the cafeteria for ten cents a bowl of boiled wheat with raisins and all the sugar and thick cream needed. This was simple food but very good and much better, I think, than the kind you eat today.

While all of us were poor, the teaching was excellent. Jobs were so scarce that everyone who had one tried to do his very best. In four years I never had a teaching assistant. Every one of my teachers was a full professor who did all of the work connected with teaching, including the reading of papers. I think every one of my professors had a doctorate in his or her chosen discipline. They were solicitous and seemed to have a great concern for us, their students.

I took a number of classes from the first Jewish professor hired in the state of Utah. I came to know him while I was here and even better afterwards. He was very bright and a very good teacher. He came from Philadelphia, apprehensive concerning what he was getting into. He told me that when he walked up South Temple from the Union Pacific Depot, he saw Temple Square. He asked a stranger what the large building in the square was. He was informed it was the temple. The word *temple* had special meaning for him, a Jew. He looked at the building, his apprehension left him, and he felt a certain peace about being here in this community.

There was no Huntsman Center, of course, at that time. Graduation was held in Kingsbury Hall, with diplomas handed to each of us by the president of the university, who never seemed to smile and acted as if he had been handing out diplomas for a hundred years. Graduation was a long and tedious experience, and for the life of me I cannot recall the name of the speaker or anything he said. It will be the same with you. It will be a little like the man who was seen on his knees in the gutter with his ear to the curb. A policeman came along and asked what was going on. "Get down and listen," the man said. The policeman knelt in the gutter and put his ear to the curb. He listened intently and finally stood up, dusted off his uniform, and said, "I don't hear a thing." "I know," the man said. "It's been that way all morning."

We were graduated in 1932 into an employment vacuum, with an education but no jobs. No graduating class ever faced a more dismal future. But somehow we made it.

The years that have followed between then and now have included the Great Depression, the terrible Second World War, the Korean War, the Vietnam War, the wild sixties, and the affluent nineties.

Never has there been a graduating class that has stepped into a better employment market than you are doing. Your prospects are so very, very good. The *Wall Street Journal* recently reported, "There has never been a job market even close to this" (Mitchell S. Fromstein, in "A Special News Report About Life on the Job—and Trends Taking Shape There," May 26, 1998, A1). You are indeed a very fortunate body who face a wonderful time of great opportunity. Our very best wishes go with you. Our hope goes with you. Our trust and respect go with you.

What a truly remarkable and exciting time is this season in which we live. There has been more of scientific discovery during my lifetime than during all previous centuries of the history of the world. When I was born, the life expectancy in the United States was 50 years. It is now 75 years plus. It seems almost unbelievable that 25 years have been added to the life of the average man and woman in this country. Certainly most of the great discoveries of medicine have occurred during this time. Smallpox, which once destroyed entire populations, has now totally disappeared. Polio, once the summer dread of every mother, is almost entirely gone. It is hard to believe. The miracle drugs that have saved the lives of millions, open-heart surgery, organ transplants, and many other similar procedures have now become commonplace. Even the complex door of cancer cures appears to be opening a crack.

Like the man on the flying trapeze, we fly through the sky with the greatest of ease. Computers have changed the way of our lives. Books will continue to be printed, but the future opportunity lies in electronic publishing. In our hands, if used properly, is the wonderful tool of the Internet, with which we can pick knowledge from across the globe. The atom has been harnessed for good or for ill. The creations of science are endless and almost too great to even dream of.

Now here you are as university graduates, set down in the midst of this world of miracles. These tools will be your tools. This world will be your world. You will marry and rear families, and I hope that you will be strong and loving parents. The family is falling apart all across the world. Please, my dear young friends, do not add to this catastrophe, but rather do your part to diminish it. Nothing will be of greater importance in your lives than the role you play as parents.

Hopefully each of you will make a great and significant contribution to the society of which you will be a part. You have trained yourselves to earn a living. I hope that you are eminently successful. The world needs your skills, and I am confident that you will make your contributions and be compensated generously by the society you serve.

However, with all the wonders of the age that is upon us, we have the same old social problems—and much worse—than when I was here seven decades ago. There is still so much of poverty and stark want across the world, so much of rebellion and meanness, so much of sleaze and filth, so many broken homes and destroyed families, so many lonely people living colorless lives without hope, so much of distress everywhere.

And so I make a plea to you. I plead with you that with all your getting you also give to make the world a little better.

I brought with me today my old Shakespeare text from which I read so long ago in English 171. It is filled with wisdom concerning the matter of which I speak. For instance, Romeo declares, "He jests at scars that never felt a wound," (*Romeo and Juliet,* act 2, scene 2). There are thousands out there who nurse wounds and carry scars from the buffetings of life. In Shakespeare's *Tempest,* Miranda, speaking of the wrecked ship and its passengers, sadly says, "O, I have suffered with those that I saw suffer" (act 1, scene 2). I hope each of us will suffer a little as we look about and see how so many others are suffering.

I think of Pamela Atkinson, who sits here on this platform, who has served so well in our own community. I salute her for the great and singular service she has given. She has gone out among the poor, the neglected, the forgotten, the sick, and the friendless and made them feel that somebody cares. She knows those men and women who live under the viaduct and beside the tracks, who think the world has passed them by. They dwell in shoddy and cold and miserable circumstances. She brings the warmth of a friend. She even carries in the trunk of her car a case of dog food to give sustenance to the only friends some of these neglected people have.

Lowell Bennion was my neighbor. He lived just across the fence. I knew him well. I knew the circumstances of his life. He not only made a great and significant contribution as a member of the faculty of this university, but he gave of himself in a most interesting and remarkable way. He had his students working on the yards and painting the homes of those who had no capacity to take care of these things themselves. He set up a boys' ranch in Idaho to afford young men the opportunity to straighten their lives and taste a new kind of experience. He too walked through the shadows of this city, imparting sustenance and hope to those desperately in need. His memorial on this campus celebrates the vast good he did with his avocation rather than the accomplishments of his vocation.

In the Philippines, a place with which I am somewhat familiar, an able doctor, an American, in his spare time, gathered Filipino doctors around him and taught them and worked with them to make possible restorative surgery that has taken away the cleft palates and the facial disfigurements of children whose lives have been dramatically and wonderfully changed as they have emerged from the operating room handsome and beautiful boys and girls. Now he has greatly enlarged his efforts and involved many others in a number of countries.

I was in the Dallas airport one day, waiting for a plane. A man walked up to me and introduced himself. He was a medical doctor on his way to Central America. Every year he goes there for a month to perform, without fee, numerous operations to help those who are utterly helpless without some assistance of the kind he can give.

My message to you today, my dear friends—and I need not belabor it—is that you resolve to dedicate a part of your time, as you map out your life's work, to those in distress and need, with no consideration of recompense. Your skills are needed, whatever they may be. Your helping hands will lift someone out of the mire of distress. Your steady voice will give encouragement to some who might otherwise simply give up. Your skills can change the lives, in a remarkable and wonderful way, of those who walk in need. If not now, when? If not you, who?

It is not enough that you get a job, that you get married, that you feverishly work to produce the kind of income which will make possible the luxuries of the world. You may gain some recompense in all of this, but you will not gain the ultimate satisfaction.

As Isaiah has declared: "Strengthen ye the weak hands, and confirm the feeble knees. Say to them that are of a fearful heart, Be strong, fear not: behold, your God . . . will come and save you" (Isaiah 35:3–4). I believe that when we serve others, we best serve our God.

Your strong hands and determined wills can improve the world and the condition of its people. I have a friend, a very successful attorney in Seattle. When he was married, his bride said to him, "Let's give a quarter of our time for the rest of our lives to the improvement of the world and the blessing of its people." They have kept that promise. His wife is now gone, but Jim Ellis is recognized for the wonders he has done for the Northwest. Leading out, he has attracted others to work with him to clean up the waters of the Seattle area, to preserve the great forests of the Northwest, to build a beautiful new civic center which is constructed over the freeway and utilizes the air rights above it. He is now growing old. I think he will not be remembered for the cases he argued brilliantly in the courts of law. I think he will be remembered for the great projects and the humanitarian aid he undertook and carried through to fulfillment in blessing his community and its people.

I commend you on your accomplishments this day. I wish for you great success in your chosen fields. I can only hope for you that yours may be the rich and satisfying pleasure of going beyond your regular vocational pursuits and pausing to do that which will help in some way someone in distress to raise his or her eyes and look up to you and say, "Thank you. Thank you, for what you did for me."

It will not be enough to be an able lawyer, a man of medicine, a skilled architect, a proficient engineer, or whatever. There will be the need for another dimension in your life—that of reaching down to someone who may be in distress to offer your strong hand to lift him up.

Wendell Phillips once made this significant observation: "How prudently most men creep into nameless graves, while now and then one or two forget themselves into immortality!" (in John Wesley Hill, *Abraham Lincoln—Man of God* [1927], 146).

God bless you, my beloved friends. Go forward. Remember, as James Russell Lowell wrote long ago in "The Vision of Sir Launfal":

> *Who gives himself with his alms feeds three,*
> *Himself, his hungering neighbor, and me.*
> *[part 2, stanza 8]*

Thank you.

# Address to the General Society of Mayflower Descendants

## September 12, 1998

*This address was given at the annual convention of the board of assistants of the Mayflower Society of America.*

GOVERNOR GENERAL MAXWELL and other officers of this great organization, members of the board of assistants, ladies and gentlemen, it is nice to be with you, to look into your faces.

I hope you have had a good time. Thank you for coming to Salt Lake. This is a good city. It was first settled 151 years ago by those seeking the right to worship according to conscience, just as our Pilgrim forebears determined to come to this land where they might enjoy freedom of conscience and freedom of worship.

I hope you have visited the family history resources of the Church. I am told that these are the largest of their kind in the nation, if not in the world. We have been at it for a long time and have put very much into it. We have drawn on the resources of the Mayflower Society and other historical groups in gathering together a vast storehouse of genealogical information. We now have 3,200 satellite facilities where patrons may have access to this gold mine of family history. We welcome you to use these. More than half of all who do so are not members of the Church, and we extend to each of you an invitation to utilize these facilities in your family history research.

You have visited other places of interest in and about the city. I am advised that many of you will be attending the weekly nationwide broadcast of the Mormon Tabernacle Choir in the morning. I hope that you enjoy it. It has been on the air for 69 years. It is the oldest network radio broadcast in the nation, if not in the world. It has outlasted all of the radio and television programs which have been your favorites over a period of many years. It has become a great national treasure.

I am honored to have membership in the Society of Mayflower Descendants, as has been noted here tonight. I do not have opportunity to get together with my associates very often, but it is a source of pride to me that I am of the 11th generation from Stephen Hopkins, who, with his wife and three children, traveled on the *Mayflower.* He was not one of the original group—the Purists, the Separatists, who came to be known as Pilgrims as William Bradford used that word. There were only 35 of the original members on the *Mayflower.* The others had dropped away for one reason or another. To increase their number, the Pilgrims invited to travel with them a group whom they called Strangers. Hopkins was one of these. He was the only passenger who had been to America previously, having visited Jamestown some 11 years earlier. He was 39 years of age at the time of the *Mayflower* trip, according to my history. Someone else mentioned that he was 35. I won't quarrel with you over that.

As I have read extensively the history of the brave souls who made that voyage, I have often wondered why they traveled so late in the season. They left Southampton on August 15, 1620. They must have realized that under the very best of circumstances they would arrive in the New World in the very late fall or early winter. They would be faced with high seas on the Atlantic. They would be faced with a fierce winter before the warmth of spring again touched these shores. It took an unusual amount of faith. It took a tremendous sense of adventure. It took hope and courage and fortitude.

The *Mayflower* was a small ship, and the *Speedwell* even smaller. When they were 300 miles west of Land's End, the *Speedwell* was leaking so seriously that they decided to abandon her. They sailed back to Plymouth, which caused a serious further delay. Here goods and passengers from the *Speedwell* were transferred to the already heavily laden *Mayflower.* Some few gave up and did not make the journey. Possibly they were the wisest of all.

The meal they had in Plymouth the night before they sailed was the last good meal they would have for a year or more.

They pointed west and raised their sails. Three hundred and seventy-eight years ago today they were wallowing in the Atlantic through high seas caused by equinoctial storms. As their little ship tossed on the waters, they must at times have been absolutely terrified.

Because of the rocking of the ship, they could not wash their clothes. They could not cook. They lived on dried beef and ship biscuit with Holland cheese. Elizabeth Hopkins, the wife of Stephen, gave birth to a child, which they named Oceanus because he was born at sea.

But they were a tough group, accustomed to perils. They were among the Puritans of England, who wanted to clean up the church. They were among the Separatists, who, when they discovered they could not change the church, wished to separate themselves. In a little village west of Sheffield, called by the unglamourous name of Scrooby, they had met and worshipped together. But they knew no peace.

Holland had recently settled her score with Spain and was regarded as a place where freedom of worship could be enjoyed. These Separatists determined to go to Amsterdam. But the captain of the ship they had hired betrayed them. They were arrested and imprisoned in Boston, Lincolnshire. At length they were given their freedom and made their way to Holland. They were poor and largely without resources. But by dint of hard work they were able to take care of their needs. Most of them moved to Leiden, but after some years there they determined that Holland was becoming worldly and they had better seek their fortune somewhere across the sea. With their meager savings they chartered the *Mayflower* and bought the unseaworthy *Speedwell*.

After a long and fearsome journey, on November 19, 1620, they sighted land. Before leaving the ship, as we have been reminded tonight, they met together and drafted a compact, which was signed by the male passengers November 21—in our reckoning of time—in the cabin of the *Mayflower*. This historic document, the first of its kind in America, became the basis of their living together under rule of law. The compact has been interpreted as the first modern example of a system of government instituted as the result of voluntary agreement by men accepting equal rights.

Following this signing, 16 men went ashore in a longboat. With their feet again on solid earth, the first thing they did was to get on their knees and express thanks to the Almighty for bringing them safely to these shores.

It was now late November. Their condition must have looked desperate. William Bradford wrote: "They had now no friends to welcome them nor entertain or refresh their weather-beaten bodies, nor houses or much less towns to repair to. And for the season it was winter, and they that know the winters of that country know them to be sharp and violent and subject to cruel and fierce storms. Besides, what could they see but a hideous and desolate wilderness, full of wild beasts and wild men."

They finally made their way across the bay, landing at Plymouth Rock. Three days after landing they began the construction of a common house. They ate the meager provisions they had carried with them aboard the ship and stole a little corn from the Indians. But their worn bodies could not stand such rigors. Many of them died of starvation. All of them must have sickened. Malnutrition and disease took their toll. The cemetery on the hill was added to almost daily. Half of their small number perished.

Lives were saved by the Indians who, at the end of February, walked into the settlement. One of the natives said, "Welcome, Englishmen." His name was Samoset. He left and returned with Squanto, who had lived in England for a time. He spoke the language. Massasoit, the chief, subsequently came. He was welcomed. He signed a treaty of peace. The Indians brought food. Without that help, all of them might have starved to death.

Notwithstanding the terrible ordeals through which they had come, when the *Mayflower* left to return to England in April, not one of them returned with it. This to me is a most remarkable and interesting thing. They had passed through that bitter winter. They had buried half their number. They had never plowed a furrow or planted a seed. I think they did not know how they would live. With no other resource, they put their faith in God and remained to establish this outpost in the land of America.

Other colonies had been planted before that time, but there was something unique and wonderful about this little body at Cape Cod. Over the years that followed, their numbers were added to.

As you have been reminded tonight, my first American ancestor of the name Hinckley came in 1635. He settled at Barnstable. His son, Thomas Hinckley, served as governor of Plymouth Colony for a period of 11 years. He lies buried in the old Lothrop Cemetery, not far from Barnstable. I have visited the place a number of times and always experience a feeling of gratitude. In the years that followed, these colonies grew and others were established. They were British colonies, and the colonists for the most part swore allegiance to the king. But as the years passed and the Crown became increasingly abusive, these men of independent thought took independent action. Confederation came. There followed the Declaration of Independence, the Revolutionary War. With their blood, they paid for the liberty they finally won. A nation came into being and grew under the banner of the magnificent Constitution. Some of its provisions had descended from the Mayflower Compact. Those who gave life to those ideals were descendants, in large measure, of the courageous men and women of faith who laid the foundations of the British colonies in Massachusetts.

Now, all of you, I know, are familiar with this history. I have spoken of it simply as a reminder of the marvelous inheritance we have from these men and women who, in the midst of adversity, put their trust in the Almighty and worked endlessly to make their dreams come true, who lived with hope and faith, eventually to bring to pass the nation that would someday grace this land.

Now I look back to our forebears and then to the present, and I ask them, "What has happened to your America?"

With the motto In God We Trust, this has become the world's mightiest power, militarily and economically. But some destructive force has been at work. America is still strong, but there is a serious unsteadiness in her stance in terms of morality, ethics, principles, behavior.

I feel sorrow in my heart for the president of the United States, the man who occupies the chair once occupied by George Washington. We have seen him damage, if not destroy, the great and sacred trust he holds because of acts unbecoming a man in his position. He has squandered the confidence of the people. He has abandoned their trust. He has forsaken self-discipline and picked up a whole train of miserly and beggarly evils.

There is a constitutional process to which he is entitled. But when all is said and done, his problems are only symptomatic of many other problems we have as a people.

For instance, in recent years the Boy Scouts of America have been attacked because of the language in the Scout Oath: "On my honor I will do my best to do my duty to God and my country" (*Boy Scout Handbook,* 10th ed. [1990], 5). That statement is an acknowledgment of the Almighty. It gives civility and refinement to our actions. It is an expression of gratitude for the gracious favors that God has bestowed upon us. We are forgetting Him and indulging a secularization of our society, which can only lead to further trouble.

Marriage was once regarded as the most sacred of institutions, to be upheld through sunshine and storm. Now an epidemic of divorce rages through the land. Parents quarrel, and children suffer. Marriage, with our forebears, was regarded as a sacrament. But now so many—so very, very many—have cast aside these binding contracts. They have given up on the family.

The report of the Carnegie Task Force on meeting the needs of young children paints a dismal picture. It says:

Our nation's infants and toddlers and their families are in trouble. Compared with most other industrialized countries, the United States has a much higher rate of babies born to adolescent mothers. "Of the 12 million children under the age of three in the United States today, a staggering number are affected by one or more risk factors that [undermine] healthy development." One in four lives in poverty. One in four lives in a single-parent family. One in three victims of physical abuse is a baby under the age of one. (See *Starting Points: Meeting the Needs of Our Youngest Children* [1994], 3, 4, 20).

It is a startling fact that 28 percent of the children born to white mothers in this nation are born to single women. That is more than one in four. Sixty-eight percent of children born to black mothers across the nation, and 80 percent in our larger cities, are born to single women. That is four out of five. The burdens imposed by these statistics are staggering. Taxes must be levied to care for the needs of such children and their mothers. The Carnegie Report continues, saying that "of teens who give birth, 46 percent will go on welfare within four years." That is almost one out of every two. "Of unmarried teens who give birth, 73 percent will be on welfare within four years." That is almost three out of every four. (See *Starting Points*, 21.)

Every young man ought to realize—ought to be made to realize—that in fathering a child, he takes upon himself a responsibility that will endure as long as he lives. Every young woman must know that in giving birth to a child, she places upon herself a responsibility from which she will never be entirely free. How tragic is the desolate and ever-increasing picture of illegitimate births. With each such birth comes responsibility to the mother—and to the father if he stands up to it—and, inevitably, to society at large. The lack of self-discipline and a sense of responsibility on the part of those who sire these children are some of the fruits of the increasing secularization of our society.

I recently read that between 1972 and 1990 there were 27 million abortion procedures performed. Think of it! What is happening to our concept of the sanctity of life?

Can there be doubt that there is a sickness in America today? We cannot build prisons fast enough to accommodate the need. We have in this nation more than a million people in prison, and the number is constantly growing. Why is this happening? I believe that in a very substantial degree it is happening because we as a nation are forsaking the Almighty and He is forsaking us. We are shutting the door against God, whose sons and daughters we are. We sing, "My country, 'tis of thee, Sweet land of liberty." We need to sing again and again the fourth verse of that hymn:

> *Our fathers' God, to thee,*
> *Author of liberty,*
> *To thee we sing;*
> *Long may our land be bright*
> *With freedom's holy light.*
> *Protect us by thy might,*
> *Great God, our King!*
> *["My Country, 'Tis of Thee,"*
> Hymns, *no. 339]*

Polls indicate that a majority of Americans believe that the private lives of public officials need not be considered as a factor in their eligibility for public office. How far we have come from the time of George Washington, who stated in his first inaugural address in 1789 that "the foundations of our national [society] will be laid in the pure and immutable principles of private morality" (in Charles W. Eliot, comp., *Harvard Classics,* 50 vols. [1910], 43:227).

It was said of old, "Where the Spirit of the Lord is, there is liberty" (2 Corinthians 3:17). The Psalmist wrote, "The counsel of the Lord standeth for ever, the thoughts of his heart to all generations. Blessed is the nation whose God is the Lord" (Psalm 33:11–12).

There is a divine mandate which states, "Look to God and live" (Alma 37:47).

We try to gamble our way into prosperity, and in the process further impoverish ourselves. A recent article in the *Wall Street Journal* stated that "in 1994 alone Americans spent $482 billion on gambling; that's more than they spent on movies, sports, music, cruise ships and theme parks combined" (Adam Wolfson, "Life Is a Gamble," Aug. 14, 1998, W11).

Once, lotteries were forbidden by law in this land, and that not very long ago. Now they are a common thing in most of our states. The *Journal* continues, "When states conduct lotteries, they are simply finding a noncoercive alternative to raising taxes." And studies indicate that these hidden taxes are paid, for the most part, by those least able to do so.

We read of a great upsurge in the use of drugs by youth. We see account after account of children killing children, of the rapacious acts of street gangs in the cities of the nation, whose activities lead only to death or prison.

Can we doubt that a great sickness has spread across the land as we witness the evils of pornography, with all the sleaze that can only lead to trouble?

Our forebears knew nothing of these things. Marriage was sacred, to be endured and made the very best of. But it was usually a very happy adventure. Children and families were regarded as a gift from God, with a responsibility to nurture them and bring them up in understanding and light and truth. Work was a thing to be enthroned as the enhancement of human dignity. Worship—worship of God; worship of the Almighty; worship of Jesus Christ, for these people were Christians—was as fundamental to our forebears as was eating and drinking.

Now, I might go on, but you know the whole litany of things.

To those of you who are here, I say that the time has come to look back to the virtues and the values which made America great—not only militarily, not only in wealth, but in moral leadership. To my Pilgrim forebears; to those of the colonial days of America; to those who wrote the Articles of Confederation, who drafted the Declaration of Independence, who fought in the Revolutionary War, and who wrote and loved the Constitution, I say that there is a sickness in the land.

But there is a remedy also, and that will begin when each of us returns to the code of ethics, to the pattern of values, to the canons of divine truth by which our honored forefathers lived.

I conclude by assuring you that even with all I see, I am an optimist. I believe that there is a tremendous residual of goodness in the people of America. For the most part, they appreciate the good, the beautiful, and those values which lead to peace, to goodwill, to behavior based upon personal integrity. They love this nation. They love its history. They love its traditions. They are proud to be known as those who put their trust in the Almighty, as declared on the coins they carry in their pockets.

This is a good land, a great land, with a glorious past and a bright future.

We can clean up the sickness which afflicts us. We need to work on the strengthening of families, on establishing a good father as the head of every household. John Lukacs wrote, "It is not impossible that the true revolutionaries of the twenty-first century will be the fathers of decent and civilized children" (*The Passing of the Modern Age* [1970], 82). And special mothers are needed. It is mothers who mold the children and who are the great carriers and purveyors of faith.

Fathers and mothers, husbands and wives and children, living together with love and appreciation and respect for one another. The roots of civility are planted in the soil of the home. This is the way it was at Plymouth. This is the way it can and must again be to keep America strong and robust, its people happy, as in virtue they look ever to the future.

Thank you, ladies and gentlemen.

# U.S. Conference
## of Mayors

SEPTEMBER 25, 1998

*Salt Lake City mayor Deedee Corradini was president of
the U.S. Conference of Mayors and invited President Hinckley
to speak at the annual convention.*

I AM HONORED IN MAYOR CORRADINI'S invitation to speak to you.
I am glad you have come to Salt Lake City. It is a good city—not
without its problems, but a good place to live. It is a city with a
unique beginning and a great history.

I think I have been in most of the cities from which you come.
Each city has its own individual personality, its own attractions, and
its own set of problems—although they are much alike, particularly
the problems.

I hope that while you are here you will visit our Family History
Library. I am told that it is the largest of its kind in the world. It is
a great treasure-house of genealogical information, and I will be
surprised if you cannot find something of your family roots. In
addition to this central resource, we have 1,674 satellite facilities
across the nation. They are open to everyone. Half of those who
use them are not members of the Church. You will be welcome in
any one of them. In many instances you will find them in the cities
from which you come.

I hope you will also visit the Sunday morning broadcast of the
Tabernacle Choir. I think you will enjoy it. This body of 300 volunteer singers has been broadcasting to the nation for 69 years. There

is nothing to compare with it in broadcast history. The choir has become a great national treasure.

Now, Mayor Corradini has suggested I talk on family values.

I need not remind you that the cities of America are in trouble. They have been for a good while, and in most cases the situation is growing worse.

I should like to briefly highlight a few of the problems of which you are all well aware. I do so to set the stage for what I wish to say later. Perhaps the most serious of these is the growing number of families without fathers. In 1996 there were 7,874,000 fatherless families with children under 18 in the United States. This represents 23 percent of all families with children under 18. They are headed by single women who struggle to make a go of things. Forty-one percent of these have never been married. This according to the National Center for Health Statistics.

In 1996 there were 1,260,000 children born to single mothers. This represents 32 percent of all live births.

Every young woman should know that in giving birth to a child, she places upon herself a responsibility from which she will never be entirely free. How tragic is the desolate and ever-increasing picture of illegitimate birth. With each such birth comes responsibility to the mother and, inevitably, to society at large. A lack of self-discipline, of a sense of responsibility, in my judgment, is symptomatic of the troubles that afflict us in growing numbers.

An editorial in the *Wall Street Journal* speaks of a report issued by the Council on the Family in America after two years of intense study. The conclusion of that report is this: "American society would be better off if more people got married and stayed married." What a remarkable conclusion that is. Any of us in this hall could have said that without a long and costly study.

In support of its conclusion, the study states that "children who don't live with both parents are more likely to grow up poor, have problems in school and get into trouble with the law. . . . Children in fatherless homes are *five times* more likely to be poor than those who live with both parents. [In] black families, where the decline in marriage has been most acute, 57% of children in fatherless households live in poverty while only 15% of children in intact families are poor."

The editorial in the *Journal* concludes, "Marriage may be an imperfect institution, but so far in human history no one has come up with a better way to nurture children in a stable society" ("Married With Children," Apr. 25, 1995, A20).

Marriage was once generally regarded as a sacred sacrament. Fortunately it still is with many, but with the people of the nation as a whole it is becoming an increasingly secular experience. We are losing something. We are losing something that speaks of accountability—not only to one another but to God, who is our Father and who will stand in judgment upon us.

The Centers for Disease Control and Prevention states that in the United States in 1994 there were 1,400,000 abortions. Such a figure is indicative of the moral indifference that has overcome so many in this nation. It says something about the value we place on human life. Have we forgotten that all of us are sons and daughters of God?

The scourge of drugs is a national disgrace. A lying sophistry lurks behind the invitation to partake of these illegal substances. As you so well know, their use leads only to degradation; to a terrible gnawing dependency; to absolute loss of self-control, of one's health, of one's happiness. A 1997 University of Michigan study concluded that 18 percent of all 8th graders and 35 percent of all 10th graders had tried marijuana within the previous year. What has become of self-discipline? What has become of self-esteem? You are all too familiar with this problem. You know of its cost, of its consequences, of the dreadful loss of human productivity because of these lost values.

The terrible blight of gangs affects our cities. These young men and women scheme, they roam, they destroy property, they fight, they murder one another and innocent victims who happen to get in their way. They are an ill-begotten lot of young people who drift in a mire of terror and whose lives lead in only one direction, if they survive, and that is to prison. We cannot build jails and prisons in this nation fast enough to accommodate the need.

I might continue, but you are all too familiar with this litany of urban troubles. These and others are your problems with which you constantly wrestle. What is the answer? What can be done about it? Long term, these problems will not be remedied by increasing taxes and spending more money. You might put more policemen on the beat. You might build more jails. But the problems will largely continue until many more people get at the root. That root, I believe, lies in two places: in our schools and in our homes.

Unless there can be some reformation here, it is not likely to occur anywhere. It will not happen in a day or a year, but it could happen in a generation.

When I was a boy, I attended public school in this city. The name of the school was Hamilton. It was named after Alexander Hamilton, one of the great Founding Fathers of our nation, and the name of our school was a constant reminder to us of strength and greatness in men. We did not slouch into the classroom each morning. Weather permitting, the flag was raised above the school. We lined up on the walk in front, saluted, and gave the Pledge of Allegiance. We then marched to our classrooms.

We had heroes in those days. Among them were George Washington and Abraham Lincoln. Their birthdays in February were holidays. There was none of this so-called Presidents' Day, which simply affords a day off to go to the mall without any thought whatever of great leaders who have preceded us.

In our public school we were taught honesty through the examples of these men. We learned love of country. We learned respect for the flag. We learned the meaning of citizenship. We learned respect for our principal and our teachers and our parents. We learned respect for one another.

What has happened to our schools? There are still many that are excellent, but there are very many that are failing. What has become of the teaching of values? We are told that educators must be neutral in these matters. Neutrality in the teaching of values can only lead to an absence of values. Is it less important to learn something of honesty than to learn something of computer science?

What has happened to the discipline we knew? Not the sometimes absurd punishment arbitrarily meted out to a child for a frivolous offense, but the self-discipline which is born of respect for others and an accountability for one's actions. Discipline is not just a matter of punishment for wrongdoing, but of teaching our youth not to do wrong in the first place.

When I was in the seventh grade, a number of us boys did not like an action taken by the school. We talked the matter over out on the school grounds. The next day we went on strike to protest. We wandered around for a day, hoping the truancy officer would not see us, wasting our time and grumbling about an injustice the school had dealt us.

The next morning when we came to school, Mr. Stearns, our principal, stood at the front door. He firmly advised us that we were suspended and could not come back until we brought a note from home. At that early age we learned the meaning of a lockout.

I recall walking home and entering the house. My mother asked what was wrong. I told her the whole story. She did not sympathize with me. She did not try to justify or defend my behavior. She told me I had done wrong and taught me that if we had a complaint to make, there was a better way to address it. She finally wrote a note, which I sheepishly carried back to school. One by one, all of the boys came, each with a note in hand.

We never tried that tactic again. From our teacher and our parents we had learned a lesson in following the proper avenues for settling grievances.

In the normal course of our lives in that school, we were far from perfect. We had fistfights with one another until our noses ran with blood. We were not very good athletes, but we were very determined in our competition. But so far as I am able to ascertain, no boy in that class was ever arrested for anything worse than a traffic violation. All went on to higher study and productive lives. How grateful I am for the values we were taught, for the discipline that was expected of us, for parents and teachers who pointed a better way to live.

Where today are the heroes from whose lives we learned honesty and integrity and the meaning of work? The debunkers of Washington and Lincoln have done their job, and we all are the poorer for it.

To you men and women of great influence, you who preside in the cities of the nation, to you I say that it will cost far less to reform our schools, to teach the virtues of good citizenship, than it will to go on building and maintaining costly jails and prisons in which to warehouse the many who violate the law.

But there is another institution of even greater importance than the schools. It is the home. I believe that no nation can rise higher than the strength of its families. And yet the family is falling apart—not only in America but across the world.

Long ago, 40 years ago, back in 1958, I read an article in the *Reader's Digest* entitled "Put Father Back at the Head of the Family." It was written by a Judge Liebowitz of New York City. In his capacity as judge, he spent his days listening to evidence and handing down sentences. He traveled to Europe and discovered that the conditions among the youth there were often much better than in America. He investigated and thought and pondered and out of a vast experience came to the conclusion that the easiest, most simple remedy in reducing delinquency among the young was to put the father back as head of the family.

The God of heaven designed the family as the basic unit of society. He did not design that children should be begotten and left to a single—and often poor—mother to rear. He designed that a father should stand as a pillar of strength in every household.

I do not believe that women resent the partnership, even the leadership, of a good man in the home, and I emphasize the word *good*. They welcome it. He becomes the provider, the defender, the counselor, the companion who will listen and give support when needed. There is no adequate substitute for husband and wife, father and mother, working together to strengthen each other and guide the destinies of their children.

How do we get father to take his place? It may be a slow process, but it is worth the effort. We begin with very young boys and teach them and motivate them and point them in this direction. It will not be easy. We will not save them all. But we can save many who are now being lost.

It is my belief that no one else, other than a good and exemplary father, can so effectively teach children the value of education; the dead-end nature of street gangs; the utter stupidity of partaking of drugs; the miracle of self-esteem, which can change their lives for good.

I remember reading in the *Wall Street Journal* four or five years ago of a lawyer in Ohio, a well-educated African American whose name was King. He spoke of his boyhood and told of his father taking the family for a ride on a Sunday afternoon in their old car. While they were going down the street, a fancy red Cadillac passed them.

The boy asked his father why some people had Cadillacs while theirs was an old jalopy. His father responded that everyone couldn't have the same but that he, his son, had something that was of absolutely tremendous worth, which many others did not have, which was of greater worth than any Cadillac. He said that his boy was a son of the King family and of the Jones family and that there flowed in his veins the best blood of each of those families. He taught his son that while all could not achieve temporal equality, everyone could cultivate those wonderful values which we speak of as self-esteem and self-discipline. The boy grew to manhood, studied law, and is today a successful practitioner.

I read this from Jenkins Lloyd Jones some years ago:

"The kid who isn't loved knows it. There is no trauma so excruciating as parental rejection. No other form of human cussedness can more efficiently wreck a human life. Yet there persists a superstition that 'advantages' are a substitute for affection. They aren't.

"The finest of the advantages a family can offer can't be found in a department store, a car dealer's showroom or a prep school. The only priceless one is a sense of belonging. Otherwise, the family becomes a combination cafe and dormitory. There's no glue in it" ("Needed: Device To Point Out Unfit Parents," in *Deseret News*, July 13, 1968, 12A).

I think we must point out to our youth of all races that there is a better way than the way so many are now going. It will take patience. It will take persuasion. It will take the counsel of good and loving and wise fathers. I believe it will take a great improvement in our homes. I believe it will take prayer.

The problem we face with family life in America is a greater problem than any of us can solve with our own wisdom. It is a problem for which we need inspiration and spiritual guidance. The things of God are understood by the Spirit of God, and I submit that what is needed is that motivating and powerful spiritual inspiration which is real and which can come into the lives of those who seek it.

I put the father back as head of the family, and while doing so, I plead with him to institute and follow a practice which was commonplace in the homes of America a century ago. We have largely lost sight of it. That is the practice of prayer.

Regardless of religious affiliation, a father who will kneel with his wife and children will do wonders for them. The very act of getting on one's knees before a higher power becomes an acknowledgment of our need for help. To thank the Lord in the presence of one another for life, health and strength, and family carries with it a wonderfully salutary effect. Remembering the poor and the unfortunate before the Almighty has an inevitable effect upon children. It leads to unselfishness, to concern for others, to a desire to lift and bless those in distress. To pray for guidance in one's life, to offer an invocation for the blessings of heaven upon children inevitably has a positive effect.

In the Church which I have the honor to represent, we stress a basic and fundamental teaching, and that is that each of us is a child of God. It matters not the race. It matters not the slant of our eyes or the color of our skin. Each of us is a son or daughter of the Almighty, who loves us and who stands ready to listen to our pleadings and help us with our problems. When a child comes to realize that there is something of divinity within him, then something wonderful begins to happen.

We have issued a proclamation on the family, which has received wide acceptance. I brought some copies with me should you care to read it.

What I have suggested may sound a little strange as I speak to you, the mayors of the cities of America. Am I getting into a field where I do not belong when I take the liberty of suggesting to you able and concerned people that the time has come for the citizens of this land to acknowledge our failures and our weaknesses in dealing with some of these terrible problems and to get on our knees and seek the wisdom of heaven? The marvelous thing is that it works. I have seen it. I have experienced it.

I conclude by repeating that I believe that only to the degree that we reform young lives will we reform our society. And that reformation must occur with a return to the teaching of values in our schools and in putting a good father who will stand beside a good mother in a home where virtue, honesty, integrity, and a reliance upon God will be taught by example as well as by precept.

I believe there is no simpler thing we can do, none less costly, none greater, and none more fruitful of good. God bless you, my dear friends, in your very serious work. Thank you.

# INDEX

569

# C